D1549264

CL

Book No 0404881
30109 004048818

# The Official Centenary History of the
# AMATEUR ATHLETIC ASSOCIATION

The Amateur Athletic Association gratefully acknowledges the assistance given by its sponsors, Nationwide Building Society, in the preparation of this book.

# The Official Centenary History of the AMATEUR ATHLETIC ASSOCIATION

**Peter Lovesey**

**Harold M. Abrahams suggested that this book should be written, and contributed substantially to the research. It is dedicated to his memory.**

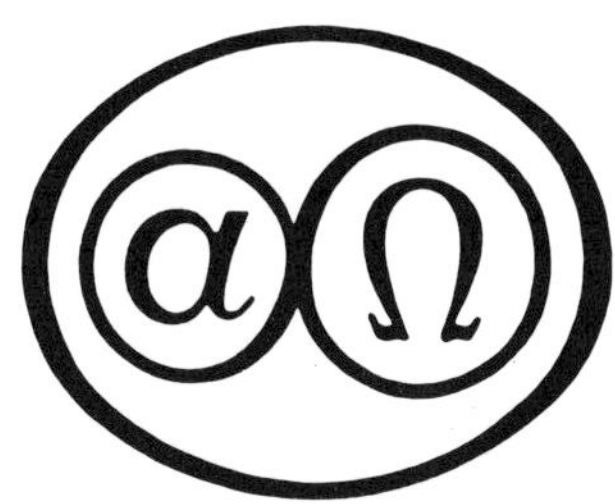

GUINNESS SUPERLATIVES LIMITED
2 CECIL COURT, LONDON ROAD, ENFIELD, MIDDLESEX

# Acknowledgements

The initial research for this book was made with the help of the late Harold Abrahams. He put his collection of notes, books and press-clippings at my disposal. He offered to share the marathon assignment of extracting information from a century of minute books, and he made three hours of tape-recordings, all meticulously indexed. I shall remember with affection his company at the National Newspaper Library, Colindale, as for weeks we scanned the accounts of events related in these pages, cautioned only occasionally for disturbing the silence of the reading room. I am indebted, too, to his son, Alan, and Sue, his daughter, for allowing me to borrow books and materials from Harold's library after his death. The collection is now in the care of the National Centre for Athletics Literature, University of Birmingham.

Several others gave considerable help. I should like in particular to thank Barry Willis and John Martell of the AAA; George Dunn of the University of Cambridge Library; John Bromhead of the National Centre for Athletics Literature; John Goulstone, Editor of *Sports Quarterly Magazine*; the athletics historians, John Keddie and Dave Terry; Stan Greenberg and Peter Matthews, of Guinness Superlatives and the National Union of Track Statisticians, who prepared the lists of Championship results; and Béatrice Frei, who edited the text.

The bibliography indicates principal sources used and other works are mentioned in the text.

BEXLEY LIBRARY SERVICE
ACC No. M33014
Bk Si
16 NOV 1979
£7.95
796.406241 LOV

Editorial: Beatrice Frei, Stan Greenberg, Peter Matthews, Norris McWhirter.

Photo Research: Beverley Waites

Design and layout: David Roberts

Copyright © Peter Lovesey Limited and Guinness Superlatives Ltd. 1979

ISBN 0 900424 95 8

Published in Great Britain by
Guinness Superlatives Ltd., 2 Cecil Court, London Road, Enfield, Middlesex

'Guinness' is a registered trade mark of Guinness Superlatives Ltd.

Colour separation by Newsele Litho Ltd., London and Milan
Set in 11 pt Times Roman
Printed and bound by Bemrose Specialist Print, Derby

# Contents


Acknowledgements 4
Starting Lines 8
What the Records Mean 11
First Away 13
The Pace-Setters 14
Mr Chambers' Championships 19
Battle of the Bridges 24
AAA: Start of a Century 29
Athletics Victorian-Style 35
The First Records 40
The AAA Shows its Muscle 41
World Championships 47
Fixing the Rules of the Game 59
Presidents One and Two 63
From Trenches to Tracks 65
The Middle Men 68
Enter Achilles 75
The Man Who Trusted Athletes 79
To the White City 81
Willy the Conqueror 90
Wooderson in War and Peace 92
The Fitful Fifties 99
Flesh-Gloves to Five Stars 117
The Sixties and the Start of Sponsorship 125
Unbroken Contact 136
Kings of the Crystal Palace 146
AAA 1 167
The Confidence of the Long Distance Runner 169
Over to Harold Abrahams 175
Principal Officers of the AAA, 1880–1979 178
AAA Championship Results 179
Bibliography 207
Index of Names 209
Index of Subjects 217

BUCKINGHAM PALACE

(Camera Press Ltd/Peter Grugeon)

As Patron I send my warm congratulations to the Amateur Athletic Association on its 100th birthday. On reaching this anniversary the Association can look back on a history of distinguished service and notable achievement.

I value the links between the Association and my family and find it a happy coincidence that the 100th anniversary of the foundation of the Association coincides with the 70th anniversary of King George V's acceptance of the office of Patron. I am delighted to keep up this tradition of Royal Patronage and look forward to a continuing association with the parent body of organised athletics in Britain.

**ELIZABETH R.**

# Starting Lines

1866 Amateur Athletic Club Championships
1876 International Match, Ireland v England
1877 English Cross-Country Championships
1879 Northern Counties AA
1880 Midland Counties AAA
**Amateur Athletic Association**
AAA Championships
1883 Southern Committee
English Cross-Country Union, first known as National CCU
1896 Modern Olympic Games
1907 Race Walking Association, first known as Road Walking Association
1912 First AAA Coaching Scheme
1914 Appointment of Professional Chief Coach
AAA formally joins International Amateur Athletic Federation
1921 Modern International, France v England
1925 Schools AA
Inter-County Championships
1926 Counties Athletic Union
1931 AAA Junior Championships
1932 British Amateur Athletic Board, first known as International Board
Championships staged at White City
1934 AAA Summer School at Loughborough
1935 AAA Indoor Championships
1946 Post-war Coaching Scheme
1947 GHG Dyson appointed Chief Coach
1948 Welsh AAA
1949 Championships televised
1952 HM The Queen attends her first Championships. Record attendance, 46 000
1958 Tug-of-War Association
1961 Southern Counties AAA replaces former Southern Committee
Sponsored Championships
1962 Indoor Championships revived
1967 AAA Youth Championships
1968 Byers Report on British Athletics
AAA Five Star Award Scheme
1969 Championships go metric
British Athletics League, first known as National Athletics League
1970 Championships move to Crystal Palace
1973 British Athletics Cup
1975 The 100th Championships since 1866
1980 AAA Centenary

The Modern Starter — wired to microphone and automatic timing/photo-finish equipment. (All Sport/Tony Duffy)

# What the Records Mean

In the AAA's history, a number of different categories of records have been recognized. The principal ones mentioned in the text are:

**WORLD RECORDS**
Instituted by the International Amateur Athletic Federation in 1921.

**BRITISH RECORDS**
Instituted by the AAA in 1887 for performances made in the United Kingdom by athletes from anywhere in the world. Superseded in 1948 by:

**BRITISH (ALL-COMERS') RECORDS**
Instituted by the British Amateur Athletic Board in 1948. For definition see British Records. Superseded in 1960 by:

**UNITED KINGDOM (ALL-COMERS') RECORDS**
Instituted by the British Amateur Athletic Board in 1960. For definition see British Records.

**BRITISH (NATIONAL) RECORDS**
Instituted by the British Amateur Athletic Board in 1948 for performances made in the United Kingdom by athletes born in the British Commonwealth. Discontinued in 1960.

**UNITED KINGDOM (NATIONAL) RECORDS**
Instituted by the British Amateur Athletic Board in 1960 for performances made anywhere in the world by athletes eligible to represent the United Kingdom in international competition.

**ENGLISH NATIVE RECORDS**
Instituted by the AAA in 1928 for performances made in England or Wales by athletes born in England or Wales. Superseded in 1960 by:

**AAA NATIONAL RECORDS**
Instituted by the AAA in 1960 for performances made in England or Wales by athletes born in England or Wales, or by bona fide members of clubs under the jurisdiction of the AAA whose fathers were born in England or Wales.

The metric system was adopted for the AAA Championships in 1969. Performances recorded prior to this date are given in the imperial measure, with the metric equivalent added for reference. Performances recorded subsequently are given in the metric measure, with the imperial equivalent added for reference.

**Brief table of basic equivalents**

| | |
|---|---|
| 100 yd | 91.4 m |
| 220 yd | 201.1 m |
| 440 yd | 402.3 m |
| 880 yd | 804.6 m |
| 1 mile | 1609 m |
| 2 miles | 3218 m |
| 3 miles | 4828 m |
| 4 miles | 6437 m |
| 6 miles | 9656 m |
| 7 miles | 11.26 km |
| 10 miles | 16.09 km |
| 100 miles | 160.9 km |
| 3 ft 6 in | 1.06 m |
| 16 lb | 7.25 kg |
| 56 lb | 25.40 kg |

The now obsolete term 'pole jump', used in the AAA Championships until 1931, is used in referring to performances prior to that year.

# The Pace-Setters

**'The towne talk this day is of nothing but the great foot-race run this day on Banstead Downes, between Lee, The Duke of Richmond's footman, and a tyler, a famous runner. And Lee hath beat him; though the King and Duke of York, and all men almost, did bet three to four to one upon the tyler's head.'**

The *Diary* of Samuel Pepys attests royal interest in a race in 1663. Whether King Charles II ever tried athletics — of the conventional sort — we do not know, but some of his predecessors did. Henry V could outrun a wild buck and Henry VIII, before he started his matrimonial marathon, vented his vigour hammer throwing, shot putting, leaping and running. Nobles of the Tudor and Stuart periods liked to be known as first-class athletes. It is on record that Sir Philip Sidney (1554–86), the ideal of Elizabethan manhood, excelled at running and jumping; it was said of the 1st Duke of Buckingham (1592–1628), favourite of the Court of James I, 'no man runs or jumps better'; and James Scott, the Duke of Monmouth (1649–85), claimant to the throne, 'won foot-races in his boots against fleet runners in shoes'.

Athletics in England can be traced back to the seventh-century saint, Cuthbert (*c* 634–87), who excelled in jumping, running and wrestling, according to the Venerable Bede. The centuries since are rich in references to the activities basic to the modern track and field meeting. Right up to the formation of the AAA in 1880, there were two strong and separate traditions: the upper classes practised 'manly exercises' and the common people amused themselves competing in rural sports.

The labouring class treated athletics as a form of revelry after the more serious business of worship and trade on days of church festivals and fairs. Foot-racing, jumping and hurling weights were well established in the Middle Ages, with dancing, wrestling and football, as popular amusements. Men and women, old and young, competed for prizes that were generally of practical use — shirts, smocks, hats, cheeses and joints of meat. And sometimes there was more to run for. Addison, reporting for the *Spectator* on the sports at a wake in Bath early in the eighteenth century, revealed that a successful competitor was likely to win a mistress as well and 'nothing is more usual than for a nimble-footed wench to get a husband at the same time as she wins a smock'. Despite periodic attempts to suppress the fun and games — Edward III, alarmed that the English yeomen were neglecting archery, prohibited shot putting, and at a later date the Puritans censured 'all sports and publick pastimes' — they outlasted the festivals that spawned them. Most fairs and wakes died out in the first quarter of the nineteenth century. In many towns their traditional place in the calendar at Easter, Whitsun or Midsummer was taken over by athletic meetings.

Running for smocks and cheeses held no appeal for the upper class. For them, there had to be a higher justification for athletics. It was a preparation for life. In his influential work on the education of the ruling class, *The Boke Named the Governour* (1531), Sir Thomas Elyot commended running, jumping and throwing as 'sundrye forms of exercise necessarye for a gentilman'. Running, he claimed, is 'bothe a good exercise and a laudable solace', a sentiment joggers everywhere would support. There is evidence that the message was enthusiastically received in at least one public school. Richard Mulcaster, the first headmaster of Merchant Taylor's, devoted six chapters of his book, *Positions* (1581), to athletics. Sadly, the educationists of the seventeenth and eighteenth centuries were less enlightened. At best, sport in schools was improvised by the boys and ignored by the masters. Not until 1834 do we hear of a Steeplechase at Rugby, where the famous Crick Run was established in 1837, the year hurdle races were reported at Eton. Progress was even slower in the universities. It was 1850 before the first annual sports meeting was instituted, at Exeter College, Oxford.

Yet the upper class had not neglected athletics. They arranged private running-matches like the one reported by Pepys. Pedestrianism, as running for wagers came to be known, was promoted and patronized by the gentry, although their servants were usually the performers. The footmen of the seventeenth century were professional runners employed to carry messages between town and country houses. On the roads of the period they were faster and more reliable than horse-drawn coaches. Their masters matched them against the footmen of rival households or anyone with a reputation as a runner. When the quality of the roads improved, the footmen were assigned to other duties, but by the middle of the eighteenth century, running-matches were part of the sporting scene and there were runners who made a living from pedestrianism.

By the beginning of the nineteenth century, there were signs that the aristocracy no longer controlled pedestrianism. There were runners who dispensed with top-drawer patrons and got

# First Away

**At the start a man waited in the rain. Tall and gaunt, he wore a black running-costume that covered him from neck to knees. The saturated fabric clung to his skin. His hair, usually crinkled, lay flat to his skull. Drips fell from his moustache.**

It was Saturday, 3 July 1880. The first Amateur Athletic Association Championships were about to begin at the Lillie Bridge Athletic Ground in West London. The opening event, the mile, had drawn this one competitor. He was 21 and his name was Walter Goodall George. There were stories that in training he had run the distance in less than 4 minutes 20 seconds. The record for an amateur was 4 minutes 24.5 seconds. Nobody wanted to be beaten out of sight. So when the starter, frock-coated and in a silk hat, lowered his umbrella and fired the starting-pistol, George set off alone. No race, then, but a solo run by the young man destined to become the outstanding athlete of his age. No ceremony either: pure chance decreed that it was George who first-footed a century of athletics.

He splashed through the mile in 4 minutes 28.6 seconds. That afternoon the downpours were more sensational than the sport. The 1200 in the covered stand saw little to excite them. But it was momentous in the history of sport. Much that is now universal in athletics was initiated by the Amateur Athletic Association. As a national governing body it provided a model for associations the world over. It opened the sport to amateurs of all classes. It codified the basic track and field programme. For years the AAA staged what were regarded as the Championships of the World. And when the Olympic movement began, the AAA Laws for Competition were adopted for the first Games. The AAA and the organizations it created have substantially influenced developments in athletics ever since.

At the start is Walter G. George, the first AAA champion and the fastest miler of the nineteenth century.

their backing from the new rich. The response of the upper-class was to make their own matches. A young Scottish landowner, Robert Barclay Allardice, known later by his military rank as Captain Barclay, wagered a thousand guineas that he could walk 90 miles in 21½ hours. He caught a cold and lost. Tenaciously, he raised the bet to two thousand guineas and made a second attempt. He lost again. His bookmaker needed no persuading to raise the stake to the prodigious sum of 5000 guineas, but Barclay was not so foolhardy as he seemed. On 10 November 1801, he completed the walk with over an hour to spare. This success encouraged him to take up running. In a series of matches he was unbeaten at distances ranging from 440 yd to 2 miles. All this created a great vogue for pedestrianism. Peers, army officers and gentlemen of fortune could be seen sprinting at Lord's or striding between the mileposts on the Uxbridge Road. As a spectator sport, it rivalled pugilism. Over ten thousand flocked to Newmarket in 1809 to see the not so dashing spectacle of Captain Barclay walking 1000 miles at the rate of 1 mile in each of 1000 hours. For this he pocketed a cool £16 000 (over £180 000 in modern money value), probably the largest amount ever earned by an athlete for a single race.

For the next 40 years pedestrianism grew in popularity, though its social heyday had been reached about 1810. The steady urbanization of England led to strongholds of professional athletics being established in the great industrial cities. Control of running shifted from gentlemen's club and officers' mess to the taprooms of public houses in Birmingham, Manchester, Newcastle, Sheffield and London. Increasing numbers of the poor class took to running as a source of income, even if the winnings were paltry by pre-Victorian standards. The stake was usually £5 a side, rising to £100 for a race of championship quality. Exploitation was rife, for few athletes could manage without backers. Inevitably there were malpractices: 'roping'*, 'running to the book'† and 'ringing in'‡. The awe-inspiring names adopted by the pedestrians — Young England, the North Star, the Crowcatcher, the Gateshead Clipper — could not disguise the shabby reputation of the sport.

But there is another side to the coin. Pedestrianism was a great innovator. Sufficient credit has never been given to the nineteenth-century managers of professional running-grounds for laying the foundations of the modern athletics meet. The first purpose-built tracks of modern times were constructed in the late 1830s; by 1850 at least a dozen were in use in the principal cities. Size and shape varied — the first, around the cricket ground at Lord's (1837), was a narrow path designed for two-man races — but they were generally faced with gravel and measured by surveyors. More stringent timekeeping enabled reliable records to be published. The standard events of the modern track and field programme began to emerge, as championship cups and belts were offered for competition over popular distances: 110 yd, 440 yd, 880 yd, 1 mile, 2 miles, 4 miles, 6 miles, 10 miles and jumping. There was a strong enthusiasm, too, for hurdling in the forties. And in dress the 'ped' of 1850 looked distinctly modern. He wore spikes and

**Captain Barclay Allardice (1779–1854), who won £16 000 by walking 1000 miles in 1000 hours in 1809.**

*Holding oneself back in order to lose a race.
†Disguising one's form, to conserve a generous handicap.
‡Promoters conspiring to fix the handicapping unfairly.

brief silk shorts. Only if ladies attended would he put on tights and a long-sleeved vest.

Running had never been so popular. Crowds of 25 000 would come to watch, and wager on, a single race. The keen competition produced some talented athletes. They ran for results, not records, yet George Seward (1817–83), an American who had settled in England, was credited in 1844 with 100 yd in $9\frac{1}{4}$ sec (timing was to the nearest quarter-second) and had many other clockings below 'evens'; Henry Reed (1825–74) ran 440 yd in $48\frac{1}{2}$ sec in 1849 and 880 yd in 1 min 58 sec in 1854; and William Jackson (born William Howitt, 1821, and known as the American Deer) ran 11 miles 40 yd in 1 hr in 1845.

Although pedestrianism had achieved a technical revolution, it was tangibly a working man's sport. In a society where class was paramount, what happened if a rich man wanted to put on spikes? A few army officers, like Sir John Astley (1828–94), brazenly made matches at the running-grounds, describing themselves as amateurs, so that they should not be classed with the 'peds'. It did not matter that they ran for staked bets, for, as Astley recalled in his memoirs, 'In those days, mind you, an amateur meant a gentleman, whether he ran for money or honour, or both — I used to combine the two.' Others, less bold, used to meet at dawn to run races at Primrose Hill and other open spaces in London.

In the next decade, athletics burgeoned in the universities. Its beginnings at Exeter College, Oxford, in 1850, were bizarre. A group of undergraduates, dispirited by their poor riding in the College steeplechase, staged a 'foot grind', across country, and an Exeter Autumn Meeting, on Jockey Club lines, even to the weighting of top runners and the inclusion of a Consolation Stakes for beaten 'horses'. Soon other colleges at Oxford and Cambridge started sports, for this was the era of 'muscular Christianity' when games-playing became practically an article of faith in public schools, certain in time to evangelize the universities. Cambridge in 1853 invited the astonishing professional long-jumper, John Howard (1824–75), to jump before an audience of dons and students; using weights, he cleared 28 ft 0 in/8.53 m. The initiative seems to have passed to the light blues, for they were first with a University Sports, in 1857, Oxford following in 1860. About this time, a Cambridge solicitor, Jack Macdonald, who like Astley made 'amateur matches' on the running-grounds and knew some of the pedestrian stars, acted as adviser to the University athletes, persuading them out of flannels and cricket boots into shorts and spikes. In December, 1861, Macdonald brought the most famous of all pedestrians, the American Indian, Deerfoot (Hagasadoni, known as Louis Bennett, 1828–97), to Cambridge. A crowd of 6000, including the Prince of Wales, watched the visitor win a 6 mile race. That the future King should have patronized a pedestrian match and afterwards received the runner and dined with him in Trinity College caused a minor scandal, but manifestly strengthened the athletic movement, at Cambridge and more widely.

Athletics became respectable again. It was the turn of the middle class. Outside the closed communities of school, university and regiment were people ambitious to run like Deerfoot. Businessmen desiring exercise on Saturday afternoons could row or play cricket, but there were no athletic clubs. In the winter months rowing and cricket stopped. The West London Cricket Ground at Brompton was used by pedestrians for running-matches. Why should it not be used by more reputable people? On 30 November 1861, the West London Rowing Club daringly hired the Brompton ground and held some track races for its members. They were so popular that the sports were regularly repeated, and opened to non-members. Not to be outdone, William Price, the astute manager of the running-ground at Hackney Wick, offered a silver cup for a handicap open to 'gentlemen amateurs'. It was held on 26 July 1862. Walter Chinnery (1843–1905), destined to become the first amateur to run a mile in under $4\frac{1}{2}$ min, recalled that he turned up there in a pair of side-spring patent leather boots, 'but Teddy Mills, the celebrated long-distance runner, who was acting as attendant to one of the competitors, took compassion on my ignorance, and lent me a pair of running shoes'. He was still beaten, by Mr Spicer, of the Honourable Artillery Company. Chinnery had to wait almost a year before an athletic club opened in London. It was founded by some City businessmen who held some races at Brompton in June, 1863, and called themselves the Mincing Lane Athletic Club.

London was not alone in developing athletics. Dramatic things were happening in Liverpool. Two strong advocates of muscular Christianity, Charles Melly and John Hulley, had founded Liverpool Athletic Club in January, 1862. It developed hand in hand with the local Volunteer Brigade. The Volunteer movement had been revitalized in 1859 when it was feared Napoleon III had plans to invade Britain. Hundreds of thousands up and down the country had joined part-time defence units, parading for drill each weekend. Sport was included in the training. On 14 June 1862, the parade ground at Mount Vernon, Liverpool, was the scene of an 'Olympic

*Above:* Victorian professional athletics — Deerfoot (Louis Bennett) v the American Deer (William Jackson) at Brompton in 1861. (Mary Evans Picture Library)

*Right:* The American Indian, Deerfoot, whose running as a professional helped to inspire the early amateur athletes. (Radio Times Hulton Picture Library)

Festival' arranged by the Liverpool AC. The programme included events untried in London, for as well as running and walking races, there were high and long jumps, pole leaping, throwing the cricket ball and throwing the disc, interspersed with boxing, wrestling, fencing and gymnastics. Up to 10 000 spectators 'of a highly respectable class' attended. In 1863 the Festival was repeated with such success, drawing athletes and spectators from other parts of the country, that Melly and Hulley grandiosely restyled the organizing committee the Athletic Society of Great Britain. Further Festivals were held in 1864 and 1865 and out of them developed several individual matches between Liverpool and London athletes in both cities.

Athletics prospered. On 5 March 1864, Oxford University met Cambridge for the first time in what was to become one of the most fashionable meetings in the athletic calendar. On 22 and 23 April, the Civil Service held its first sports in the grounds of Beaufort House, in West London.

By now there was a band of enthusiasts in London who competed regularly at the running-grounds at Brompton, Hackney Wick and Bow. Members of the Stock Exchange, civil servants, army officers, solicitors, they were solidly middle class. Although they categorized themselves as 'amateurs', they were not shy of running for money prizes. They were amateurs in the sense that they did not rely on running for a living. Because they were a small group who soon knew each other's form, they introduced handicapping to keep up the interest. As a further diversion, they went 'pot-hunting' out of London, for 'strangers' handicaps' were fast becoming a feature of school and college sports. Athletics was a freelance activity. No one in London thought of organizing it on a national scale. That was Liverpool's idea.

On 6 November 1865, the enterprising John Hulley and Charles Melly opened a vast new gymnasium in Liverpool. The same evening, Hulley chaired a meeting of delegates from the North, Midlands and South that resolved to form a National Olympian Society 'for the encouragement and reward of skill and strength in manly exercises by the award of medals and other prizes, money excepted'. Besides Hulley and Melly, the founders included William Penny Brookes, a devotee of the Olympic idea who as early as 1850 had formed an Olympian Society in Much Wenlock, Shropshire; EG Ravenstein, President of the London-based German Gymnastic Society; and Ambrose Lee, who was pioneering amateur sport in the Manchester area.

A shock-wave ran through the running-grounds of the capital. The prospect of athletics controlled from anywhere but London was unthinkable. Never mind that Liverpool had staged four Olympic Festivals on a scale grander than anything seen in the South. The London contingent mobilized as fast as if the French had landed.

The rural games of Merrie England had their dangers. The Patent Rolls and Calendar of Assize Records show that between 1566 and 1622 at least six fatalities occurred in games of throwing the sledge-hammer, bar or coulter. Serious accidents were not uncommon in the early years of the modern athletic era, for the hammer 'cage' was not introduced in Britain until 1927.

# Mr Chambers' Championships

**In the 40 years of his life, John Graham Chambers rowed for Cambridge, founded the inter-varsity sports, became English Champion Walker, coached four winning Boat-Race crews, devised the Queensberry Rules, staged the Cup Final and the Thames Regatta, instituted championships for billiards, boxing, cycling, wrestling and athletics, rowed beside Webb as he swam the Channel and edited a national newspaper. He was the architect of modern athletics.**

John Graham Chambers (1843–83), the architect of modern athletics. (By permission of the British Library)

The *Sporting Gazette* for 23 December, 1865, announced:

'The Amateur Athletic Club will hold their first annual champion games on the day immediately preceding the University Boat Race, on some ground in London. The programme will probably consist of the following events:

Flat races: 100 yd, 440 yd, 880 yd, 1 mile, 4 miles, 7 miles walk.

120 yd hurdle race over 10 flights of hurdles 3 ft 6 in high.

High running jump, long running jump and high pole jump.

Putting the weight (16 lb) and throwing the hammer (16 lb).

The entrance fee for each of these competitions will be one guinea. The competitions will be open to any gentleman amateur, and the club lays down the following rule, which will be strictly enforced: "That no gentleman who has ever run in any open race or handicap can enter for the club races."

C. Guy Pym. Secretary *pro tem.*'

The new club was managed by a dazzling committee. They included a VC (Col the Hon HH Clifford), two winners of the Diamond Sculls (CB Lawes and EB Michell), a future Lord Chief Justice of England (RE Webster), a future Governor of New South Wales (the Earl of Jersey), a future High Sheriff of London (C. Guy Pym) and JG Chambers, in many ways the most remarkable of the lot. The son of a Welsh landowner, Chambers was educated at Eton and Trinity College, Cambridge, where he won the Colquhoun Sculls and became President of the University Boat Club. He was one of those rugged Victorians who excelled at any sport he tried, but his genius was in bringing order into sport. As self-appointed manager of Cambridge University athletics, he regularized the schedule of events, substituting shot putting and hammer throwing for such aberrations as sack racing and pole jumping for distance. By insisting on accurate timing and measurement, he made a serious sport of athletics. A contemporary, PM Thornton, wrote, 'It was to this great athlete's inspiring mind being directed to such matters that we owe the spirit which enabled the athletic revival to culminate in the Inter-Varsity Sports.' Certainly the programme of that first meeting between the Universities was mainly drawn up by Chambers. And when the AAC Championship programme was discussed, he made sure that some events Oxford had blocked in 1864 were included. The 880 yd, 7 mile walk and pole jump appeared. The hammer throw displaced the cricket ball and the distance-run was raised from 2 miles to 4. The programme he devised has formed the basis of track and field meetings ever since. Of the eleven events in the AAC Championships of 1866, nine,

or their metric equivalents, are still contested in the Olympic Games. The hammer and shot still weigh 16 lb and the hurdles are still 3 ft 6 in high.

John Chambers had more than his share of bad luck. On leaving Cambridge in 1865, he learned that his father had invested rashly and was quite unable to support him as a gentleman of leisure. He took a job as a journalist with the weekly, *Land and Water*, which printed an editorial strongly in favour of the AAC: '. . . There can be but one locality for the formation of such a club and that is London. The Amateur Element, though mustering from the Universities and large cities and towns in every part of the kingdom, can only hope for undivided success by making London its headquarters. It will receive strong accessions of support from Ireland and Scotland, from Liverpool, which has itself held a meeting as early as November of last year for the establishment of a National Olympian Association, and probably from the capital cities and chief towns of every shire. But London as a centre is as essential to its success as Newmarket to a Jockey Club.'

*Above:* Chambers with Mr Kotze, the winner of the pole jump.

*Left:* The pole jump in the University sports at Cambridge, 1864, supervised by John Chambers.

Chambers had a vision of the Club exercising control over athletics as the Jockey Club did over racing and the MCC over cricket. He failed to appreciate that these were institutions dating from the eighteenth century whose authority over their respective sports was part arrogation, part tradition. The second half of the nineteenth century required something less feudal in concept. If he had applied himself as energetically in committee to establishing a *modus operandi* for the Club as he did to planning the Championship Meeting, he would have saved himself much heartbreak later. It has to be said that the AAC prospectus, published in February, 1866, bears signs of having been cobbled together over Christmas with no more purpose than to thwart the National Olympian Association. Far from providing an organization that could legislate for athletics generally, the AAC set itself up as an exclusive club, its only declared object 'to supply a want which exists of some established ground on which the numerous competitions in athletic sports and foot races may take place'. It invited three-guinea subscriptions from officers of the army and navy on full pay, and members of the Civil Service, the Universities, the bar and the principal London clubs. Anyone else had to be balloted for 'in the usual manner'.

The immediate consequence was that the Mincing Lane Athletic Club viewed the AAC as a potential rival. It called a meeting on 16 January 1866, and changed its name to the London Athletic Club. This was the first shot in a 14-year war.

Beaufort House was chosen for the Championships, and they were held on 23 March 1866 — a cold, blustery afternoon. If March seems an odd choice for the main athletic meeting of the year, it has to be remembered that most of the competitors were from Oxford and Cambridge, where athletics was a winter sport, crowded out of summer by cricket and exams. The wind ripped away the canvas roof of the grandstand, but numbers of lady spectators 'braved the weather as best they could' and saw a 17-year-old Eton schoolboy, John Ridley, sporting a moustache, win the 440 yd. John Chambers himself won the walk, and his friend Charles Lawes took the mile. The entries for each event were stronger than anyone had hoped, and the only flaw in the organization was that an overweight shot was used. All in all, the committee could be pleased, more so the following August, when the National Olympian Association held its first meeting on the grass track at the Crystal Palace, London, in which the only notable event was the appearance of 18-year-old WG Grace while he was officially fielding in a cricket match at the Oval. He won the hurdles and scored a double century in the match. But the rest of the athletics was unremarkable.

The AAC was an overnight success. Subscriptions flooded in. A Club gymnasium was opened off the Strand. The committee took over the management of the Beaufort House ground, put Chambers in charge, and replaced the old gravel track with a new circuit of cinders. They staged a range of other sports: football, cricket, swimming, billiards and boxing. The Marquess of Queensberry donated a set of challenge cups for the first national amateur boxing championship (1867), so Chambers sat down and wrote the famous Queensberry Rules. And, incredibly, the Amateur Athletic Club organized regular meetings for pedestrians, the first at Crystal Palace on 8 October 1866. The Earl of Jersey, destined to become the first President of the AAA, offered one of the £30 money prizes, Charles Lawes another. Richard Webster, who as Lord Alverstone would become the second President of the AAA, was a steward; Chambers was the starter; and the Marquess of Queensberry handed the winners their money. There was no discredit in the enterprise. They undertook it in the best tradition of Victorian philanthropy. Since Deerfoot had returned to America, pedestrians had fallen on hard times. No one thought it improper for an amateur organization to resuscitate professional athletics.

But what *was* an amateur? The word had been used in cricket and rowing since the eighteenth century. In athletics, the first 'amateurs' were spectators; 'fans' is the modern equivalent. One of Captain Barclay's races at Lord's in 1806 was watched by 'the amateurs of speed of foot'. Early definitions of the word as applied to sportsmen came from the world of rowing, whose links with athletics have been made clear. In 1835 *Bell's Life* defined an amateur as anyone who rowed and was not a waterman or otherwise engaged in rowing for a living. By mid-century there was a distinct narrowing of emphasis; the term was used to dignify people of the middle and upper classes who indulged in sports also practised by the low class. An amateur was a gentleman. *The Rowing Almanack* (1861) defined amateurs by listing the universities, schools and institutions that nurtured these superior beings, ending with an absolute exclusion of 'tradesmen, labourers, artisans or working mechanics'.

To its credit, the AAC began with a definition that opened the sport to all classes: 'An amateur is any person who has never competed in an open competition, or for public money, or for admission money, and who has never at any period of his life taught or assisted in the pursuit of athletic exercises as a means of livelihood.' Although it omitted to mention private matches for staked bets, this was an honest attempt to define amateurism in the context of the sport. It proved too liberal for the membership. In 1867 a significant tag was added: '. . . or is a mechanic, artisan or labourer.' In 1868 the first words of the definition were amended to 'An amateur is any gentleman . . .' By then the AAC had its own private club-rooms at 6 Pall Mall Place.

The Club was exclusive, but not the Championships. They were open to all except professionals. Certain gentlemen might cavil in the club-rooms at entering a race with persons in trade, but the chance of winning an English Championship was not to be missed on any account. In 1867, John Chambers lost his title in the 7 mile walk by half a yard to JH Farnworth, who worked in a public bar in Liverpool. Alfred Wheeler, for 3 years (1871–3) runner-up in the 4 miles, was a London cart-driver.

Beaufort House had a good track, but presented occasional hazards because the ground was shared with a farmer. In the 1868 Championships, Edward Colbeck (1848–80), trying for a double in the 880 yd and 440 yd, collided with a sheep which stood in his way 'presumably amazed at the remarkable performance which the runner was accomplishing'. Colbeck broke the animal's leg and the world record for 440 yd, with 50.4 sec — a time that stood for 11 years! It was still a relief when the AAC achieved its target of supplying a home for amateur athletics. The Lillie Bridge ground was opened on 18 March 1869.

The new ground was conveniently placed, beside West Brompton Station, with its own hotel and stables for sportsmen visiting London. The worst it threatened in the way of hazards was the odd football or tennis-ball, for it was conceived as a nineteenth-century equivalent of the National Sports Centre, with facilities for athletics, cricket, cycling, football, tennis, rackets, gymnastics and billiards. John Chambers, as ground manager, plunged into the task of popularizing Lillie Bridge with the zeal of an impresario. He persuaded Middlesex Cricket Club to play its home fixtures there; organized the first amateur cycling championship, in August 1871; staged the 1873 FA Cup Final; started an amateur wrestling championship; and saved pedestrianism from virtual extinction in London.

In those years Chambers drove himself with almost manic energy. He coached the Cambridge eight to victory 4 years in a row (1871–4); took over as editor of *Land and Water* (1871); re-wrote the rules for billiards; started a Thames Regatta; and opened a Welsh shop in Chelsea. People said it was all too much: a recipe for disaster.

> '. . . we of the old Amateur Athletic Club regard with justice the AAA as to a large extent our child. And, you know, any of you who have been connected with the Association, as many of you have, from its actual nominal foundation in the year 1880, you know that it really was the outcome of the movement which had given rise to the Amateur Athletic Club some 16 years before.'
>
> Lord Alverstone, AAA President, 1891–1915, speaking at the AAA Coming-of-Age Dinner, 1901.

# Battle of the Bridges

**The running-grounds of Lillie Bridge and Stamford Bridge faced each other across open country, like mediaeval castles, but there was no chivalry in the fight for control of English athletics.**

Into our story step two brothers, as infamous a pair as you would find in any Victorian melodrama. They were James and William Waddell, who had joined London Athletic Club as middle-distance runners, discovered they were poor athletes, and diverted their energies to winning control of the Club. They introduced a number of non-athletic friends, and outvoted the committee at a general meeting in October, 1870. As members of the new committee — James was treasurer — they set about unifying the membership by launching an offensive against John Chambers and the AAC. Lillie Bridge, the AAC stronghold, with its one-third of a mile track of hard-packed cinders, was so superior to the old running-grounds that the London AC had been compelled to swallow its pride and hire the place for meetings. It was a sore point with many members, and the brothers seized on it as a crucial issue. If they could find a way of overthrowing Chambers and taking over the management of Lillie Bridge, they would have London AC in the palm of one hand and the English Championship in the other.

James Waddell.

William Waddell.

They issued invitations to all the principal clubs up and down the country, and in Ireland, to send delegates to a meeting at the Cannon Street Hotel on 8 November 1871, 'to consider who are, or are not, eligible to compete at amateur sports, and for the purpose of forming an association of athletic clubs'. It was a neat manoeuvre, for, by ignoring the existence of the AAC, it implicitly dismissed its authority.

The response was less enthusiastic than they would have wished. In particular, Oxford and Cambridge declined to send anyone. But twelve clubs did send representatives, including two from the North. It was clear as soon as James Waddell opened the discussion that the burning issue was the gentleman amateur question. GP Rogers, the London AC secretary, explained that their desire was 'to put down the attendance of roughs and extirpate betting men and bad language'. His words were chosen to reassure the Northerners that working class athletes were not under attack, but Walter Rye (Thames Hare and Hounds), who had resigned the secretaryship of London AC in protest at the Waddells, lit a fuse to the meeting by proposing 'that it is not desirable to include in this Association clubs who admit as members men who are not gentlemen by position or education'. Someone asked how a gentleman could be defined. A. Saward (S. Norwood AC) said no one who kept a shop, or was in any way connected with one, could lay claim to the title. By contrast, E. Ravenstein, from the less exalted German Gymnastic Society, said it would be unfair to exclude working men from the Championship, and JW Thomas (Stoke-on-Trent AC) wanted to bar only those who had competed for money. With the meeting hopelessly split, James Waddell cut his losses by appointing a sub-committee to draft a set of rules for the new Association. When these were published, the definition of an amateur was practically the same as the AAC's, except for a footnote declaring that 'some amateurs . . . may still be considered objectionable on other grounds'. The Athletic Association lasted for two more meetings. It had succeeded only in demonstrating that athletics, like much else in Victorian England, was riddled with social prejudice.

The Waddells were shrewd enough to see that power in athletics was not compatible with snobbery. They made it their aim to combat class distinction in London AC by increasing the

**The England team that met Ireland in the first ever international match, on 5 June, 1876.**
**Back row from left**: James Waddell (manager), Tom Stone (shot put), Montague Shearman (sprints), William Waddell (manager), William Fuller (4 miles), Gerard Blathwayt (high jump) and Walter Chinnery (London AC President).
**Middle row from left**: Charles Mason (4 miles), William Winthrop (shot and tug-of-war), Harry Venn (3 miles walk), Walter Slade (880 yd and 1 mile), Alfred Powles (sprints), Charles Lockton (high jump and long jump) and HW Hill (440 and 880 yd).
**Reclining**: Nat Perry and Bob Rogers (trainers).

membership and eroding the diehard attitudes. It was not easy. In November, 1872, they accepted the entry of a tradesman — and future champion — William J. Morgan, for their autumn meeting, and 60 members of the club resigned in protest. Not until they devised a new system of vetting non-members' entries would the objectors return.

Their most bitter critic was Walter Rye (1843–1929). One of the group who had pioneered athletics in the early sixties, he was a practising solicitor who wrote a weekly column in the *Sporting Gazette*. His blend of bigotry and wit was entertaining to read if you were not in the firing line. Of the German Gymnastic Society, he wrote, 'The members are unpleasantly notorious for bumptiousness, disagreeableness and wrangling.' Of John Chambers, 'For any leading London or southern athlete to receive civility let alone favour from the owner of Lillie Bridge is a thing seldom heard of.' And of Fred Elborough, winner of five AAC Championships at 440 and 880 yd, 'To a certain extent a champion is public property, and I should not be doing my duty if I did not point out that the systematic giving way to habits of inebriation must tell its tale sooner or later, especially on a constitution already undermined by venereal disease.' Sports journalists are not renowned for discretion, but no modern paper would print such vitriol. Through the 1870s Rye trumpeted the cause of the gentleman amateur, and attacked the 'lamentable results' of 'the buffoons, James and William Waddell'.

But the tide of events was against elitism. Athletics was growing in popularity everywhere. In the North and Midlands, crowds of 10 000 and more attended even cricket club sports. In Ireland, the annual Lurgan AC meeting attracted huge crowds, who watched races Lord Lurgan had decreed should be 'open to all, except professionals'. Athletes of the 'mechanic, artisan and labourer' class were increasingly tolerated, if not welcomed, by club secretaries.

In 1874, William Waddell was elected Secretary of London AC and with James as Treasurer effectively controlled a membership approaching 900. If the old guard suspected that standards had slipped, they could not ignore the annual profits, which soared to over £1000 in 1875. Nor could they deny that the brothers were raising the club's prestige. In June, 1876, William arranged the first athletics match between Ireland and England, in Dublin. In that year, also, they stepped up the war against the AAC.

It was common knowledge that the AAC was a spent force. A joke was circulating that it was down to three active members — John Chambers, the pony and the roller. The truth was that it had ceased to function as an athletic club. Chambers still devoted himself passionately to sports management, whether it was accompanying Captain Webb on his Channel swim or supervising long-distance walks. But his single-

**A view from the grandstand of the Stamford Bridge ground opened by the Waddell brothers for London AC in 1877. (By permission of the British Library)**

Stamford Bridge in the nineties.

mindedness made him a difficult man to work with. The committee left him to manage Lillie Bridge alone. Middlesex now played its matches at Prince's Ground, Sloane Street. The FA Cup Finals were played at the Oval. True, the two major athletic occasions, the Oxford and Cambridge Sports and the Championships, still took place at Lillie Bridge in March or April, but it needed more than those to pay for the upkeep of the ground. He relied heavily on the income he derived from letting it to the London AC.

The clash, when it came in 1876, was over gate-money. Blaming an increase in overheads, Chambers asked for a larger share of the proceeds from the six London AC meetings at Lillie Bridge. The brothers came to terms with him, but started a subscription fund to secure the lease of a piece of ground a few hundred yards south-east of Lillie Bridge. They quickly raised the £2899 required, putting in, it was said, a substantial sum themselves.

The track at Stamford Bridge was laid, and the grandstand built, in a matter of months. It was opened on 28 April 1877. Its proximity to Lillie Bridge was more than provocation; it was a challenge to the death.

The AAC faced defeat. The Championships that year had drawn a contemptible total of 26 athletes for the twelve events. The question was not *whether* the London AC should take over the organization, but when. The Waddells were determined to move cautiously; the failure of their Athletic Association had been a bitter lesson. So they simply suggested to Chambers, in a letter issued to the press, that the 1878 Championship Meeting should be held in the summer, instead of the spring. Chambers was bound to resist this. It would not be favoured by the athletes of Oxford and Cambridge, who still competed in the winter. He counted on support from Cambridge, his own University, where his successes coaching Boat Race crews were fresh in the memory. He staged the Championships as usual at Lillie Bridge in April, 1878. Cambridge provided five winners, Oxford two.

The Waddells acted. They served notice that in 1879 the Championships would take place in the summer, at Stamford Bridge, under the management of a committee 'of the representatives of the leading clubs'. Chambers refused to capitulate. From Lillie Bridge he announced that the Championships would take place there, in April, under AAC management. So the battle-lines were drawn.

The result was a stalemate. The Lillie Bridge meeting was practically an Oxford and Cambridge affair, boycotted by London AC members. The Stamford Bridge meeting drew only four entries from outside London. Athletics was close to anarchy.

On 14 June 1879, the day of the Stamford Bridge 'Championships', came a timely reminder that the power struggle in London would not automatically decide who controlled the sport nationally. Representatives of nine Northern clubs met in Southport, their aim firstly to improve the government of athletics by forming a committee with power of disqualification; secondly, to arrange an Amateur Championship Meeting in the North; and thirdly, to provide a definition of an amateur. Further meetings at Crewe, Stoke and Manchester settled the name of the organization as the Northern Counties Athletic Association, drew up rules for the management of athletic meetings and defined an amateur, using the words of the AAC definition, but pointedly deleting the 'mechanic, artisan or labourer' tag, and any reference to the word 'gentleman'. That autumn, there were suggestions that the Midland Counties should form a similar association.

Unless someone made concessions, 1880 would bring chaos, with up to four meetings purporting to be Championships. In January, William Waddell wrote to John Chambers suggesting that the committees of the London AC and AAC should confer over the date and location of the Championship Meeting. In *Land and Water*, Chambers blazed defiance: 'It would be as well, perhaps, if the opposition were to state their reasons for any alteration of the existing date when the opinion of every champion has been applied for by the AAC and nine-tenths are in favour of the spring fixtures.'

The pace of events quickened. On 14 February, Frank Smith, secretary of Birmingham AC, invited clubs in the Midlands to send delegates to a meeting on 1 March, 'to consider the advisability of forming a Midland Counties Amateur Athletic Union'.

Like a general marshalling his depleted officers for a last stand, Chambers called a meeting on 26 February of the AAC committee and donors of the challenge cups. They included an earl, two baronets, a colonel, an MP and three old colleagues from Cambridge. They decided that the Championships of 1880 would take place as usual at Lillie Bridge on the Monday after the Boat Race. Once again, they were relying on the Universities to keep the meeting alive. At Oxford, if not Cambridge, people were beginning to ask if the life was worth saving. There was not much honour in a Championship disregarded by everyone outside the Universities.

No compromise seemed possible. Athletics was torn between Lillie Bridge and Stamford Bridge; between the Universities and London; between North, Midlands and South; and between gentlemen and those they did not regard as gentlemen. The main antagonists were implacably committed. None of them could repair the damage now. There was too much suspicion between them. It required a mediator — in modern idiom, a trouble-shooter — with the ability to extract concessions all round.

The eight original AAC Championship cups are still competed for at the AAA Championships. The donors, most of them personal friends of Chambers, included some distinguished names:

- 100 yd (now 100 m): His Highness Prince Hassan, the son of Ismail Pasha, the Khedive of Egypt. Prince Hassan, a student at Oxford, presented the cup in 1871, when he attended the Championships.
- 440 yd (now 400 m): Kenelm Thomas Digby, MP for Queen's County, Ireland.
- 880 yd (now 800 m): Percy Melville Thornton, MP for Clapham and Battersea, and the first amateur champion for 880 yd.
- 1 mile (now 1500 m): Charles Bennet Lawes, who became Sir Charles B. Lawes-Wittewronge, Bart. He was the first amateur champion for the mile, and also won the first Oxford v Cambridge mile. Well known as a sculptor, he occasioned one of the most celebrated libel cases of his time, by accusing the sculptor Richard Belt of representing other people's sculptures as his own. After an action heard in Westminster Hall, lasting 43 days, damages of £5000 were awarded against Lawes.
- 4 miles (now 5000 m): The 7th Earl of Jersey, first President of the AAA.
- 120 yd hurdles (now 110 m): Thomas Arthur, Viscount Southwell.
- 7 mile walk (now 10 000 m): John Graham Chambers himself.
- High jump: Sir Claude Champion de Crespigny, Bart.

# AAA: Start of a Century

**'People who see the tremendous reputation the Championship Meeting has now acquired know very little of the difficulties encountered at the inception of the AAA, which was inaugurated by a few young men at Oxford, who found chaos reigning in amateur sport.' Sir Montague Shearman, 1927.**

They were Clement N. Jackson, 33, a tutor at Hertford College; Bernhard R. Wise, 21, a scholar at Queen's College and President of the University Athletic Club; and Montague Shearman, 22, a graduate of St John's College and former President of the University Athletic Club, at this time reading for the bar.

Clement Jackson (1846–1924), Senior Treasurer, coach and mentor of Oxford athletics, had run in the first AAC Championships in 1866, finishing third in the 120 yd hurdles. Known throughout Oxford as 'the Jacker', he was the man whose stewardship had brought the Athletic Club out of a swampy cricket field at Marston to its cinder track at Iffley Road. He still held the best time on record (16 sec) for the high hurdles, made at Cowley on 14 November 1865, but his active career was cut short by a foot injury sustained when he spiked a hidden oyster shell while trying to match the hurdling of WG Grace. 'From that day forth,' he once wrote, 'I have never run again, never tasted an oyster, never spoken to WG the Great!'

Wise (1858–1916), born in Sydney, Australia, of English parents, was a brilliant scholar, a winner of the Cobden Essay Prize and a future Attorney-General of New South Wales. In 1879 he had won the mile both at the Inter-Varsity Sports and the AAC Championships. Now, as President of Oxford, he faced an exacting problem. The moribund AAC was turning to the Universities for a stay of execution. Cambridge were sure to back John Chambers, but if the Championship Meeting were to have credibility, it needed the active co-operation — or complicity — of Oxford. Was it justifiable to urge the Oxford team to compete in a 'Championship' that amounted to little better than a re-match of the Inter-Varsity Sports? Wise took his problem to Jackson.

They faced facts. Athletics had undergone a transformation since the AAC was founded. It was no longer the exclusive pastime of a few enthusiasts in London and the Universities who styled themselves gentlemen. It had become a popular national sport. The upsurge of interest among working men in the North and Midlands now made nonsense of the AAC ban on mechanics, artisans and labourers, which had never been strictly enforced at the Championships. Unless action was taken, the sport would

The three young men at Oxford who founded the AAA Clement N. Jackson (*above*) Montague Shearman (*right*) Bernhard R. Wise (*below*)

soon be split between regions, each with its own set of rules. There was an obvious need for a governing body everyone would respect. If Oxford scuppered the AAC, what would replace it? James and William Waddell?

There had to be an alternative to that. Jackson and Wise contacted Montague Shearman (1857–1930), who opportunely was both a former President of Oxford and a well-established member of the LAC, which he had joined in 1876. In the same year, within a few days of his nineteenth birthday, he had won the AAC Championship for 100 yd. He was now on the threshold of a distinguished legal career, in which he would feature in some of the classic trials of the twentieth century: he was counsel for the defence of George Joseph Smith, the 'Brides in the Baths' murderer (1914), and as a judge he presided at the acquittal of Harold Greenwood (1920) and the conviction of Frederick Bywaters and Edith Thompson* (1922). He was knighted in 1914. In a speech at the AAA 'Coming of Age' dinner in 1901, Shearman made it clear that he was not the 'father' of the Association: 'Mr CN Jackson, I know, has as good a claim as any; Mr Bernhard Wise has also claims, and I think really it was hatched between them. I think on one occasion — after dinner — I laid some claims to the honour myself. I withdraw these claims now. I should perhaps be more aptly described as the nurse of the young infant.'

So Jackson and Wise put their plan to Shearman. They proposed calling a meeting at Oxford with the aim of forming an Amateur Athletic Association. It would be composed of all the principal clubs in the country, and it would legislate for athletics and take over the running of the Championships. It offered a way of ending the war between the AAC and the London AC, and preventing a break with the North and Midlands. But it was vital to secure everyone's co-operation. Wise believed he could persuade Cambridge to participate by offering to present the plan as the joint suggestion of both Universities. Once Cambridge were in, John Chambers' last support would go and the AAC would be at an end. The danger was that the brothers Waddell would take this as the opportunity to impose their own Championships on the country. They must be left in no doubt that this would be resisted by both Universities, as well as the North and Midlands. If the London AC sought to influence athletics, its best chance was from within the AAA. Montague Shearman agreed to take this message back to London, and Bernhard Wise went to talk to Cambridge. 'The support given by Cambridge to the AAA at this time was very lukewarm,' Shearman recollected in 1927. 'The support of the London AC was less than lukewarm. Two gentlemen — Messrs James and William Waddell — had run rival Championships to our Championship Meeting which now exists and I had no assistance from them.'

The vital elements in the equation were the North and Midlands. For them, two issues were paramount. They wanted to prevent professionals from masquerading as amateurs; and they wanted the removal of the 'mechanic, artisan and labourer' clause from the definition of an amateur. The latter was the bigger problem, for a powerful group of diehards were entrenched in London, led by that old intransigent, Walter Rye, still championing exclusiveness in the *County Gentleman* (formerly the *Sporting Gazette*). He regularly published a list of athletic clubs classified as: '1. Recognized Gentlemen's Athletic Clubs. (They included London AC and Thames Hare & Hounds, which he had founded.) 2. Athletic Clubs not generally recognized, some of whose members, however, are gentlemen. 3. Unrecognized Athletic Clubs, wholly or in the greater part consisting of tradesmen, tradesmen's clerks, warehousemen or railway clerks.'

The Oxford trio decided that the North and Midlands were right: the day of the gentleman amateur was over, and it was in the interest of athletics to recognize this. They would find a way to deal with Walter Rye.

For John Chambers, the spring of 1880 must have been exceptionally bleak. On 13 March, the sports press published a letter proposing the formation of an Amateur Athletic Association. It was signed by BR Wise and E. Storey, the Presidents of the two University Athletic Clubs. To Chambers, this could only seem a betrayal. His bitterness unconcealed, he announced in *Land and Water* that the AAC Championships would be postponed: 'The Monday after the Boat Race was arranged for the Championship Meeting, because it appeared to be the unanimous opinion of the University athletic authorities that it was impossible for any Oxford or Cambridge runners to compete at other time. Now, however, the two presidents appear to have entirely altered their views, and therefore the AAC consider it far better to withhold their meeting until the utopian theories of the University athletes are a little more

*Coincidentally, it was revealed at the trial that Mrs Thompson herself had some success as an athlete. Four months before the murder of her husband, she wrote to Bywaters, '. . . your own pal is getting quite a sport. On Saturday I was first in the Egg & Spoon race & first in the 100 yard Flat race & 3rd in the 50 yards race.' *The Trial of Frederick Bywaters and Edith Thompson*, Filson Young (Editor) in the *Notable British Trials* series (Hodge, 1923).

matured and developed. The birth of the new Amateur Athletic Association and the millennium may be expected at one and the same time.'

Undeterred, Jackson, Shearman and Wise booked the banqueting hall of the Randolph Hotel, Oxford, for Saturday 24 April. Delegates were invited from the Northern Counties AA, the Midland Counties AAA and all the main athletic and cross-country clubs in the South. But the crucial work was done in the weeks before, as Shearman and Wise consulted individuals and negotiated the terms for their co-operation. It was a brilliant exercise in diplomacy. While a largely sceptical press talked of 'boy legislators' and University exclusiveness, a set of proposals was drawn up that provided for a Championship Meeting open to all amateurs, and a definition that made no social discrimination. James and William Waddell agreed to abandon the London AC 'Championships' when an assurance was given that the AAA Championships would be a summer meeting and could include the two events, 10 miles and 2 mile steeplechase, the brothers had introduced. Their satisfaction at this is perpetuated in the AAA Challenge Cup for the steeplechase. John Chambers was consoled by a promise that Lillie Bridge would be the venue for the first Championships. As 24 April approached, his column in *Land and Water* became significantly more conciliatory: 'It is the first time such a thing has been attempted with any chance of success, and the thanks of all amateurs are due to the two University Clubs for the energy they have displayed in arranging and working up the meeting.'

The single person left who was capable of causing havoc was Walter Rye, who would attend as the representative of Thames Hare & Hounds. He had scotched the attempt to form an Athletic Association in 1871 and he could do it again. What advocacy Shearman brought to bear on this notorious opinionist we do not know. We only have Rye's statement in the *County Gentleman* of 20 March: 'Having been for many years one of the spokesmen of the "gentlemen amateurs" who have considered, and who still consider, that the meeting should be confined to men who are "gentlemen by profession and education", I am bound in common honesty to admit that there seems to be a growing feeling that in running, walking and jumping contests anyone who has never competed for money or against a professional should be allowed to enter.' After 20 years of intolerance, this was an astonishing about-turn. Possibly a psychologist would find some evidence of deep-seated inadequacy in Rye, for he had never attended university. He had left school at 14 and completed his education in evening classes. Certainly it was inspired psychology to invite him to dinner in Oxford on the eve of the meeting. He was treated as a privileged being and taken into the confidence of the three founders of the AAA. What was said that night is not on record. All that is certain is that Walter Rye said hardly a word next day at the inaugural meeting, and he was one of the ten who formed the first General Committee.

The groundwork had been so thorough that on the day of the meeting, the column *Oxford Notes* — possibly contributed by Wise — in *Land and Water* claimed: '. . . on the whole the meeting promises to be most effectual and harmonious. If it succeeds, as undoubtedly it will, the record of its triumph will have contributed a lasting page to the history of athletics, and one which will never be read without a most just appreciation of the very honourable services rendered by the OUAC at a most important crisis.'

When the 28 delegates arrived at the Randolph, they were handed a draft of resolutions, among them the all-important definition of an amateur already adopted by the North and Midlands. With Bernhard Wise as Chairman, and a general invitation to dinner afterwards, the AAA was formally set up in as harmonious a session as the Oxonians could have wished. The Objects of the Association were agreed *nem. con.*:

1. To improve the management of athletic meetings, and to promote uniformity of rules for the guidance of local committees.
2. To deal repressively with any abuses of athletic sports.
3. To hold an annual championship meeting.

It was further agreed that the Association should be managed by a General Committee composed of representatives of the AAC, CUAC, Civil Service Club, LAC, German Gymnastic Society, Eastern Counties Association (when formed), MCAAA, OUAC, a West of England Athletic Club, NCAA, one representative of the Cross Country Clubs, and ten members elected at the Annual General Meeting.

When the staging of the Championship Meeting was discussed, the Cambridge representatives read a letter from Richard Webster, QC, a future President of the AAA, proposing alternate Easter and summer meetings, but the feeling of the meeting was strongly in favour of a summer fixture. Cambridge also opposed Wise's resolution that the Championships should be held in rotation in different parts of the country, but it was easily carried. Lillie Bridge was confirmed as the venue for the first meeting.

This was the cue for the Chairman to ask about the AAC challenge cups. It was a tense moment: the call for John Chambers to make his formal declaration of surrender. With dignity he announced that he had consulted the donors, and the cups would be handed over to the new Association. He added, 'In 1866, when the thing was started, athletics was in its infancy, and a great deal of the criticism that has been passed on to us is, to a certain extent, deserved. We could not be infallible, and where we have made mistakes, we will be glad to remedy them in future.' There was applause at this.

It should have been his last word, for when the definition of an amateur came up for discussion, he challenged the wording on the agenda, and suggested they used the AAC definition. He read it out.

Murmurs of dissent started round the table. As if he had not heard correctly, Clement Jackson asked, 'Do I understand you leave out the words "mechanic, artisan or labourer"?'

'No,' answered Chambers emphatically. 'The definition includes them.'

'Then I must press my proposition,' said Jackson.

Whereupon James Waddell took the opportunity to make a pious little speech to the effect that Championship Meetings ought to be above questions of class.

Jackson agreed, and said he would accept Chambers' amendment if he would leave out the words 'mechanic, artisan or labourer'.

'That I will do,' said Chambers, and closed the era of the gentleman amateur.

The Oxford three had brought it off, and only they knew how. 'It is very doubtful whether ever a meeting which had threatened to prove so stormy has culminated in so amicable an adjustment of difficulties,' commented the *Athletic World*. 'Mr Chambers was the very personification of all that is meek and mild. If that commodity known as humble pie could in any way satisfy the hungry, Mr Chambers must have satisfied his appetite and something more.'

In justice it should be said that Chambers had done more to foster amateur sport than anyone in his century. And the AAC had brought some fine athletes before the public, among them Robert Mitchell, the winner of eleven titles over a range of four events; Marshall Brooks, the first high jumper to clear 6ft; Alick Tosswill, who raised the world long jump record from 20 ft 11 in/6.37 m to 22 ft 2 in/6.75 m; Louis Junker, the only Russian ever to win an English title (the 100 yd, in 1878); and the prodigious Charles Lockton, who won the long jump of 1873 at the age of 16 years 9 months, to become the youngest-ever champion.

Within a short time of the AAA's foundation, the old protagonists made their different exits from the scene. Walter Rye gave up his column in the *County Gentleman* in 1882, devoted himself to genealogy, but caused a brief and characteristic flap as Mayor of Norwich in 1909 when he refused to put on a top hat and frock coat to meet the King. 'Walter Rye was Mayor when the King came and he was Walter Rye when he left,' records his obituary. John Chambers continued trying to manage Lillie Bridge, involve himself in numerous sports and edit *Land and Water*. His health broke under the strain and he died a few days after his fortieth birthday, in March, 1883. Had he lived till August it would have interested him to learn that his old rivals, the brothers Waddell, had caused a sensation by failing in business and fleeing the country, leaving liabilities of £30 000. When the books were checked at Stamford Bridge, it was found that London AC was £1000 in the red.

## THE ORIGINAL RULES

[illegible] Championship Meeting in 1880, the AAA published its first Rules for Competition, [illegible] below. It is notable that the essentials of the modern internationally recognized rules, including sizes and shapes of weights and throwing areas, were here established. A century later, there are 114 AAA Rules for Competition.

1.—No attendant to accompany a competitor on the scratch, or in the race.

2.—Any competitor starting before the signal to be put back at the discretion of the starter, who shall have power to disqualify him on a repetition of the offence; all questions as to starts to be at the discretion of the starter.

3.—In Hurdle races each competitor to keep his own hurdles throughout the race. The hurdles to stand 3 ft 6 in out of the ground.

4.—In Sprint racing each runner to keep his own side of the course.

5.—Wilfully jostling, or running across, or obstructing another, so as to impede his progress, to disqualify the offender.

6.—In Pole Leaping and High Jumping, three tries at each height allowed. Each height to be determined by the Judges; displacing the bar only to count as a try.

7.—In Broad Jumping, Putting the Weight, or Throwing the Hammer, three tries only to be allowed. The best three competitors of the first trial to be allowed three more tries each for the final. The farthest Throw, Put, or Jump of the six attempts to win.

8.—The Hammer to be thrown from a circle of 7 ft diameter; the throw to be measured from the nearest point of the edge of the circle to the edge of pitch of the ball of the Hammer.

9.—In Broad Jumping, Weight Putting, and Hammer Throwing, crossing the Scratch in the attempt, to count as 'A Try'; all Broad Jumps to be measured from the scratch to the nearest place where any part of the body touches the ground.

10.—The weight of the Hammer (head and handle) and Weight to be 16 lbs respectively.

11.—The Weight and Hammer head to be of iron and spherical, and the Hammer handle to be of wood.

12.—The length from the end of the handle of the Hammer to bottom of the ball not to exceed 4ft over all.

13.—The Weight to be delivered from the shoulder with either hand, from a seven feet circle; no 'Put' to count if delivered or followed with any part of the body touching the ground over the mark; all puts to be measured from the nearest point of the circle, to the edge of the pitch of the Weight.

14.—In Walking Races cautions and disqualifications to be left to the discretion of the Judges.

15.—The decision of the Judges in each competition to be final.

16.—All cases of dispute and any questions that may arise, not provided for in these rules, or the interpretation of any of these rules, to be referred to the Committee of Management at the time, whose decision shall be final.

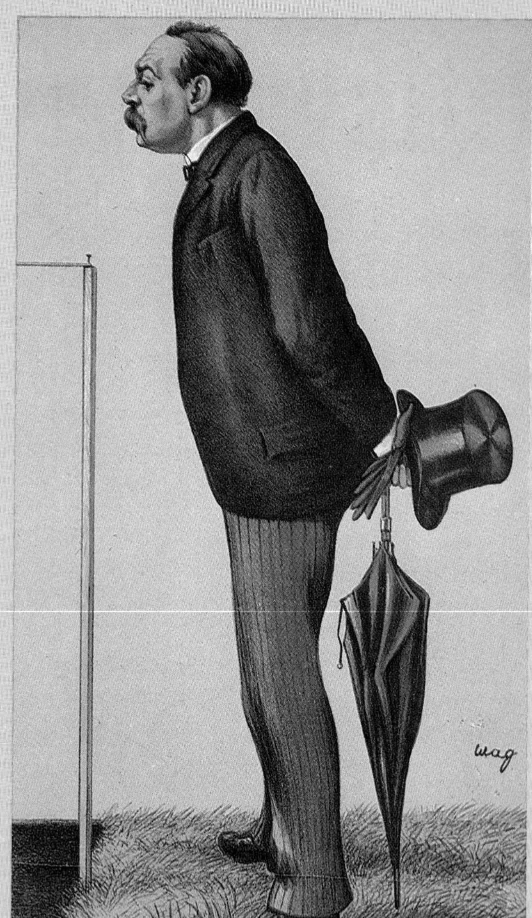

The first three Presidents of the AAA as caricatured in *Vanity Fair* magazine.

*Above left:* Victor Albert George Child Villiers, 7th Earl of Jersey (term of office 1880–90).

*Left:* Richard Everard Webster, Viscount Alverstone (1891–1915).

*Above:* Sir Montague Shearman (1916–30). (Radio Times Hulton Picture Library)

# Athletics Victorian-Style

**Torrential rain ruined the first AAA Championships, but in 1881 the sun shone on a crowd of 12 000. They had come to Birmingham to see the Americans, Myers and Merrill, bid for English titles. Shock followed shock in an afternoon that became a legend in Victorian athletics.**

A vital part of the agreement that sealed the foundation of the AAA was the commitment to the Championships rotating between the South, Midlands and North. The Midlands had their turn in 1881. They were determined to do better than the South, whose rain-soaked meeting had forced the treasurer, Clement Jackson, to levy a rate on all member-clubs to recover a £31 deficit. Happily, Saturday, 16 July turned out a fine day. By early afternoon it was obvious that a thumping profit was in prospect as thousands converged on the Aston Lower Grounds, Birmingham. The weather helped, and so did the stories of two athletes who had crossed the Atlantic to compete. Their short tour of England had already produced some unbelievable times and a disgraceful riot. Just a week before, the crowd had surged across this track with shouts of 'Stop the Yankee!' as EE Merrill had looked certain to win the 1 mile walk after the disqualification of a local man. Betting, not patriotism, was to blame for the fighting that followed. Bookmakers were part of the athletic scene on every ground. Merrill and the race officials had left Aston with a strong police escort. And this afternoon police were posted at 30 yard intervals round the track.

The other American, Lawrence Myers (1858–99), would be the first to test the mood of the crowd as he took part in the first heat of the opening event, the 100 yd. While he was changing, he heard an official in the dressing-tent remark, ''Pon my soul, the fellow's nothing but skin and bone and porous plasters.' Ill-mannered as it was, the comment was not far short of the truth. Myers was thin almost to emaciation. His mother had died of tuberculosis, and the family doctor had told Myers he, too, was at risk, and suggested he joined Manhattan Athletic Club to exercise his lungs. Encouraged by a win in a handicap race, he had asked for help from John Fraser, a New York trainer. Mrs Fraser, an Englishwoman, warned her husband to have nothing to do with Myers: 'That boy has consumption; and if you train him it will kill him, and his people will blame you for it.' Fraser disregarded the advice, and within a year Myers was American champion at 220, 440 and 880 yd. He was sick after each race, yet he forced his 8 st 2 lb/52 kg frame to new US records for each event from 100 yd to 1 mile. People in England frankly refused to believe he had covered 440 yd in 49.2 sec and 880 yd in 1 min 56.1 sec. They shrugged their shoulders at the information that in 1880 he had won the 100, 220, 440 and 880 yd in the US Championships, and repeated the feat in the Canadian Championships. They put it down to mediocre opposition. They were even inclined to dismiss the fast times he had put up since arriving in England. The ones that counted were this afternoon: his clashes over 100 and 440 yd with William Page Phillips, the 6 ft $2\frac{1}{2}$ in/12 st 2 lb/1.89m/77 kg old Etonian who was reigning champion at 100 yd.

The track was watered to lay the dust that threatened to swirl up in the runners' faces. There was still a sharp breeze as the first four came under starter's orders, but no delay in getting them to their marks because they came from the dressing-tent ready to run; anything so unmanly as a tracksuit would have caused hoots of derision. They all used an upright stance for starting. Myers was easy to spot in the white strip, with Manhattan's cherry diamond on his chest, a slight, dark man with a carefully trimmed moustache, more like an Italian waiter than a runner. The gun fired. Myers got an appalling start, possibly from nerves. By halfway he caught the others, but it cost too much in effort, and he faded to fourth at the finish. The Champion of America eliminated in the heats! 'I told you so,' was practically heard in chorus round the ground.

Attention switched to the first final of the afternoon, the 1 mile. The betting — officially banned, but impossible to control — was heavily on two men from the local club, Moseley Harriers. Walter George (1858–1943), as champion and record-holder, had a strong following, but it was known that illness and a bad spiking had hampered his preparation, so William Snook (1861–1916), a shorter, barrel-chested man who had recently beaten the 2 mile record, was favourite. They lined up with HD Thomas (London AC) and Bernhard Wise, now Vice-President of the Association he had helped to found, making his last appearance for Oxford, where he had just graduated with a First Class in Jurisprudence. In 1879, Wise had won the AAC title, but the schism in athletics had cheapened its worth. He keenly wanted to emulate Montague Shearman, who in 1880 had added an AAA Championship to one of AAC currency.

The local men's experience of the awkwardly sized, 501 yd 1 ft/458.4 m track with its gently undulating contours, looked sure to be a factor in the race as Snook, and then George, set the pace, but after two laps Wise spurted into the lead. George drew level as they went into the final lap, but the Oxford man was stronger, and won in 4 min 24.4 sec. The crowd applauded him generously. Snook, who should have finished third, had dropped out 150 yd from home, to save himself for the 4 miles.

The police were strongly in evidence as the walkers came on to the track, among them Merrill, the American record-holder, and Whyatt, the local man whose disqualification had triggered the previous week's rumpus. Race walking was bedevilled with controversy in the Victorian era. The three leading walkers of the 1860s happened to be John Chambers, Walter Rye and Tom Griffith, the athletics correspondents of *Land and Water*, the *Sporting Gazette* and *Bell's Life* respectively, so when incidents occurred, they were argued over for weeks in the press. It happened, too, that walkers were the cause of some of the fiercest wrangles over the gentleman amateur question. In the field this afternoon was Harry Webster, a wheelwright from Knotty Ash, Liverpool, whose victories in two previous Championships had not pleased the diehards in the least. Disagreement between the judges over Webster's style in 1880 had led to his disqualification after he had finished 3 min ahead of the field. Nothing so unfortunate was allowed to happen in the present race, for Webster had not gone three miles before he was disqualified. Soon after, Whyatt pulled up exhausted, leaving only Merrill and JW Raby, a novice from Elland, Yorkshire, walking together in impeccable style. Just as this duel between America and England was rousing the crowd, Merrill threw up his hands and collapsed in a dead faint, overcome, it was said, by nerves. Raby walked the second half of the race alone, finishing in 54 min 48.2 sec, and bringing a very good return to anyone who had backed him.

It was left to Myers to repair America's reputation in the 440 yd. It seemed unlikely as he stood beside the man who had just won the 100 yd, the towering William Phillips; impossible, when Phillips powered into a three yard lead. Nothing so eccentric as Myers' style had been seen in England. He let his arms dangle at his sides like a puppet's and concentrated his movement in a long, deceptively indolent stride. In the back straight he suddenly accelerated and swept past Phillips with devastating ease. It was the biggest shock of a shattering day, that humbling of England's best quarter-miler. Myers had the race in his pocket, and he knew it. Before reaching the tape, he turned and beckoned repeatedly to Phillips to make a race of it, finally trotting in five yards clear in 48.6 sec. The British record was 50.4 sec. Because of the unevenness of the Aston track, Myers' time was discounted as a record by the press, who were the only arbiters, but his mastery was imprinted on the memories of the 12 000 present that afternoon.

Meanwhile one family from Ireland had taken charge of the field events. Patrick Davin (1857–1949), a Carrick-on-Suir solicitor, had set Championship records for the high jump (6 ft 0½ in/1.84 m) and long jump (22 ft 11 in/6.98 m), while his brother Maurice (1842–1927), at 39 the oldest man in the Championships, had won the shot (39 ft 6½ in/12.05 m) and hammer (98 ft 10 in/30.12 m). If the performances seem modest, it should be noted that the jumping was from a grass take-off on to grass, and the hammer was wooden-shafted. The pole jump, the remaining field event, was the most formidable, for the standards were simply set up on the turf in the centre of the arena. The defending champion, Edward Strachan (1858–1953), used a mattress for landing, but he was easily beaten by a sturdy 19-year-old who spurned that facility and literally landed on his feet. Tom Ray (1862–1904), from the Lake District, where pole jumping was a strong tradition, had developed the ability to 'climb' the pole by slipping his hands up the shaft as it became vertical — a style now banned, but permitted by the AAA until as late as 1920. The resilience of glass-fibre has anyway made modern pole vaulting into a different event from the one Ray practised with a pole of stiff hickory tipped with three steel spikes to pierce the turf. Here at Birmingham he was in brilliant form, hoisting himself to a world's best of 11 ft 3 in/3.43 m. After that it was not Tom Ray who failed, but the Aston ground staff, who had raised the bar to its absolute limit. 'There is no knowing how much higher he might have done,' commented the *Midland Athlete*. 'It is difficult to understand why proper posts were not provided.'

On the track something yet more precocious was happening. In the 4 miles a lad of 18 had opened a long lead. Behind him toiled three world record holders, Walter George (1 mile), George Dunning (15 miles) and William Snook (2 miles). Such was young George Nehan's pace that neither George nor Snook finished the race. His lead over Dunning at the finish was 50 yards, and his time of 20 min 26.2 sec was a Championship record. With the self-confidence that makes and breaks distance-runners, Nehan was also to turn out for the 10 miles, the following Monday, to lead for two miles and then collapse with cramp.

The first of the foreign stars in the AAA Championships — Lawrence 'Lon' Myers, who won the 440 yd in 1881. (By permission of the British Library)

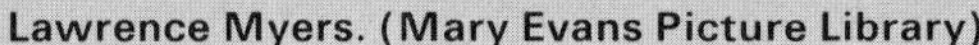

Lawrence Myers. (Mary Evans Picture Library)

The collapse of EE Merrill (USA) in the 7 miles walk at Birmingham in 1881. (By permission of the British Library)

In a day of upsets, it was almost a relief to see the old Etonian, George Lawrence, clear his row of ten sheep-hurdles without mishap to retain the title he had won the previous year at Lillie Bridge. A previous champion, Samuel Palmer, was less fortunate and fell at the sixth. Hurdling was strictly a field event, staged on grass in the centre of the arena, more to stake the hurdles stoutly than provide soft landings. The winner's time was 16.2 sec. Not until 1895 was 16 sec beaten in an English Championship. Faster times were common in America, where hurdling was a track event, over purpose-built barriers with moveable top-rails. But that was 'clothes horse hurdling', according to the English.

There remained two track events — the half-mile and the steeplechase — but the big names of the afternoon were back in the dressing-tent. If there was disappointment that the Moseley Harriers, George and Snook, had run below form, there had been compensations enough in the electrifying speed of Myers, the brave front-running of Wise, Raby's confident win in the walk and the astonishing talent of the under-twenties, Nehan and Ray. They were the new names, and they seemed certain to dominate the Championships for years to come.

With hindsight we can trace what the future really held for those stars of 1881. 'Lon' Myers continued accumulating world records and championships until he turned professional in 1885, the world's fastest runner for each standard distance from 100 yd to 1000 yd — a unique achievement. Ill each winter with bronchitis, he made no concessions to his state of health, and was known to sit up all night playing poker, sustained by two apples and a cup of coffee, and go straight to the track and set a world record. It was not a recipe for long life. He died of pneumonia at 40. Sir Montague Shearman wrote of him: 'Certainly Myers was unlike any of his predecessors. Whether another will ever appear

Tom Ray winning the third of his seven pole jump titles, in 1884. (By permission of the British Library)

Ray also won the high jump. Note the landing areas in both events. (By permission of the British Library)

like unto him it is hard to say.'

Bernhard Wise retired from running to concentrate on his studies in law. He returned to Australia in 1883, but made one more contribution to the history of athletics shortly before leaving England. At a meeting of the AAA General Committee on 10 February 1883, the Rules for Competition were discussed, and Clement Jackson proposed that four attempts, rather than three, should be allowed at each height in the high jump and pole jump. The voting was level, so it was the casting vote of the chairman, Wise, that fixed the rule at three attempts. In Australia, he had a distinguished legal career as Attorney-General of New South Wales. He returned to London as Agent-General for the State in 1915, and died there the following year.

The newcomers, Raby and Nehan, did not appear in the Championships again. Raby turned professional and modernized the records for each distance from 2 to 15 miles, but his style was said to have acquired 'a little artificial cultivation'. Nehan must be recorded as an early example of a brilliant junior who dropped out of athletics altogether.

But Tom Ray, the pole jumper, became a well-known figure at the Championships, winning a total of eight titles, including the high jump in 1884. His beer-drinking was a problem, and his weight increased from 12 st 0 lb/76 kg in 1881 to 14 st 11 lb/94 kg in 1887, yet he repeatedly improved the pole jump record, and in the latter year won the Championships of USA and Canada. He retired in 1891 and trained Richard Dickinson, another of the long line of Lakeland pole jumpers, who won the title five times. Sadly, Ray, like Myers, was careless of his health, and died at 42.

When Jackson drew up the accounts, he found that the AAA had profited from the meeting by £325, a very substantial sum in 1881. This was gratifying news to the Midlands group, a vindication of the policy of moving the venue out of London. To Montague Shearman, who by his own account had 'nursed' the young Association on pens, ink and paper for a year, a healthy bank balance bolstered the authority of the General Committee and enabled it to establish control of athletics. Reminiscing in 1901 at the AAA Coming-of-Age Dinner, he said, '. . . it put us in funds and it made the country and the world at large respect us for the way in which we conducted our Championship Meeting, and from that time until now I do not think we have ever gone one step backwards.'

One morning in 1883, a sporting daily reported the death of William Page Phillips, who had run against Myers in the 1881 Championships. To the embarrassment of the paper, Phillips wrote from abroad, where he was serving with the West Suffolk Militia, stating that he was alive and in the best of health. By a bizarre twist of circumstance, he died four months later, of quinsy. He was 25.

# The First Records

On 16 April 1887, the AAA ratified a list of British records. It was the result of 16 months' investigation by a special sub-committee. The records were the first to be ratified by an official governing body anywhere in the world. Below are listed the inaugural records for events still contested (although over metric equivalent distances) in the Championships.

| | min | sec | | | |
|---|---|---|---|---|---|
| 100 yd | | 10.0 | Arthur Wharton | Stamford Bridge | 3 July 1886 |
| 220 yd | | 22.0 | William Phillips | Stamford Bridge | 25 May 1878 |
| 440 yd | | 48.8 | Lawrence Myers (USA) | Lillie Bridge | 6 June 1885 |
| 880 yd | 1 | 56.0 | Lawrence Myers (USA) | Stamford Bridge | 2 July 1881 |
| mile | 4 | 18.4 | Walter George | Birmingham | 21 June 1884 |
| 3 miles | 14 | 39.0 | Walter George | Stamford Bridge | 17 May 1884 |
| 6 miles | 30 | 21.5 | Walter George | Stamford Bridge | 28 July 1884 |
| 120 yd hurdles | | 16.0 | Clement Jackson | Oxford | 14 Nov 1865 |
| | | 16.0 | Samuel Palmer | Lillie Bridge | 15 Apr 1878 |
| | | 16.0 | Charles Daft | Stamford Bridge | 3 July 1886 |
| 2 mile walk | 14 | 21.4 | Henry Meek (USA) | Stamford Bridge | 12 July 1884 |
| 6 mile walk | 45 | 04.0 | Harry Webster | Lillie Bridge | 7 Apr 1879 |
| high jump | 6 ft $2\frac{3}{4}$ in/1.90 m | | Pat Davin | Carrick-on-Suir | 5 July 1880 |
| pole jump | 11 ft $5\frac{1}{4}$ in/3.48 m | | Tom Ray | Whitehaven | 13 Aug 1886 |
| long jump | 23 ft 2 in/7.06 m | | Pat Davin | Monasterevan | 30 Aug 1883 |
| | 23 ft 2 in/7.06 m | | Pat Davin | Portarlington | 27 Sept 1883 |
| shot | 43 ft 9 in/13.33 m | | James O'Brien | Dublin | 3 July 1886 |
| hammer | 119 ft 5 in/36.40 m | | James Mitchell | Limerick | 16 June 1886 |

This was practically, in effect, a world record list. Only in the 880 yd was a superior record known, and that was by Myers, with 1 min 55.6 sec in America. The same runner's 48.6 sec for 440 yd in the 1881 Championships was disallowed as a record because of the gradient in the Aston track.

# The AAA Shows its Muscle

**'Watchful as Fatima in Bluebeard's chamber, the members of the Amateur Athletic Association.' (*The Sporting Life*, 6 July 1896.) From the start, the AAA set out to govern fairly and firmly and punish malpractices. An erring athlete in Victorian times could find himself serving a prison sentence.**

One of the three declared objects of the AAA when it was set up was to deal repressively with any abuses of athletic sports. The Northern and Midland Associations had been formed out of deep concern at the extent of corruption in the sport. The problem arose directly from betting, which had been linked with pedestrianism for centuries. When amateur athletics had blossomed in the 1860s, the bookmakers had simply moved in on the new business. To the end of his life Clement Jackson remembered with distress the 'awful strife of 1866', when the last event in the Inter-Varsity Sports, the 2 miles, had resulted in a dead heat between the leading runners from Oxford and Cambridge, each heavily backed by his supporters, who vented their frustration in a series of scuffles 'the sounds of which, dinning into the midnight, I can still hear'. The scandalized authorities reacted by banning the Sports from the two University towns, so they were moved to London. In *Land and Water*, John Chambers, who had just formed the AAC, commented: 'I hear that academic ears are offended by the sounds of "Two to one bar one!" "Long odds against some of these runners," and the like; and that the dons will not allow the inter-University sports to take place any more at Oxford or Cambridge. And I am sure London will be a far better place for them, and there will be many more spectators, and there will be much more complete arrangements, and there will be much more betting; and as for these things coming off without betting, you might as well have a dinner at Greenwich without whitebait!'

Betting led inevitably to malpractices. Athletes were persuaded to lose races they could have won. Professionals posed as amateurs. And sometimes one amateur impersonated another. The prevalence of handicaps provided an extra temptation. It paid a man to run below his real ability to earn long odds against himself and ransack the bookmakers later. These and other dodges led to charges and counter-charges, hostile crowds and gang violence. On 19 September 1887, a pedestrian match between two sprinters, Harry Gent and Harry Hutchens, failed to start because each of the rival gangs wanted to arrange for their man to lose; the angry crowd set Lillie Bridge ablaze and ended its chequered history.

It was plain to the founders of the AAA that they must take a firm line if they were to win respect as a governing body. Within weeks of the 1881 Championships they were faced with a case that threatened the unity of the Association. On 26 August 1881, the Northern Counties AA suspended the Midland distance-runner, William Snook, until the end of 1882 for conniving at the entry of a professional in an amateur meeting at Southport. Snook, the world record-holder for 2 miles, had a strong following in the Midlands. He continued competing at the meetings of clubs not affiliated to the AAA. It seemed as if the member-clubs were being punished instead of Snook. The General Committee considered the case in October, and it was decided to issue a circular to explain the effect of the suspension, and make it clear that any athletes who competed with Snook would be liable to suspension. Montague Shearman's advocacy was invaluable in steering the Committee through these difficult waters. The circular made Snook's suspension effective.

Certain offenders were outside the scope of AAA laws, so an important principle was established in May, 1882, when the General Committee voted £30 to cover the NCAA's expense in prosecuting a man for fraud. He was a professional who had masqueraded as an amateur in a Nottingham meeting. He was sentenced to one month's imprisonment with hard labour. The AAA Minute Books over the next 20 years recorded many similar cases involving impersonation by amateurs and professionals. Sentences of six months with hard labour were not unusual. Imprisonment may seem an excessive punishment for malpractices in athletics, but it is notable that, far from deterring clubs from joining the new Association, the stringent action boosted recruitment dramatically. The 45 member-clubs at the AAA's foundation increased to 75 in 1883, 185 in 1887 and 296 in 1897.

Scarcely a meeting passed in those early years without decisions being taken on issues of principle that determined AAA policy for years to come. On 30 September 1882, the General Committee considered a letter from Walter George seeking permission to run against the leading professional distance-runner of the day, William Cummings. George by this time had won every honour open to him in the amateur ranks. At the Championships of that year he had taken the 880 yd, 1 mile, 4 miles and 10 miles. With

The riot and burning of Lillie Bridge in 1887. (Mary Evans Picture Library)

Another view of the Lillie Bridge riot — the outcome of a dispute over a professional sprint match. (Mary Evans Picture Library)

Snook still under suspension, there was no amateur capable of giving him a race. Cummings had put up a series of brilliant times in professional matches, and was confident that he could defeat George. But the amateur champion was reluctant to sacrifice his eligibility, so he suggested in his letter that he would race Cummings for nothing, donating his share of the gate-money to a charity, the Worcester Infirmary. There was great enthusiasm for the match in the sporting world. The press urged the AAA to grant George a dispensation to run. It was an issue that struck at the bedrock of the Association's existence, for its definition began with the words, 'An amateur is one who has never competed with or against a professional . . .' To have made an exception of George would have been popular at the time, but it would have set a fuse to the Association. Unanimously the Committee turned down the application. George remained an amateur for another two years and improved every world record from 1 mile to 10 miles before signing articles to run a series of races with Cummings, climaxed by his celebrated mile in 4 min $12\frac{3}{4}$ sec in 1886.

The AAA also ruled in 1883 that professional cricketers were not eligible to compete in amateur athletics meetings. Soon other professional sports were added to the list. Curiously, Association Football was not considered until 1899, although the FA had recognized from 1885 that players were paid wages. Arthur Wharton, the first man to win the AAA 100 yd in 10 sec flat — and, incidentally, the first black athlete to win a Championship, in 1886 — was goalkeeper for Preston North End, who had paid wages to their players for years, but no one challenged his right to run. In time, rulings were given on all major professional sports, but certain members of the Committee could be relied upon for years to come up with unconsidered suggestions for the list. One suspects frivolity in such nominations as chess-players, billiard-markers, punt-racers and fire-men competing in fire drills. A useful covering phrase in AAA Rule 1 has thankfully ended the debates.

Meanwhile the structure of the AAA was strengthened by the formation on 2 August 1883 of the Southern Committee, the counterpart of the NCAA and MCAAA. There were obvious advantages in the area associations dealing first with matters of discipline and using the General Committee where appropriate for referral or appeal. The detection and punishment of offenders formed the bulk of the work in the early years, but the area associations gradually took on a more constructive role, with power to initiate legislation, appoint County Associations and deal with the application of the Laws and Rules for Competition. A further development was the introduction in 1884 of Local Officers, who represented the AAA in country districts, partly to promote the Association, partly report on infringements of the Laws. Among the first Local Officers representing Bristol, was that magisterial cricketer, Dr WG Grace.

**William Snook of Moseley Harriers won eight AAA titles and was National cross-country champion, but also earned notoriety as the first man to be suspended by the AAA. (By permission of the British Library)**

**The first West Indian born athlete to win an AAA title, Arthur Wharton, clocking a British record of 'evens' in the 100 yd of 1886. (By permission of the British Library)**

In 1885, the phenomenal American middle-distance runner, Lon Myers, visited England for the third time and competed each week through the season. There were persistent rumours that he was receiving 'appearance money' for competing at certain sports meetings. The matter was raised at the General Committee in November, and a resolution passed 'that it is undesirable in the opinion of this Committee that any payments should be made to any amateur athlete on behalf of a club he is alleged to represent, or for his own benefit, by any athletic club in consideration of his becoming a competitor at any sports'. Since Myers had by this time returned to America and accepted $4000 from a 'benefit' meeting, this seemed a classic case of locking the stable door too late, but if there was a feeling that the AAA had shirked an embarrassing enquiry while Myers was in England, no one could accuse them of procrastination in the next important case that came their way. For the second time it concerned William Snook.

In the National Cross-Country Championship of 1886, held at Croydon on 6 March, Snook finished second to JE Hickman, of Godiva Harriers. The bookmakers — always prominent at cross-country events — had made Snook, the defending champion, strong favourite to win again. There were pointed allegations that he was guilty of 'roping', by deliberately allowing Hickman to win. On 30 April, the Southern Committee suspended him permanently from amateur athletics. This was a sensation in the athletic world, for, since Walter George's defection to the professional ranks, Snook had become the king of English distance-running. In 1885, he had capped one of George's most amazing feats by winning the 1 mile, 4 miles and 2 mile steeplechase on the Saturday of the Championships, followed by the 10 miles on the Monday. Now 25, he could have looked forward to several more years at the top. It was thought a stiff sentence in many quarters, notably the Midlands, where Snook was a great crowd-puller.

On 22 May, Snook appealed against the suspension, explaining that he had been below his usual weight on the day and was suffering from sore feet. This was set against the evidence of AAA officials present, who had formed the impression he was not trying. The sentence was confirmed by 15 votes to 11. A second appeal, backed by the MCAAA, was lost in February, 1887; by 13 votes to 12, it was decided that Snook's case could not again be considered by the General Committee. Doggedly, the Midlanders raised the matter at the Annual General Meeting. After a discussion lasting until 11.15 pm, the motion was lost by 16 to 26. Snook — the man Walter George described as the greatest of all his opponents ('He worried the life out of me in scores of races') — was finished as an amateur. The harshness of the sentence, allowing that the evidence was entirely circumstantial, underlines the strength of feeling about the menace of roping.

The AAA's determination to govern was made clear in January, 1889, when its Rules for Competition, previously *recommended* at all meetings held under AAA Laws, were made compulsory. In the same year a joint committee of the AAA, National Cyclists' Union and Amateur Swimming Association declared themselves unable to find a remedy for open betting. 'Persons who hire a ground are in a very helpless condition. They have of themselves no legal power to expel offenders, and, though they are often expelled, those expelling them lay themselves open to harassing and legal proceedings.'

Most of the abuses in athletics in the first 20 years of the AAA were attributable to betting, but the biggest scandal of all, in 1896, arose from payments of money by clubs to athletes as inducements to appear at their meetings and boost attendances. The suspicions over Lon Myers in 1885 first alerted the AAA to this practice, and it was recognized in 1892 by the introduction of a new law: 'A competitor who asks for and/or receives expenses ceases to be an amateur.' The wording could not have been more blunt, but it still went unheeded by some. On 25 July 1896, a Special General Meeting of the AAA was called at Anderton's Hotel in Fleet Street 'to consider what sentence should be passed upon CA Bradley, AR Downer, FE Bacon, H. Watkins, G. Crossland and A. Blair, Jun., for receiving cash to compete under AAA Laws'.

In the words of one of them, 'the news came like a bombshell into the athletic world'. Between them, these athletes held three world records, seven British records and eleven English Championships. Charles Bradley (1870–1940),* of Huddersfield, had won the AAA 100 yd 4 years in succession; the Scot, Alf Downer (1874–1912), was the second-ranking sprinter in Britain, and at Stoke the previous August had shared a 9.8 sec clocking with Bradley, unacceptable as a record

*In the AAA Championships at Northampton in 1893, Bradley was informed that there was no possibility of his breaking the 100 yd record that afternoon as the course dropped 1½ ft in 100 yd and there was a following wind. He retorted, 'Then I'll run oop hill and against t'wind, and then nobody can say nowt against it,' and he did exactly that, winning in a record-equalling 10 sec flat. AAA result-lists have always included a note with the word 'uphill' against Bradley's name.

because it had been timed with one watch only; Fred Bacon (b. 1870) (Reading AC) had won AAA Championships at 1, 4 and 10 miles and set a world record for the mile of 4 min 17 sec in 1895; Harry Watkins (1872–1922) (Walthamstow H.) had won the Southern Cross-Country Championship in 1894 and 1895 and been runner-up in the 1895 and 1896 10 mile Championship; George Crossland (Manchester H.) was the reigning National Cross-Country Champion and world record-holder for 20 miles and the 2-hour run; the least known of the group was Alexander Blair, 19, (Airedale H.), the Yorkshire mile champion, who was the only one to be reinstated after his appeal was heard. There was firm evidence against the others. The clubs concerned had actually obtained receipts from the athletes for the £5 that seemed to be the standard hand-out. When Downer had tried to raise the Burnley Cricket Club to £8 instead of the £6 they wanted to pay, the club retaliated by providing the AAA with the evidence it needed.

There was no doubt that payments were common; Downer admitted later, in his autobiography, that there were few meetings at which he was not paid. The athletes found guilty generally accepted that they had been caught out, and deserved suspension. But there was bitterness that no action was taken against the clubs who had made the payments. Several of the club secretaries named in the inquiry actually sat in judgement on the athletes. One was a Local Officer of the AAA. The Committee had adopted the principle of Queen's Evidence: indemnification of those who were willing to provide evidence.

After that, the seasons of 1896 and 1897 had a distinctly impoverished look. In the absence of so many well-known names, attendances at the Championships were sparse. Conversely, there was a resurgence of interest in pedestrianism, as several of the suspended athletes made professional matches. A serious blow to amateur athletics was the voluntary decision of Edgar Bredin (1866–1939), the country's leading 440 and 880 yd runner, to join the renegades in 1897. That summer, yet another top athlete was permanently suspended by the Southern Committee. Sid Thomas (1868–1942), world record-holder for 3, 6 and 15 miles and winner of five AAA Championships in 4 miles and 10 miles events, appealed to the General Committee, but they confirmed the suspension in December. So by the end of 1897, the leading British runners for each event from 100 yd to 20 miles had been disqualified from ever competing again as amateurs.

The purge had a more positive consequence. In 1897 the AAA officially approved travelling expenses incurred by competitors in AAA Championships, international, inter-club, inter-team, inter-college or inter-school contests. Sports meetings arranged by individual clubs were deliberately excluded, the distinction being that, except for the Championships, expenses would be awarded only to athletes in representative matches. In connection with this, the 'First Claim Rule', relating to club representation, was drafted; re-drafting it was to become a ritual of AAA meetings for many years.

**Alfred Shrubb, winner of ten AAA titles and holder of the first official world distance-running records.**

With the cream of English distance-running removed, it took several years for another runner of quality to reach the top. Alfred Shrubb (1878–1964) proved to be more brilliant than Bacon, Watkins, Thomas or Crossland, greater, arguably, than George. AAA Champion at 1 mile, 1903–4; 4 miles, 1901–4; and 10 miles, 1901–4; National

Cross-Country Champion, 1901–4; and International Champion, 1903–4, Shrubb was rarely tested by his contemporaries. At the start of the twentieth century, athletics was becoming truly international. In the first months of 1905 Shrubb toured New Zealand and Australia at the expense of the NZAAA, setting a string of national records. Invitations arrived the same year at the AAA office from South Africa and Canada, but it was decided to decline them. Angered at what he considered high-handed treatment, Shrubb made other arrangements to embark on the Canadian tour. On 29 September 1905, he was suspended for misleading the Southern Committee 'concerning a ticket which he possessed which entitled him to travel by one of the Allen Boat Lines to Canada'. In November, an article in the *Sporting Life* made further allegations regarding Shrubb's expenses. The Southern Committee investigated them at two special meetings. Shrubb's permanent suspension was confirmed by the General Committee on 20 January 1906. Like others before him, he became a professional.

A happier outcome of that year was the passing of the Street Betting Act, which at last provided the AAA with a remedy for many of the abuses it had wrestled with for the first quarter-century of its existence. When the Bill was going through Parliament, Montague Shearman, Harry Venn and Percy Fisher (then acting Hon Secretary) had joined representatives of the NCU in a deputation to the Home Secretary to ask that a clause be inserted giving power to sports promoters to control betting at amateur sports meetings. On 20 April 1907, the General Committee was able to publish the following resolution: 'This Association therefore requests that every sports committee carry out the regulations of the Street Betting Act and obtain the services of sufficient Police to rigorously enforce the penalties under that Act.'

The bad old days were over.

> 'it is extremely undesirable that clubs affiliated to the AAA should include in their list of officials professional pugilists.'
>
> Ruling of the General Committee, 1892

# World Championships

**From the start, the AAA Championships were open to the world. By 1900, the roll of medal-winners took in five continents. The AAA was the pace-setter in international athletics.**

In June, 1894, Baron Pierre de Coubertin initiated a Congress at the Paris Sorbonne that led to the revival of the Olympic Games. 'At the head' — to quote Coubertin — 'an immovable trinity composed of three members: C. Herbert, Secretary of the Amateur Athletic Association (London), for Great Britain and the British Empire; WM Sloane, professor at the University of Princeton, for the American continent; and myself, for France and continental Europe.' Coubertin had met Charles Herbert (1846–1924) the previous December in London. He had found him 'quite taciturn but more understanding than he appeared at first sight.' Crucially for the Olympic movement, Herbert 'had at his disposal, as administrative head of the AAA, a whole propaganda network already organized on a wide footing'. Whether the AAA regarded itself as a propaganda organization is questionable, but it is beyond dispute that by the last decade of the nineteenth century its experience and authority had made it the premier athletic association in the world.

Charles Herbert, AAA Hon Secretary 1883–1906, who was one of the 'immovable trinity' who founded the modern Olympic Games.

Charles Herbert's term as Secretary from 1883 to 1906 saw the AAA — by definition a national governing body — increasingly involved internationally. His taciturnity in 1894 may have been a reflection of character — he was an impassive man who at eleven had suffered the trauma of losing parents, brother and sisters in the massacre at Cawnpore, India, in 1857 — but it is significant that Coubertin's conception was one of several master-plans for international athletics the AAA was urged to support in the nineties, and there was coolness in the General Committee about each one. The AAA seal of approval was not easily acquired. For years J. Astley Cooper tried to win support for a 'Pan Britannic Contest and Festival' — an embryonic Commonwealth Games — but he was unable to satisfy the AAA that it was a feasible project.

The plain fact was that throughout the nineteenth century the Championships were the world's principal athletic meeting. Not until 1908 did the Olympic Games really take off, and then the AAA had a large hand in the organization. The earlier Olympics, of 1896, 1900, 1904 and 1906, were blighted either by organizational problems or mediocre competition.

Overseas challengers came regularly to England from 1881 onwards. The most numerous and successful were the Irish. They had a great tradition in athletics, reaching back to the Tailteann Games, four centuries before any record of the ancient Olympics. In the modern era, they had hosted the first international match in athletics in 1876, when William Waddell's England team had visited Ireland, and they had visited Stamford Bridge for the return fixture the following year. Once the AAA Championships were established, gold medals were shipped to Ireland with astonishing consistency; the legendary crock of gold is filled with AAA Championship medals. There was not a year between 1881 and 1912 when an Irish-born athlete did not win at least one Championship. They collected 85 in those years, mostly by jumping and throwing. In 1889, a Manchester AC shot putter, RA Greene, succeeded in tying with the 6 ft 4 in/16 st 4 lb Dr William 'Jumbo' Barry (b. 1863) from Co. Cork. When Sir Richard Webster presented Greene with his medal, he remarked that it was splendid for once to find an Englishman among the honours. 'English?' put in Barry with a great laugh. 'Did you not know the man was born in Ireland?'

Durability was a hallmark of the Irish 'heavies'. Barry won his seventh title in 1895 at the age of 32; Tom Kiely was the same age when he won his sixth hammer Championship in 1902; James Mitchell, winner of five titles in shot and hammer between 1886 and 1888, was still active in athletics at 41 in 1906. Yet one man's achievement is unequalled. Thirteen of Ireland's victories were collected in the shot by Denis Horgan (1871–1922), between 1893 and 1912. This is the record number of wins for a single event. Horgan's warm-up for his event was said to be a dozen eggs broken into a pint of sherry. The best of the many stories told of this literally great (17 stone/108 kg) athlete came out of his defeat in the AAA Championship of 1900 by Richard Sheldon (USA), who went on to become Olympic Champion the same month in Paris. Horgan decided to seek revenge in the American AAU Championships. He posted his entry, threw up his job and worked his passage across the Atlantic on a cattleboat, arriving in Boston on the eve of the meeting. He travelled through the night to New York, found some Irish friends and warmed up in his usual style. Suitably refreshed, he turned up at Manhattan Field just as his event was announced. The huge crowd who had come to see America's ten new Olympic Champions in action were unaware that Horgan was in America. So was Richard Sheldon. The judge for the shot called over the list of entrants and came to *Denis Horgan, Ireland.* A voice in the crowd shouted 'I am here'. Over the barrier stepped Horgan, ready changed, in as devastating a display of gamesmanship as Stephen Potter ever devised. He heaved the shot 46 ft 1¾ in/14.06 m and took his revenge with over a foot to spare.

Denis Horgan (Ireland) winning the tenth of his record thirteen shot titles, in 1908. (Syndics of Cambridge University Library)

Horgan made a second trip to New York in 1907, obtained a job as an auxiliary policeman, and got into a brawl with some Italians, one of whom crashed a shovel into his head. He was taken unconscious to hospital, where a metal plate was inserted into his skull. The following year, at the age of 37, he won his tenth AAA title and took the silver medal in the Olympic Games.

Of the Irish jumpers who picked up AAA titles in the early years — they included Pat Davin, who won two, John Purcell, two, Dan Bulger, five, James Ryan, two, the Leahy brothers Pat, two, and Con, four, and Walter Newburn, two — Peter O'Connor (1872–1957) was the most outstanding. In the nineteenth century it was common for athletes to double at high and long jumping. The techniques were not dissimilar, for high jumpers tended to dash straight at the bar and rely on raw spring to get them over, while the 'sail' style of long jumping also required a combination of speed and elevation. O'Connor won the AAA high jump twice and the long jump six times between 1901 and 1906. Winning leaps of 23 ft 8½ in/7.22 m, 23 ft 7½ in/7.20 m, 22 ft 9½ in/6.95 m, 23 ft 2½ in/7.07 m, 23 ft 9½ in/7.25 m and 23 ft 5½ in/7.15 m indicate his consistency. Twenty years passed before his 23 ft 9½ in/7.25 m was beaten in the Championships. His world record of 24 ft 11¾ in/7.61 m, made in Dublin on 5 August 1901, lasted as long, and remained the Irish All-Comers Record until 7 August 1968, when Lynn Davies finally beat it with a modern hitch-kick. O'Connor once confided *his* technique to an American journalist: 'Well, y'see, I have a mark at so far back, and another mark beyond that. I hit the first mark easy like, then I run harder for the near one; and when I'm after hitting that, I go for all that's in me, and about four steps from the take-off, I shut my eyes, and put my trust in God.'

One suspects just a trace of the blarney in the statements of Horgan and O'Connor; they were far too proficient to owe everything to sherry or

*Above:* Pat Leahy (Ireland) wins the 1898 high jump at Stamford Bridge. (Syndics of Cambridge University Library)

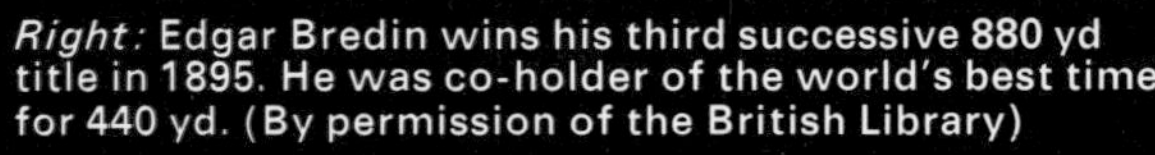

*Right:* Edgar Bredin wins his third successive 880 yd title in 1895. He was co-holder of the world's best time for 440 yd. (By permission of the British Library)

*Below:* Mortimer Remington (USA) wins the 440 yd in 1891 utilizing the low-arm style favoured by early American runners. (By permission of the British Library)

Remington wins with ease.

The Start for the Quarter Mile.

The start of the 100 yd final of 1896 — the winner was Norman Morgan (Ireland) (2nd from right). (Syndics of Cambridge University Library)

the Almighty. Nothing so frivolous was claimed by the other nation regularly seen at the Championships. The Americans unashamedly made a study of training and technique. It yielded good results: 41 Championship medals by 1914. After Myers and Merrill first crossed the Atlantic to compete in 1881, groups of Americans regularly competed, and they generally contributed something new in style or technique. In the eighties, American running was characterized by the strange style used by Myers, in which the arms were held low at the sides. It was more of an idiosyncrasy than an aid, but both Tom Conneff, world record holder for the mile and AAA Champion in 1888, and Mortimer Remington, 440 yd Champion in 1891, doggedly used it.

There was a more useful innovation in the high jumping of William Byrd Page (1866–1940). This Philadelphian cleared 6 ft/1.83 m with the traditional head-on rush at the bar with which he simultaneously covered 18 ft/5.48 m in distance, but achieved greater heights by modifying his style. Using a short approach with the effort concentrated in upward thrust and movement in the air, he raised the world record to 6 ft 4 in/1.93 m, over 9 in/23 cm above his own height. At the Championships of 1887 he was hampered by a foot injury, but still jumped 6 ft 0 in/1.83 m, to tie with the Englishman, George Rowdon (Teignmouth).

A technician equally remarkable in his event was the Canadian-born US shot putter, George Gray. At 5 ft 10½ in/11 st 4 lb/1.79 m/72 kg, he was surely the slightest-built of all the champions of the 7 ft square, yet succeeded in breaking the world record four times and winning the AAU title on ten occasions. On his one visit to England, in 1888, he set a Championship record of 43 ft 7 in/13.28 m, to win by over 3 ft/92 cm.

The Americans made their biggest impression at the AAA Championships of 1900, when there was an added reason for coming to Europe: the Paris Exposition Games — curiously, no one

An historic figure, Charles Bennett, here winning the 1 mile in 1900, was the first British athlete to win an Olympic gold medal. (Syndics of Cambridge University Library)

Future double Olympic champion Alvin Kraenzlein, of the University of Pennsylvania, in the long jump, 1900. (Syndics of Cambridge University Library)

Alvin Kraenzlein (USA), (on right) showing remarkably modern form over the fearsome high hurdles of 1900, winning from Norman Pritchard (India) and Alfred Trafford. (By permission of the British Library)

described them at the time as the second Olympic Games. At Stamford Bridge, the best 'gate' since 1881 saw a 44-strong US team pick up eight of the 14 Championships. The outstanding athlete of the afternoon, and of the Olympics, was Alvin Kraenzlein (1876–1928), who beat Peter O'Connor in the long jump (22 ft 10¼ in/6.96 m to 22 ft 4¼ in/6.81 m) and then brought hurdling into the twentieth century by using the straight-leg lead he had perfected, to win in 15.4 sec. It was an astonishing time for a grass course over hurdles you could not afford to skim, even allowing for a following wind. Kraenzlein repeated the feat in Paris. The runner-up in both races was Norman Pritchard, of India, who was awarded a silver medal by the AAA and a penknife worth half a crown by the French Olympic Committee.

Those 1900 Championships provided spectacle as well as sensation. The crowd's amusement at the multi-coloured dressing-gowns worn by the Americans evaporated when Arthur Duffey, Frank Jarvis and John Tewkesbury (all USA) filled the first three places in the 100 yd. Duffey equalled the record with 10 sec flat, a time he was to match in successfully defending the Championship in each of the next 3 years. In New York in 1902, he recorded the first 9.6 sec 100 yd to be ratified as a record, but when the AAU later declared him a professional they removed his name from all record and championship lists.

Irish-American John Flanagan's 1900 AAA hammer win heralded three consecutive Olympic titles. (Syndics of Cambridge University Library)

A clean sweep for America in the 100 yd final of 1900. Arthur Duffey (far right) wins from Frank Jarvis (21) and John Tewkesbury (4). Jarvis and Tewkesbury later won the Olympic 100 metres and 200 metres titles respectively. (Syndics of Cambridge University Library)

Irving Baxter wins the 1900 high jump. (Note the position of the crossbar against the uprights.) (Syndics of Cambridge University Library)

Germany's popular Hans Braun carried in triumph after winning the 1911 half-mile championship. (Syndics of Cambridge University Library)

Worse shocks followed for the crowd. American pole jumpers dominated the event England considered its own, Bascom Johnson winning with a Championship best of 11 ft 4 in/ 3.45 m. In the hammer, Irish-born New Yorker John Flanagan stretched the record by over 20 ft/ 6 m, to 163 ft 4 in/49.78 m. Irving Baxter came within a fraction of the high jump record and Richard Sheldon beat Horgan in the weight. 'In every sport requiring skill and agility we were completely outclassed,' admitted Harold Graham, one of the demoralized English.

Other nations were less successful. Frenchmen and Belgians regularly challenged for AAA titles, but won nothing until the new century. Teams from New Zealand (1892) and South Africa (1895 and 1898) returned home without a single gold medal. But athletics was increasingly popular in Europe, and in 1902 the Hungarian pole jumper, Jakab Kauser, became the first Continental to capture a title. English chauvinists explained that pole jumping had fallen into neglect; there were suggestions that it should be removed from the list of events. No alibis were possible when the Europeans started winning on the track. The first was Hans Braun of Germany, champion over 880 yd in 1909. A distinctive figure with his red-gold hair and broad smile, Braun became a great favourite with the Stamford Bridge crowd — they called him 'Fritz' — and he won again in 1911 and 1912. Finland won its first title in 1911, through Hannes Kolehmainen (1889–1966), who took the 4 miles; the following year he dominated the Olympic Games, with three victories in distance running. Even the AAA mile title was ultimately claimed by a European, the Swede, John Zander, in 1913; during World War I, he became world record holder at 1500, 2000 and 3000 metres.

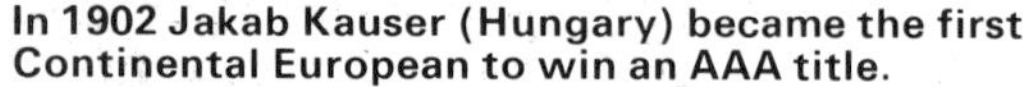

In 1902 Jakab Kauser (Hungary) became the first Continental European to win an AAA title.

John Rimmer (later the Olympic steeplechase champion) wins the 4 miles in 1900. (Syndics of Cambridge University Library)

The first of the 'Flying Finns', Hannes Kolehmainen, outsprints Walter Scott to win the 4 miles in 1911. (Syndics of Cambridge University Library)

Peter O'Connor (Ireland) set a Championship long jump record in 1905 which lasted for 20 years. (His 24 ft 11¾ in/7.61 m jump in 1901 was a world best for 20 years and a UK best for 59 years.) (Syndics of Cambridge University Library)

Joe Binks (3) sets a British mile record of 4 min 16.8 sec to win the 1902 mile from Henry Hawtrey. Binks later became the athletics reporter of the *News of the World.* (Syndics of Cambridge University Library)

In those pre-war years, the entries for the Championships gave a fairly accurate picture of the development of the sport internationally. Well into the twenties, the Dublin paper, *Sport*, referred to the AAA meeting as the World's Athletic Championships. This was never a title the Association would have used; it had no ambition to rival the Olympic movement. It had given Baron Pierre de Coubertin its support from the start. The International Olympic Committee — of which Charles Herbert, AAA Hon Secretary, was a founder-member — was permitted to announce that the field events at the Games of 1896 would be held under AAA Laws. The *Olympic Review* No 2 (1894) had reported, 'The Amateur Athletic Association . . . exercises complete control over almost all the athletic sports societies, even outside England; its regulations are observed throughout the British Empire; they are generally considered as being superior to all others.'

Tom Nicolson, seen here in 1907, won the hammer six times and the shot once. (Syndics of Cambridge University Library)

There was no national team for the 1896 Olympics; a few individuals made their own way to Athens and participated, but none was in the top class, and there were no British victories in athletics. For the next Games, at Paris in 1900, the AAA provided £100 and selected a team after the Championships. They won four events: Alfred Tysoe (1874–1901) took the 800 m, Charles Bennett (1870–1949) the 1500 m, John Rimmer (1878–1962) the 4000 m steeplechase, and a group of five won the 5000 m team race. The expense prevented a British team from being sent to St Louis for the 1904 Games, but there were three British winners in the intercalated Games at Athens in 1906: Henry Hawtrey (5 miles), Con Leahy (high jump) and Peter O'Connor (triple jump), though it is right to note that the latter two were born in Ireland.

In 1906 poor Charles Herbert suffered a serious head injury when he fell from the top of a London horse bus, so it was his successor as AAA Hon Secretary, Percy L. Fisher, who served as the Association's representative on the British Olympic Association when the Games came to London in 1908. He stated the AAA's terms: it would support the Games provided that they were scheduled some time after the Championships had taken place, and that the AAA had sole control of the athletic portion of the Games. This was conceded; the athletic events in the new White City Stadium were held from 13–25 July, under AAA Laws and Rules, and all officials were appointed by the Association. It must be said that this created problems. There was an atmosphere of international rivalry in the stadium quite outside the experience of athletes and officials. The most publicized of a number of incidents were the disqualifications of the American, John C. Carpenter, in the 400 metres, and the Italian, Dorando Pietri, in the marathon. At the conclusion of the Games James E. Sullivan, President of the American AAU, charged the British officials with being the most prejudiced and unfair in the world. The AAA and the BOA jointly published a 60-page booklet, *A Reply to Certain Criticisms*, defending each decision that had aroused controversy. De Coubertin's considered judgement in his *Mémoires Olympiques* (1932) was that there was no real foundation for so much bitterness on the part of the critics. 'I just could not understand Sullivan's attitude here. He shared his team's frenzy and did nothing to calm them down.' Happily the acrimony between the

**The first Royal visit to the Championships, 1908. Prince Albert of Wales, the future King Edward VIII, and his tutor, with AAA President, Lord Desborough. To the right, Con Leahy, the winner of the high jump, with Percy Fisher, AAA Hon Secretary, 1906–15. (Syndics of Cambridge University Library)**

AAA and the AAU was temporary; by 1925 relations had improved to such an extent that the two signed a formal working agreement.

It is interesting that the distance of 26 miles 385 yd/42 195 m which became standardized for marathons in 1924 was fixed by the four AAA officials who formed the Olympic Track Committee: Percy Fisher, Charles Val Hunter, George Schofield and Harry Venn. The distance from the East Terrace of Windsor Castle to the White City was 26 miles/41 843 m. The distance from the stadium entrance to the finish, below the Royal Box, was 385 yd. If this seemed a considerable increase on the 40 km (24 miles 1504 yd) originally scheduled — and possibly accounted for Dorando's collapse and disqualification — at least there were ample refreshments along the route. At four points runners were offered rice puddings, raisins, bananas, milk, soda, Oxo and (for external use) eau-de-Cologne, thus qualifying them as the best fed and most fragrant marathon runners in history.

Britain's eight victories in 1908, through Wyndham Halswelle (400 m), Emil Voigt (5 miles), Arthur Russell (3200 m steeplechase), George Larner (3500 m and 10 mile walks), Tim Ahearne (triple jump), the 3 miles team and the tug-of-war team, amounted to her best performance in any Olympics. Yet it was a shock that Britain had not done better. The Americans had won 15 track and field events and paraded a 'British lion' on a chain at their reception at City Hall, New York.

Strenuous efforts were made to rehabilitate British athletics before the next Olympics. An Amateur Field Events Association was formed in

**Emil Voigt wins the 4 miles in 1908, the year he became Olympic champion for 5 miles. (Syndics of Cambridge University Library)**

In 1909 Alfred Flaxman, despite this failure, won the pole jump. The following year he won the hammer event. (Syndics of Cambridge University Library)

The water seems unusually deep in the 1912 AAA 2 miles steeplechase won by Sydney Frost. (Syndics of Cambridge University Library)

John Zander (Sweden) wins the mile in 1913. He became world record holder for 1500, 2000 and 3000 metres. (Syndics of Cambridge University Library)

1910 by FAM Webster and other enthusiasts, with Sir Arthur Conan Doyle as President. The AAA permitted it in 1911 to arrange Championships in a number of events not included in the main July programme: standing jumps, the triple jump, 220 and 440 yd hurdles, discus and javelin (each in both styles practised in the Olympics), slinging the 56 lb weight and putting the 16 lb weight for height. In 1912, FW Parker was appointed Chief Athletic Adviser to the AAA. A Chief Trainer, and Trainers to the North, South and Midlands were also appointed. Meanwhile a series of invitations to compete in full international matches with Sweden and France were declined. When the tentative programme for the 1912 Olympic Games was published, the AAA made strong representations to have additional events included. Percy Fisher was able to report in October, 1910, that through the good offices of the British representatives on the International Olympic Committee, the 800 m, 10 000 m walk and a cross-country race of 5 miles (actually 8000 m) had been added. The General Committee instructed him to thank the British representatives for their efforts and ask for the inclusion of a 2 mile steeplechase. This proved too much for the IOC to swallow.

Unhappily for British hopes, other nations had learned the lesson of the London Olympics and trained assiduously for Stockholm. The tally of British victories in 1912 was two. Ironically, one of them was in an event the AAA had suggested should be *deleted* from the Olympic programme: the 4 × 100 m relay. The other was a superbly judged 1500 m by Arnold Strode-Jackson (1891–1973). He was the nephew of Clement Jackson, co-founder of the AAA, who had promised in 1911 that if he gave up rowing he would make him into a miler. The training was not too Spartan. 'I invariably had a bottle of Guinness for lunch and a nice glass of Burgundy for dinner,' Col Strode-Jackson recalled in a 1965 interview. 'That's what my Uncle Jacky, bless him, prescribed.'

One important outcome of the 1912 Olympics was the Congress at Stockholm on 17 July that drafted rules for an International Amateur Athletic Federation. The need for internationally respected regulations governing athletics had been made clear at each of the Olympic celebrations. AAA delegates attended this and the second Congress in Berlin in August, 1913. SG Moss (Assistant Secretary) was one of the committee that drew up the first official world record list which, however, was not submitted until the 5th Congress at Geneva in 1921. The AAA formally joined the IAAF at its Congress at Lyons in June, 1914.

*Above:* George Hutson overtakes a lapped runner to win the 1913 4 miles in record time. He had won two bronze medals at the 1912 Olympics. (Radio Times Hulton Picture Library)

*Right:* Willie Applegarth wins the 1914 220 yd in 21.2 sec — a world record. (The late Sir Adolphe Abrahams)

It was made clear by the 1912 Olympics that Britain no longer called the tune in world athletics. The Games had taken over from the Championships as the premier international meeting. The AAA found itself charged with a new obligation: to raise the standard of national athletics. For the first time, there was talk of asking Parliament for a grant from public funds. Local authorities were urged by the AAA to include athletics in the school curriculum and to provide facilities for athletes to train in public parks. A full-time Chief Coach, Walter Knox, was appointed in 1914 on a 3-year contract. In the same year, the Championship programme was expanded to two days, and the 440 yd hurdles, discus, javelin and triple jump were dignified with inclusion. Not without reservation. 'In the event of any of these events not being included in the standard programme for the Olympic Games, they will be deleted,' reported the Championship Committee. The 1 mile relay, instituted in 1911, was also incorporated in the Championship meeting for the first time.

The possibility of official international matches had often been raised at General Committee meetings, but financial considerations had always ruled it out — except for a modest five-event contest between the United Kingdom, Australasia and Canada in connection with the 1911 Festival of Empire. A start was finally made near home on 11 July 1914, with the match between Scotland, Ireland and England at Hampden Park. England won six events, Scotland three and Ireland two. That brilliant sprinter Willie Applegarth (1890–1958) repeated his Championship double in the 100 and 220 yd. His time in the latter was a Scottish record of 21.4 sec, one-fifth slower than the world record he had set a week previously round the narrow, banked bend at Stamford Bridge.

Less than a month later, Britain was at war. At its October meeting the AAA Olympic Committee was disbanded. The Games of 1916 had been scheduled for Berlin. The specially constructed stadium would wait 20 years for the Olympic flame to arrive.

### AAA REPRESENTATIVE MATCHES

In 1911, Philip Baker, now Lord Noel-Baker, then President of Cambridge University AC, wrote to the AAA suggesting a match between the University and the AAA. It was held at Cambridge on 7 December 1911, and the AAA won by seven events to three. From that time, matches between the AAA, universities, clubs and forces became regular features of the athletic calendar. In World War II, AAA teams helped to keep the sport alive, and the first post-war meeting at the White City in 1945 between the AAA, the Army, the RAF and the US Forces drew the biggest crowd seen for athletics since 1908. It was in the AAA v Oxford University AC match in 1954 that Roger Bannister achieved the first sub-four-minute mile. After 1970 the list of AAA fixtures was reduced to two, against the past and present students of Loughborough and Borough Road Colleges. However, the Area Associations contest a number of representative matches.

# Fixing the Rules of the Game

**The laws of athletics are repeatedly adjusted to take account of technical innovation and human ingenuity. In 1880 the 16 rules for competition could be printed on a single page. A century on, there are 114 rules occupying 69 pages of the AAA Handbook. Behind each new rule there is usually a story.**

A civil servant in spectacles, Ernest Pelling, caused a small sensation at the Championships of 1889 by getting on all fours for the start of the 100 yd. The crouch start, said to have been invented in Scotland in 1884 by Bobby Macdonald, of Maori origin, made no real impact in competition until 12 May 1888, when a Yale student, Charles Sherrill, used it in a meet at Cedarhurst, Long Island, mainly to remedy a problem of unsteadiness in the upright position. A sketch of Sherrill's start appeared in the *Athletic Journal* (Manchester) on 17 July, and Tom Nicholas (Monmouth AC) began to use it towards the end of that summer. An attraction of the new style was that there was nothing in the rules to prevent the runner from placing his hands beyond the start-line, provided he did not *overstep* the mark. The 'Nicholas start' was debated by the General Committee in May, 1889. They ruled by 6–5 that 'no part of the body of the athlete must touch the ground in front of the mark before the pistol fire'. Nicholas did not appear for the 1889 Championships (he won the 440 yd in 1890, and soon after turned professional), and it was Pelling who first used the crouch start under the new rule. He won by a yard in 10.4 sec. 'Previous to 1889,' he later recalled, 'I was one of the slowest starters in London.'

High jumping was for a long time regarded as akin to hurdling, with special praise for 'a downright honest leap at the bar' in the styles of the Irishmen, Pat Davin and James Ryan. In 1888, the AAA prohibited diving and somersaulting, and there was an attempt to introduce a rule that every competitor should land on his feet. It was not carried. Even so, it was as late as 1912 before the AAA conceded that 'a pit of sand or soft earth may be dug for competitors to alight in'. More stunning than that, pole jumpers also had to wait till 1912 for softer landings.

In long jumping, too, there were few concessions to comfort. To discourage overrunning, the ground immediately beyond the line was dug out to a depth of 3 in/7 cm. Measuring was strictly from the take-off line to the heel-mark. Anyone who fell back, or made a mark with another part of his anatomy, suffered a no-jump.

The shot put had a curious evolution. From 1866 to 1877, the throwing area was a pair of lines 7 ft/2.13 m apart. In 1878 the prodigious law-maker, John Chambers, introduced the 7 ft/2.13 m diameter circle for the AAC Championships, and this was adopted by the AAA and used until 1882, when a motion from his old rival, William Waddell, supplanted the circle with a 7 ft/2.13 m square. For a quarter of a century the Championship was decided in a square; in the Olympic year of 1908 the AAA reverted to Chambers' 7 ft/2.13 m circle, which had been used in America since 1888, and is still in use. The stop-board was introduced by the AAA in October, 1911.

Of all events, hammer throwing underwent most changes. Originally, throwers were allowed a free run and follow. They were limited by John Chambers in 1876 to a 7 ft/2.13 m throwing area between two lines, as in the shot put. He introduced the 7 ft/2.13 m circle in 1878 and this was used for each Championship up to 1886. Thereafter, there was a period of anarchy in hammer throwing. The AAA switched to a circle of 9 ft/2.74 m; the Americans threw from a 7 ft/2.13 m circle from 1888; the English universities used a 30 ft/9.14 m circle; and

Ernest Pelling, the first man to use the crouch start in the Championships. (University of Birmingham)

Tom Nicolson puts the shot in the 1903 Championships. The 7ft square was used from 1882 to 1907. (Syndics of Cambridge University Library)

John Barrett (Ireland) wins the shot in 1911 from an open circle. After this the AAA introduced the stop-board. (Radio Times Hulton Picture Library)

London AC frequently used one of 20 ft/6.09 m. The 7 ft/2.13 m circle was not reintroduced by the AAA until October, 1907, in time for the Olympic Games. Stiff wooden-handled hammers went out of use (except in Highland Games) soon after 1896, when the AAA legalized the piano-wire handles already in use in America and at the Universities. But problems persisted. There was strong opposition to the event; Charles Herbert tried to have it expunged from the Championships, and almost succeeded at the AGM of 1902, losing by 16–19; another attempt to ban it was made in 1905. In 1906 there was an 'unholy' incident when the Rev EEB May was disqualified from the Championship for attempting to use a hammer more than the 4 ft/1.22 m regulation length. Even after the rules were internationally standardized for the Olympic Games of 1908, there was an attempt, in 1912, to introduce a stop-board, as in shot putting. After one year it was abandoned as dangerous.

Two burning issues of the pre-1914 period have happily long since cooled. Handicap races — a legacy of pedestrianism — predominated in club athletics into the 1940s. For example, when Arthur Astley (Salford H.) won the 1906 880 yd Championship, it was the first scratch race he had run in his life. Before 1890, handicapping was arranged at a local level by club secretaries and local experts who kept up with the 'form'. In the

**Charles Pearce defeats Charles Willers in the 1893 4 miles and the crowd invade the track. (By permission of the British Library)**

North and Midlands there was a strong feeling that the AAA should take control by appointing its own licensed handicappers. This was opposed by the South, who were satisfied with the informal arrangement. Voting *en bloc*, the North and Midlands won by a single vote, and AAA handicappers were licensed annually from 1890 and allowed to charge fees for their services. In 1901, the system was further tightened by the creation of Area Boards of Control, and a similar arrangement still exists for the relatively few handicap events still contested.

The other great controversy concerned the National Cyclists' Union. The first cycle races in England took place in 1869 and the first Championship was organized by John Chambers, under AAC auspices, in 1871. The new sport was often included as a novel event in track and field meetings, and the connection persisted even after the formation of the Bicycle Union, soon restyled the NCU, in 1878. The problem was that the NCU, unlike the AAA, was conceived as a controlling body for amateurs *and* professionals. Its meetings could include races in either class.

Whenever athletics and cycling appeared on the same programme, there was a chance of the AAA's firm laws on amateurism being broken. After much acrimony, a working agreement was hammered out in 1885 between the two bodies, Montague Shearman leading the AAA delegation. Twenty-one years later, the NCU flouted the agreement by permitting professional running at its meetings. The AAA terminated the 1885 agreement, and the NCU retaliated by forming its own organization to promote amateur and professional foot-racing. The AAA's response was to promote its own amateur cycling championships in 1910 and 1911. This nonsensical situation ended in the spring of 1912, when Shearman's advocacy was once again deployed to reach an agreement with the NCU, and the two organizations reverted to promoting only their own sports.

Legislation provides athletics with its structure, but the people in the sport determine its character. Contrary to popular belief, the Victorians were more interested in winning than playing the game. A few examples will illustrate this. In races of 880 yd and upwards it was usual for a runner to drop out as soon as he realized he had no chance of winning. Nobody set much store on finishing the course. On the rare occasions a man persevered, he was more likely to be censured than applauded. 'Dixon kept plodding away,' reported *Bell's Life* of John Fowler-Dixon (AAA Vice-President, 1922–43) in the 1883 4 mile Championship, 'though for what purpose it would be curious to ascertain, as he was about a quarter of a mile behind.' Athletics was all about winning. When Charles Pearce (Birchfield H.) entered the 4 miles at Northampton in 1893, over 1000 of his fellow workers at the Wolverton railway depot came to support him. They rushed the track when their man took the lead in the last lap, oblivious to other runners trying to finish. The most horrendous tales come from the pole jump. In 1899, James Poole (Windermere) travelled to Wolverhampton with the ambition of emulating his fellow Lakelanders, Ray and Dickinson, with a third consecutive Championship. Somehow he lost his pole changing trains. The other competitors refused to lend him theirs, so Poole had to watch his title taken at 9 ft 1 in/2.77 m, the lowest winning jump of the century. In 1901, Irving Baxter (USA), the Olympic Champion, also arrived for the AAA Championship without a pole, and got a similar rebuff when he asked to borrow one. Undaunted, he took a look round the ground, uprooted a flagpole and vaulted with that, sharing the Championship at 9 ft 10 in/2.99 m.

**Irving Baxter uses a flag-pole to tie for the 1901 pole vault title. (The Mansell Collection Ltd)**

**WH Hodgson using his own pole to tie for the Championship at 9 ft 10 in/2.99 m. (The Mansell Collection Ltd)**

'Egg and Spoon Races do not come under the jurisdiction of the AAA.'

Ruling of the Southern Committee, 1897.

'A competitor is disqualified for jumping over the worsted.'

Ruling of the General Committee, 1898.

'When a competitor's head touches the tape first, he wins; it is not absolutely necessary to breast the tape.'

Ruling of the General Committee, 1899.

# Presidents One and Two

**Richard Webster (left) defeats Lord Jersey in the mile in the 1865 Oxford and Cambridge Sports. These athletes became the first two Presidents of the AAA, Lord Jersey from 1880 to 1890, and Sir Richard Webster from 1891 to 1915. Both died in 1915.**

The 7th Earl of Jersey (Victor Albert George Child-Villiers), (1845–1915), was the inaugural President. One of the pioneers of amateur athletics, he had won the Eton mile in 1862 and represented Oxford in the second Inter-Varsity Sports in 1865, finishing second in the mile and fourth in the 2 miles. He was a member of the AAC committee that organized the first Championships in 1866, and he staunchly supported John Chambers through the AAC's beleaguered existence. Appreciative of the ability of the young AAA committee when he was elected President in 1880, he was content to be mainly a figurehead, providing an occasional exotic note for the minutes that he was unavoidably absent in Monte Carlo. In 1890, Lord Jersey was appointed Governor-General of New South Wales, and resigned the Presidency.

His successor, Sir Richard Everard Webster (Viscount Alverstone) (1842–1915), curiously had an athletic career that closely paralleled Lord Jersey's. He won the Charterhouse mile in 1861, went up to Cambridge and became Hon Secretary of the University Athletic Club — which in 1864 was the equivalent of President. He penned the historic challenge to Oxford that instituted the world's oldest athletics match, and finished second in the steeplechase. In the 1865 match he met Lord Jersey in the mile and 2 miles, winning both. He, too, was a close colleague of Chambers, active in the organization of the AAC, and maintained a constructive interest in athletics throughout a momentous legal career. 'It is unlikely that in thirty-two years at the bar any man ever had more work to do, or earned more money,' states his entry in the *Dictionary of National Biography*. He was Attorney-General when he became President, and Lord Chief Justice of England from 1900 to 1913, yet regularly attended the Championships and the Oxford and Cambridge Sports and often took the chair at AAA committee meetings. No chairman was more effective at bringing an AGM to order than the Judge of the Dr Crippen case (1910). In *Recollections of Bar and Bench* (1914), Viscount Alverstone claimed credit for two innovations in throwing events, the 7 ft/2.13 m square for the shot, and the 9 ft/2.74 m circle for the hammer,* but by the end of his life each had been discarded for the earlier 7 ft/2.13 m circle. However, his

*He claimed to have *suggested* the changes. The formal proposals came, respectively, from William Waddell (1881) and H. Beardsell (1887).

interest in the heavy events probably ensured the survival of the hammer in the standard track and field programme, for there was persistent pressure to abandon it from Clement Jackson (Hon Treasurer) and Charles Herbert (Hon Secretary). The event was deleted from the Oxford and Cambridge Sports a few years after his death. He is more likely to be remembered in athletics as an early holder of the best amateur time on record for 2 miles, 10 min 5 sec, set in the Cambridge Sports of 1865. The University's Alverstone Club (1920) was named in his honour.

Victor Albert George Child-Villiers, 7th Earl of Jersey (1845–1915), the first President of the Amateur Athletic Association. (Radio Times Hulton Picture Library)

Richard Everard Webster, Viscount Alverstone (1842–1915), the AAA's second President. (Radio Times Hulton Picture Library)

# From Trenches to Tracks

**Interest in athletics erupted after World War I. New clubs affiliated to the AAA at the rate of 100 a year. Crowds of 30 000 filled Stamford Bridge for the Championships. Regular international matches began. Athletics had become a major national and international sport, and crucial developments took place in its organization.**

In the 1914–18 war, the AAA was kept in being by a small Special Committee. They organized athletics meetings for home-based forces at Brighton (1915) and Stamford Bridge (1916, 1917 and 1918), but the focus of attention was the Front. Among the former AAA Champions killed in action were the hurdler, Gerard Anderson, hammer throwers Alfred Flaxman and Henry Leeke, middle distance runners Hans Braun (Germany) and Olympic Champion, Wyndham Halswelle, and distance runners George Hutson and Douglas McNicol.

Nothing was quite the same again. The key figures in the AAA had changed. Sir Montague Shearman, its founder, had been elected President in January, 1916, and Harry Barclay (1861–1933) had succeeded Percy Fisher as Hon Secretary in 1915. WM Barnard was Treasurer, Clement Jackson having retired from the office in 1910. When the full General Committee met to take stock in January, 1919, it found that, far from being impaired by the war, athletics had emerged stronger than before. Just as the Volunteer movement of the 1860s had given an impetus to the sport by its emphasis on physical training, so the widescale enlistment of 1914–18 made millions conscious of the importance of fitness. Moreover, physical education was at last developing in the national school system. In 1909 a new *Syllabus of Physical Training* had been issued by the Board of Education, and physical training made compulsory in training colleges. The demobilized forces and school-leavers looked to sport as a way of sustaining their fitness.

Encouraging as this was, the AAA, as constituted, was in no shape to cope. Its structure, laws and rules for competition required substantial revision. Cobwebs of the nineteenth century had lain undisturbed for years. Hurdle races were permitted only on grass tracks; the 'climbing' style could still be used by pole jumpers; relay teams were expected to carry a handkerchief or flag; and all competitors were instructed to wear costumes that covered them from shoulders to knees. More serious than that, the three-tier structure of General Committee, Area Associations and Clubs was incapable of providing facilities for competition on the scale now demanded.

The problem was met by setting up the AAA Reconstruction Committee, its purpose 'to cater for (1) the thousands of new athletes made as a result of the war, and (2) the more or less athletically trained youth leaving college or school'. At the Annual General Meeting of 1919, the Committee recommended the creation of County organizations, with the object of promoting County Championships in track and field, road walking and cross-country. The new County Athletic Associations would also be responsible for encouraging the sport in schools, scout groups and similar organizations. They were charged to 'bring all possible influence to bear on local and other bodies to provide playing fields' and to form athletic associations 'in each Borough, Urban and Rural District in the County'. True to the post-war philosophy, the emphasis was to be given to team, rather than individual, competition.

The Committee also recommended revising and regrouping the Laws and Competition Rules. The first batch of proposals passed at the AGM of 1920 excised some of the more outdated rules. *Out* went the stipulation that hurdling should always be on grass; 'climbing' in the pole jump; and the rule banning long jumpers from sitting back or making any mark behind the heelmarks. *In* came batons for relays, although handkerchiefs were still permitted until 1922, when a second set of revisions was approved. In that year the rule governing clothing was amended to 'a half-sleeved vest and loose drawers, reaching at least halfway to the knees, with slips'. High jumpers must have cursed those loose drawers, for a 'fair jump' in 1922 was defined as 'one where the head does not go over the bar before the feet and is not below the buttocks in clearing the bar'. Few modern styles would have satisfied judges of the twenties.

In the same set of new rules (1922) appeared the first-ever definition of walking for competitive purposes. Previously race walking operated, like the British Constitution, on an unwritten principle. Judges formed their own opinions as to what was a legitimate walking style. The Road Walking Association (known since 1954 as the Race Walking Association), formed in 1907 and affiliated to the AAA, now provided a formal definition: 'Walking is progression by steps so taken that the heel of the foremost foot must reach the ground before the toe of the other foot leaves it.' This was altered in 1928 to: 'Walking is progression by steps so taken that unbroken contact with the ground is maintained.' The AAA thus accepted the IAAF definition. Without surrendering its autonomy, the Association steadily adapted its rules to international standards in the mid-twenties.

Memories of route marches must have discouraged some from participating in race walking, but the enthusiasm for athletics in post-war Britain was overwhelming. At the outbreak of war the number of affiliated clubs was 582; through the 1920s the figure grew by up to 100 annually, so that in 6 years the AAA doubled in size. Entries for the Championships tested the programme organizers. In 1924 there were 50 names for the 100 yd, compared with 17 in 1914. The field for the mile – dignified in the first AAA Championships in 1880 by the solitary presence of Walter George — rose to 48 in 1924, and in 1926 the Championships Committee took the unprecedented step of introducing heats in this event. The meeting was extended to three days in 1927, one innovation that was not successful. But public interest in the twenties practically guaranteed a Saturday gate of 25 000 at Stamford Bridge, with 30 000 not unusual. In 1922, HM King George V, the AAA's Patron since 1910, attended, and the profit on the Championships topped £1000 for the first time.

The stimulus to the AAA's finances meant that some cautions of the pre-war years could be set aside. An agreement was made with the *Union des Sociétés Françaises des Sports Athlétiques* for an annual international match (except in Olympic years) between England and France, first staged at the Stade Colombes, Paris, on 11 September 1921, before the largest crowd yet assembled for an athletic meeting in France. The pleasure of England's narrow victory was slightly soured by the stoning of the English team bus, but it was explained that this was a political demonstration against the British Treasury, whose exchange control policies had depressed the franc. A political issue of greater consequence, the partitioning of Ireland in 1922, was destined soon to threaten England's other international fixture, the triangular match between the home countries, resumed in 1920.

Plenty was happening on the domestic scene. Eleven provincial universities combined to form the Inter-University Athletic Board of Great Britain and Ireland (now known as the Universities Athletic Union) in 1919. The following year the Achilles Club was founded to unite the talents of the two oldest universities, with the result that Oxbridge within a year or two dominated English athletics as triumphantly as Shearman and his contemporaries in the 1870s.

Among so many new ideas came a move to give formal recognition to women's athletics, which had unofficially taken place under AAA auspices since at least 1907. The General Committee first discussed the matter in October, 1920, but no resolution was put, and the ladies waited until February, 1922 — by which time English athletes led by Mary Lines had swept the board at the first women's international meeting at Monte Carlo and defeated France in an unofficial international match. A letter was read requesting the AAA to accept control of women's athletics; this was approved in principle and the procedure suggested that 'it would be advisable that an Athletic Association for women should be formed and application made to the AAA for affiliation'. The WAAA was clearly intended to function within the AAA, as the Race Walking Association or the English Cross-Country Union do. Traditionally it is a woman's prerogative to change her mind, but in 1922 the General Committee changed theirs. When the duly formed WAAA applied for affiliation in October, the AAA refused the application, adding 'if the Association is properly formed, the AAA will be prepared to enter into a working agreement'. What prompted this *volte-face* we may never know. Whether male chauvinists won the day, or the AAA simply took fright at controlling what was regarded in some quarters as at best *risqué* and at worst dangerous to health, the WAAA went its own way, and the working agreement took 10 years to emerge.

In 1925 came encouraging evidence that the Reconstruction Scheme was achieving results. The Schools Athletic Association was founded, and held its first Championships at Crystal Palace. And the first Inter-County Championships, which began as a relay and team contest, presaged the formation of the Counties Athletic Union in 1926, though it must be said that this was largely a Southern affair until the thirties.

One venture tried at this time and not persisted with was an English Championship Meeting open only to athletes born in England and Wales. It was held in 1923, 1924 and 1925. When support lessened, the idea was put on ice, to be defrosted 52 years later by the British Amateur Athletic Board as the United Kingdom Championships, open to athletes of British nationality only.

The formation of the BAAB in 1932 was the most significant development of the inter-war period. It was triggered by the Scottish AAA announcing that it had decided to seek independent membership of the IAAF. Relations between the governing bodies of the home countries had become strained to crisis-point by the struggle for control of the sport in Northern Ireland. After the creation of the Irish Free State in 1924, two organizations, the National Athletic and Cycling Association of Ireland and the Northern Ireland Amateur Athletic, Cycling and Cross-Country Association, claimed jurisdiction over the six counties of Ulster. The AAA had a working agreement with the NACAI, and the triangular international match between England, Ireland and Scotland continued until 1930, controlled by an International Board representing the three countries. But then the Irish dispute boiled over, the Northern Ireland Association suspending certain athletes connected with the rival Association, and the AAA was compelled to make its own position clear. It withdrew from the triangular international. Scotland, deprived of its only international fixture, decided this was the time to apply to the IAAF for separate representation.

This complex problem was tackled by a new generation. At the AGM of 1931, Sir Harry Barclay* tendered his resignation as AAA Hon Secretary, and was succeeded by Douglas Lowe, the Olympic 800 m Champion of 1924 and 1928. Ably supported by his contemporary, Harold Abrahams (1899–1978), the Olympic 100 m Champion of 1924, also a lawyer by training, Lowe first negotiated the restyling of the Northern Ireland AA and CCA as the Northern Ireland AAA. The two then drafted the constitution of an International Board representing England and Wales, Northern Ireland and Scotland. The Board, composed of representatives of the AAA, NIAAA and SAAA in the ratio 5:2:3, would replace the AAA as the body affiliated to the IAAF. The British Amateur Athletic Board, as it became known in 1937, was a major innovation. It meant that international teams could in future represent Great Britain and Northern Ireland, as distinct from England and Wales. Moreover, it allowed the hard-pressed General Committee to give its main attention to domestic athletics.

The Scots were satisfied with the draft, and withdrew their application to the IAAF. The Irish dispute was the subject of a joint commission set up by the IAAF, on which Lowe and Abrahams represented the AAA, out of which enough harmony emerged for the NIAAA to lift its suspensions. The difficulties between North and South in Ireland had eased enough by 1938 for a joint Irish team to be selected, and in consequence the triangular international match between the home countries was revived.

A further advantage of the BAAB was that it forged a link with women's athletics. After the IAAF assumed control of women's athletics internationally in 1936, the Board the following year signed an agreement with the WAAA by which two of its representatives were co-opted, with the right to exercise one vote. The formality over, a good understanding was established, and the hurts of earlier years were mitigated by the advice and help AAA representatives were able to supply.

If the most obvious successes of the Board were diplomatic, it also addressed itself to practical problems. Britain's lamentable weakness in field events was the subject of a special report by the Board in 1934. Out of this emerged perhaps the most constructive development of the thirties: the AAA summer schools at Loughborough under the direction of Capt FAM (Michael) Webster, Evelyn Montague and Malcolm Nokes. Over a hundred students attended the first in 1934, and it was repeated annually until the war.

'The Athletes to and from Abroad Committee asked for guidance upon the question whether an athlete should be accompanied by a lady as an "attendant". It was the opinion of the meeting that such a practice was undesirable.'

General Committee Minutes, 21 Nov 1931.

*His knighthood in 1930, the Jubilee year, after 16 years as Hon Secretary, was the highest honour conferred on an AAA official for services to the sport.

# The Middle Men

**Between the wars Britain excelled at middle distance running. The Olympic 800 metres was won by Albert Hill in 1920, Douglas Lowe in 1924 and 1928 and Tommy Hampson in 1932. The two-lap race seemed as British as a bowler hat.**

Frustratingly for foreign coaches trying to draw deductions from Britain's success, the three were most unlike each other. Hill was broad in build, with a well-muscled trunk and legs almost disproportionately long. At 31, he had the look of a veteran, eyes that had seen 3 years' war service in France, and a dab of moustache exactly right for his job as a railway guard. Lowe, trim and dark, with sleek hair parted in the centre, had clean-cut features and a glittering smile that might have made him a matinée idol; in fact he was a serious-minded man, firm in principle, who became a QC and ultimately the Recorder of a Crown Court. Hampson was the tallest, over 6 ft, a schoolmaster, sensitive in expression, but elusive behind a thin moustache and round-rimmed spectacles that flashed in the sun. Three immortals of Olympic history. Three individuals.

The 800 m perfectly expresses the AAA motto, taken from one of Pindar's Olympian Odes: *Swiftness of foot and the flower of strength.* Traditionally a meeting point for two classes of runner, the 400/800 m man and the 800/1500 m specialist, it has tempted some of the great names in athletics to try for a double victory in the Championships. Over 440 and 880 yd the spindly American, Lon Myers, had an easy task in 1885, with 52.4 sec and 2 min 1 sec. He was emulated in 1889 by the Rev Lenox Tindall (1863–1940) with Championship records of 48.5 sec and 1 min 56.4 sec. 'Come tell us where to find Tindall's fellow beyond the white cliffs of "Perfide Albion",' rhapsodized the *Sporting Life*. His quarter-mile time lasted 48 years, but the half-mile record fell to the next double winner, Edgar Bredin (1866–1939), a not so reverend character who liked a cigarette between finals. He ran 49.2 sec and 1 min 55¼ sec in 1893 and repeated the feat in 1894, with 50 sec and 1 min 56.8 sec. Eventually he went to Canada and joined the Mounties. The 880 yd and 1 mile double was achieved by Walter George in 1882, with 1 min 58.2 sec and 4 min 32.8 sec; and 1884, 2 min 2.2 sec and 4 min 18.4 sec; and by Francis JK Cross (1865–1950) in 1887, with 1 min 59 sec and 4 min 25.4 sec. The following year, at Oxford, Cross set a world 880 yd best performance of 1 min 54.6 sec that lasted until 21 September 1895, which happened to be his wedding day.

In 1919 the 880 yd/1 mile double was completed by a 30-year-old back from France, where he had served 3 years with the Royal Flying Corps as a wireless operator. Albert Hill (1889–1969), who had won the 4 miles as far back as 1910, evoked memories of Walter George's eventful afternoons, for within three hours he ran the heat and final of the 880 yd (1 min 55.2 sec), the mile (4 min 21.2 sec) and the 880 yd leg in Polytechnic Harriers' win in the 1 mile medley relay. He was theoretically past his peak as an athlete, but he set his sights on a double victory in the 1920 Olympic Games.

There were serious misgivings about sending a team to Antwerp. Britain's one individual victory in the 1912 Olympics had been shockingly below expectations. After 4 years at war, how could this nation expect to match others who had conserved their neutrality and continued with athletics? Scandinavians won five of the 15 titles in the 1919 AAA Championships; if the discus, javelin and triple jump had not been omitted, they would probably have won more. Britain's best athletes were either near-veterans, who had learned their athletics before the war, or raw youngsters. In the General Committee in August, 1919, the AAA discussed the matter; four British athletes — Albert Hill, Howard Baker, Robert Bridge and Guy Butler — had beaten strong Swedish opposition in the Championships. It was announced that a British team would compete.

Before the Games came the 1920 AAA Championships. Sensationally, Albert Hill was beaten in the 880 yd in 1 min 55.8 sec by Bevil

Albert Hill winning the Olympic 800 metres in 1920, the first of his two gold medals. On the left is Edgar Mountain (GB) and on the extreme right, Bevil Rudd (S. Africa), the AAA champion.

Rudd (1894–1948), of Oxford University, who went on to join the select group of double winners with a 440 yd victory over Butler in 49.2 sec. Although his father was a South African diamond merchant, Rudd had been born in Devon, done his best running for Oxford and fought with the Argyll and Sutherland Highlanders and the Tank Corps. The AAA invited him to compete for Britain in the Olympics, but he decided his loyalty must be with South Africa. He was permitted to travel with the British team and share their accommodation.

Albert Hill knew that a leg injury had hampered him in the 880 yd championship. His heart was still on the double in Antwerp. 'I well remember the strong argument I had with the late Sir Harry Barclay, the secretary to the AAA . . . for the committee were opposed to my attempting the 800 and 1500 metres. But I was adamant on tackling the double and in the end Sir Harry bowed to my arguments.'

Athletics is about self-assertion, and Hill was a forthright man, but that was not the whole of the story. Nor is it right to account for his running in Antwerp simply as a tactical triumph earned by years of experience. In 1919 he had begun to be advised by that shrewd trainer, Sam Mussabini. Together, they made a study of the normal race tactics of Hill's potential rivals — information not easily gleaned from Europe and the United States. In the US Championships Earl Eby (1 min 54.2 sec) and Joie Ray (4 min 16.2 sec) each won in times faster than Hill had ever achieved. Fortunately Hill had one other priceless asset — an unflappable temperament. 'While others were counting aches and pains and biting nails,' recalled his team captain, Lord Noel-Baker, 'Hill would have an early lunch and then sleep soundly for three hours.'

Antwerp was no place for the highly strung. The war-weary Belgians had been awarded the Games more in sentiment than confidence. It was impossible to forget the war. In 1919 the AAA had considered the draft programme distributed by the Belgian Olympic Committee and recommended that 'throwing the grenade' be deleted 'this being a purely military efficiency test'. The British were billeted in an Antwerp school and slept on camp beds that were liable to collapse. They were transported to the stadium over cobbled roads in an army lorry fitted with wooden seats. The track was not much firmer than Flanders mud and the organization was like the army at its most exasperating, with Olympic finals being run as early as nine in the morning.

Hill took it like the old soldier, drinking lager in preference to the suspect water and eating out 'until the cooking arrangements improved at our quarters'. Even the erratic seeding, which brought Eby, Rudd and himself together in one 800 m heat, did not perturb him. He used the race to check that he and Mussabini were right about his adversaries' form, and qualified in second place, behind Rudd. He had a second look at Eby in the semi-final and decided Rudd was the man to beat.

In the final, Eby, as Hill had anticipated, took the field through a fast first lap (54.2 sec) and then Rudd made his customary challenge 300 m from home and opened a four metre gap. 'Everyone expected an easy victory,' Hill recalled, 'but I was watching him closely, and noticed his arms beginning to come up high, and his body getting stiff.' Like a coursing greyhound, Hill struck 20 m from the tape and won — 'hardly blowing', according to a witness — in 1 min 53.4 sec. Eby was a metre behind, and Rudd, who had wrenched an ankle on the pitted track, limped in third.

Forty-eight hours later, Hill appeared with a fresh set of runners for the final of the 1500 m, his fifth race in as many days. The rain bucketed down throughout. Philip Baker (Lord Noel-Baker) ran as he had in Stockholm 8 years before, unselfishly lifting some of the pressure from his team-mate by taking the lead. Hill expected Joie Ray to use his telling strategy of a fast third lap, but the American had injured a leg in training and faded quickly. Hill took the lead at the bell and led Baker to the tape in 4 min 1.8 sec. His double victory stands as one of the most authoritative performances by an Englishman in the Olympic Games. Afterwards he said with simple candour, 'My races went as I expected'.

Hill had a final ambition: to break the world record for the mile. Norman Taber, a 23-year-old American, had set it at 4 min 12.6 sec in 1915, when Hill was 26, and fighting in France. At the AAA Championships of 1921, Hill, now 32, made his attempt. He and Mussabini believed he was capable of four 62 sec laps, but a field of 21 put even-paced running out of the question. To get a clear run, he covered the first lap in 59.6 sec and reached the half-mile in 2 min 4 sec. The pace burned off everyone except Hyla 'Henry' Stallard, 20, the Oxford and Cambridge winner. Bravely, the willowy Stallard ran at the Olympic champion's shoulder, matching his long stride. It was obvious that the venerable British record of 4 min 16.8 sec made by Joe Binks (1874–1966) in the 1902 Championships was sinking, and a section of the crowd who had spotted Binks improvised a chorus of 'Poor old Joe'. Hill, sensing that Stallard would not give up, eased perceptibly in the third lap (67.2 sec) to conserve his finish. Right through the final lap (62.6 sec) he

Hill beats Hyla Stallard in the 1921 mile Championship in a British record time of 4 min 13.8 sec, and gets a champion's reception, twenties-style. (Syndics of Cambridge University Library)

held off the challenge, and won in 4 min 13.8 sec, to Stallard's 4 min 14.2 sec. The world record had eluded Hill by little more than a second, but his reputation as a great competitive runner was secure.

If Hill had been the sentimental favourite in 1921, it was in the knowledge that Stallard represented a new generation. With his Cambridge colleague, Edgar Mountain, 20, who won the 880 yd that afternoon from Bevil Rudd, and had actually finished fourth in the Olympic 800 m final the previous year, Stallard seemed set to spearhead Britain's defence of the Olympic 800 and 1500 m titles in 1924. They confirmed their form in the Championships of 1922, when Mountain won the half-mile and Stallard was second to Duncan McPhee in the mile, and in 1923, Stallard winning the mile, and Mountain second in the half-mile.

In 1924 it was Stallard who won the AAA half-mile. His time of 1 min 54.6 sec was a fraction outside the American Homer Baker's Championship record, set in 1914. Second, less than a yard back, finished Douglas Lowe.

Like Alfred Tysoe, a predecessor (in 1900) as Olympic 800 m champion, Lowe had been born in Manchester. While at Highgate School he won the Public Schools half-mile, and in 1921 went up to Cambridge. Like so much else in Lowe's athletic career, it was happily timed. In Stallard and Mountain he had team-mates of international class. As a member of the recently formed Achilles Club, he took part in tours and matches against stiff opposition in Europe and America. In 1923 he won the first of three victories in the Oxford and Cambridge half-mile; in 1924 he tested his stamina by also winning the mile.

The preliminary rounds of the 800 m in the Paris Olympic Games in 1924 were rough. In his semi-final Edgar Mountain stumbled badly and was eliminated. When the finalists — three Britons, four Americans, a Swiss and a Norwegian — came to their marks they were lectured on the matter by the French starter. The British had a plan, described by Stallard: 'It was thought that if one of the three British in the final made a hot pace the Americans could be broken and either Lowe or I would get through. Lowe had no experience of pace-making and the team manager thought that Houghton, the other Englishman in the final, could not be asked to do so, so I had to make the pace.' Stallard did, for 700 m, but the effort took a toll. Lowe and Paul Martin (Switzerland) got by and battled for the title all the way past the grandstand to the finish. Lowe reached it first, in 1 min 52.4 sec. One of the

Americans edged the exhausted Stallard out of a bronze medal.

Next day, in the 1500 m heats, Stallard sustained a stress fracture of the scaphoid bone in his right foot and ruptured a ligament. In great pain, he contested the final the following afternoon, won by Paavo Nurmi, and finished third, collapsing across the line. Lowe was fourth.

Douglas Lowe was an Olympic champion at 21, and he had won the title handsomely. Yet in a curious way there was still something to prove. Accounts of the Paris races praised Lowe, but were heavy in sympathy for the luckless Stallard. It was pointed out that Lowe had yet to win an AAA Championship, still regarded by many as the real criterion of success. In 1925 Stallard won the AAA 440 yd (50 sec), to round off an unprecedented sequence of victories at 1 mile (1923), 880 yd (1924) and 440 yd (1925). While this was happening, Lowe was in America, winning for Oxford and Cambridge against the American universities. He had yet to show his best form on an English track. A dignified, self-possessed man, he made no promises, but waited for the right opportunity.

It came at the Championships of 1926, for which the AAA had lifted its ban — imposed in 1918 — on German competitors. The large contingent included Dr Otto Peltzer, 26, German champion at 400 m, 1500 m and 400 m hurdles. His half-mile race with Lowe has passed into legend as the classic duel of all AAA Championships. It had everything: Stamford Bridge packed with 27 000 roaring spectators; Lowe's decision to make the pace, and make it scorch; England v Germany, with a world record as the prize. If doubts persisted as to Lowe's calibre, he destroyed them that afternoon, covering the first lap in 54.6 sec, answering Peltzer's challenge in the back straight so that the two ran stride for stride for a hundred yards, before the German eased, seeming beaten, then summoned a last grimacing effort and came back to win. Peltzer's 1 min 51.6 sec decisively beat Ted Meredith's world record of 1 min 52.2 sec, and Lowe, who was untimed three yards back, certainly got inside the old time as well.

In analysing his defeat, Lowe could not fail to note that Peltzer had also finished second in the 440 yd. He decided to include the quarter-mile in his own race repertoire, with conspicuous success. In 1927 he achieved the elusive AAA Championship victory in *two* events, the 440 and 880 yd, and repeated the double in the Olympic year of 1928, including a good tactical win over the German, Hermann Engelhard, in the half-mile (1 min 56.6 sec). That same day, in Cambridge, Massa-

In this epic 880 yd race in 1926 Otto Peltzer (Germany) beat Douglas Lowe in the world record time of 1 min 51.6 sec. (Syndics of Cambridge University Library)

Prior to retaining his Olympic 800 metres title in 1928, Douglas Lowe won an AAA Championship double — the 880 yd and 440 yd. (The Press Association Ltd)

Tommy Hampson wins the half-mile in his AAA debut in 1930 in 1 min 53.2 sec, an English Native record. (The Press Association Ltd)

chusetts, Lloyd Hahn won the American title over 800 m in 1 min 51.4 sec, improving on the world record. A week later, Sera Martin (France) reduced it further, to 1 min 50.6 sec. Lowe was not distracted; his peak was timed for 31 July, in the Amsterdam Olympic stadium. At the AAA Championships a friend had remarked that he was looking fit. 'Am I?' Lowe had said. 'I hope not.'

Hahn and Martin were there when the draw for the Olympic final took place. And so was Lowe. He stood back while the eight other finalists selected their cards. He picked the one remaining, and smiled, for it gave him pole position. It was pure chance, but it must have seemed to the others that the champion was in control.

The impression remained. Lowe moved into the lead, ensured a brisk start, then allowed Hahn to make the pace. At the bell, in 55.2 sec, Lowe was second. He waited till the last turn and then devastated the field with a finish that won him the race by a full second, from Byléhn (Sweden) and Engelhard. Throughout his career Lowe had consistently declined to talk about his running. His new Olympic record of 1 min 51.8 sec was his statement; the manner in which he achieved it was eloquent beyond words.

There remained one formality. Otto Peltzer had injured himself shortly before the Games and had run below form, eliminated in the semi-finals. Lowe had written in sympathy, expressing the wish that they would meet when fully fit. The opportunity came in Berlin on 19 August; in beating his old rival, Lowe ran his fastest time, 1 min 51.2 sec, to Peltzer's 1 min 52.2 sec. That done, he rested his case.

Within 2 years of Lowe's retirement, his English Native record was beaten in the 1930 Championships by a new star, Tommy Hampson (1907–65), who recorded 1 min 53.2 sec. Moreover, he defeated the world record-holder, Sera Martin, and Cyril Ellis, who had won both the 880 yd and the mile in 1929. Astonishingly, this was Hampson's AAA debut, but the Hampson story is wholly astonishing. The son of a middle-distance runner, he had been encouraged in athletics from childhood, taken to the 1914 Championships when he was six, the year Albert Hill finished runner-up to Homer Baker in the half-mile, and duly made his own public debut in the Public Schools 880 yd in 1925. No Douglas Lowe as a schoolboy, Hampson just qualified for a standard medal at a second try, in 1926. At Oxford, he scraped into the team in his final year (1929) and finished last in the Inter-Varsity half-mile.

Five months later he ran for England against Germany and defeated Engelhard, the Olympic bronze medallist. From also-ran to international in one season: it was a transformation straight out of boys' adventure fiction. To strain credibility still more, he sat his final exams that spring.

The explanation is that between finals and starting work as a schoolmaster in September he applied himself to athletics as never before, training hard and competing often. He broke 2 min in May and after that his times improved week by week. By June he was down to 1 min 57.6 sec and was included as a last-minute substitution in the Oxford and Cambridge team leaving for America. There he twice ran 1 min 56 sec and was the only man undefeated in three meetings. On his return he was picked to lead off the 4 × 880 yd relay for England against Germany. The team set a British record.

Hampson piled success on success in 1930. After that English Native record in the Championships, he went to Canada and became the first British Empire champion for 880 yd, winning by 20 yd in 1 min 52.4 sec. Behind his improvement was a training schedule probably more demanding than any middle-distance runner had attempted up to that time. Hampson defied the bogeys of staleness and athlete's heart. 'My own success', he wrote, 'would not have been possible if I had not, over the previous two years worked to pretty stringent training schedules which I had prepared myself... and if I had not pushed myself very close to my physical limits at regular intervals during my training...'

At about this time he decided that the most effective way to run a half-mile was at an even pace. The idea was not new — Albert Hill had planned his 1921 Mile in 62 sec laps, although the practicalities of competition had thwarted him — but in 1930 it was flying in the face of the best advice available. Douglas Lowe himself had written, 'It is extremely doubtful whether the attempt to run two consecutive quarters in the same time can ever be more successful than the hitherto satisfactory method of making the first some two or three seconds faster than the second.'

Hampson believed he could win the Olympic 800 m in Los Angeles in 1932. He calculated that a time of 1 min 50 sec or less would suffice. This would mean running a world record in an Olympic final. He planned to achieve it in two 55 sec laps. He worked on it through the next two seasons, at first holding a watch and drawing derisory shouts of 'Nurmi!' — and later relying on his own judgement of pace.

He won the AAA Championships in 1931 and 1932, and was also runner-up in the 440 yd that year. Vitally for his plan, his lap times were now practically identical each time he ran, consistently within two-fifths of a second of each other.

Just how courageous Tommy Hampson's plan was became dramatically clear in that Los Angeles final. Phil Edwards (Canada) led off at a near-sprint to cover the first 200 metres in 24.4 sec and the first lap in 52.8 sec, while the Englishman ran his own race 15 metres adrift, passing the bell fifth, in 54.8 sec, exactly on schedule. Then as the hares slowed, Hampson's steady pace began to reclaim the lost metres. By the back straight he had overtaken them all without injecting any apparent speed. But there was one conceivable flaw in the plan, and another Canadian, Alex Wilson, had found it by dogging Hampson from the start and deriving the same benefit from the even pace without the strain of setting it. Off the final bend, Wilson moved into the lead. Hampson's concentration was equal to the challenge. He held his form, kept his stride, knowing that this was world record pace and simply to maintain it should suffice. To the crowd it was a thrilling duel all the way to the finish, with first one runner showing ahead, then the other. In Hampson's recollection the important thing was that 'except for the last two or three yards my style did not go to pieces', but he admitted to 'the wonderful relief when out of the corner of my eye I saw the white form of Wilson gradually disappear and felt the worsted break across my chest.' The time was 1 min 49.7 sec. Hampson's laps had been run in 54.8 sec and 54.9 sec.

There, Britain's run of successes in the Olympic 800 m ended. The closest since — and it was desperately close — was Derek Johnson's silver medal in 1956. Despite wins in the European Championships by John Parlett (1950) and Mike Rawson (1958) and in the Commonwealth Games by Parlett (1950) and Johnson (1954), the period between the wars remains the golden era of British middle-distance running. It was given a final burnish by Sydney Wooderson on 20 August 1938 with world records of 1 min 49.2 sec for 880 yd and 1 min 48.4 sec for the metric distance in a race at Motspur Park, Surrey.

Developments since have neither confirmed nor disproved Hampson's theory. Great judges of pace like Mal Whitfield (USA) have won gold medals with practically even laps, but others like Peter Snell (NZ) and Alberto Juantorena (Cuba) have been successful with a discrepancy between laps of up to four seconds. Probably the only conclusion to be drawn is that Hill, Lowe and Hampson had one thing in common: they were all supremely certain that they had found a way to beat the world.

# Enter Achilles

**That dazzling decade, the twenties, saw athletics transformed into a major sport as stars like Nurmi, Abrahams, Liddell, Lowe and Burghley burst into prominence. It was a legend-making era. Achievements of heroic quality — the stuff of schoolboy fiction — happened at the Championships and the Olympics.**

### 1920 — HODGE AND A SHOE

In the AAA steeplechase of 1920, Percy Hodge (1890–1967), the holder, was badly spiked at the water-jump in the second lap. He stopped and removed his shoe to examine the wound, then replaced it and laced it up. A hundred yards behind the field, he set off in pursuit. In four laps he had caught them and taken the lead. He won by twenty yards. At the Olympic Games that year he won the steeplechase by a hundred metres, but to the end of his life he regarded that AAA victory as his finest.

There was one Championship win in 1920 that made no headlines, but signalled a development of strong significance in British athletics. The 1 mile relay (880 × 220 × 220 × 440 yd) was won by the Achilles Club. This fusion of the light and dark blues — founded 27 March 1920 — was the work of Arnold Strode-Jackson (Oxford), Philip Baker (Cambridge), Bevil Rudd (Oxford) and Arthur Anderson (Cambridge). From the outset it was clear that Achilles was not just another athletic club. Within weeks of its foundation it organized the first post-Olympic match between the British Empire and the USA. Its frequent tours abroad provided members with international experience which helps explain why as many as eleven were to win Olympic gold medals between 1920 and 1936. By fostering athletics in the public schools through matches in which members were heavily handicapped, and instituting the public schools relay meeting, it did much to enthuse the next generation of Oxbridge athletes.

**A unique treble was achieved in 1922 by Harry Edward, who added the 440 yd to his 100 and 220 yd titles. (Syndics of Cambridge University Library)**

If all this seemed like a return to AAC days when Oxford and Cambridge regularly carried off most of the Championships, there were now strong clubs to provide resistance, high among them the Polytechnic Harriers, whose Kinnaird Trophy and Marathon was the principal inter-club fixture of the season. Poly's trainer, Sam Mussabini, had advised Willie Applegarth in pre-war days, and in 1920 he sent another brilliant sprinter to the Championships, in Harry Edward (1895–1973), who won the 100 yd in 10 sec and the 220 yd in 21.6 sec. Edward, 25, a Chartered Secretary born in British Guiana, had been interned by the Germans in the war. In the 1920 Olympic Games he took bronze medals in the 100 and 200 metres.

### 1921–2 — EDWARD MAKES HISTORY

In 1921, Mussabini's men had Achilles by the heel at the Championships, for not only did Albert Hill beat the young Light Blue, Stallard, in the mile, but Harry Edward twice defeated Harold Abrahams, the Oxford and Cambridge sprint champion, in 10.2 sec and 22.2 sec, and Polytechnic won the relay. But Edward's most sensational performance came at the Championships of 1922, when within an hour he won the 100 (10 sec), 220 (22 sec) and 440 yd (50.4 sec), a triple no one has ever matched. In an era when style was believed to be practically synonymous with success, Edward could not be faulted. 'He was one of the most impressive sprinters I have ever seen,' wrote Harold Abrahams, a judgement he affirmed in 1924 by asking Mussabini to prepare him for the Olympic Games.

The 1922 Championships were notable also for the appearance of five foreign Olympic champions. Paavo Nurmi celebrated his English debut with a rare double in the 4 miles (19 min 52.2 sec)

The brilliant Finnish runner, Paavo Nurmi (in black kit) clears the water jump in the 1922 steeplechase, which he won, as well as the 4 miles race. (Syndics of Cambridge University Library)

Paavo Nurmi (Finland) at Stamford Bridge in a flat distance race.

and 2 miles steeplechase (11 min 11.2 sec); his personal hero, Hannes Kolehmainen, now 32, was fourth in the steeplechase; the entertaining and scrupulously fair walker, Ugo Frigerio (Italy), known affectionately at Stamford Bridge as ''appy-'earted Ugo', won the 2 mile walk; Ville Porhola (Finland) set a Championship record of 47 ft 10 in/14.58 m in the shot; and his countryman Vilho Tuulos won the triple jump. But the outstanding competitor in the field was the Norwegian, Charles Hoff, who won the long jump (23 ft 3 in/7.08 m) and the pole vault (12 ft 0 in/3.66 m) and finished second in the triple jump. As if that were not enough in versatility, in the 1924 Olympics he reached the final of the 800 metres. One other Championship and British record was set, by Carl-Johan Lind (Sweden), who threw the hammer 172 ft $3\frac{1}{2}$ in/52.50 m at the age of 39. The runner-up, Malcolm Nokes (Achilles), was the only British athlete to gain a place in the eight field events.

## 1923 — FLYING SCOTSMAN

1923 was Eric Liddell's year. Making his debut in the Championships, the 21-year-old Scot ran inside 'evens' for the first time in his life in the second round of the 100 yd, with 9.8 sec, equalling the British record, and then improved it in the final with 9.7 sec. In the 220 yd he twice recorded 21.6 sec. Harold Abrahams, weakened by a septic throat, had failed to survive the heats, but came within three-quarters of an inch of Peter O'Connor's long jump record, with 23 ft $8\frac{1}{4}$ in/7.24 m. The Frenchman, Pierre Lewden, set a Championship record in the high jump (6 ft 4 in/1.93 m) and also won the pole vault without having to record a jump. The other Championship best of the afternoon went to Fred Gaby, an ex-sprinter converted by Sam Mussabini into Britain's most consistent high hurdler of the decade. His 15.2 sec was the second of five AAA hurdles victories.

Future Olympic 400 metres champion, Eric Liddell, wins the 1923 220 yd from Tom Matthewman (15) and William Nichol. He had previously won the 100 yd in a British record of 9.7 sec. (Syndics of Cambridge University Library)

## 1924 — PRELUDE TO PARIS

The Olympic year of 1924 was one of the greatest in British athletics, but the Championships gave little indication of what was to come. Harold Abrahams — who years later in a radio interview revealed that so much was expected of him that he was on the verge of a nervous breakdown at the Championships — won the 100 yd in 9.9 sec and the long jump with 22 ft $8\frac{1}{2}$ in/6.92 m. Eric Liddell (1902–45), a strong sabbatarian, aware that the Olympic 100 m heats were scheduled for a Sunday, concentrated on the 440 yd, which he

Harold Abrahams employs the dip finish taught him by Sam Mussabini to win the 1924 100 yd. (Syndics of Cambridge University Library)

Harold Abrahams also won the 1924 long jump with 22 ft $8\frac{1}{2}$ in/6.92 m. (Syndics of Cambridge University Library)

won in 49.6 sec, a time that could have perturbed none of his potential rivals. The only Championship record of the afternoon fell to Syd Atkinson (S. Africa), 15.1 sec for the 120 yd hurdles. Possibly the most notable feature of the meeting was the success of the Achilles Club in winning eight titles.

Paris three weeks later was another story. Abrahams, resolute with such determination that half a century later it still animates photographs of the race, beat four Americans and Arthur (now Lord) Porritt, of New Zealand, in the 100 m in 10.6 sec. Liddell, head towards Heaven, body almost in a backward lean, set a pace in the 400 m that said more for his heart than his experience, for he had drawn the outside lane and covered the first 200 m in 22.2 sec, yet had the strength to win in 47.6 sec, a world record. And Douglas Lowe, as already related, won the 800 m. Britain's performance in the Olympic track events, with nothing worse than a bronze medal between 100 and 1500 m, has not been bettered since.

**1925 — THE MAN WHO CHANGED A RULE**

1925 brought the Olympic high jump and decathlon champion, Harold Osborn (USA), to the Championships. There was almost a sensation when he tried clearing 5 ft 9 in/1.75 m in sweater and trousers and failed twice. He stripped for the third attempt and just got over, leaving the bar quivering. Osborn had developed a trick of pressing the bar against the uprights of the standards as he executed the Western roll; as a result, the IAAF introduced a rule by which the pegs faced inwards, so that the bar could be dislodged in either direction. But on this occasion he went on to equal the Championship best of 6 ft 4 in/1.93 m, and proved his all-round ability with second place in the triple jump and standard medals in the pole vault, long jump and discus. He shared the Harvey Cup* with Jack Webster (Birchfield H.), winner of the 10 miles and the steeplechase. Sam Ferris (RAF) won the inaugural marathon Championship.

**1926 — GERMAN RAID**

The AAA's decision to lift its ban on German competitors in 1926 had a dramatic consequence when no less than five Germans qualified with Jack London (Poly H.) for the 100 yd final. The winner, Richard Corts, defeated London in 10 sec, but in the 220 yd, that talented but highly strung athlete, Guy Butler (Achilles), held off the challenge of Joachim Büchner (Germany) in 21.9 sec. If the day was dominated by Dr Peltzer's world record in the 880 yd, there was also brilliant hurdling from Fred Gaby, in defeating George Weightman-Smith (S. Africa), who had set a Championship record of 15 sec in the 120 yd hurdles heats, and from Lord Burghley (now the Marquess of Exeter), with 55 sec over 440 yd, a British record. There was another fine double from Jack Webster, this year in the 4 miles (19 min 49.6 sec) and 2 miles steeplechase (10 min 34.2 sec), the latter a Championship record.

*This award for the best performance in the Championships is a solid gold cup presented in 1906 by Gordon C. Harvey, MP for Rochdale (1906–18), in memory of his brother, Charles Harvey (1860–1906), a former president of the NCAA, and starter at the Championships of 1891, 1897 and 1901.

### 1927 — LORD BURGHLEY'S WORLD RECORD

The 3-day Championships of 1927 brought a spate of records. Lord Burghley's 54.2 sec in the 440 yd hurdles was a world record of short duration, for it was beaten the same day by John Gibson (USA) in Lincoln, Nebraska. Fred Gaby for the second year defeated Weightman-Smith in the 120 yd hurdles, in the excellent time for a grass course of 14.9 sec. Wim Peters (Holland) got within 2¼ in/5 cm of the world record for the triple jump, with 50 ft 9 in/15.47 m, the first of six British titles he won over a period of 10 years. The discus record went to Kalman Marvalits (Hungary), with 145 ft 8½ in/44.40 m, and his compatriot Bela Szepes threw the javelin 212 ft 7½ in/64.80 m.

### 1928 — HURDLERS HIGH

1928 was Olympic year. Again the hurdlers impressed, as Syd Atkinson repeated his 1924 120 yd hurdles victory over Fred Gaby, this time in 14.7 sec, a British record, with Lord Burghley third. In Amsterdam, Atkinson secured the gold medal that had eluded him by inches in Paris in 1924. Lord Burghley, too, produced a British record in the Championships (54 sec) and capped it with a marvellous Olympic victory. His 53.4 sec for the metric distance was too good for the Americans, who included the defending champion, Morgan Taylor (third), and the world record holder, Gibson (eliminated in a semi-final). Lord Burghley's greatest British rival, Tom Livingstone-Learmonth (Achilles), three times runner-up in the AAA race, finished fifth; sadly, he died at 25, in 1931. Britain's other gold medallist in 1928, Douglas Lowe, was one of two double winners in the Championships, winning the 440 and 880 yd; the other was the consistent Jack Webster, who took the 10 miles and his fourth successive steeplechase. Two British records fell in field events: Ernst Paulus (Germany) threw the discus 147 ft 0 in/44.80 m and the New Zealander, Stanley Lay, sent the javelin 222 ft 9 in/67.90 m, a distance that took 29 years to better in the Championships.

### 1929 — ONE FOR LONDON

In 1929, the Olympic silver medallist for 100 m, Jack London (1905–66), like Harry Edward a British Guianan, trained initially by Mussabini and later by Albert Hill, won the AAA 100 yd. It was his only English title, but he was a natural sprinter of great ability. In that fine book, *Testament of a Runner*, by WR Loader, London's running was encapsulated in a memorable sentence: 'The man's will vibrated down the track like the twanging of a great bow-string.' But the headlines in 1929 were captured by dual winners John Hanlon (Poly H.), in the 220 and 440 yd, and Cyril Ellis (Birchfield H.) in the 880 yd and 1 mile. The Italian, Luigi Facelli, emphatically defeated Lord Burghley in his main event, but the future President of the AAA had already won a Championship 35 min earlier in the 120 yd hurdles. The marathon, since 1928 incorporated in the Championship meeting, finished in the darkness of the Friday evening, Harry Payne (1892–1969) (Woodford Green AC) winning by over 8 min from Sam Ferris in 2 hr 30 min 57.6 sec, a British record secure till 1951. When Jim Peters finally beat it, Payne, the race referee, was the first to shake his hand.

Jack London wins the 1929 100 yd from WJ Simmons (45) and E Toetti (18) (Italy). This was the only English title won by the Olympic silver medallist from British Guiana. (Syndics of Cambridge University Library)

Steeplechaser Jack Webster, seen in 1929 running round the second water jump to avoid injuring other competitors, was subsequently disqualified and missed a fifth consecutive title. (Syndics of Cambridge University Library)

# The Man Who Trusted Athletes

**It was 2 April 1927. The main business of the AAA Annual General Meeting was over, completed in under 90 minutes. A vote of thanks was made to the chairman, and, unusually, he responded to it. Almost 70, and handicapped by a worsening speech impediment caused by an old rugby injury, Sir Montague Shearman made his last public statement as President of the Association he had founded 47 years before.**

For a few minutes he reminisced about the first Championship meeting on a rainy afternoon in 1880, when he had run through sheets of water to win the 440 yd in the 'absurd' time of 52.2 sec. Then he turned to modern athletics. What he said was not what his audience expected. It was sharply critical of the younger generation, but not for infringements of AAA laws. 'Many of the younger men come to these meetings with the idea that the AAA is a Parliament and that they intend to legislate. If they really think so, I wholly disagree with them . . . The Association has, I think, a great many regulations which are unnecessary, because I have always found that when somebody does something, or a club does not do what is quite the thing, and of which anybody disapproves, many people want to pass a resolution against somebody being allowed to compete. They trust the clubs; they do not trust the athletes. I do. All should have the interest of the sport at heart, and the best test for athletics is a wholesome public opinion and not punitive legislation.' Half a century later, the principle is as sound as when Shearman expressed it. His thinking on athletics had been progressive in 1880, and it remained so to the end of his life.

The son of a Wimbledon solicitor, Montague Shearman attended Merchant Taylor's School, where he was captain of rugby. In the season 1875–6, he, at 18, and his older brother John (1855–1940) were members of the famous Wasps team that went through the season without a single try scored against it. He won a scholarship to St John's College, Oxford, and made enough impression as a sprinter to draw a comment from the splenetic correspondent of the *Sporting Gazette*, Walter Rye: 'He has more speed than anyone would think from his extremely elephantine appearance, and may make a good man yet, though I should fancy him more likely to prosper at shot-putting.' Shearman made a good man sooner than Rye expected, for in his first year he represented the University against Cambridge and won the 100 yd by three yards in 10.2 sec. Four days later he won the English (AAC) Championship in the same time. In June, barely 19, he ran for England against Ireland in the first-ever international match, finishing fourth in the 100 yd and third in the 220 yd. In subsequent seasons he represented Oxford again in the 100 yd, the 440 yd and — here Rye was prophetic — the shot put. He was President of OUAC in 1878 and played rugby twice against Cambridge. He left Oxford with a first in *literae humaniores* in 1879 and was called to the bar by the Inner Temple in 1881.

Shearman's part in the formation of the AAA has already been described. For him the meeting at Oxford in 1880 began a lifetime of service to athletics. He was Hon Secretary until 1883, when legal commitments compelled him to resign, but as Vice-President he frequently chaired meetings of the General Committee. Officially or unofficially he was consulted over almost every issue of importance that arose: the drafting of rules, the preparation of the first British record list, the dispute with the NCU, the suspension of lawbreakers. 'Time and again when difficulties arose he was available,' wrote Harold Abrahams, who as a young AAA official knew Shearman well, 'always anxious to hear every side of the question; never prejudging an issue, or allowing conservative notions to influence his opinions.'

In 1887 was published Shearman's classic *Athletics and Football**, in the Badminton Library series. It ran to five editions, and remains the most comprehensive account of the development of athletics in Britain from earliest times, meticulously researched, and written with an elegance and authority that enhanced the popularity of the sport in Victorian England.

His legal career was not as meteoric as that of Viscount Alverstone, his predecessor as President of the AAA. Tact and a gentle, persuasive manner were his strengths in advocacy, and in 1903 they were recognized when he took silk. In 1914 he became a judge in the King's Bench division, and was knighted. It is unfortunate for his reputation that, of the many cases he tried, the one remembered is that of Frederick Bywaters and Mrs Edith Thompson for murder in 1922; they were convicted and hanged after a controversial summing-up by Shearman.

---

*The 1898 and subsequent editions were issued under the title *Athletics*.

After Alverstone died, Shearman succeeded him in 1916 as President of the AAA. He was a considerate chairman; he would interrupt an overlong speech by gently saying, 'Mr —, I think the meeting sees your point,' but generally he was at pains to ensure that everyone received the same patient hearing.

In 1920 Shearman was invited to be the first Chairman of the Achilles Club Committee. He had also served as President of London AC from 1905 to 1908. He resigned his various offices in 1929, when he knew he was incurably ill. He died on 6 January 1930, a few months before the AAA celebrated its Jubilee.

The Right Hon Sir Montague Shearman (1857–1930).

# To the White City

**Stamford Bridge had been the home of British athletics for half a century, but by the thirties it was time to quit.**

On 24 April 1930, the AAA celebrated its Jubilee with a dinner at the Park Lane Hotel, London. Among many distinguished guests were the first AAA champion, Walter George, the first long jump champion, Charles Lockton, and two of those present at the founding of the Association at Oxford 50 years previously, John Fowler-Dixon and RH Macaulay. If Sir Montague Shearman had lived a few months longer, and attended the dinner, he would certainly, as the founder and main support of the AAA in all that time, have received a standing ovation. Towards the end of his life his main concern had been that athletics should one day have a national ground of its own. The arrangement at Stamford Bridge, where the new sport of speedway was savaging the cinder surface, was increasingly under strain. Shearman had planned to use the Jubilee dinner as the occasion to launch a Ground Fund. A few days before his death, he asked the Secretary and Treasurer to visit him. He made a gift of £500 to the Association to start the fund, and requested that this be announced at the dinner. It took another 41 years for his vision to be fully realized, when the Championships moved to the Crystal Palace sports complex in 1971.

The immediate problems at Stamford Bridge were resolved by accepting an offer from the White City Stadium Ltd to make the White City the AAA headquarters from 1 January 1932. A new quarter-mile track would be built to AAA specifications, replacing the old one-third of a mile circuit used for the 1908 Olympic Games and practically abandoned afterwards. The use of the stadium would be shared with the Greyhound Racing Association, so it was not the national ground Shearman had visualized, but dogs on their own circuit were preferable to motorcycles on the running track.

A view of the Stamford Bridge crowd watching the 4 miles at the 1930 Jubilee Championships. In 1932 the AAA moved to the White City. (Syndics of Cambridge University Library)

### 1930 — HAMPSON ARRIVES TO MUSIC

There was understandably some nostalgia about the last two Championship meetings at Stamford Bridge. A feature of athletics meetings for the first half-century of the AAA's existence had been the programme of music played by a military band. In 1930 the London Victoria — the regular band at Stamford Bridge since the nineties — played its repertoire of overtures and waltzes for the last time. But there was nothing backward-looking about the running. Tommy Hampson set an English Native record (a category introduced in 1928 and applied to performances in England and Wales by native-born athletes) of 1 min 53.2 sec for 880 yd. Lord Burghley defeated his great rival, Luigi Facelli (Italy) in the 440 yd hurdles in an English Native record of 53.8 sec, and also beat Fred Gaby in the high hurdles in 15.2 sec. Reg Thomas (RAF) was in irresistible form in the mile (4 min 15.2 sec), defeating Jerry Cornes (Achilles) and Luigi Beccali (Italy), who were to finish second and first respectively in the 1932 Olympic 1500 m. Another future Olympic champion, Janusz Kusocinski (Poland), qualified for the mile, but elected to run instead in the 4 miles, in which the Finn, Lauri Virtanen, burned him off to fourth place.

In Hamilton, Ontario, the same year were held the first British Empire Games (known after 1952

Though behind at this hurdle, Lord Burghley, (left) defeated Luigi Facelli (Italy) in the 1930 440 yd hurdles. Their duels were a feature of many Championships. (Syndics of Cambridge University Library)

as the British Empire and Commonwealth Games and now more shortly as the Commonwealth Games). In as many as seven events British athletes repeated their AAA victories: the 220 yd, Stanley Engelhart (21.8 sec); 880 yd, Tommy Hampson (1 min 52.4 sec); 1 mile, Reg Thomas (4 min 14 sec); marathon, Dunky Wright, representing Scotland (2 hr 43 min 43 sec); 120 and 440 yd hurdles, Lord Burghley (14.6 and 54.4 sec); and 2 mile steeplechase, George Bailey (10 min 55.4 sec). Stan Tomlin (1905–69), who never won an AAA title but served as Championship secretary from 1949 to 1957, became the Empire champion for 3 miles (14 min 27.4 sec); and 'Nokey', the popular Malcolm Nokes, who for 10 years had finished first of the British hammer throwers in the Championships, was rewarded with the Empire title, with 154 ft 7½ in/47.12 m. England's rich haul was completed by the 4 × 440 yd relay squad of Ken Brangwin, Lord Burghley, Roger Leigh-Wood and Stuart Townend.

**1931 — THE LAST OF STAMFORD BRIDGE**

In 1931 Douglas Lowe succeeded Sir Harry Barclay as AAA Hon Secretary and the number of affiliated clubs reached precisely 1000. Field events unusually stole the show at the Championships. The Harvey Cup was awarded to the Hungarian shot putter, Jozsef Daranyi, whose British record of 49 ft 11½ in/15.23 m beat by over 2 ft the Championship best set by the 1920 Olympic champion, Porhola, in 1922. Even so, he was hard-pressed by a future world record holder, Frantisek Douda (Czechoslovakia). In the triple jump, a 4-year run of successes by Wim Peters (Holland) was ended by his countryman Jan Blankers, who later became the coach and husband of the brilliant Fanny Blankers-Koen. On the track, another AAA tradition ended when the 440 yd was run in lanes for the first time. The stagger obviously suited Godfrey Rampling (Milocarian AC), who won from three foreign athletes in 48.6 sec, and was awarded the Jackson Cup for the best performance by a British competitor.

**The 120 yd hurdles was staged for the last time on grass in 1931. Lord Burghley, second from right, is seen beating Don Finlay in 14.8 sec. (Syndics of Cambridge University Library)**

**1932 — FINLAY HOT ON CINDERS**

With the move to the White City in 1932 came more innovations. The 120 yd hurdles, until then (except in 1908) staged on the grass in the centre of the arena, became a track event. It was won by Don Finlay (1909–60) in 14.9 sec, the first of seven successive victories. The old 4 mile event, the standard distance-running Championship since 1866 — and in professional running since the eighteenth century — was displaced by 3 and 6 mile Championships, approximating to the 5000 and 10 000 m of the Olympic Games. Walter Beavers (14 min 23.2 sec) and John Potts (30 min 23.2 sec) set the inaugural records. In the programme, the Americanism pole *vault* appeared; as if in defiance, a British athlete, Patrick Ogilvie (Achilles), won for the first time in 20 years. Best Championship performances were set in both walks: by Bert Cooper (2 miles) in 13 min 44.8 sec and Alf Pope (7 miles) in 51 min 25.4 sec. Robert 'Bonzo' Howland (Achilles) set an English Native record of 47 ft 8½ in/14.54 m in the shot, but finished second to Harry Hart (S. Africa); between 1929 and 1939 he was second on nine occasions. The most precocious victory of the day was by 17-year-old Sergeant Boy William Land (Royal Engineers) in the high jump (6 ft 1 in/1.85 m). At 16, Land had jumped 6 ft 2¾ in/1.90 m against Germany as Britain's youngest international athlete, but later he concentrated on the javelin, in which he set an English Native record in 1935.

An ocean and a continent away, another stadium had been given a face-lift. The Olympic Games of 1932 were held at the Los Angeles Coliseum. The British athletic team was restricted to 19 men and five women, all considered capable of reaching at least the semi-final stages of the competitions. In fact, 13 returned with medals. The golds were won by Tommy Hampson in the 800 m, and Tommy Green — winner of just about

A thrilling end to the 1932 AAA marathon as Dunkie Wright (left) and Donald McNab Robertson enter the White City Stadium together. (Syndics of Cambridge University Library)

every important road walk in Britain in the previous 2 years — in the 50 km walk, by a 7 min margin. Sam Ferris, 32, who had last won an AAA marathon 5 years before, but made the team on his performance in the Polytechnic race, won a silver medal and finished so strongly behind the wilting Juan Zabala (Argentine) that it was clear he could have won. The AAA mile champion, Jerry Cornes, finished second in the 1500 m to Luigi Beccali (Italy), whom he had edged into third place in the 1930 AAA race. In an extraordinary steeplechase an extra lap was run by mistake; Tom Evenson, the AAA champion, clung on to second place. Crew Stoneley, Tommy Hampson, Lord Burghley and Godfrey Rampling upheld Britain's strong tradition in the 4 × 400 m relay with a time of 3 min 11.2 sec that beat the world record, but not the powerful American team. Bronze medals were won by the women's sprint relay team, and Don Finlay in the high hurdles.

Robertson wins one of the closest finishes ever seen in an AAA marathon. (Syndics of Cambridge University Library)

### 1933 — THE FINNS IMPRESS

Fine distance running distinguished the 1933 Championships. Lauri Lehtinen (Finland), the Olympic 5000 m champion, consigned to history Alf Shrubb's 30-year-old British record for 3 miles by returning 14 min 9.2 sec. And in the 10 miles an even more venerable record, Syd Thomas's 1889 Championship best of 51 min 31.4 sec, finally fell to George Bailey (Salford H.), with 50 min 51 sec. The Olympic steeplechase champion, Volmari Iso-Hollo — improbably, a Finn reputed not to have had a serious attitude to training — improved the 2 mile steeplechase best to 10 min 6.6 sec. The outstanding performance in the field was the British record of 51 ft $8\frac{1}{4}$ in/15.75 m by Zygmunt Heljasz (Poland) in the shot.

Not yet a marathon runner, Jack Holden wins the 6 miles in 1933. (Syndics of Cambridge University Library)

*Above:* Volmari Iso-Hollo (Finland) the winner of two Olympic steeplechase titles, easily beat the British record in 1933. (Syndics of Cambridge University Library)

*Above:* Lauri Lehtinen (Finland) beat Alfred Shrubb's British 3 miles record in 1933 with 14 min 9.2 sec. (Syndics of Cambridge University Library)

## 1934 — LOVELOCK LEAVES NOTHING TO CHANCE

The Championships of 1934 were rather eclipsed by the second British Empire Games, held that August in London. Much had been expected of the AAA mile, with the world record holder at 4 min 7.6 sec, Jack Lovelock (New Zealand) facing challenges from a 19-year-old named Wooderson who had unexpectedly beaten him in the Southern Championship, and Jerry Cornes, the Olympic silver medallist. On the day, nobody was prepared to sacrifice himself as pacemaker. After a funereal two laps (2 min 21 sec), Lovelock won the dash for the tape in 4 min 26.6 sec. It was the only AAA title won by the talented Rhodes Scholar, whose running had moved into top gear after he had started at Oxford in 1931, but the Championship meant a lot to him. 'Two years ago,' he wrote in his diary after the race, 'I should most certainly have gone out. But I have now learned better than to have my races dictated by the public and the press, so I did not throw away a certain championship merely to amuse the crowd and be spectacular.'

One athlete who could amuse and be spectacular was the Irish hammer thrower, Dr Pat O'Callaghan, the Olympic champion in 1928 and 1932, who won his first and only British title in 1934, with 168 ft 6¾ in/51.38 m. In 1937, in Fermoy, Co. Cork, O'Callaghan threw 195 ft 4⅞ in/59.56 m, well beyond the world record, but it could not be ratified, as the NACAI was not recognized by the IAAF. Nevertheless, the German Olympic champion, Karl Hein, and the silver medallist Erwin Blask, visited Ireland to try to improve it. The story is that they were each offered a pint of Guinness before the attempt, and assured that O'Callaghan had drunk a glass of the same before the great throw. The Germans failed to match it, and uncharitably suggested that perhaps it was the judges who had been drinking before they measured the throw.

The Empire Games took place at the White City three weeks after the Championships. The track and field programme was organized by the AAA and dominated by United Kingdom athletes, who won 17 of the 30 men's and women's events. Only four of the AAA champions, Godfrey Rampling (440 yd), Jack Lovelock (1 mile), Don Finlay (120 yd hurdles) and Stan Scarsbrook (2 mile steeplechase), repeated their victories. Dublin-born Arthur Sweeney (1909–41), representing England, won both sprints, although he had yet to win an AAA title. Walter Beavers — second to the Olympic 10 000 m champion, Kusocinski, in the AAA 3 miles — and Arthur Penny — beaten by Jack Holden in the

Arthur Sweeney (right) wins the 1935 100 yd (10.2 sec) from Martinus Osendarp (Holland). (Syndics of Cambridge University Library)

AAA 6 miles — won the distance events. Alan Hunter (Scotland), the son of the Games Secretary, Evan Hunter, took his revenge on the winner of the AAA 440 yd hurdles, Ralph Brown (now Hon Mr Justice Kilner Brown), by beating him into third place in the Empire race. Both relays went to England and the English women won six of their nine events. The United Kingdom had just one success in men's field events: at 37, Malcolm Nokes retained his hammer title with 158 ft $3\frac{1}{2}$ in/48.24 m.

### 1935 — WOODERSON'S FIRST

In 1935 two AAA champions beat all previous best performances in the meeting by extraordinary margins. The discus thrower, Harald Andersson (Sweden), stretched the Championship record by almost 23 ft/7.01 m to 169 ft $11\frac{3}{4}$ in/51.80 m, and the pole vaulter, Keith Brown (USA), added 15 in/38 cm by clearing 13 ft 10 in/4.21 m. Each was a British record. But the sensation of the Championships was the defeat of

Jack Lovelock's mile victory over Sydney Wooderson and Jerry Cornes in the 1934 Championship was slow in time, but a tactical triumph.

Dr Pat O'Callaghan, twice Olympic hammer champion, took the AAA title for Ireland in 1934. (Keystone Press Agency Ltd)

**Sydney Wooderson sensationally defeats Jack Lovelock (NZ) in the 1935 AAA mile. (Syndics of Cambridge University Library)**

Jack Lovelock, the recent winner of the 'mile of the century' in America, by 20-year-old Sydney Wooderson. What seemed more significant than the time, 4 min 17.4 sec, was that Wooderson had outsprinted the famous Lovelock finish. He did it again in 1936, this time in 4 min 15 sec. Photographs of both races show Lovelock smiling as he finishes, as if even in defeat he was amused by the unlikely spectacle of the small, pale man in spectacles going at full steam like a goods train passing an express. Sadly, Wooderson injured an ankle and did not survive the heats in the 1936 Olympic 1500 m, won by Lovelock in world record time of 3 min 47.8 sec.

1935 saw the introduction of the AAA Indoor Championships at the Empire Pool, Wembley. Despite the statement in many works of reference that indoor athletics originated in New York in 1868, the credit should go to the proprietor of the Cremorne pleasure gardens in Chelsea, who adapted the Ashburnham Hall for the West London Rowing Club to hold their sports indoors by gaslight on 7 November 1863. Other London venues prior to 1868 were Lambeth Baths and the Agricultural Hall, Islington, and Liverpool also staged indoor meetings. But it must be admitted that indoor athletics since owes its development mainly to America. Meetings in England were so sporadic — there was one at Islington in 1909, and some in Regent Street Polytechnic in 1919 — that the AAA was virtually breaking new ground in 1935. The standard of performance in the five pre-war Indoor Championships reflected the difficult conditions on the 142 yd 1 ft 9 in/130.3 m track; the pole-vaulter, Richard Webster (the son of FAM Webster), was invariably the star, and in 1937 cleared 12 ft 9½ in/3.90 m, 1½ in/4 cm better than his own outdoor English Native record, though he had cleared 13 ft 1½ in/4.00 m in the 1936 Olympic Games. Perhaps the main achievement of those pioneering years was the co-operation of the AAA and the WAAA in organizing joint Championships.

**Keith Brown (USA) releases his bamboo pole as he vaults 13 ft 10 in/4.21 m in 1935 for a British record. (Syndics of Cambridge University Library)**

## 1936 — BROWN, SILVER, GOLD

The 1936 outdoor Championships were notable for British records by Don Finlay — whose consistency not only in winning, but improving from year to year was remarkable — in the 120 yd hurdles, with 14.6 sec; and William Eaton in the 10 miles, with 50 min 30.8 sec, which finally disposed of Alf Shrubb's 1904 record. But the Harvey Cup for the best performance of the Championships went to neither of these, nor to the Polish athlete Jozef Noji, who set a Championship record in the 6 miles, with 29 min 43.4 sec. It was awarded to Godfrey Brown, winner of the 440 yd in 48.6 sec. Brown more than justified the award by coming to within two-hundredths of a second* of the Olympic title in Berlin, in a time of

*Official times given were Archie Williams (USA) 46.5 sec, Brown 46.7 sec, but subsequent investigation of photo-timings, used only as a guide for the judges, indicate timings were 46.66 and 46.68 respectively.

Harald Andersson (Sweden), world record holder for the discus, beat the British record easily in the 1935 Championships. (Syndics of Cambridge University Library)

Luz Long, the German remembered for his Olympic long jump duel with Jesse Owens in 1935, won the 1937 Championship with a record 24 ft $8\frac{3}{4}$ in/7.48 m. (Syndics of Cambridge University Library)

46.7 sec. To his silver medal he added a gold in the 4 × 400 m relay, running the last leg after Fred Wolff, Godfrey Rampling and Bill Roberts had built a five-metre lead which he turned into a fifteen-metre victory, in 3 min 9 sec.

Britain's other medals in Berlin were the gold won by Harold Whitlock in the 50 km walk; and silvers by Don Finlay (110 m hurdles), Ernie Harper (marathon), Dorothy Odam (women's high jump) and the women's 4 × 100 m relay squad of Eileen Hiscock, Violet Olney, Audrey Brown and Barbara Burke.

## 1937 — LONG LONG JUMP

Germany sent a small, but strong team to the 1937 AAA Championships. Karl Hein, the Olympic hammer champion, set a British record of 183 ft 3 in/55.86 m. Luz Long, whose long jump duel with Jesse Owens (USA) had been one of the most exciting and civilized contests in the Games, won the British title with a Championship best of 24 ft $6\frac{3}{4}$ in/7.48 m. And the first male German athlete ever to win an Olympic gold medal, Hans Wöllke, demonstrated his ability in the shot with a put of 50 ft 6 in/15.39 m. Wöllke, a Nazi, was put to death in 1943 by the French Resistance for his crimes in concentration camps.

A Swede, John Mikaelsson, was the outstanding winner of 1937, for he set a world record in the 7 mile walk, 50 min 19.2 sec. Eleven years later he returned to London to win the 10 000 m walk in the first Olympic Games held after the war, and at the age of 39 he retained the title in Helsinki in 1952. But there were doughty performances, too, from Britons. At last the Rev Lenox Tindall's best Championship performance for 440 yd, 48.5 sec set in 1889, was beaten, by Bill Roberts, with 48.2 sec. Don Finlay cut his own hurdles time to 14.5 sec. And Sydney Wooderson got inside Albert Hill's 1921 mile performance with 4 min 12.2 sec.

Don Finlay (2nd from left) on the way to a record seventh successive win in the 120 yd hurdles, in 14.4 sec, in 1938. John Thornton (4th from left) was second, with Jan Brasser (Holland) (nearest camera) third. (Syndics of Cambridge University Library)

Godfrey Brown (49.2 sec) wins the 1938 440 yd from Alan Pennington and Bill Roberts. (Syndics of Cambridge University Library)

Tom Lockton, who won the 1938 decathlon, was the grandson of the winner of the first AAA long jump title. (Syndics of Cambridge University Library)

## 1938 — TWO MAKE SEVEN

The British Empire Games of 1938 took place in Sydney before the British season began. Although some 90 competitors from the home countries made the long sea voyage, they had to be satisfied with fewer successes than in previous Games. Cyril Holmes won an excellent double (9.7/21.2 sec) in the sprints; Bill Roberts took the 440 yd in 47.9 sec; Jim Alford, in the 1 mile, won the first-ever gold medal for Wales in 4 min 11.6 sec; and Dorothy Odam, using her scissors technique, won the high jump, with 5 ft 3 in/1.60 m.

Jack Emery wins the 1939 3 miles in 14 min 8.0 sec from Peter Ward and beats Lauri Lehtinen's British record. (Syndics of Cambridge University Library)

Two athletes in 1938 won their seventh successive AAA titles, a distinction till then achieved only by Denis Horgan in the shot put between 1893 and 1899. They were Don Finlay — who yet again improved, to 14.4 sec — and Bert Cooper, in the 2 mile walk. But twelve of the 25 events were won by foreign athletes. Among six Italian winners were Adolfo Consolini, who in 1948 would become Olympic discus champion, and a pole vaulter named Romeo, whose 13 ft 0 in/3.96 m clearance, someone wryly commented, was about the height of a balcony.

To round off a crowded year, Britain competed for the first time in the European Championships, held in September, 1938, in Paris. Not one of the four British winners had made the trip to Sydney the previous winter. Godfrey Brown easily won

*Above:* Great rivals of the thirties, Arthur Sweeney (14) and Cyril Holmes (23) finish first and second in the 1939 100 yd. Behind them European sprint champion, Martinus Osendarp, pulls a muscle.

*Right:* Sydney Wooderson wins his fifth successive AAA mile from Dennis Pell in 1939. Pell and Arthur Sweeney were both killed in wartime flying accidents.

*Below right:* Bert Healion upholds the Irish hammer throwing tradition in 1939, his second victory. In a comeback 16 years later he threw over 5 ft further, but was placed only sixth.
(Syndics of Cambridge University Library)

the 400 m (47.4 sec). Sydney Wooderson defeated the old Italian campaigner, Luigi Beccali, over 1500 m (3 min 53.6 sec). Don Finlay did a lifetime best, equalling the European record, in the 110 m hurdles (14.3 sec). And Harold Whitlock in the 50 km walk (4 hr 41 min 57 sec) added a European gold medal to the Olympic one he had earned in 1936.

### 1939 — CHURCHER AND CHAPELLE

The last Championships before World War II saw Sydney Wooderson, by then world record holder for 880 yd and 1 mile, collect his fifth successive title in the mile, by defeating for the second year Dennis Pell, a runner of great promise who was killed flying for the RAF in the war. The time, 4 min 11.8 sec, was a Championship record. Jack Emery in the 3 miles set a new British record of 14 min 8 sec that won him the Jackson Cup. The Harvey Cup was awarded to the Belgian, Jean Chapelle, winner of the 10 miles and steeplechase. Another good double, the 2 and 7 mile walks, was achieved by Harry Churcher, who thus deprived Bert Cooper of an unprecedented eighth successive title. The Empire champions Arthur Sweeney (100 yd) and Cyril Holmes (220 yd) shared the sprints; among those who did not reach the finals were two young men who would be heard of later: Jack Archer, 17, of High Pavement School, Nottingham, and Emmanuel McDonald Bailey, 18, of Trinidad.

# Willy the Conqueror

**The song '*Anything you can do I can do better*' might have been written for Baron Desborough of Taplow (1855–1945), the AAA President from 1930 to 1936. His immediate predecessor, Sir Montague Shearman, had a marvellous record as a sportsman, but Willy Desborough topped it in every way. At Oxford, Shearman was President of Athletics: Desborough was President of Athletics and the Boat Club; Shearman was an international sprinter at 19: Desborough fenced for Britain in the Olympic Games at 50; Shearman swam across Niagara (1881): Desborough did it twice (1884 and 1888), the second time in a snowstorm.**

William Grenfell, Baron Desborough, AAA President 1930–36, in characteristic roles as big-game hunter . . . and champion puntsman.

He also set a record for the Harrow School mile (4 min 37 sec) that lasted over 60 years; played cricket against Eton (1873 and 1874); rowed twice for Oxford against Cambridge (1877 and 1878); won the Punting Championship of the Thames three successive years (1888–90); climbed the Matterhorn three times by different routes (1876–9); stroked an eight across the Channel (1885); and was an outstanding big game hunter. He faced death several times; once, as special correspondent of the *Daily Telegraph* in the Suakin campaign in the Sudan (1888), he confronted the advancing enemy alone, with an umbrella as his weapon. Yet he survived, lived to a great age, and at 74 succeeded Shearman (who had died at 72) as AAA President. There were not many challenges left, but chairing the AGM was one he enjoyed.

As William Henry Grenfell, the son of an MP, he earned the reputation early in life of an achiever in everything he tried. He was himself elected to Parliament four times between 1880 and 1900, characteristically giving both parties a turn, as a Liberal and a Conservative. In 1885, he was private secretary to the Chancellor of the Exchequer. After being raised to the peerage in 1905 he involved himself so strenuously in local government that at one time he was serving on 115 committees. He was Chairman of the Thames Conservancy Board for 32 years and became President of the London Chamber of Commerce. In 1921 he was offered, but declined, the Governor-Generalship of Canada. He was made GCVO in 1925 and a Knight of the Garter in 1928.

Grenfell was an able distance runner. He finished second in the 3 miles for Oxford against Cambridge in 1876. Although President of OUAC the following year, he missed the sports because he was down to row in the Boat Race next day. When the British Olympic Association was founded, in May, 1905, he was the obvious choice as Chairman. Succeeding Charles Herbert as one of two British representatives on the International Olympic Committee in 1906, Lord Desborough returned from Athens (where he competed that year in the fencing) with the proposal that London should stage the Games of 1908. His enthusiasm, influence and organizing ability substantially ensured the success of those London Olympics. After them, he was elected a Vice-President of the AAA. In March 1920, when the Achilles Club was formed, he became its first President. Uniquely, he held office as President of five national sports associations: the MCC, the Lawn Tennis Association, the Amateur Fencing Association, the National Amateur Wrestling Association and, in 1930, the AAA.

Although 74 when he became President, Lord Desborough took a lively interest in the Association, often chairing meetings of the General Committee as well as AGMs. An entertaining speaker with a quick sense of humour, he made sure that meetings were never dull, and his executive experience was particularly valuable to the young officials steering the AAA through the choppy waters of the early thirties. In 1936 he retired, as he explained, to make way for a younger man able to accompany the British Olympic team to Berlin, so Lord Burghley (now the Marquess of Exeter) succeeded him.

# Wooderson in War and Peace

**In August, 1940, Sydney Wooderson should have been challenging for an Olympic gold medal in Tokyo. Instead, as a member of the Auxiliary Fire Service, he was in London fighting the Blitz. He was 26. The Olympics — his Olympics — were cancelled. So were those of 1944. Like his coach, Albert Hill, he was robbed of the years that promised most. And like Hill he refused to be beaten.**

Wooderson's war is interesting because it provides a picture of what activity there was in athletics. When the Blitz was over, this man who outranked everyone on the track joined the unprestigious Pioneer Corps and became a corporal. His poor eyesight precluded him from active service, so he was based in Britain. After the 'phoney war', when all athletics stopped and the AAA reverted to the 1914–18 arrangement of an emergency committee, meetings began to be organized in the services and at club level. The pre-war stars, Wooderson and the sprinter Cyril Holmes, a Company Sergeant-Major in the Physical Training Corps, were pressed to appear at meetings in aid of war charities. Jack Crump, the AAA team manager, estimated that they raised many thousands of pounds. Untrained by international standards, Wooderson used his leave allowance to compete whenever he could, regularly running inside 4¼ minutes for the mile. Meetings were organized on a limited but wider scale than in the previous war. There were the usual inter-service matches and a series between the AAA and combined Oxford and Cambridge teams, the University of London and the services. Wooderson also represented the AAA in events staged by Glasgow Rangers FC and Manchester AC. In July, 1944, after winning the 'Stalin Mile' in Manchester (4 min 12.8 sec), he developed rheumatic fever, and spent four months in hospital and another two convalescing. He was advised by the doctors to give up all ideas of running again.

**1945 — LOCKOUT AT THE WHITE CITY**

Frequently during the war the British press reported phenomenal times recorded in neutral Sweden by Gunder Hägg and Arne Andersson. By 1945 they had set 19 world records between them. In 1942 the Swedish Athletic Association had requested that Hägg visit England, but the AAA had declined. When the war ended they issued an invitation to Hägg and Andersson for the match between the AAA, the Army, the RAF and the US Forces, arranged for August Bank Holiday. It was announced that Wooderson would run.

Long before the action began, the White City gates were closed on 52 000, the largest crowd seen for athletics in England since the day of the Olympic marathon in 1908. At one gate, those locked out rushed a police barrier. It was estimated that a further 7000 gained admission as a result. Swept inside were Ralph Bannister and his 16-year-old son. 'As boys we all have our sports heroes,' wrote Sir Roger Bannister in his book *First Four Minutes*, 'and Wooderson from that day became mine.'

He was an unlikely hero. Pale, slight in build, gaunt-featured behind wire-framed spectacles, and looking markedly older than 31, he scarcely reached the shoulder of Andersson, his main rival in the mile. Nor did the impression alter when they started running; Sydney's overlong shorts flapped as he followed the trimly-kitted Swede. But the crowd adored him, for he embodied all that was best in wartime Britain. He had the pep of Arthur Askey and the will to win of that other small man, Montgomery. Before the bell, he scampered into the lead and the crowd roared for a miracle. That day it did not happen, for Andersson was fitter, and won in 4 min 8.8 sec. The following month in Gothenburg the result was the same, but Wooderson improved to 4 min 4.2 sec. 'It was most gratifying after spending the war years running times of between 4 min 11 sec and 4 min 16 sec on bumpy grass tracks to improve over two seconds so long after I'd set my record,' he said later.

That first post-war meeting was a marvellous boost for athletics — a thumping success in spite of the eclipse of Wooderson, the inability of Doug Wilson to stay with Gunder Hägg in the 2 miles and the wrecking of the public address system by a thunderstorm, obliging the announcers to tour the stadium with hand-held megaphones.* Hopes were raised of a post-war revival, as in 1919. No one cared to admit it, but in the late thirties athletics had gone into a decline. Attendances at the Championships in the 4 years before the war had fallen from over 30 000 to below 22 000. The number of clubs affiliated to the AAA had slumped from 1000 in 1931 to 483 in 1939.

*Megaphones had been used at AAA meetings until 1928, when for the first time an announcer, Harold Abrahams, addressed the crowd through a loudspeaker system.

Sydney Wooderson. (The Press Association Ltd)

Special circumstances had contributed to the success of the Bank Holiday meeting. The interest in the Swedes and the popularity of Wooderson had made it a star attraction. So had the fact that it was the first big meeting at the White City for 6 years. Whether athletics could keep its new public remained to be seen. The possibility of a return visit by Hägg and Andersson ended early in 1946 with their suspension by *Svenska Idrottsförbund* for infringements of the amateur code. Wooderson could not go on pulling in the crowds much longer. Fortunately some intriguing new talent had surfaced in the latter years of the war. In the match events of that Bank Holiday meeting, Aircraftsman Emmanuel McDonald Bailey had twice finished second to Cyril Holmes in fast-run sprints, while a 6 ft $4\frac{1}{2}$ in/1.94 m Flying Officer, Arthur Wint, had seemed to amble his 440 yd in 49.7 sec.

**1946 — WOODERSON'S GRAND FINALE**

Both these stylish West Indians appeared at the 1946 AAA Championships, the first since the war. Bailey won the 100 yd in 9.8 sec and the 220 yd in

In the 1946 AAA 3 miles, Sydney Wooderson is too fast for the man with the tape, as he sets a British record in beating Willy Slykhuis (Holland). (The Associated Press Ltd)

22.3 sec, with Jack Archer second each time. Wint, too, scored a double victory, in the 440 yd, 48.4 sec, and 880 yd, 1 min 54.8 sec. But in 1946 Wooderson was still the draw, and over 25 000 came mainly to see his début over 3 miles. What a race it was, with Wim Slykhuis (Holland) tagging him all the way to the bell and then darting into the lead, only to succumb to Sydney's full-steam finish in the home straight. The time was a British record: 13 min 53.2 sec.

The only other record of the day was the profit — £2070. The expense of keeping the Association going through the war had been a steady drain on funds, so this was a timely boost. A post-war planning scheme, with strong emphasis on coaching and the development of junior athletes, had been drafted as early as February, 1944. Now it could go ahead.

There were no congratulations on the organization of the Championships, which the AAA admitted in its Annual Report 'was found to be a little rusty in places after a break of seven years'. The arena had been cluttered with athletes, officials and pressmen; the team of eight announcers had compounded the confusion; and the scheduling of events caused problems and ultimately chaos when the leaders in the marathon entered the stadium while the 2 mile steeplechase was in progress. How Squire Yarrow (2 hr 43 min 14.4 sec), and Donald McNab Robertson (2 hr 43 min 14.6 sec) contended with hurdles and harassed officials and still staged the most exciting finish in marathon history is a story in itself. In 1978 the winner, Squire Yarrow, became seventh President of the AAA. Probably only the experience of the runners — they were both 40 and had rivalled each other for years — enabled the race to come to a result. At the next General Committee meeting a full report was ordered into the organization and management of sports meetings. There was a positive improvement in presentation in 1947.

Great Britain entered the 1946 European Championships in Oslo with hope squarely on the slender shoulders of Sydney Wooderson in the 5000 m. The running of Jack Archer in the 100 m was a revelation, for at home the speed of McDonald Bailey (ineligible for the European Championships) had taken yards from British-born sprinters. Archer did an 'Abrahams', by winning the heat, semi-final and final in 10.6 sec, each faster than he had ever shown before. On the same afternoon Wooderson faced Viljo Heino (Finland), 'Willy' Slykhuis (Holland), Gaston Reiff (Belgium) and a Czech runner new to the international scene, Emil Zatopek — 'probably running out of his class' said Abrahams in the radio commentary. Wooderson, one week from his 32nd birthday, judged the pace impeccably, refusing to be drawn by Heino's then breathtaking first kilometre of 2 min 46 sec, but drawing steadily into contention to take the lead with 150 m to go. Sydney Wooderson in full cry was a match for anyone. His winning time of 14 min 8.6 sec was the second fastest recorded up to that time, and in his own words, written more in surprise than self-congratulation, 'caused quite a stir'. On Wooderson's retirement from top-class athletics in 1947, the AAA arranged a dinner in his honour, a unique tribute to a phenomenal runner and a man as popular with other athletes as with the public. There is a postscript: vowing to devote himself to club running in his retirement, Wooderson in 1948 won the National Cross-Country Championship for Blackheath Harriers.

Honour of another kind came Britain's way in Oslo, for Lord Burghley, the AAA President, was elected Chairman of the IAAF. The headquarters therefore moved to London, and EJH 'Billy' Holt, AAA Hon Secretary since 1938, became Hon Secretary/Treasurer of the International Federation. This, coupled with his responsibility as Treasurer of the British Olympic Association, necessitated his retirement at the next AGM (1947), when Ernest Clynes was elected in his place. It is noteworthy that Billy Holt advised the appointment of a professional Secretary, but the General Committee decided to keep the position honorary, and so it has remained.

The bold decision in March, 1946, to hold the 1948 Olympic Games in London — allowing just over 2 years to prepare — put immense pressure on the Organizing Committee, chaired by Lord Burghley. He tackled the responsibility, among the most onerous ever undertaken in British sport, with the zest and energy he had characteristically put into his own athletics.

### 1947 — THE JUMPING PRINCE

The 1947 Championships were dominated by athletes from abroad, who took two-thirds of the titles — not so auspicious for British chances in the Olympic Games. Sandor Garay (Hungary) set a Championship best of 4 min 10.6 sec in the mile in beating Willy Slykhuis. McDonald Bailey, believed to be likely to represent Trinidad in 1948, notched his second double in the sprints, taking the 100 yd three yards clear in 9.7 sec, to equal Liddell's 1923 performance. And Prince Adegboyega Adedoyin, son of the royal house of Ijabu-Remo in Nigeria, gave the announcers a testing time by competing in three events. He won the high jump, equalling the Championship record of 6 ft 4 in/1.93 m; was second in the long jump and fourth in the high hurdles. The winner of the long jump at 23 ft 9½ in/7.25 m, Captain Harry Whittle, was the discovery of the afternoon, for he also took the 440 yd hurdles (55 sec), the first, as it turned out, of seven successive wins in that event.

**Arthur Wint, a great favourite of White City crowds, is seen beating the veteran Bill Roberts to take the 440 yd title in 48.4 sec. (Central Press Photos Ltd)**

### 1948 — THE OLYMPICS COME TO WEMBLEY

A major structural change took place in 1948 with the creation of a fourth Area Association, the Welsh AAA. Reorganization of the AAA had been hotly debated at intervals through the Association's history. The latest blueprint, an outcome of the post-war planning scheme, had met strong opposition from the Area Associations, but they conceded that some decentralization was desirable, so when Wales applied for separate recognition as an Association with the same powers as the NCAA and the MCAAA, it achieved the first change in the basic structure of the AAA in nearly 70 years. The new arrangement was embodied in the articles of incorporation when, on 12 August, the AAA became a Company limited by guarantee, with a licence to omit the word 'Limited' from its title. Soon afterwards the new Company achieved exemption from Entertainment Tax, to which all athletic meetings had been liable since 1916. The AAA was the first national sports organization to win this concession.

The 1948 Championships were a curtain-raiser for the Olympics, with many foreign entries, and home athletes did encouragingly well. If there was disappointment that McDonald Bailey, who had elected to represent Britain, was hampered by injury and below his scintillating form of the previous two seasons, it was tempered by the sharp running of a new 'find'. Coldstream Guardsman Alistair McCorquodale finished only a yard down on John Treloar (Australia) in the 100 yd (9.8 sec) and won the 220 yd (22.2 sec). John Parlett with a late run overtook Arthur Wint and Doug Harris (NZ) to win the 880 yd in 1 min 52.2 sec. That elegant runner, Bill Nankeville, convincingly won the mile from a field that included Josy Barthel (Luxembourg), second, and 19-year-old Roger Bannister, fifth. Injury prevented Don Finlay from taking on some strong Australians in the 120 yd hurdles, but young Joe Birrell, of Barrow Grammar School, beat them instead in 15.1 sec. Harry Churcher, who won the 7 mile walk, and Jack Holden, the marathon, were regarded with Parlett as Britain's best prospects for Olympic medals.

The 4099 Olympic competitors from 59 countries seem a modest entry by 1980 standards, but it more than doubled the numbers of 1908, when Britain had previously hosted the Games. The staging of anything so spectacular in austerity Britain was an astonishing achievement, in which the AAA was substantially involved. The overall direction of the Games was a professional assignment ably undertaken by 'Billy' Holt, the former AAA Hon Secretary, but much of the work in individual sports devolved on amateur officials. In athletics, Donald Pain headed the committee responsible for the layout of the Wembley track, the daily programme and the technical direction of the athletic events. He regularly worked into the night, yet was up in time each morning to do a day's work as manager of a large City bank. Among several technical innovations he provided that became standard in athletic meetings later was the amplification system on staggered starts. It would be invidious to list the numerous individuals who sacrificed time and energy to make the Games a success; Don Pain must represent them.

**_Above:_ Neither hurdles nor puddles trouble Don Finlay as he wins his eighth AAA high hurdles title in his last appearance, at the Championships of 1949. (Keystone Press Agency Ltd)**

**_Left:_ John Parlett (24) surprises Doug Harris (New Zealand) with a late burst to win the 1948 880 yd title. In 1950 Parlett won the Commonwealth and European gold medals. (Central Press Photos Ltd)**

The main events were seen live on television for the first time, although the majority of the public followed them on radio and in the press. When it was over there was disappointment that there had not been a single British victory in the stadium. In men's athletics there were silver medals for Welshman Tom Richards, 38, in the marathon, and the sprint relay team of Alistair McCorquodale, Jack Gregory, Ken Jones and Jack Archer, and a bronze for the remarkable Tebbs Lloyd Johnson, at 48 then Britain's oldest-ever international, in the 50 km walk. The women's team gained four silvers through

Dorothy Manley (100 m), Audrey Williamson (200 m), Maureen Gardner (80 m hurdles) and Dorothy Tyler (*née* Odam) (high jump). There was consolation in the fine running of Arthur Wint, representing Jamaica, but long since adopted as British by White City crowds; he was second in the 800 m to Mal Whitfield (USA), yet took the 400 m, the event most experts thought him less likely to win. And what of those British hopes? John Parlett reached the final of the 800 m, but was heavily bumped at the start, and finished last; Harry Churcher, cautioned by a judge, walked safely and sadly into fifth place; and Jack Holden for the first time in his career was forced by blisters to retire from a marathon.

### 1949 — MAC AT HIS BEST AGAIN

Ironically, all three won their events at the 1949 Championships, but the honours that year went to McDonald Bailey, who had finished sixth in the Olympic 100 m. He was back in form with a 9.7 sec/21.7 sec double on a rain-soaked track in the sprints. Bill Nankeville, also sixth in his event in the Olympics, now beat the Championship best in the mile by 1.8 sec, and made 4 min 8.8 sec look devastatingly easy. Three British high jumpers, Alan Paterson, Ron Pavitt and Peter Wells, were placed in that order yet each jumped 6 ft 4 in/ 1.93 m, to join a Frenchman, a Prince and two Olympic champions as holders of the Championship record. These were the first AAA Championships to be televised: a development whose full significance was difficult to foresee in 1949.

The forties ended in an upbeat way with Britain defeating France in their fourth post-war international match, distinguished by a British National and English Native record of 14.4 sec in the high hurdles by silver-haired Don Finlay, 40, in his final international appearance at the White City. Wooderson, Finlay and, next, Holden — men who had magicked away 6 years of war — were closing their careers as winners.

# The Fitful Fifties

**Many followers of British athletics remember the era of Bannister, Chataway and Pirie as the most glorious in the history of the sport. Certainly the four minute mile, the last-gasp defeat of Kuts and the deeds of 'Galloping Gordon' gave the fifties a golden glow. Huge crowds filled the White City to see records shattered regularly. Yet the same decade saw British hopes dashed at two Olympic Games and serious rifts develop between athletes and administrators.**

The year 1950 belonged to two athletes of different generations, Jack Holden, 43, and John Parlett, 25. Each achieved the rare double of Commonwealth and European gold medals. It began in Auckland, New Zealand, in February. Parlett — a ghostlike runner with the habit of materializing just when the leaders felt safe — snatched the Commonwealth 880 yd title in 1 min 53.1 sec. Another canny tactician, Len Eyre, took the 3 miles (14 min 23.6 sec) for England. Tim Anderson produced his best-ever form in steady rain to win the pole vault (13 ft 0$\frac{1}{8}$ in/3.96 m) and Duncan Clark, with 163 ft 10$\frac{1}{4}$ in/49.94 m won the hammer for Scotland. In the women's high jump, consistent Dorothy Tyler (5 ft 3 in/1.60 m) defended the title she had won in 1938. But there was no question who was the hero of the Games. The veteran, Jack Holden, one of the first distance men to run 100 miles a week in training, led the marathon field through the rain until his shoes split, then discarded them and ran the last eight miles on bare, bleeding feet. Despite also being attacked by a Great Dane two miles from the finish, he won by over four minutes.

The Championships that year brought a rich crop of records and best performances. Duncan Clark started it by throwing the hammer to a British National record of 178 ft 4$\frac{1}{2}$ in/54.36 m. McDonald Bailey, who won his usual double next day, ran a heat of the 100 yd in 9.6 sec, to equal his own British all-comers' and National records and improve Liddell's 27-year-old meeting record. The same evening, Dr Frank Aaron modernized the British National and Championship records for 6 miles, with 29 min 33.6 sec. In wind and rain on the Saturday, the record spree continued. Roland Hardy walked 7 miles in 50 min 11.6 sec, the best ever on British soil. Petar Segedin (Yugoslavia) set an unofficial world record in the 2 mile steeplechase of 10 min 2.4 sec, just 3 sec ahead of young John Disley. And Championship best performances were equalled by Alan Paterson (6 ft 4 in/1.93 m in the high jump), Les Lewis (48.2 sec for 440 yd) and Arthur Wint (1 min 51.6 sec for 880 yd), who beat Roger Bannister and John Parlett. Jack Holden, recovered from his Auckland experience, had already won two marathons since returning; in July, he won the AAA race in a lifetime best of 2 hr 31 min 3.4 sec.

Jack Holden wins his fourth and fastest AAA marathon in 1950. (HW Neale)

Bill Nankeville winning his third successive AAA mile in 1950. (Central Press Photos Ltd)

'Galloping Gordon' Pirie won six AAA titles over a ten-year period and made British distance running respectable. (All Sport/Konig)

*Above:* Three times AAA and twice Commonwealth pole vault champion Geoff Elliott was also Britain's leading decathlete in the early 1950s. (All Sport/Konig)
*Right:* Three distance runners of the fifties who achieved world-class performances — Fred Norris (17), world-record holder for 10 miles, Frank Sando (16), twice International Cross-Country Champion, and George Knight, UK record-holder for 10 000 metres. (All Sport/Konig)

*Below:* Olympic 800 metres silver medallist in 1956, Derek Johnson (4), won two AAA junior titles over 440 yards and was the 1955 senior 880 yards champion. (All Sport Photographic)
*Right:* In a five-year span as AAA Champion (1957–61), Arthur Rowe, European and Commonwealth Champion, improved the Championship shot put record by over 2 metres. (All Sport/Konig)

In Brussels, Great Britain had its most successful European Championships, winning eight events. Holden set the standard on the first day with yet another convincing marathon victory, shrugging off the challenge of Feodosi Vanin (USSR). 'It was either King George or Joe Stalin,' he explained afterwards. Brian Shenton's three-metre victory in the 200 m was as marvellous a bonus as Jack Archer's in 1946; but for injuries to John Wilkinson and Nick Stacey, he would not have made the team. Derek Pugh convincingly won the 400 m. John Parlett's spectral form crossed the 800 m line first, with Bannister third. Alan Paterson was over an inch clear in the men's high jump (6 ft 5 in/1.96 m) and Sheila Alexander won the women's, from Dorothy Tyler, who cleared the same height. Britain also won two relays, the men's 4 × 400 m, with Martin Pike, Leslie Lewis, Angus Scott and Derek Pugh, and the women's 4 × 100 m, with Elspeth Hay, Jean Desforges, Dorothy Hall and June Foulds.

### 1951 — THE GLINT OF GOLD

Predicting Olympic medals is a time-honoured pastime in the build-up to the Games, but hopes have never been so high in Britain as they were for Helsinki, 1952. It became a gold rush. The beginnings can be traced to Auckland and Brussels, where success obliterated memories of Wembley, 1948. Through 1951 the prospectors filed their claims. At the AAA Championships McDonald Bailey twice equalled his 100 yd

*Above:* 'Mac', the popular E. McDonald Bailey, wins the 100 yd in 9.6 sec. in 1951. He achieved the sprint double on seven occasions. (Keystone Press Agency Ltd)

*Below:* In 1951 Ron Pavitt, with a jump of 6 ft 5 in/1.95 m removed a 26-year-old Championship record from the books. (Keystone Press Agency Ltd)

record of 9.6 sec and easily won the 220 yd in 21.4 sec. Derek Pugh cut the English Native record to 47.9 sec in the 440 yd. Arthur Wint came within half a second of Wooderson's world record for 880 yd, winning in 1 min 49.6 sec. Roger Bannister (4 min 7.8 sec, a Championship best), Bill Nankeville (4 min 8.6 sec) and John Parlett (4 min 9.2 sec) all got inside 4 min 10 sec for the mile. Gordon Pirie, 20, set new figures for the 6 miles of 29 min 32 sec. And Ron Pavitt at last raised the Championship record for the high jump — by then it was shared by nine men — to 6 ft 5 in/1.95 m. If foreign athletes bettered the Championship records in the steeplechase (Petar Segedin of Yugoslavia, 9 min 58.6 sec), the shot (Gunnar Huseby of Iceland, 52 ft 0¾ in/15.87 m) and the discus (Giuseppe Tosi of Italy, 175 ft 9½ in/53.58 m), there were still promising British performances by the fast-improving John Disley in the steeplechase and John Savidge in the shot.

### 1952 — A RECORD SEND-OFF TO HELSINKI

In 1952 the largest attendance ever at the Championships, over 46 000, filled the White City. The meeting was honoured by the presence of Her Majesty the Queen, Patron of the AAA, in the first year of her reign, and HRH Princess Margaret. Britain's greatest living athletes mustered in the centre to be presented, among them Abrahams, Brown, Burghley, Green, Hampson, Lowe, Rampling, Roberts, Whitlock and Wint — all Olympic gold medallists — and Wooderson. Also in the line were the leading candidates for Helsinki. It was premature, but the newspapers were talking of up to seven gold medals.

**The supreme newsmaker of the fifties, Gordon Pirie, leads Len Eyre and Fred Green in the 1953 AAA 3 miles. Pirie set a Championship record of 13 min 43.4 sec. (ED Lacey)**

Nothing in the Championships modified that expectation. McDonald Bailey (9.6 sec/21.4 sec) was as sharp as ever. Bannister won the half-mile by a long way in 1 min 51.5 sec. Bill Nankeville defeated the new Australian miler, John Landy, in 4 min 9.8 sec. Chris Chataway got inside 14 min for 3 miles. Gordon Pirie set a 6 miles record of 28 min 55.6 sec. John Disley ran a world's best, 9 min 44 sec, for the 2 mile steeplechase. Peter Hildreth, in almost beating Ray Weinberg (Australia), equalled Finlay's 14.4 sec for the high hurdles; and Harry Whittle set a new British record in the 440 yd hurdles of 53.3 sec. Roland Hardy walked faster than ever before in the 2 and 7 mile events. John Savidge restored the Championship record for the shot to Britain after 39 years, with 54 ft 1¾ in/16.50 m. And Mike Denley set an English Native record of 216 ft 1 in/65.86 m in the javelin. In the marathon, held that year in conjunction with the Polytechnic Harriers' race, Jim Peters (2 hr 20 min 42.2 sec) and Stan Cox ( 2 hr 21 min 42 sec) bettered all previous records by a sensational margin.

Bailey, Bannister, Chataway, Disley, Hardy, Peters, Pirie and Sheila Lerwill, world record holder for the women's high jump: on paper it still looks as strong a squad of gold-diggers as ever left these shores. Yet the men between them returned with nothing better than bronze. Sheila Lerwill struck silver; Shirley Cawley, in the long jump, bronze; and the women's sprint relay team, bronze. What went wrong? It was a combination of miscalculation and misfortune. An unscheduled qualifying round, a disqualification, a fall at the final turn — each athlete had his individual calamity, but if a general observation is possible it is that the team lacked the competitive edge that frequent top-class international experience provides. Since 1950, Great Britain's international programme had consisted of one meeting with France and a short tour of the Balkans in 1951.

The two men who earned bronze medals were McDonald Bailey in the 100 m and John Disley in the 3000 m steeplechase. 'Mac' shared the winning time of 10.4 sec, but lacked the finishing technique of Lindy Remigino (USA) and Herb McKenley (Jamaica); he crossed the line with that elegant, upright action he had never needed to modify against British opposition. Disley, tracking the pre-race favourite, Helmut Gude (Germany), was seventh with two laps to go, when Geoff Dyson shouted from the edge of the track, and, in Disley's words, 'I woke up and began to chase the leaders. I had been running in a vacuum . . .'. He caught up four places and missed the silver medal by one-fifth of a second.

Basil Heatley's two AAA titles were in the 10 miles, but his peak performance was finishing second in the 1964 Olympic marathon. (All Sport/Konig)

1958 European 1500 and 800 metres champions Brian Hewson (2) and Mike Rawson (4) closely tracked by the 1960 Olympic 1500 metres champion Herb Elliott (far left). (All Sport/Konig)

Mike Lindsay's tally of AAA titles in shot and discus was four as a junior, four as a senior and two in the indoor Championships. (All Sport/Konig)

**Five AAA Champions who between them won ten distance-running titles — Stan Eldon (2), Frank Salvat (20), Derek Ibbotson (behind Salvat), George Knight (10) and Bruce Tulloh (8). (All Sport/Konig)**

## 1953 — PIRIE'S WORLD RECORD

'Mac' made his farewell appearance at the Championships of 1953. In winning the sprint double for the seventh time since 1946, he overhauled Denis Horgan's record of 13 Championship wins. One meeting record he failed to dislodge was Willie Applegarth's 21.2 sec for 220 yd, set in 1914, but with 21.3 sec in a heat, he came tantalisingly close. He and Arthur Wint, who retired in September, 1952, with the rare tribute of a lap of honour, will forever be associated with the White City in its heyday. These two West Indians, both great gentlemen of the track, enlivened British athletics with world-class running over a period of 6 years. It would be hard to over-estimate the service their popularity did to community relations, a service Arthur Wint performed more formally as Jamaican High Commissioner in the United Kingdom from 1974 to 1978.

Another compulsive collector of titles who retired after the 1953 Championships was Harry Whittle, British team captain in the 1952 Olympics, whose seventh successive win in the 440 yd hurdles in a Championship record time of 52.7 sec made eleven Championships since 1947, for he had also won the decathlon (1950), the long jump (1947 and 1949) and the 220 yd hurdles (1953). But the headline-maker at these Championships was Gordon Pirie. On the Friday evening, he pounded through the twilight for 28 min 19.4 sec to set a world record for 6 miles, over 11 sec faster than Heino's figures of 1949. And on the Saturday, blisters notwithstanding, he wiped out Wooderson's best for 3 miles by nearly 10 sec, with 13 min 43.4 sec, for a double that won him the Jackson and Harvey cups. Even Roger Bannister's Championship best in the mile, 4 min 5.2 sec, was upstaged by Pirie. So was a significant English Native record by Don Anthony in the

**Harry Whittle won the 440 yd hurdles seven years in succession between 1947 and 1953, and was also AAA champion in the 220 yd hurdles, long jump (twice) and decathlon. (HW Neale)**

hammer, 174 ft 8 in/53.24 m, thrown for the first time at the White City from a concrete circle; significant because four of the first five in a close competition belonged to the Hammer Circle, the first of the specialist clubs to focus attention on a technical event.

### 1954 — BANNISTER SUPREME

By 1954 the interest of sports fans was concentrated on a race within a race that spanned three continents. John Landy (Australia), Wes Santee (USA) and Roger Bannister (GB) were chasing the world's first mile in under four minutes. The possibility had been argued over in schoolrooms and bar lounges for a generation.

The location for Bannister's attempt, on a damp, blustery evening on 6 May, was appropriately Oxford, where amateur athletics had begun. The meeting was the annual match between the AAA and Oxford University. Roger Bannister, Chris Brasher and Chris Chataway wore AAA vests — which would have pleased the founders of the Association — but of course it was an Oxbridge triumph. Brasher, formerly of St John's, Cambridge, was the scrupulous pacemaker for the first two laps. Then Chataway, formerly of Magdalen, Oxford, towed Bannister into what he described in *First Four Minutes* as 'the place where no man had yet ventured'. The running of the four minute mile, by six-tenths of a second, was and remains the sublime achievement of British athletics. It is not improbable that the subsequent triumphs of Chataway and Brasher were sparked by their share in that unforgettable evening at Iffley Road.

It was a summer replete with incident. In Turku, Finland, in June, John Landy improved the mile record to 3 min 58 sec (actual time 3 min 57.9 sec). Bannister won the AAA mile in 4 min 7.6 sec, failing to please a crowd so gluttonous for a four minute feast that the significance of the last lap in 53.8 sec eluded them. It was a message to John Landy, destined to meet Bannister in the Commonwealth Games: in a slow-run race, the Englishman would win.

The race of the AAA Championships was the 3 miles, enlivened by the uninhibited running of a Kenyan, Nyandika Maiyoro, a forerunner in more senses than one, who set such a pace that Chris Chataway and Freddie Green found themselves in the last laps battling not merely for the title, but the world record. At the bell, Green appeared to concede the race, waving Chataway ahead, then sensed that for once the 'Red Fox' could be caught, and he was. Green was clearly the winner, but the record of 13 min 32.2 sec was shared. In the steeplechase, run over a 3000 m course for the first time in the Championships, another close finish meant that two runners, Ken Johnson, first, and Laszlo Jeszenszky (Hungary), second, shared the inaugural record of 9 min 0.8 sec. Championship bests were also achieved by the winners of the high jump, Brendan O'Reilly (Ireland); the pole vault, Dr Tamas Homonnay (Hungary); and the hammer, József Csermak (Hungary), the Olympic champion. In the marathon, Jim Peters yet again put up a world's best performance, with 2 hr 17 min 39.4 sec.

Three weeks after the Championships, the fifth British Empire and Commonwealth Games opened in Vancouver, Canada, with the mile as the star event on the last day. The United Kingdom had some dazzling successes, none more gratifying than in the field events, where two Dyson-trained athletes, Geoff Elliott in the pole vault (14 ft 0 in/4.26 m) and John Savidge in the shot (55 ft 0¼ in/16.77 m) were decisive winners; and Ken Wilmshurst scored an inspired double in the long jump (24 ft 8¾ in/7.54 m) and triple jump (50 ft 1½ in/15.28 m). On the track, England won gold, silver and bronze in the 880 yd, Derek Johnson winning in 1 min 50.7 sec; the 3 miles, where Chataway took revenge on Green in 13 min

**Roger Bannister won the 1954 mile in 4 min 7.6 sec, but failed to please the crowd, looking for another 4 minute mile. His sights were on Vancouver. (Keystone Press Agency Ltd)**

35.2 sec; and the 6 miles, won by Peter Driver in 29 min 09.4 sec. There was also an English victory in the 4 × 440 yd relay, through Peter Higgins, Alan Dick, Peter Fryer and Johnson.

As for the mile, it completely fulfilled its promise. John Landy courageously elected to draw the finish from Bannister by setting the four minute pace only those two were capable of sustaining. In the second lap a gap of 15 yards opened between them, but by the bell Bannister had closed to Landy's shoulder. The decisive moment came 80 yards from the finish, when Landy glanced left to see where Bannister was, just as the Englishman surged into the lead. In his account of the race Bannister admitted he was actually slowing all the time, but he reached the tape to win in 3 min 58.8 sec, to Landy's 3 min 59.6 sec.

In 20 minutes the sight of those marvellous milers in full stride was replaced by a puppetlike figure shambling into the stadium, arms dangling, legs refusing to function. Jim Peters, dehydrated by the extreme heat, was attempting to finish his last marathon. Nothing so harrowing had been seen since the Dorando marathon of 1908, for Peters fell repeatedly, crawled and staggered towards the line Bannister had crossed in triumph. When he reached it, the AAA Hon

Secretary, Ernest Clynes, and the team masseur, Mick Mays, supported him to a stretcher. The assistance automatically disqualified Peters, because the marathon finish was 200 yd farther on. The official winner was Joe McGhee of Scotland, who had fallen five times on the roads outside and was sitting waiting for the ambulance when he heard that Peters was out. He got up and finished the race in 2 hr 39 min 36 sec.

That same month, the Great Britain team travelled to Berne for the next stage of its most exhausting season. Success in the European Championships was limited to Bannister's crushing victory in the 1500 m (3 min 43.8 sec), with a 25 sec last 200 m, and wins in the women's events by Jean Desforges in the long jump and Thelma Hopkins in the high jump, who joined Bannister by taking gold medals of the Commonwealth and European varieties. The sensation of the Championships was the world record 5000 m win by Vladimir Kuts (USSR), who defeated Chris Chataway and Emil Zatopek by haring into an extravagant lead early in the race and holding it to the finish. The re-match between Kuts and Chataway in the London v Moscow match under floodlights in October was by common consent the most exciting race ever seen at the White City. Chataway, who seemed dedicated to demonstrating the need for photo-finish at whatever distance, never cut it finer than this, taking the lead only five metres from the tape to win in a world record of 13 min 51.6 sec.

**A happy moment for Jim Peters as he enters Chiswick stadium in the 1954 AAA marathon when he set a world best performance of 2 hr 17 min 39.4 sec. (Central Press Photos Ltd)**

**Fred Green pips Chris Chataway in the 1954 AAA 3 miles, but they share a world record of 13 min 32.2 sec. (Keystone Press Agency Ltd)**

High jumper and meteorologist Crawford Fairbrother, three times AAA outdoor champion between 1959 and 1964 and twice indoor champion, investigates the stratosphere. (All Sport/Konig)

Roger Bannister completes his marvellous year with victory in the 1954 European Championship 1500 metres. (ED Lacey)

### 1955 — PIRIE'S COLLAPSE

In the fifties the biggest newsmaker in Britain was the incident-prone Gordon Pirie, whose fearless front running helped lift British standards from mediocrity in the post-Wooderson era to world class. The 1955 AAA 6 miles was run with the temperature at 79°F/26.1°C. Pirie, who had retired from the previous year's race with a foot injury, started as if determined to recapture the world record from his hero, Emil Zatopek. But by halfway, Ken Norris took over the lead. It was Pirie's custom to drink no liquid on the day of a race, and as it progressed he became increasingly dehydrated. In the 23rd lap, under the impression it was the last, he raised a sprint and passed Norris. Before he crossed the line, his sight failed and he crashed into the outside rail and collapsed. Norris won by half a minute in 29 min 0.6 sec.

On the Saturday of those 1955 Championships, the temperature rose to 88°F/31.1°C, but that did not prevent John Disley from setting a British All-Comers' record in the 3000 m steeplechase of 8 min 56.6 sec, with Chris Brasher also beating 9 min. Brian Hewson missed Bannister's Championship record in the mile by the smallest margin, winning in 4 min 5.4 sec. Derek Pugh's 1951 best for the 440 yd (47.9 sec) fell to two runners, Peter Fryer and Mike Wheeler, who each recorded 47.7 sec. There were best performances, too, in the hurdles events over 220 yd and 440 yd by the Achilles men, Paul Vine (23.7 sec, a British all-comers' record) and Bob Shaw (52.2 sec), while the Rumanian javelin thrower Dumitru Zamfir exactly matched Stanley Lay's 222 ft 9 in/ 67.90 m of 1928.

Derek Ibbotson leads the eventual winner, Chris Chataway in the 1955 3 miles. (ED Lacey)

In 1956 Ibbotson (2) gained his revenge over Chataway (1). (ED Lacey)

### 1956 — BRASHER GETS THE GOLD

Unrelenting rain depressed performances in the 1956 Championships, honoured on the first day by the presence of Her Majesty the Queen and HRH the Duke of Edinburgh. Ken Norris and Frank Sando produced a 6 miles of high quality and excitement, Norris, in 28 min 13.6 sec, beating Pirie's British record, with Sando closing fast a mere six-tenths of a second behind. The steeplechase was won by stylish Eric Shirley, 1.8 sec ahead of John Disley in the British record of 8 min 51.6 sec. Chris Brasher, who was to beat the world before the year's end, was 11 sec adrift. Creditably, in the conditions, Championship bests were set in the 440 yd, by Mike Wheeler, 47.7 sec, equalling his time of 1955; the 440 yd hurdles, 52.2 sec, by Ilie Savel (Rumania); and the shot, 54 ft 2 in/16.51 m, by Barclay Palmer. John Young, aged 18 years 10 months, became the youngest-ever winner of the AAA 100 yd (9.9 sec), although the Eton schoolboy John Ridley in 1867

*Above:* The last British male sprinter to gain an individual Olympic sprint medal — Peter Radford, 100 metres bronze medallist in 1960. (All Sport/Konig)

*Right:* Steeplechaser Maurice Herriott, one of only five men ever to win seven consecutive AAA titles (1961–7). (All Sport/Konig)

**John Disley (2) leads Chris Brasher (4), the man who beat the world in the 1956 Olympics. Disley won this 1956 event against Czechoslovakia. (Central Press Photos Ltd)**

had won the AAC Championship when one month younger. And Chris Chataway was involved in yet another cat and dog finish, this time with Derek Ibbotson, who took the 3 miles title by two feet, sharing the time of 13 min 32.6 sec.

The Melbourne Olympic Games were in more than one respect pivotal in the history of British athletics. The outstanding achievement was Chris Brasher's in winning the steeplechase (8 min 41.2 sec) with a sustained sprint in the final lap that devastated his rivals and beat the Olympic record. The jury-room drama that followed, confirming Brasher as champion after a precipitate disqualification, has tended to distract from the stunning success of a third-string athlete inspired to the race of his life on the day it mattered.

British distance running was never stronger than in Melbourne. Gordon Pirie's herculean struggle with the eventual winner, Vladimir Kuts, for 21 laps of the 10 000 m was a highlight of the Games; it says much for his famed irrepressibility that Pirie, who finished eighth, won the silver medal five days later in the 5000 m. In this, Ibbotson was third, and for most of it he, Pirie and Chataway (who had stomach cramp and finished eleventh) provided the only challenge to Kuts. In the 800 m Derek Johnson won the silver medal, a mere half-metre behind the American, Tom Courtney, whom he led until the final strides. Johnson also earned a bronze medal in the 4 × 400 m, with Peter Higgins, Mike Wheeler and John Salisbury. Britain's women had two silver medal placings, through Thelma Hopkins in the high jump and the sprint relay quartet of Anne Pashley, Jean Scrivens, June Foulds-Paul and Heather Armitage-Young.

Viewed historically, 1956 ended an era, the third flowering of Oxford and Cambridge talent. The first, 1866–90, dated from days when the entry conditions ensured the perennial eminence of University athletes; the second, 1920–36, was the dazzling show of the Achilles Club between the wars, with Abrahams, Lowe, Burghley, Tisdall, Hampson and Godfrey Brown; and the third —

the briefest, and arguably most brilliant — was the mid-fifties, with Bannister, Chataway, Brasher and Johnson, and the four minute mile as the most exquisite bloom. After 1956 even the presence of Adrian Metcalfe and Herb Elliott could not alter the fact that the Oxbridge garden had wilted.

A reason often suggested for the success of University athletes in the twenties and thirties is that they had the leisure to train, whereas men in employment worked long hours. Paradoxically, the post-war generation of Oxford and Cambridge runners — notably Bannister and Chataway — trained to schedules ridiculously light by comparison with employed athletes such as Gordon Pirie and Derek Ibbotson. But the pace of improvement in athletics meant increasingly that top-class athletes could spare little time for anything but training. To contribute to the administration of national athletics was difficult, if not impossible. Yet issues were arising that caused unrest and concern among international athletes. They reached crisis-point in Melbourne. 'It was not as if 1956 was a particularly black year,' wrote John Disley, 'it was just that at Melbourne we had time to organize our bickerings.'

The immediate problem was pocket money. Other teams in the Olympic village were paid a weekly sum, in anticipation of a relaxation in the IAAF rule, to which the British management conscientiously adhered. But the resentments went deeper, and members of the team went on to formulate proposals to reform the administration of British athletics.

On their return to England, three representatives were invited to a meeting of the AAA Finance and General Purposes Committee. In consequence a new Athletes' Consultative Committee was set up, composed of athletes' representatives, national coaches and officials of the BAAB, AAA and Women's AAA. The next step was the formation on 19 October 1958, of the International Athletes' Club, which became a strong organization not only as a ginger group, but by contributing constructively to the development of the sport by promoting highly successful meetings, sponsoring coaching and encouraging its members to participate in administration and coaching. Since 1965 two international athletes and the two principal national coaches have attended meetings of the BAAB.

### 1957 — IBBOTSON BLAZES BACK

In 1955 the AAA had introduced a new system for its qualifying heats for certain events by which only the winners automatically progressed to the final, and the remaining places were secured on the basis of fastest times. This triggered a shock result in 1957. Derek Ibbotson, the new British record holder for the mile (3 min 58.4 sec), finished second in a slow heat and was eliminated. As title-holder, he was automatically entered for the 3 miles, which he had intended to miss. Yorkshire pride was at stake next afternoon when, after all, he turned out, and went hunting the British record. In steady rain, but with the crowd's warm support, he ran alone for most of the race to win by over 20 sec in 13 min 20.8 sec, a 2.4 sec improvement on Chataway's record. Six days later he set a world record for the mile of 3 min 57.2 sec.

Another great miler, Ron Delany (Ireland), the Olympic 1500 m champion, won the AAA 880 yd in 1 min 49.6 sec, equalling Arthur Wint's 1951 time. More Championship records were set by Peter Higgins, with 47.6 sec for 440 yd; Tom Farrell, 440 yd hurdles in 52.1 sec; and Oladipo Okuwobi, with a 6 ft 5 in/1.95 m high jump. The highest honours in the field were won by Mike Ellis, 20, with a British all-comers' record in the hammer of 197 ft 9 in/60.28 m; a few weeks later, he became the first UK athlete to throw over 200 ft/61.00 m. And Peter Cullen won the javelin after a titanic competition with Colin Smith, in which the Championship best was beaten five times, and Cullen set new British National and English Native records of 236 ft 7 in/72.12 m.

### 1958 — THE COMMONWEALTH INVASION

On a proposal passed at the 1957 AGM, the 10 miles, one of the original AAA Championship events, was revived in 1958 after an eleven-year break. Fred Norris, the winner in 49 min 39 sec, cut nearly a minute from Bill Eaton's previous best. In subsequent years this rarely run event was won in world record time by Basil Heatley, 47 min 47 sec in 1961; Mel Batty, 47 min 26.8 sec in 1964; and Ron Hill, 47 min 2.2 sec in 1968. But after 1972 it was discontinued, and is no longer in the IAAF schedule of world records.

The strongest foreign 'invasion' since 1900 was the feature of the 1958 Championships, the year the Commonwealth Games were held in Cardiff, but some of the outstanding performances were by United Kingdom athletes. Brian Hewson faced master-miler Herb Elliott in the 880 yd without fear of defeat. 'I had never regarded Elliott as a world-class half-miler,' he wrote in *Flying Feet*, 'and I was confident of my ability to claim another AAA title.' This he did, in a Championship best of 1 min 48.3 sec. Mike Rawson, too, finished in front of Elliott, but the tough

**Perils of the steeplechase in 1957, as Eric Shirley (1) and John Disley (4), the eventual winner, try to avoid the fallen AC Porter — who got up and finished in the best time of his career. (Bippa)**

Australian was to take his revenge in Cardiff.

Graham Everett outsprinted Murray Halberg (NZ) in the AAA mile in 4 min 6.4 sec. John Salisbury comfortably defeated Mal Spence (S. Africa) over 440 yd in a Championship best of 47.2 sec. A triumphant distance-running double was achieved by Stan Eldon; among those he beat in the 3 miles were Ibbotson and Pirie, and his 6 miles time, 28 min 5 sec, was a British all-comers' record. Eric Shirley marginally improved his own Championship best for the steeplechase (8 min 51 sec) in a close finish with John Disley (8 min 51.2 sec); in third place finished the future General Secretary of the BAAB, David Shaw. Arthur Rowe, the Barnsley blacksmith who was Mr Adonis of 1958, obliterated the British shot put record with a mighty effort of 56 ft 9 in/17.30 m. Mike Ellis in the hammer defeated Commonwealth champion Mohamed Iqbal (Pakistan), and stretched the Championship best to 203 ft 2 in/61.92 m.

To be fair to the visiting athletes, they did claim British National records in the high jump, 6 ft 8 in/2.03 m by Patrick Etolu (Uganda); the 120 yd hurdles, 14.1 sec by Keith Gardner (Jamaica); the 440 yd hurdles, 51.2 sec by Dave Lean (Australia); and the triple jump, in which Dave Norris (NZ), with 51 ft 4 in/15.64 m edged out Jack Metcalfe's 1934 mark by one half-inch. The oddest result was the long jump, for Paul Foreman (Jamaica), who was to win in Cardiff, equalled the 20-year-old Championship record of 24 ft 8 in/7.52 m in the qualifying round, but finished fourth in the final, won by Karim Olowu (Nigeria), with 23 ft 10½ in/7.28 m.

For the United Kingdom, the fifties remained fickle to the end. For the first time ever, there was not a single individual track victory by a runner from one of the home countries in the Commonwealth Games. England did win the men's and women's sprint relays, but mainly it was left to the field event competitors to salvage national pride. Their efforts gave England six more gold medals, a striking testimony to the AAA Coaching Scheme, considering that before it existed only one Englishman had ever won a field event in the Games — he was the chairman of the Coaching Committee, Malcolm Nokes. The successful six were Geoff Elliott (pole vault, 13 ft 8 in/4.16 m), Arthur Rowe (shot, 57 ft 8 in/17.57 m), Mike Ellis (hammer, 206 ft 4½ in/62.90 m), Colin Smith (javelin, 233 ft 10½ in/71.28 m), Sheila Hoskin (women's long jump, 19 ft 9 in/6.02 m) and Suzanne Allday (women's discus, 150 ft 7½ in/45.90 m). There were no Welsh athletes among the winners, although John Merriman chased Dave Power to within a second in the 6 miles. This must have been disappointing to the Welsh AAA, whose organization of the Games was a triumph.

The press were generally pessimistic about British chances in the European Championships that summer, held in Stockholm. It was agreed that our Commonwealth champions in the field events would be outclassed by the strong men and women of East Europe, and there was sharp criticism of the track selections, notably Brian Hewson's omission from the 800 m, his own preferred event, in favour of the 1500 m. The *News Chronicle* in a leader wrote, 'The selectors seem to have been capricious in their choices. They may have some far-sighted plan for improving long-term British prospects, but they have certainly made our hopes of winning gold medals at Stockholm more remote.'

This time, the critics had to eat their words. The team performed magnificently, spurred by the forceful Leslie Truelove in his first year as BAAB Team Manager. They won seven gold medals. John Wrighton, regarded as our second-string 400 m runner, beat John Salisbury in 46.3 sec. Mike Rawson won the 800 m in 1 min 47.8 sec, then had to endure an experience similar to Chris Brasher's in Melbourne, as the jury of appeal considered whether his being barged off the track at the start meant he had not run the full course. The 1500 m was won — to his great credit — by the still smarting Brian Hewson in 3 min 41.9 sec. Stan Vickers took the 20 km walk in 1 hr 33 min 9 sec, Arthur Rowe, with his last effort, the shot, at 58 ft 4 in/17.78 m, Heather Young the women's 100 m, and the men's quartet of Ted Sampson, John MacIsaac, John Wrighton and John Salisbury won the 4 × 400 m relay.

### 1959 — THREE FOR THE SIXTIES

The decade ended with athletics in a quieter phase. The 1959 Championships were watched by one of the smallest crowds for years. There were just two Championship best performances, by Ken Matthews in the 2 mile walk, 13 min 19.4 sec, and the steadily improving Arthur Rowe in the shot, 58 ft 10¾ in/17.95 m. The interest otherwise was in the advent of new champions, among them three who would carry Britain's hopes in the sixties: the 19-year-olds, Peter Radford, winner of the 100 yd, and Maurice Herriott, the steeplechase, and the barefoot 3 miler, Bruce Tulloh.

### TUG-OF-WAR

In 1958, twelve British clubs formed the Tug-of-War Association, to which the AAA delegated control of the sport. Tug-of-war became a AAA Championship event in 1910, but its links with track and field can be traced to the Woolwich Garrison Sports of 18/19 August 1874. It became rapidly popular everywhere. A single-handed tug-of-war was included in the first international match between Ireland and England in 1876; William Winthrop (England) was the winner. The first rules for tug-of-war were probably those framed by the New York AC in 1879. The AAA formulated rules in 1887. In the Olympic Games, tug-of-war first appeared in 1900. At the London Olympics of 1908, it provoked a bitter row between Great Britain and the USA, when the Americans accused UK Team II (Liverpool Police) of wearing specially prepared boots with prongs and heel-plates. Although the judges examined the boots and found nothing projecting, the Americans, after one ignominious pull in a heat, abandoned the contest. Nor did they seem to appreciate the policemen's offer to pull in their socks.

The first AAA Championship, in 1910, was a 90-stone contest, won by Central London Railway. For some years the Championship was decided at the same meeting as the 10 miles and 7 mile walk, but from 1927 to 1970 it appeared on the main Championship programme, with two contests, at 100 stone and catchweight. Until 1955 the sport was dominated by teams from the police, fire service and armed forces, but since the TOWA was formed, clubs from industry and local communities have come to prominence. The most successful team ever are Wood Treatment of Bosley, Cheshire, who won 15 consecutive catchweight titles between 1959 and 1974.

Tug-of-war is passionately contested, not least by the team coaches. One pull in the 1958 AAA catchweight final between New Haw & Woodham and Ford Sports lasted 5 min 10 sec, and after it the New Haw coach needed a new set of false teeth.

# Flesh-Gloves to Five Stars

**When Lynn Davies won the Olympic long jump in 1964 he completed a unique double for Britain, for Mary Rand had already won the women's long jump. Each was an individual triumph by a supremely talented athlete, yet each had been trained to Olympic pitch in a technical event by an AAA national coach. Their victories rewarded not only John Le Masurier and Ron Pickering, but thousands who had shared in the development of British athletic coaching.**

Athletic training a century ago was practically as clandestine as smoking opium. Few admitted to indulging. Those who did made sure they were not observed. Secret time trials took place at first light, with athletes and trainers looking over their shoulders to see who was watching. One reason for the secrecy was that betting still pervaded athletics, even in the amateur sphere. Another was that no gentleman-amateur liked it to be known that he was too serious about his sport. Yet a number of trainers, ex-professional runners, made a living 'assisting gentlemen with their breathings'. For a fee they administered massage, using the gruesome-sounding flesh-gloves, and disclosed the lore of tactics they had learned on the old running-grounds. In the Victorian social order, the athletic trainer ranked rather lower than a servant. The best-known was Jack White, the old 'Gateshead Clipper' of Deerfoot's era, retained in the 1880s by London AC and in the early nineties by Cambridge University AC. Oxford relied for nearly half a century on the advice of Clement Jackson, the AAA founder, whose position as don, treasurer and trainer was exceptional.

In 1895 English athletics suffered the shock of the century when a London AC team that was virtually England travelled to New York to meet a New York AC team that was virtually the USA and lost by eleven events to nil. The Americans set world records in five events. They had been trained by Mike Murphy (1861–1913), the Yale University coach, whose knowledge of athletics far exceeded that of old Jack White, who travelled with the Englishmen. 'Compared with the Americans our time of training was very short and haphazard,' recalled Frederick Horan, the English distance-runner. 'We suffered a staggering defeat on that September 21, 1895.' It took a long time for the lesson to sink in. In 1900, there were similar recriminations when the American team *en route* for the Paris Olympics cleaned up with eight wins in the AAA Championships. In the 1908 Olympic Games, held in London, the USA, still coached by Murphy, won 15 of the track and field events, to Britain's eight.

Shortly before the next Olympic Games in 1912 the AAA appointed FW Parker, the London AC secretary, as Chief Athletic Adviser, with the responsibility of visiting training centres through-

Lynn Davies, trained by National Coach Ron Pickering, won Olympic, European and Commonwealth gold medals in the long jump. (ED Lacey)

Mary Rand, coached by AAA National Coach John Le Masurier, won the Olympic women's long jump in 1964 with a world record. (ED Lacey)

**Walter Knox (*inset*) was the first full time AAA Chief Coach in 1914, the year his successor, Geoff Dyson, was born. Here Dyson, at the blackboard, with John Le Masurier (behind him) and Jim Alford (with towel) coaches young athletes at Motspur Park in January 1952. (Canada's Sports Hall of Fame; HW Neale)**

out England to supervise possible candidates for the Games. He was supported by a Chief Trainer, Alec Nelson, and subsidiary trainers for the North, Midlands and South. The scheme sounded impressive; on closer analysis, however, it is clear that the 'training centres' were simply existing sports grounds, and that funds were so limited that Parker and his team were on four-month contracts. The British team won only two events in the Games.

To the AAA's credit, it learned from the experience and invested some of its limited funds in a salaried Chief Coach. In February, 1914, a three-year contract for a salary of £400* was signed by Walter Knox (1878–1951), a Scots-Canadian and possibly the most colourful character ever to be employed in English athletics. Knox prided himself on his power to persuade, justifiably, considering that in him the reputable AAA took on to its payroll a tough professional athlete who for years had barnstormed his way round America and Europe, often using false identities to upset the betting odds. Each summer since 1911 he had toured the Scottish Highland Games, picking up as many as 50 first prizes on the circuit. Out of season he lived like a character in a Jack London novel, moving among the gold-mining camps of the Klondike, living rough and buying and selling claims and shares. His richest strike in sport was getting appointed coach to the Canadian Olympic team in 1912. This, and his brilliance as an all-round athlete — he had sprinted 100 yd in 9.6 sec, long jumped 24 ft 2 in/7.36 m, pole-vaulted 12 ft 6 in/3.81 m and put the shot 46 ft 5 in/14.15 m — convinced the AAA that this rough diamond could put the sparkle back into English athletics.

Knox sensibly decided to give his main attention to field events, which the Amateur Field Events Association was already making attempts to foster. Britain fell short in these events, he concluded, because there were not enough competitions; most sports meetings were confined to running and walking. So he began touring the country giving demonstrations of jumping and throwing, in an effort to persuade meeting

*Incidentally, this was equivalent to the salary of a British Member of Parliament at that time.

**Howard Baker won the 1912 title at 6 ft 0 in/1.83 m, using the scissors style, but as one of the first to benefit from AAA coaching, he changed to a more efficient style and improved to an English Native record of 6 ft 5 in/1.95 m. (Radio Times Hulton Picture Library)**

organizers to introduce field events, and athletes to support them. At 36 he was still a better pole vaulter and shot putter than anyone in England. As a back-up to his efforts the AAA intended appointing nine regional coaches. One early coaching success by Knox was to persuade the champion high jumper, Howard Baker, to abandon the schoolboyish scissors style and use a cut-off technique, with which he eventually set the inaugural English Native record of 6 ft 5 in/1.95 m.

What transformations Knox might have made in the overall strength of the nation's athletics we can only speculate, for with the outbreak of war his contract had to be terminated, and he returned to Canada. It was 33 years before another full-time Chief Coach was appointed.

The first national coaching scheme was a victim not of the war, but the peace. In the twenties massive public interest in athletics practically overwhelmed the AAA. Priority had to be given to meeting immediate needs for competitive facilities, and there was no reference to coaching in the reconstruction plan. Athletes requiring assistance made private arrangements with professional trainers in attendance at the tracks, just as the Victorians had. Certain trainers were retained by particular clubs: Cambridge University employed Alec Nelson, the Chief Trainer to the 1912 Olympic team, who was a former professional half-miler; Oxford had the illustrious distance champion, Alf Shrubb; and Polytechnic Harriers had the best of them all in Sam Mussabini. The flaw in the arrangement is that all were essentially, if not quite exclusively, coaches of *running*. In 1923 a British Olympic Association Commission met to discuss training facilities in athletics, and Michael Webster, founder of the Amateur Field Events Association, told them, 'We cannot find anyone in England who can teach field events.' The AAA in the same year nominated Alfred George, another ex-champion at running and the journalist brother of 'WG', as Honorary Manager and Chief Coach to the 1924 Olympic team, and as many as five additional trainers and three masseurs travelled with the team to Paris. For the 1928 Olympics, the number of masseurs — one was known as Jack the Rubber — was increased to five. But if such reliance on massage seemed like a regression to Victorian methods, it should be said that the twenties saw the introduction of slow-motion films as technical aids and the publication of several forward-looking books on training.

The real breakthrough in British coaching was the BAAB report that set up the first AAA summer school at Loughborough in 1934; with Michael Webster and Malcolm Nokes among the organizers, no apology was offered for restricting the programme to field events. Foreign coaches as eminent as Boyd Comstock (USA), Charles Hoff (Norway), Pierre Lewden (France), Armas Valste (Finland) and Jaako Mikkola (Finland) — world authorities on jumping and throwing — came to Loughborough each summer and with the British staff taught techniques to schoolmasters, club officials and athletes wishing to qualify as AAA honorary coaches. In 1936 Webster founded the School of Athletics, Games and Physical Education at Loughborough College. With it were soon associated British coaches whose contribution since to the sport has been immense — Geoff Dyson, John Le Masurier and Denis Watts. The importance of Loughborough lay less in immediate results — cut short by World War II — than in laying the foundation of the post-war AAA coaching scheme. By 1939, there was a real impetus in coaching. The AAA obtained the financial backing of the Government National Fitness Campaign to appoint three full-time professional coaches. CFR Hilton was named as full-time organizer. Then, with timing depressingly reminiscent of 1914, war scotched the project.

This time, only for as long as the war lasted. In the General Committee on 12 October 1946, Lt Col Roland Harper — who had hurdled for Britain in the 1932 Olympics — formally proposed the adoption of the AAA coaching scheme. It had three objects, which can be summarized as: (1) to provide a national scheme of coaching with an approved body of professional and amateur coaches; (2) to establish a chain of communications with clubs and schools so that they would benefit from the coaching efforts; and (3) to issue

*Above:* National coaches meet at the Crystal Palace track in 1969: standing, from left, Peter Lay (Wales), Alf Cotton (Race Walking), Denis Watts (North), Peter Harper (North), John Le Masurier (South); seated, from left, David Kay (South-West), Tom McNab (South), Bill Marlow (Midlands) and Wilf Paish (North). (All Sport Don Morley)

*Right:* Geoff Dyson, the dynamic Chief Coach in charge of the AAA's post-war scheme, and big John Savidge, one of the first to show a dramatic improvement under Dyson's guidance. (All Sport Don Morley)

coaching bulletins. Three experienced athletes formed the first AAA Coaching Committee: Nokes, the senior tutor at the Loughborough summer school, was chairman; Harper was Hon Secretary; and 'Sandy' Duncan, the long jumper who had captained England in the 1938 Empire Games and became Secretary of the British Olympic Association, was Assistant Hon Secretary. It was decided to appoint a professional coach whose duties would include being in charge of AAA coaching courses and co-ordinating the work of AAA honorary coaches.

In Major Geoff Dyson, who took up his duties as Chief Coach on 17 February 1947, the AAA made an outstanding appointment. Born in 1914 (the year his predecessor as Chief Coach, Walter Knox, was serving his brief term), Dyson early in life revealed a sturdy individualism by running away from home at 15 and existing on odd jobs, sleeping rough in London until he joined the army at 16. As an army athlete he attended the AAA summer school in 1935, 1936 and 1937, and in January, 1938, joined the Loughborough College staff. The highpoint of his athletic career was finishing within 5 ft/1.50 m of Don Finlay in a 14.5 sec high hurdles race in 1938. In the war he was commissioned as a PE instructor, and served in East Africa and Italy.

Geoff Dyson's commitment to athletics was absolute. He was a natural communicator — admitting to 'a bit of a parade-ground manner, I suppose' — and, vitally, his understanding of the physiological principles on which athletics is based was unequalled. 'Whatever developments occur in the future,' wrote Roland Harper in *Athletics Weekly* in 1949, 'and however big our scheme becomes, there will be no question as to who deserves the credit for laying its foundations, and all athletes throughout the country for generations to come will owe a debt of gratitude to Geoffrey Dyson.'

The scheme was launched with the help of a contribution of £522 by the *News of the World*, whose 1946 British Games (they had organized athletics meetings since 1915) had done well at the turnstiles. In 1947 the same newspaper donated another £1000, an early instance of commercial sponsorship, from which athletics would increasingly benefit. An agreement with the Ministry of Education, whereby 80 per cent of the cost would be met from Government funds, enabled the AAA to appoint a second professional coach, Tony Chapman, in 1947, and three more in 1948, each responsible for an Area: Denis Watts (North), Allan Malcolm (Midlands) and Jim Alford (Wales). Watts in 1946 had achieved the first double in the AAA long jump and triple jump; in 1978 he completed 30 years' service in the scheme, and retired as one of the two Principal National Coaches. The other was John Le Masurier, a former 440 yd hurdler, who replaced Tony Chapman in 1949, and also served with the AAA and BAAB until 1978.

The Ministry of Education gave its backing on the understanding that the main duty of the national coaches was to train honorary coaches, who would teach the technical skills in clubs, schools and youth organizations. There was no provision for the national coaches to work with individual athletes, so that Dyson's assistance to Maureen Gardner, who won the silver medal in the 80 m hurdles in the 1948 Olympics and afterwards married him, was voluntarily given. Only after the Games was a supplementary scheme, known as the special coaching scheme, devised to enable national and senior honorary coaches to give their services to athletes of outstanding promise. But the main work of coaching the *coaches* continued. In the first 5 years the number of honorary coaches grew from 160 to 1000; by 1965 it had topped 2500.

If the real achievement of the national coaches was in training thousands of men and women to develop the skills of the sport nationally and abroad, the publicity they earned — this in itself helped the scheme — was through the star athletes they coached. By the early fifties Dyson had a small squad spearheading an improvement in events unfashionable in Britain, among them the shot putter, John Savidge (AAA champion 1952–4), pole vaulter and decathlete, Geoff Elliott (AAA champion 1952–3 and 1955), long jumper, Shirley Cawley (WAAA champion 1952) and steeplechaser, John Disley (AAA champion 1952, 1955 and 1957). John Le Masurier's charges included high hurdler, Jack Parker (AAA champion 1951, 1954 and 1955) and discus thrower, Mark Pharaoh (AAA champion 1952–3, 1955 and 1956). All achieved high standards internationally, and for a pilot group they were conspicuously successful in major Games, collecting between them two Olympic bronze medals; one European silver and one bronze; and three Commonwealth golds and one bronze. To these successes should be added Pharaoh's fourth place, ahead of all the Europeans in the 1956 Olympic discus competition — a result that took British throwing into world class.

As training methods increased in sophistication in the fifties a practical development was the formation of clubs for specialists in particular events. The trail-blazer, in 1952, was the Hammer Circle. In 10 years, each of the field events had its own club, as did milers, steeplechasers and road runners. In the same period the national coaches edited a series of AAA instructional booklets covering the standard events. *Weight Training for Athletes* reflected the emphasis on strength-training, and, with a fine counterpoise, the AAA also issued *Ballet Exercises for Athletes*.

It was not all an arabesque. Periodic differences arose between national coaches and officials. The issues most publicised concerned breakdowns in consultation over team management, but the underlying problem went deeper. It was about status. The Victorian stereotype of the wily old trainer reeking of embrocation had been allowed to linger too long in British athletics. An athletic coach is a highly professional expert in an extremely technical and developing field. Coaching as a career was a new concept, complicated by the fact that the employer was a committee of part-time amateur officials. The coaches were paid at schoolteachers' rates, but their work entailed extensive travel, unsocial hours and a demanding range of duties. As professional men they needed to keep up to date with technical developments in their field. They were better informed and more in touch with schools, clubs and individual athletes than many of the General Committee. Moreover, they were chosen because they were articulate, dynamic personalities. Geoff Dyson's achievements as Chief Coach were held in high regard by the AAA, but it was no secret that he and BAAB team manager Jack Crump had some angry clashes over decisions taken under pressure in international matches. It must also be said that they worked in close collaboration for most of Dyson's 14 years with the AAA. His resignation, when it came in September, 1961, was the consequence of a dispute over revised conditions of service. British athletics was the loser.

In the same year Ron Pickering joined the team as national coach for Wales, and almost at once discovered a schoolboy athlete of distinct promise named Lynn Davies. 'I asked him if he wanted to be the greatest long jumper that Britain had ever produced,' Pickering wrote in *World Sports*. 'He looked a little surprised, but said "Yes".' Three years — and a prodigious campaign of coaching — later, Pickering was in the Tokyo Olympic Stadium yelling repeatedly, 'Not the bronze — go for gold!' With his fifth jump Lynn the Leap responded with 26 ft 5¾ in/8.07 m. Great Britain's first-ever gold medal in the men's long jump matched one already earned in the women's event by Mary Rand. Her world record of 22 ft 2¼ in/6.76 m was her reward for persevering after a shattering disappointment in the previous Olympics, described by her coach, John Le Masurier, as 'just about the most difficult coaching challenge of my career'. Britain's first Olympic champions in field events for 56 years made 1964 a golden year for everyone connected with the coaching scheme.

But the scheme was not devised mainly to produce Olympic champions, rather to assist raw beginners, schoolchildren, club recruits to learn basic principles and, if they wished, to progress. The graded standards scheme introduced in 1959 provided measures of attainment in all events for youth, junior and senior athletes. Thousands of certificates are issued annually, and since 1968 gold and silver awards have been made for outstanding performances. The scheme is managed by a Standards Committee, whose Hon Secretary since 1959, Les Golding, is also the Chairman of the General Committee and has served the AAA and BAAB in numerous capacities — typical of so many honorary officials who give time, enthusiasm and managerial skill without thought of recognition or reward.

The AAA's most far-reaching innovation was the Five Star Award Scheme, sponsored by Wall's Ice Cream. It was championed by Tom McNab, a national coach appointed in 1963. His idea of devising a method by which *all* children — not just the precocious few who tend to dominate the school sports day — could measure their progress and win an award, has proved a block-busting success. Since it was introduced nationally in 1968 the number of certificates issued has risen to well over a million a year. About a quarter of a million badges are sold annually, and the scheme is a major source of revenue for the Area Associations, who see that much of it is ploughed back into schools' athletics in the form of grants.

In January, 1965, Arthur Gold succeeded Jack Crump (1905–66) as Hon Secretary of the BAAB. As organizer of the special coaching scheme (1957–62) and having been associated with AAA coaching since the inception of the summer school in 1934, Gold appropriately arranged for the principal national coaches, John Le Masurier and Denis Watts, to attend meetings of the Board and its selection committee.

The incorporation of the AAA scheme into a United Kingdom scheme was the next logical step, for Scotland had one professional coach, the Women's AAA had its own honorary coaches and Northern Ireland relied on local enthusiasts, with occasional help from the AAA. By patient negotiation the UK coaching scheme was finally established in 1972.

Since Walter Knox's missionary efforts in 1914, coaching in Britain has progressed to a stage where it is capable of assisting exceptionally talented athletes to achieve world class standards in any track or field event. In 1978 Daley Thompson's gold medal in the Commonwealth Games signified a British athlete's excellence over a range of ten events. Ten events taught by National Decathlon Coach, Bruce Longden. No better testimony could be supplied to the success of the coaching scheme launched 31 years before. How fitting, then, that the medal was presented by the Technical Director of the Games, the man who piloted the scheme — Geoff Dyson.

**Britain's athletic excellence over a range of ten events personified by the 1978 Commonwealth Games gold medallist Daley Thompson. (All Sport/Tony Duffy)**

'It was reported that none of the national coaches wished to be supplied with a Webley pistol. National coaches feel it is preferable to manage without a pistol.' *General Committee Minutes, 3 October 1953.*

# The Sixties and the Start of Sponsorship

**The Championships had a facelift in the sixties. And British athletics braced itself for major surgery.**

The fifties had seen spectacular improvements in each event and some unforgettable races. Yet by 1960 it was clear that public support had not kept pace with the progress on the track. Attendances at the White City had plummeted. A total of 17 000 watched the 1959 Championships, compared with 46 000 in 1952. The AAA announced a deficit of over £6000 for 1959. The new decade began with an appeal to clubs and supporters for donations.

At the AGM of 1960, Phil Gale, the newly elected Hon Treasurer, urged the immediate reorganization of British athletics, with a United Kingdom AAA replacing the four governing bodies — the AAA, Scottish AAA, Northern Ireland AAA and Women's AAA. Proposals for reorganization had often been made at AGMs, but never won a majority. Harold Abrahams, whose 1946 scheme had failed to win the support of the powerful Area Associations, argued that the AAA should first put its own house in order by obtaining a report from an independent investigator. His amendment was defeated. The proposal for a United Kingdom AAA was carried, and referred to the British Women's Council and Women's AAA, the Northern Ireland AAA and the Scottish AAA. All emphatically stated that they were fully satisfied with the existing arrangement and would not support a change.

The 1960 Championships attracted the entries of several foreign stars sharpening up for the Olympic Games, as well as such British favourites as Pirie, Ibbotson and Hewson, and the 26 650 gate must have heartened Phil Gale. The preliminaries on the first day certainly helped, for Peter Radford won a heat of the 100 yd in 9.5 sec and Dave Segal covered 220 yd in 21.1 sec, each a Championship best performance; and László Tábori (Hungary) and Michel Jazy (France) jointly improved the mile figure to 4 min 3.8 sec. That was fast running for a heat, but how about a final next day in which all eight runners beat Bannister's 4 min 5.2 sec, the Championship best listed in the programme? Tábori, the bogeyman of British milers, was first in 4 min 1 sec, but Mike Wiggs (4 min 1.2 sec) squeezed out Jazy in the run-in. British hopes for Rome were raised by Gordon Pirie's pace at the end of his personal best 6 miles, in 28 min 9.6 sec, Frank Salvat's breakthrough in the 3 miles and a stirring 2 mile walk in a new best of 13 min 2.4 sec by Stan Vickers, with Ken Matthews also inside the 56-year-old UK record. Mike Ellis in the hammer and Arthur Rowe in the shot improved their own Championship bests, and Eric Shirley matched his own in the steeplechase. Yet the abiding image of 1960 is the top-knotted Sikh, Milkha Singh, in full stride, pulverizing the 440 yd record in 46.5 sec, with 20-year-old Robbie Brightwell in pursuit.

On Great Britain's record in the three post-war Olympic Games — a single gold medal in 1956 — no one could have been over-optimistic about Rome in 1960. Don Thompson's golden 50 km walk — to which we shall return — is cherished as one of the most heartening stories in the history of sport, but otherwise the Games appeared to confirm the trend since 1948. What made it harder to accept was that many British competitors failed to show their best form. Rome was exceptionally hot when the team's plane touched down after leaving London at 55°F/13°C, and when the three 5000 m runners failed even to survive the first round, it was suggested that they had not been given sufficient time in Rome to acclimatize. In the men's team only the walkers and the sprinters won medals of any kind. Stan Vickers finished third in the 20 km walk, as did Peter Radford in the 100 m. The 4 × 100 m relay squad of Radford, David Jones, David Segal and Nick Whitehead, were awarded bronze medals after finishing fourth to the disqualified USA.

A sobering year ended with a ray of hope, when the Wolfenden Committee on Sport and the Community had as its chief recommendation the establishment of a Sports Development Council to disburse an annual sum of £5 million between national sports associations. But the politicians had to be convinced first, and it was to take five more years for the Sports Council to be set up. In the meantime, athletics was existing on a diminishing capital.

### 1961 — SPONSORED CHAMPIONSHIPS

The urge to reorganize had not achieved its main aim of a United Kingdom AAA, but one practical reform in 1961 was the introduction of the

Southern Counties AAA, which replaced the old Southern Committee set up by the founders, and put it on the same footing as the MCAAA, the NCAA and the Welsh AAA.

Montague Shearman and his generation would probably have conceded that the Southern Counties AAA would eventually emerge, but what would they have said about the other big development of 1961 — commercial sponsorship of the AAA Championships? The Carborundum Company, a Manchester firm, celebrated its 50th year in business by making donations to a number of sports. Their £5000 cheque was picked up gratefully by the AAA, already so concerned about falling attendances that they had commissioned an inquiry by Public Attitudes Survey Ltd. Leading foreign athletes were invited and certainly boosted the gate, although heavy rain kept it down to 20 000. The Commonwealth champion, Dave Power, became the first Australian for 80 years to win an AAA title in a distance event, with a Championship best of 27 min 57.8 sec for 6 miles. On the Saturday, record-breaking was limited to field events, for the White City track was under water much of the time. Gordon Pirie, pledged to 'ram it down the selectors' throats that they took us to Rome too late', won his last AAA title in the 3 miles, while Bruce Tulloh found the conditions impossible for barefoot running, and stopped after a few laps. Somehow between the downpours high jumper Crawford Fairbrother set a UK National record of 6 ft 9$\frac{1}{8}$ in/2.05 m; Michel Macquet (France) stretched the Championship best for the javelin to 253 ft 0 in/77.12 m; Risto Ankio (Finland) made the pole vault slightly more respectable by international standards, with 14 ft 6 in/4.42 m; and Arthur Rowe, who had been well below his best in Rome, and, like Pirie, blamed the team management, won the shot for the fifth and last time with a new Championship record of 60 ft 11$\frac{3}{4}$ in/18.58 m.

### 1962 — WEMBLEY REVIVED

With sponsored Championships established, the AAA in 1962 went ahead with the *Daily Herald* in reviving the Indoor Championships, last seen in 1939. Indoor meetings had been tried sporadically in the fifties under conditions of varying difficulty. Possibly the most sought-after duty ever assigned to athletics officials was embracing women sprinters at RAF Stanmore to prevent them over-running into a brick wall. The Empire Pool, Wembley, was the venue for the Championships, arranged jointly, as in pre-war years, by the AAA and WAAA. A new portable track was supplied by the newspaper, whose outlay on the venture amounted to some £20 000. The season's programme included the world's first full international match indoors, in which Great Britain defeated West Germany.

Sponsorship eased the financial problems of the AAA, but it was not successful in the sixties in bringing back the crowds to the White City. The 1962 Championships were watched by 16 300 over two days, the worst gate since the war, and for the next 4 years it improved hardly at all. The report of the public research group named a number of possible causes linked with changes in the social habits of the public, including the greater use of cars for leisure, rising fares, competition from other outdoor pursuits and the fact that the highlights of meetings were usually shown on TV. A factor not mentioned was that the crowd-pullers of the fifties — Bannister, Chataway, Pirie and Ibbotson — had achieved a status as newsmakers no one since had matched.

Paradoxically, athletic standards were stronger in the early sixties than they had been for years, or would be. The 1962 Championships, sponsored by Wall's, produced a torrent of rain and records. A fiercely contested 6 miles climaxed in a last-lap duel as close as any of Chris Chataway's 3 mile thrillers, with a new Commonwealth and UK record of 27 min 49.8 sec shared by Roy Fowler, the 5 ft 5 in/1.65 m winner, and his 6 ft 0 in/1.83 m rival, Mike Bullivant. In the 3 miles Bruce Tulloh burned off the challenge of 18-year-old Bruce Kidd (Canada), with a Championship best of 13 min 16 sec. Maurice Herriott won his third steeplechase title and improved the Championship record to 8 min 43.8 sec. And John McSorley, the latest in Thames Valley Harriers' marvellous line of javelin throwers, lofted one to a new UK and Championship record of 260 ft 0 in/79.26 m. But the Harvey cup for the best champion of the year was irresistibly claimed by Robbie Brightwell, whose 440 yd in 45.9 sec on a track made heavy by rain came within one-fifth of a second of the world record and collected every other record possible. Meanwhile, the remaining field events were wrapped up by visitors, with Championship bests in the high jump by Kuniyoshi Sugioka (Japan); the pole vault by Pentti Nikula (Finland); the long jump by Jorma Valkama (Finland); the triple jump by Tomio Ota (Japan); and the discus by Jay Silvester (USA), with a huge throw of 199 ft 7$\frac{1}{2}$ in/60.84 m, which also beat the UK all-comers' record. Silvester later completed a double by taking the shot with 59 ft 7$\frac{3}{4}$ in/18.18 m.

In Belgrade that summer Britain won five gold medals in the European Championships, more than any nation except the USSR. Bruce Tulloh, spritelike in the floodlight, jinxed a talented

5000 m field, including Pyotr Bolotnikov (USSR), by raising the pace two laps from home and running the last 800 m inside 2 min, for victory in 14 min 0.6 sec. Robbie Brightwell, with no less confidence, hared away into a long lead in the 400 m, then hung on grimly to win in 45.9 sec. Ken Matthews outclassed the 20 km walkers in 1 hr 35 min 54.8 sec, and Brian Kilby took the lead 7 miles from home in the marathon and kept it. Of the British women, Dorothy Hyman was the outstanding competitor, with a medal of each kind, the gold being for the 100 m.

The staging of European Championships and Commonwealth Games in the same year is a regular dilemma for British teams; whether these major international championships are held within weeks of each other or months apart there is a problem in achieving two physical and psychological peaks. Fortunately, when the 1962 Commonwealth Games were held in Perth, Australia, in November, England was able to compensate for some loss of form in track by winning the shot, through Martyn Lucking, 59 ft 4 in/18.08 m; the hammer, Howard Payne, 202 ft 3 in/61.64 m; and the women's javelin, Sue Platt, 164 ft 10½ in/50.24 m. The relay quartet of Peter Radford, Len Carter, Alf Meakin and Dave Jones retained the 4 × 110 yd title in 40.6 sec. And two European champions succeeded in repeating their Belgrade successes: Brian Kilby won the marathon (2 hr 21 min 17 sec) and Dorothy Hyman took the 100 yd in 11.2 sec and capped it with victory in the 220 yd in 23.8 sec. In the two major international Championships of 1962 British athletes had accumulated a total of twelve gold medals.

### 1963 — WORLD'S BEST FOR PENNEL

Pepsi-Cola began their sponsorship of AAA Championships in 1963, a year distinguished by a pole vault of 16 ft 8¾ in/5.10 m, which beat the listed world record by ¾ in/2 cm. So for once a field event stole the crowd's attention from the track; Sue Tulloh was heard amusedly protesting, 'How dare that John Pennel break the pole vault record in the middle of my Bruce's 3 miles?' As it turned out, Pennel twice went higher the following month, and his AAA vault was never ratified by the IAAF. Another Championship record was set in the hammer, little Takeo Sugawara, with 215 ft 1 in/65.56 m, confirming how seriously the Japanese were preparing for the Tokyo Olympic Games. A fine 6 miles win by Ron Hill in 27 min 49.8 sec produced the unlikely circumstance of three runners — Fowler, Bullivant and Hill — sharing the Commonwealth and UK all-comers' record. Brian Kilby, tenth in Hill's race, later that year won his fourth AAA marathon in 2 hr 16 min 45 sec, so removing the last of Jim Peters' records.

European 5000 metres champion Bruce Tulloh runs barefoot to the 1963 AAA 3 miles title. (Central Press Photos Ltd)

### 1964 — GLORY IN TOKYO

Pre-Olympic publicity and the appearance of several world-class athletes boosted the gate for the 1964 Championships to 18 486, not exactly a crush, but 7000 up on 1963. They were treated to the fastest sprinting ever in the meeting. The stocky Cuban, Enrique Figuerola, recorded 9.4 sec in the 100 yd. Henry Carr (USA), after 9.6 sec in the heats, withdrew injured, so the main opposition came from Lynn Davies (9.7 sec), building speed for long jumping; with wind assistance Davies the same afternoon jumped 26 ft 1¼ in/7.95 m, the first 26-footer in the Championships. Carr was later to win the Olympic 200 m, but his absence from the 220 yd was compensated by record-equalling runs in semi- and final by Scotsman 'Ming' Campbell. Otherwise, the most encouraging British performances were John Cooper's UK and AAA National records of 51.1 sec in the 440 yd hurdles; Maurice Herriott's runaway steeplechase win in Championship best time, 8 min 40 sec; Fred Alsop's 52 ft 3 in/15.92 m triple jump; and an epic 6 miles that settled the ownership of the European and UK records as Mike Bullivant's, with 27 min

Fred Alsop won a total of eight AAA titles in the long jump and triple jump in the sixties and achieved a career best performance in finishing fourth in the 1964 Olympic triple jump. (All Sport/Konig)

26.6 sec, although Ron Hill crossed just two-fifths of a second later.

Great Britain's most successful Olympic Games in recent times began, ironically, as the dust settled on a bitter row between the International Athletes' Club and the BAAB over the screening of a BBC *Sportsview* programme from Timsbury Manor, the Hampshire mansion made available to the IAC as a training headquarters. A blow by blow account of this dispute, which received national publicity, and from which no one emerged unhurt, is given in the late Jack Crump's book, *Running Round the World.* Crump had already signified his intention of retiring from athletics administration at the end of the 1964 season, and it was a pity that this man of integrity, who had served as AAA team manager from 1937 to 1952 and BAAB Hon Secretary since 1937, and for years fielded much

Robbie Brightwell in the 1964 AAA Championships. In the same year he was disappointed by his fourth place in the Olympic 400 metres, but compensated for this with an inspired anchor leg in the 4 × 400 metres, bringing Great Britain from fourth place to second. (ED Lacey)

One of the great moments in White City history — Ron Clarke (Australia) sets a world record for 3 miles of 12 min 52.4 sec in the 1965 Championships. (The Associated Press Ltd)

of the criticism thrown at 'officialdom', ended his service to athletics under strong attack. To the post-war generation he could seem too taken up with formality — too much the JP — but time and again this was a strength used on behalf of British teams and individuals. Jack Crump died suddenly at the age of 60 in April, 1966. Harold Abrahams, who knew him as well as anyone in athletics, wrote 'No man in my lifetime has given more unselfish service to the cause of athletics both at home and abroad. Endless service not only in the many high offices he held, but even as a minor official at local athletic meetings. And always he gave of his best.'

In Tokyo, only the USA and USSR won more athletics gold medals than Great Britain. To the dazzling successes of Ken Matthews, Lynn Davies and Mary Rand, separately described, can be added Ann Packer's triumph with a joyous burst of speed in the 800 m after she had finished second in what was thought to be her main event, the 400 m. Her future husband, team captain Robbie Brightwell, clinched a silver medal for Britain with an inspired last leg in the 4 × 400 m relay, after fine legs by Tim Graham, Adrian Metcalfe and John Cooper. Cooper (1940–74), hurdling with a verve and courage that recalled Lord Burghley, took the silver medal in the 400 m hurdles. The ultra-consistent Maurice Herriott, the only man to have won eight AAA steeplechase titles, achieved his lifetime best of 8 min 32.4 sec in finishing second. An heroic final 200 m in 32.3 sec in the *marathon* earned Basil Heatley a silver medal as he overtook the Japanese runner, Kokichi Tsuburaya, in the stadium. And Paul Nihill produced the best-ever time by a British walker in finishing second over 50 km. Britain's women completed the medal collection with a silver for Mary Rand in the pentathlon and bronzes in the 4 × 100 m relay.

### 1965 — RON CLARKE'S YEAR

From the Olympic Stadium, Tokyo, to RAF Cosford is a long hop, mentally as well as physically, so it was not surprising that the medallists missed the 1965 Indoor Championships, held on a new 220 yd track purchased by the AAA with help from the Department of Education and Science. But Derek Ibbotson, a medallist of 1956 vintage, treated Cosford to his charisma and at 32 achieved a UK best for 2 miles almost equal to his best-ever time outdoors. Regrettably, Cosford is still the only banked board indoor track in this country.

Descriptions of athletics are shackled with superlatives that confine them to their own time. A few achievements remain sharp in the memory

***Left:*** **Howard Payne won five Championship titles in the hammer and was best-placed Briton on another eight occasions. (All Sport/Tony Duffy)**

of the generation who saw them, and seem to meet the criterion of greatness: the quarter-miling of Lon Myers in 1881; Albert Hill's 1921 mile record; Peltzer against Lowe in 1926. Among scores of record-breaking feats in more recent times, Ron Clarke's 3 miles in the 1965 Championships is still the spellbinder. The facts are that he ran the distance in 12 min 52.4 sec, bettering his own world record by 8 sec. The uniqueness of the run was that Clarke remained composed, even serene, throughout, while everyone else, opponents, officials, spectators, responded in their different ways to the man's audacity. For 2 miles — the fastest ever seen in such a race — he was tagged by Gerry Lindgren (USA). In the ninth lap Lindgren could not sustain the tempo, and Clarke was running alone. He could have eased, but he still had a fight on — with his own body. He actually quickened the pace, with a 64 sec lap and then one of 64.6 sec. The crowd, by now informed that history's first sub-13-minute race was in prospect, bawled its support. Clarke raised the pace again without the least loss of form, and toured the last lap in 61 sec. If his career is analysed, Clarke falls short of greatness as a competitor in major Games, but he made new things possible in distance running. And he demonstrated that record-breaking is not the mindless activity purists would have us believe.

It happened that in the same Championships one of the supreme competitive runners, Mohamed Gammoudi (Tunisia), won the 6 miles. He controlled the race with tactics — braking and accelerating — that conserved his finishing burst for an easy win in 27 min 38.2 sec, an object lesson in why a runner of his craft would invariably defeat Clarke.

In 1965 Ernest Clynes retired after 18 years as AAA Hon Secretary, during which he was associated with many far-reaching innovations, including the post-war coaching scheme, the incorporation of the AAA into a limited company and the beginning of sponsorship. As a young member of the Polytechnic Harriers he had pioneered the pre-war Southern Amateur Athletic League, which anticipated by many years the British Athletics League of 1969. In 1954 this popular and widely respected man was awarded the OBE for his services to athletics.

He was succeeded by Barry Willis, the present Hon Secretary and only the eighth in 100 years. The AAA has been fortunate in the loyalty and length of service of its principal officers. Ray Stroud, the present Hon Treasurer, is only the eleventh in the same period (see complete list on page 178).

### 1966 — LYNN DAVIES MAKES IT THREE

In 1966 Gammoudi was back to defend his title, and was pressed to a UK all-comers' record of 27 min 23.4 sec by Bruce Tulloh and Lajos Mecser (Hungary), who were jointly credited with a new European record four-tenths slower. Clarke, too, regained his title, and made the beating of 13 minutes seem almost commonplace.

The British athlete of 1966 was Lynn Davies, whose achievements included the first 8 m long jump in the 100-year history of the Championships — it was actually 26 ft 5¼ in/8.06 m; a win for Wales (26 ft 2¾ in/7.99 m) in the Commonwealth Games; and a European Championship gold medal—to complete a unique set—with 26 ft 2¼ in/7.98 m in Budapest.

United Kingdom athletes won seven events in the Commonwealth Games in Kingston, Jamaica. A young English-born hurdler who had come to prominence on the US indoor circuit, David Hemery, won the 120 yd hurdles in 14.1 sec; Jim Alder took the marathon for Scotland; Ron Wallwork, the 20 mile walk for England; Howard Payne retained his title in the hammer, with 203 ft 4 in/61.98 m; John FitzSimons won the javelin with a Games and UK record of 261 ft 9 in/79.78 m; and Mary Rand once again matched Lynn Davies by winning the women's long jump with 20 ft 10½ in/6.36 m. Unhelpful scheduling gave them only three weeks interval before the European Championships, where an athlete who had not made the trip to Kingston, Jim Hogan, in the marathon (2 hr 20 min 4.6 sec), was the only British winner besides Davies.

### 1967 — LORD BYERS TAKES STOCK

By now it was no secret that the AAA was deeply in the red. 'Bankruptcy', stated the Annual Report for 1966/7, 'is a very real threat.' Reduced gates at the White City had forced the crisis, but essentially the problem was the cost of administering a sport so diverse that it was in reality a series of sports. Sponsorship had cushioned some of the financial difficulties, and television fees compensated for diminishing crowds, but no substantial improvement could be expected from those sources. The only hope was for a large increase in state aid. To justify that, athletics had to demonstrate to the Government and the Sports Council that it would use the money efficiently. For years there had been criticisms of the way the sport was managed, and for years the officers had admitted that the machinery was imperfect, but — given its complexity, with separate organizations for women's athletics, Scotland and Northern Ireland, all jealous of their autonomy, and the AAA's infrastructure of Area Associations, two of them historically senior to itself — it was not practicable to reconstruct from within. The remedy *had* to be an independent inquiry, for long canvassed by Harold Abrahams. So in March, 1967, the AAA and BAAB commissioned a ten-man committee under the chairmanship of Lord Byers, the Leader of the Liberal Party in the House of Lords and a former British Universities record-holder for 440 yd hurdles. Its terms were 'to examine the problems of development of athletics under the jurisdiction of the AAA and BAAB, including matters of organization, administration, finance, coaching services and competition, and to make recommendations thereon'.

While the committee carried out its inquiry, the 1967 season unfolded and, appropriately, that year's Championships fitted in with the stocktaking theme. The steeplechaser Maurice Herriott won his last title, making eight in all, and seven in sequence. So he joined the select club of champions with a run of seven wins, started by Denis Horgan (shot put, 1893–9) and joined by Bert Cooper (2 mile walk, 1932–8), Don Finlay (120 yd hurdles, 1932–8) and Harry Whittle (440 yd hurdles, 1947–53). Herriott's time of 8 min 33.8 sec was a Championship best. Another runner with a fine sense of symmetry, Ron Clarke, won his third successive AAA 3 miles in under 13 min. Andy Green, with 4 min 0.6 sec in the mile, ran the closest anyone would ever go to 4 min in an AAA Championship, for the event was altered to 1500 m in 1969, with his time remaining the Championship best. And in the 880 yd John Boulter won the last title in recent times for the once-dominant Achilles Club, with a Championship record of 1 min 47.3 sec.

Ron Clarke en route to his third successive 3 miles title, run, like the others, in under 13 minutes. (ED Lacey)

### 1968 — HEMERY'S DREAM RACE

The Byers Report, published in May, 1968, recommended the establishment of a single governing body, 'The British Athletic Federation', to represent England and Wales, Scotland and Northern Ireland, the Women's Associations, the Cross-Country Unions, the Race Walking Association, the Tug-of-War Association and the schools. It would be headed by a professional Director of British Athletics, supported by a team of professional administrators — a Chief Assistant, an Office Manager, a Chief National Coach, who would also act as Team Manager, and regional officers. The committee also recommended reorganization of the coaching scheme; proficiency awards; an annual registration fee for all athletes; and the introduction of league competitions between clubs. It was computed that in a full year British athletics needed an income of £100 000.

Weeks before the report was published, its recommendations were leaked in the press, and some hostile reactions reported. The Women's AAA were quoted as ready to fight the suggestion of a Federation 'all along the line'. The AAA and BAAB issued a statement on publication pointing out that the report included a number of statements from unspecified sources concerning the past actions of officials 'the authenticity of which we were never given any opportunity to test'. However, they expressed their appreciation

David Travis, winner of seven titles, is the most successful javelin thrower in Championship history. (ED Lacey) for the work of the committee, and undertook to do their best to produce 'a practical programme of progressive action'.

Several recommendations were soon implemented. The idea of league athletics was not new — a Southern League had operated in the thirties — and a pilot scheme for a British Athletics League was already in being when the report appeared. It began on a national scale in 1969, and is a well-supported, thriving venture. The AAA Five Star Award Scheme, piloted in 1967, was also established before the Byers Committee suggested proficiency awards for young athletes. The matter of registration fees had been agreed in principle by the AAA AGM in 1966; after a heated debate at the 1968 AGM, a referendum was held and revealed a strong preference (1172 to 415) for increased club affiliation fees as a way of financing the Association.

The AAA agreed in principle to work towards the formation of a UK governing body, with the transfer to the BAAB of responsibility for coaching as an early objective. In an article in *Athletics 1978*, Arthur Gold (BAAB Hon Secretary, 1965–77) wrote, 'it needed four years of patient, diplomatic negotiation, spiced from time to time with outspoken confrontation, before the UK coaching scheme became a viable and operational entity'.

The crucial step towards a confederation was the redrafting of the BAAB constitution in 1970. The representation was agreed at six members from the AAA; two from the Northern Ireland AAA; three from the Scottish AAA; two from the Welsh AAA; three from the Women's AAA; one each from the Northern Ireland Women's AAA, the Scottish Women's AAA and the Welsh Women's AAA; one from the men's international athletes; and one from the women's international athletes. While it was agreed that the Board would, where appropriate, 'accept responsibility for carrying out any functions which may be transferred on terms to be agreed between the Association concerned and the Board', a special clause was written into the constitution to safeguard the domestic autonomy of the Associations.

Byers notwithstanding, 1968 was Olympic year, with Mexico City as the controversial venue. The AAA welcomed its Patron, Her Majesty the Queen, to the Championships. An invitation 5000 m had been billed as the highlight, but David Hemery, back from intensive coaching at Boston University, altered that. His 50.2 sec victory in the 440 yd hurdles — a new National record — was thrilling in its possibilities, for clearly he was far from his limit. With John Sherwood, whose 50.8 sec also beat the previous best, he was sure to challenge the best Americans in Mexico City. The other outstanding champion of 1968 was Tim Johnston, with a new European record for the 6 miles of 27 min 22.2 sec, the more impressive for a final mile in 4 min 21.6 sec — sharp running for a man in training for the Olympic marathon.

David Hemery made the 1968 Olympic Games unforgettable for Great Britain. He did what every athlete dreams of doing: won an Olympic final by a street, in world record time. It is worth remembering all three of Hemery's 400 m hurdles races in Mexico City. They were of a piece, movements in a symphony culminating in the *allegro vivacissimo* of the final. In the first round and the semi-final he ran to qualify, concealing his true form, ignoring the impulse to 'psych out' his rivals with a fast time. Only one of the eight eventual qualifiers was slower than he. No one, not even Hemery himself, knew how well he would go when it counted. Those 48.1 sec of the final brought the event into a new era. He had travelled fast enough to have won the gold medal for the *flat* 400 m in each Games up to 1920.

In Hemery's race, John Sherwood was third, sharing the time, 49 sec, of the second man. His bronze medal inevitably lost some of its lustre to Hemery's gold, yet no other man in the British team did so well. His wife Sheila, the long jumper, was one of two silver medallists in the women's team. The other was Lillian Board, who was overtaken in the last strides of the 400 m by Colette Besson of France.

## 1969 — THE AAA GOES METRIC

In 1969 Hemery for the time being abandoned his gold medal event to return to high hurdling and tinkering with the decathlon. In August, he was injured, and the AAA Championships had a depleted look that extended to the White City's terraces. The Saturday attendance was 8000, the lowest since before World War I. Possibly the shade of old John Chambers had some bearing on it, for after 102 years the Imperial distances were replaced by their metric equivalents. The best performances were by new champions: a 1500 m in 3 min 40.9 sec by Frank Murphy (Ireland); 5000 m in 13 min 39.8 sec by 20-year-old Ian Stewart; and a javelin throw of 85.08 m/279 ft 1 in by Wladyslaw Nikiciuk (Poland). Two championships held elsewhere were won in brilliant times. Ron Hill took the AAA marathon for the first time in 2 hr 13 min 42 sec, and Paul Nihill walked 10 000 m in 44 min 7 sec.

The sixties ended with another upturn in British fortunes. The European Championships, usually held in the same year as the Commonwealth Games, had been brought forward to

In the late sixties Ron Hill regularly began his season with an AAA 10 miles win. Here, in 1968, he sets a world record. (ED Lacey)

1969, giving British athletes one peak to train for. In Athens in September they won six events. Paul Nihill set the team's spirits high on the first day by taking the 20 km walk. John Whetton, known in Europe as a brilliant tactician indoors — he had won three European 1500 m titles on the boards — showed he was no slouch outdoors by collecting the 1500 m in 3 min 39.4 sec. Young Ian Stewart emulated Wooderson and Tulloh convincingly in the 5000 m (13 min 44.8 sec). Over the classic route from Marathon to Athens Dr Ron Hill extended Britain's run of victories in his event to three (2 hr 16 min 47.8 sec). And brave Lillian Board not only won the women's 800 m, but brought Britain home first with a storming last leg in the 4 × 400 m relay, having been kept in contention by Rosemary Stirling, Pat Lowe and Janet Simpson.

So the sixties ended in glory, at least on the track. Already the curtain was drawn on the disappointments of the Olympic Games. It had to be admitted that the AAA was still losing money, and the revamped, sponsored and metricated Championships had failed to set the White City's turnstiles clicking. But television had made athletics known to a wider public. New developments, like the British Athletics League and the Five Star Award Scheme, were instant winners. There was no reason to dispute the conclusion of the Byers Report: 'We do not believe there is anything so fundamentally wrong with British Amateur Athletics which cannot be put right with common sense, goodwill and patience. There could be a bright future for the sport at every level in the coming years.'

# Unbroken Contact

**He resembled a deserter from the Foreign Legion as he scuttled into the Olympic stadium in strange headgear and sunglasses, and set off round the track at a furious walking pace. He was Britain's only gold medal winner of the 1960 Olympic Games. The Italians called him *il topolino* — the mouse — but his name was Don Thompson. At home in Britain he had prepared for the heat of Rome by turning his bathroom into a steam-room with the help of boiling kettles. And now he was the winner of the 50 km walk.**

Britain has an unequalled history in race walking. The sport was pioneered in this country and it was in 1908, when the Olympic Games were staged in London, that walking events were added to the Olympic programme. With its elements of perseverance, self-discipline and dignity fringing on humour, it suits the British character. Since John Chambers — who else? — became the first amateur champion in 1866, walking has attracted some of the most colourful personalities in athletics.

One suspects that in the early days, when judges had only the misleading 'fair heel and toe' as a standard, personality was a major factor. Cantankerous Walter Rye, winner of the 7 mile walk in 1868, boasted that his style was 'certainly not pretty and was cavilled at by many' but for 4 years he 'ran the gauntlet of every imaginable referee, so it must have been fair'. Likewise, the 6 ft 2 in/1.88 m red-bearded Bram Stoker, the author of *Dracula*, who came to London for the 1868 Civil Service Championships, finished first in the 5 mile walk, and was only disqualified afterwards, presumably by a judge who preferred to remain anonymous. The fastest walker of the AAC period was Harry Venn (1856–1913), a member of the prestigious London AC, who tussled year after year with Harry Webster, a wheelwright from Knotty Ash, Liverpool. Their times steadily improved until in the 1878 7 miles Championship, in the words of Sir Montague Shearman, 'the pair ran more or less the whole way, Venn running rather faster than Webster and winning in the time of 52 min 25 sec'. When the AAA drew up its first list of records in 1887, Venn's performance was rejected, which must have caused some embarrassment, as he was by then the Chief Judge at the Championships.

The first to approach Venn's time was Harry Curtis (Highgate H.), who won the AAA 7 miles title 4 years in succession, 1890–93, curiously getting slower each time. Another curiosity is that 'Harry Curtis' was a pseudonym; he appeared before the Southern Committee in 1888 to obtain permission to use it. Whatever his secret, he was a flamboyant performer on the track, usually walking with a small cap perched on the back of his head and a toothpick jutting from his mouth. In 1894, the AAA streamlined its programme,

Harry Curtis beat his arch-rival Bill Sturgess in t 1895 4 miles walk, but was subsequently disqual fied. (By permission of the British Library)

cutting the walk to 4 miles. Curtis won as usual, but the following year he had a desperate struggle with a Dublin-born Polytechnic Harrier, Bill Sturgess, who went ahead on the last lap. With a great effort Curtis overtook him and crossed the line six yards clear. The crowd swarmed across the track, oblivious of other walkers trying to finish. Then there was a near-riot when it was announced that Curtis was disqualified. The judge was Harry Venn!

Sturgess won a total of eight Championships between 1895 and 1902, and improved all the records up to 13 miles. His 1895 performances were conceded as irreproachable, but in later years his style in record-breaking failed to satisfy the purists. Significantly, he usually won his

Bill Sturgess (Polytechnic H.) won eight titles between 1895 and 1902.

George Larner leads Ernie Webb in the 1908 Olympic 3500 metres walk, in which they finished in that order. Between them, they won eleven AAA titles.

Championships at a more moderate gait, but in the 7 miles of 1903 he was stopped for 'lifting' and there his AAA career ended.

When the 1908 Olympics were held in London, Britain had two swift walkers in George Larner (1875–1949) and Ernie Webb (1872–1937). They outclassed all other competitors in the 3500 m and 10 mile walks, Larner winning each, with Webb second. Larner, a Brighton policeman, had won AAA titles at 2 and 7 miles at his first attempt, in 1904, when 19, retained them in 1905 and then given up the sport until the Olympics tempted him back. He won the AAA 2 miles in 1908, picked up his gold medals at the Games and then retired again until 1911, when he won the AAA 7 miles. For a member of the Force, Larner had some eccentric training habits: 'When circumstances permit, ALL clothing should be removed for a run round a secluded garden, especially if it be raining at the time.'

It was Larner's shadow, Ernie Webb, who finally disposed of Harry Venn's maligned Championship best for 7 miles, with 51 min 37 sec in 1910, and Venn congratulated him personally. Of all the early walkers, Webb was considered the fairest. He was a hardy individual who had gone to sea at twelve, then joined the army and served in the siege of Ladysmith. In 1912, at 40, he won a third silver medal in the Olympic 10 000 m walk.

By this time, road walking had acquired its own organizing body. The Southern Counties Road Walking Association, formed in 1907, extended its authority in 1911 to become the Road Walking Association. The AAA, to which they affiliated, retained control of track walking until 1954, when the RWA by a tidy change of title became the Race Walking Association, responsible for all competitive walking.

One of the most popular walkers after Webb was a Lancashire postman, Bobby Bridge (1883–1953), who, once seen, was not forgotten, for his left arm was amputated at the elbow. He made a sensational debut at the age of 19, winning the AAA 2 and 7 mile events in 1912 and defeating the veteran Webb in the former. He was unbeaten in the AAA Championships before the 1914–18 war, which for Bridge was a period of extreme hardship and despair, during which his young wife died. But he remarried, began a new career (amazingly, considering his handicap, as a dentist) and retained his AAA 2 miles title in 1919. 'His style throughout', reported the *Athletic News*, 'was perfection.'

Bridge was unfit in the Olympic year of 1920, when that likeable extrovert, Ugo Frigerio (Italy), won both walks in Antwerp to a selection of tunes he had arranged with the bandmaster. Charles

The one-armed walker, Bobby Bridge, wins the 2 miles in 1913. After the 1914–18 War, he was the only champion to regain his title. (Radio Times Hulton Picture Library)

Gunn (GB), a railwayman who never won an AAA title, walked to third place in the 10 000 m. Frigerio twice won AAA titles, in 1922, at 2 miles, and 1931, 7 miles, in immaculate style. He retained the Olympic 10 000 m in Paris in 1924, but Britain's tradition was upheld by Reg Goodwin, in second place.

The track walk was dropped from the Olympic Games after 1924, and not until 1932 did road walking appear on the programme. Britain's representative for the first Olympic 50 km walk, Tommy Green, went to Los Angeles after a string of victories in distance events in Britain, but how would a 39-year-old survive a five-hour race in the heat of California? He let others make the pace, yet stayed among the leaders until the three-quarter mark, when the sun got to him, and he lost a minute. Just when it seemed Tommy Green had relinquished the race, a cold sponge revived him, and he zipped through the field to win by over 7 min, in 4 hr 50 min 10 sec.

The following year Green won the London to Brighton walk for the fourth and last time. Second, over 20 min behind, was the man destined to succeed him as Olympic champion. Harold Whitlock, a motor mechanic who worked on the famous Brooklands racing circuit, devised for himself a 3-year plan of training and competition that culminated in the 50 km walk in 1936. On the day, he was actually the last of the 31 walkers to leave the Berlin Olympic Stadium, but by pacing himself judiciously he had overtaken everyone by 35 km. Then, at 38 km — just the point where Tommy Green's crisis had occurred — Whitlock had a bout of sickness, and the pack began to close. Like Green, he recovered to finish strongly, in 4 hr 30 min 41.4 sec, so winning Britain's only individual gold medal of 1936. As competitor (until the 1952 Olympics), coach, writer and administrator, Harold Whitlock profoundly influenced the development and popularity of walking.

On the track, the dominant competitors of the thirties were the Woodford Green AC walkers, Alf Pope and Bert Cooper. Pope won five AAA titles and cut the 7 mile record to 51 min 25.6 sec in 1932, while Cooper reduced the 2 miles best to 13 min 39.8 sec in 1933, and won a total of seven

**Woodford Green's Bert Cooper practically monopolized the 2 miles walk in the thirties, and won seven AAA titles in succession, which emulated the achievement of shot putter Denis Horgan.**

successive titles at the distance between 1932 and 1938, which is itself a record. Neither of these fine champions had the opportunity of competing in the Olympic Games, for not until 1948 did pressure, mainly from Britain, restore track walking to the Olympic schedule. In those London Games, the winner, over 10 000 m, was the durable John Mikaelsson (Sweden), who had won the AAA 7 miles in 1937 in a world record of 50 min 19.2 sec. In the 50 km road walk, another Swede, John Ljunggren, was the winner. Tebbs Lloyd Johnson at 48 years of age was just beaten out of second place, yet maintained Britain's proud record of winning at least one medal for walking at every Olympic celebration possible.

Controversy over style, ever a troubled issue, came to a crisis in the 1950s that virtually ended international track walking. For the 1950 European Championships Britain had two Sheffield walkers, Roland Hardy and Laurence 'Lol' Allen, whose performances in Britain (Hardy had won the AAA 2 and 7 miles in outstanding times and Allen was the RWA 10 and 20 miles champion) made them strong prospects for medals. This they confirmed by establishing such a lead in the 10 000 m that it seemed they would not be caught, until an old campaigner, Fritz Schwab (Switzerland), raised what might charitably be termed a dashing finish and reached the line first. When it was announced that the result had been referred to the Jury of Appeal, justice seemed about to be done. Yet to general amazement Schwab's victory was confirmed, and Hardy and Allen disqualified! The British team manager, Jack Crump, described it as 'the most atrociously unfair occurrence which I have ever known in more than twenty years of first-class athletics'. In the protracted debate that followed, it was argued that the human eye was incapable of telling whether an 8 mph walker was 'lifting'. Films and photographs were studied minutely; even Bobby Bridge from pre-World War I days had his reputation dented by the evidence.

Hardy and Allen continued to satisfy English judges. Hardy reduced the AAA 2 miles best to 13 min 27.8 sec and the 7 miles to 50 min 5.6 sec. They went to the 1952 Olympic Games as favourites for the 10 000 m and were disqualified in the heats. Olympic track walking was dealt its quietus in the final, when Fritz Schwab, chasing second place, produced another of his fleet-footed finishes, travelling at such speed that the Chief Judge had to run hard beside him to observe his style. Bruno Junk (USSR) manfully met the challenge, and the pair sprinted to a photo-finish which palpably showed both men running. Yet there was no disqualification. Track walking had disqualified itself from the Olympic Games.

Since 1956 the major international championships have been decided on the roads, with British walkers contributing substantially to the rehabilitation of the sport. The surprise of the Melbourne Olympics in 1956 was the 50 km win of Sussex-born Norman Read, representing New Zealand, to which he had emigrated 2 years before. British hopes were pinned on Don Thompson, who was overcome by heat and collapsed in the last stages, a disappointment he took ingenious precautions to avoid in the next Olympics; but there was pride that Read had learned competitive walking in England, and was a former AAA junior 1 mile walk champion.

The two track walks — since 1969 the 3000 and 10 000 m — have remained on the AAA Championship schedule without creating the problems experienced abroad. They serve as useful speed tests for road walkers, besides bringing their skills before a public who would not otherwise see them. In spectacle, excitement and sheer athleticism, the 1960 AAA 2 mile duel between Stan Vickers and Ken Matthews stands comparison with any of the great races in the history of the Championships. Scrupulously fair, yet at the fastest pace ever seen in Britain, the two kept within a yard or so of each other, Matthews

**Stan Vickers sets a UK 2 miles walk record of 13 min 2.4 sec at the White City in the 1960 Championships. (The Associated Press Ltd)**

leading until the bell, when Vickers powered past to cut 9 sec from George Larner's 56-year-old record, with 13 min 2.4 sec, and Matthews, 13 min 9.6 sec, also inside the old figures. That same year Matthews modernized the Championship best for 7 miles, with 49 min 42.6 sec.

Expectations soared for the 1960 Olympic Games, with Vickers already European champion over 20 km (1958), and still improving, and Matthews even faster. But Matthews, weakened by recent flu, wilted in the Rome sun. Vickers, concerned about his team-mate, eased his pace, until Matthews, who was shortly after taken to hospital, urged him on. Vickers finished in the bronze medal position, less than a minute down on the winner. The 50 km walk once again proved Britain's winning event. The way Don Thompson attacked that final lap of the stadium, then explained to the world's press the secrets of his sessions in the bathroom, confirmed him as one of the immortals of Olympic history. 'Road-walk training is a lonely thing sometimes, you know,' he told *World Sports*. 'You've got to have some spark, a sort of hope and faith about things.'

Walkers are the most persistent of all athletes. Like Thompson, Ken Matthews consigned his first Olympic disappointment to experience and prepared for the next Games. In 1962 he won the European 20 km title. He raised his tally of AAA titles to ten by 1964. And in the Tokyo Olympic Games that year he took the lead after 5 km and was never headed. So Ken beat the world. And his

Harold Whitlock in a race prior to his Olympic 50 km walk victory in 1936.

Don Thompson, dressed to combat the heat of Rome, winning the Olympic 50 km walk in 1960. (Central Press Photos Ltd)

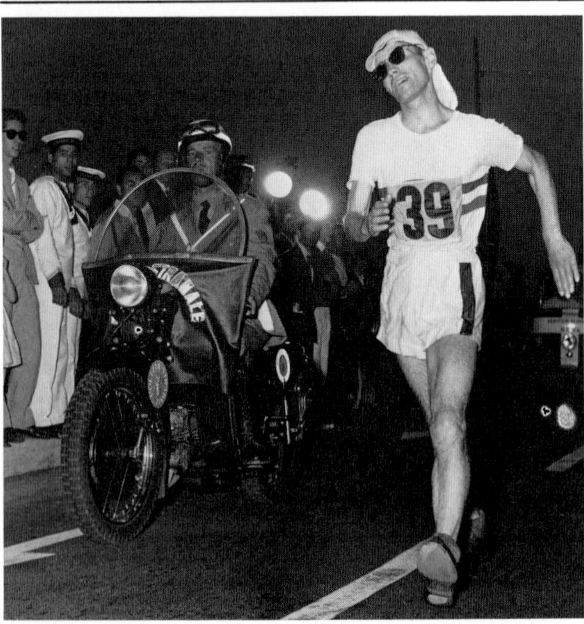


wife Sheila beat the Japanese security to embrace him on the track. Walking is not without romance.

Britain's other medal-winning walker in Tokyo was Paul Nihill, a close second in the 50 km. Less spirited in style than Thompson, less machinelike than Matthews, Nihill brought to British walking an astonishing versatility and resilience. Reluctantly abandoning his first ambition to be a professional boxer, he tried cross-country until an operation for the removal of a knee-cap forced him to modify his plans again. He won his first national walking title, the RWA 20 miles, in 1963. A year after his silver medal in the long-distance event in Tokyo, he won the AAA 2 mile walk — which might be compared to a marathon runner trying the 800 m — and the AAA 7 miles, the RWA 10 miles and 20 miles and 20 km. He suffered a serious breakdown in health in 1965 and another in 1966, when he withdrew from the team for the European Championships and decided to retire, but in 1968 he was back as the foremost British walker at each event from 7 miles to 50 km. In the Mexico City Olympics, Nihill duelled with his one great rival, Christoph Hohne (East Germany), refusing to try for anything less than the gold medal, and walked himself into a state of collapse 5 km from home. Yet the following year in the European Championships he won the 20 km, and in 1971 the bronze. In 1975, at 35, this indomitable man still had enough speed in his legs to win the AAA 3000 m.

The pace of race walking quickened markedly in the seventies. The 1972 Olympics saw East Germans take the Olympic records for 20 km below 1 hr 27 min, and 50 km below 4 hr. In 1976 the 20 km was won by Daniel Bautista (Mexico) in 1 hr 24 min 40.6 sec, walking at a rate faster than the AAA champion for 10 000 m, Brian Adams, when he set the record in 1975. The Mexicans, and, more recently, the Spaniards, have upset the pattern of international walking by demonstrating that the Russians, Germans and British are not invincible.

Britain cannot any longer bank on a medal or two from each Olympic Games, but the roots of race walking go deep. The sport owes its survival internationally to persistent campaigns by British enthusiasts to frustrate those who would ban it. Ernest Neville was chiefly responsible for its restoration to the Olympic programme in the form of a road walk in 1932. In 1948 British pressure got the track walk reinstated, but that success was short-lived. The battle after that was to win approval for the 20 km. It was introduced in 1956 and became so well established that the

**The most versatile of all British walkers, Paul Nihill, won 27 AAA and RWA championship titles between 1963 and 1975. Here he is pictured at speed in the 1971 AAA 10 000 metres. (ED Lacey)**

opponents of walking turned their opposition to the 50 km, and got that dropped from the 1976 Olympics. The RWA countered with a vigorous campaign of propaganda and persuasion that resulted in both walks appearing on the 1980 Olympic schedule.

The outstanding British walkers of the seventies, Roger Mills, Brian Adams and Olly Flynn, are faster than the medallists of earlier years, but less successful internationally. It requires a walker of exceptional talent and resource to make up the ground. Tradition argues that he must soon arrive on the scene. It is unlikely that he will train in secluded gardens or steam-filled bathrooms, but, depend upon it, he will be an individualist.

Roger Mills, the leading British speed walker of the seventies, wins the 1977 AAA 3000 metres. (George Herringshaw)

**Stan Vickers (16) and Ken Matthews in their thrilling duel for the 1960 AAA 2 miles walk title, won by Vickers in a Championship record time. (All Sport/Don Morley)**

The AAA challenge cup for the 3000 m walk was presented in 1901, when the 2 miles event was instituted, by John Fowler Dixon (1850–1943). In 1876 and 1877 Dixon had set world walking records for all distances from 26 to 100 miles and in 1884 and 1885 he set new figures for running 40 and 50 miles. A lifelong athletics enthusiast, 'Jimmy' Dixon trained regularly in Hyde Park, paced by a hansom cab containing his office clothes. In 1910 he was called in for questioning in connection with the Crippen murder, but unlike the notorious Doctor he resembled, Fowler Dixon lived to be 93, the last survivor of the meeting that founded the AAA.

# Kings of the Crystal Palace

**The AAA was 90 years old in 1970, but its chances of making 100 looked doubtful. The Championships failed to attract a sponsor, and the attendance slumped to 4721, the lowest in living memory. Happily there was a dramatic recovery, aided by Dave Bedford, the first King of the Crystal Palace.**

Few would have envied the new Hon Treasurer of the AAA, John Martell. At the October, 1970, AGM, he estimated that the Association was heading for a loss on the year of some £8000. Moreover, there was a £10 000 shortage of working capital.

The need for drastic remedies was met by a special Finance Committee. They faced the invidious task of serving notice on staff, including the two Area Administrators, simply because the AAA was no longer in a position to pay their salaries. All investments held by the Association were sold for cash. These and other stringent economies achieved the necessary swing of £18 000. This impressed the Government enough to offer the AAA a £6000 loan to carry on its work. It was repaid within a year. A £3037 deficit in 1970/71 was turned into a £14 600 surplus in 1971/72, a near-miracle in accounting and administration.

One reason for the poor attendance at the 1970 Championships may have been that the public had already feasted on richer fare, the Commonwealth Games, held that July in Edinburgh, and covered comprehensively on TV. There, United Kingdom athletes had excelled, winning 15 of the 36 events. England's winners were David Hemery, 26 on that day, who retained the high hurdles title to earn renderings of 'Land of Hope and Glory' and 'Happy Birthday'; John Sherwood in the 400 m hurdles; Ron Hill, the marathon; Howard Payne, for the third time, the hammer; Dave Travis, the javelin; Rita Ridley, the women's 1500 m; and Sheila Sherwood, the women's long jump. The achievement of the Sherwoods in each winning a gold was matched, for Howard Payne's wife, Rosemary, won the women's discus for Scotland. The host nation's list of winners was completed by Ian Stewart, with a famous victory over Kip Keino in the 5000 m; Lachie Stewart in the 10 000 m; and Rosemary Stirling, the women's 800 m. Northern Ireland took golds through Mike Bull in the pole vault, and Mary Peters, a double winner in the shot and pentathlon. For Wales, Lynn Davies retained the long jump title he won in 1966.

Dave Bedford drew the crowds to the Crystal Palace for performances such as this 1972 5000 metres, a fraction outside the world record, to complete a brilliant double victory in the AAA 10 000 and 5000 metres. (ED Lacey)

Although several Commonwealth champions appeared at the Championships, the main honours went to Dave Bedford, who had not competed in Edinburgh, and Martin Reynolds, who had placed fourth there. Bedford, a 20-year-old with a facility already for making headlines that equalled Gordon Pirie's, set a Championship record of 28 min 26.4 sec for 10 000 m. Reynolds was metres clear in the 200 m (21 sec), in which his semi-final in 20.9 sec was a Championship best. One Commonwealth champion among the record-breakers was David Hemery, with 13.9 sec, the first to beat 14 sec for 110 m hurdles in the Championships. But the main applause of the afternoon was reserved for a runner who trotted round the White City track in 80.5 sec. Ron Clarke, 33, for whom the AAA had arranged this lap of honour, was retiring from the sport, still without the gold medal he had sought in successive Commonwealth and Olympic Games, but with 17 world records to his credit, and the universal respect and affection of athletics followers.

### 1971 — BEDFORD IN HIS PALACE

The spectacular recovery in the AAA's finances was helped in 1971 by the overdue move of the Championships to the Crystal Palace track. Opened in 1964, the track had been relaid with an all-weather surface in 1968. John Martell and National Coach Tom McNab between them mounted a lively promotional campaign and the meeting was a sell-out. The centrepiece for the 14 000 crowd was Dave Bedford's attack on Clarke's world record for 5000 m. Already that year Bedford had won the National and International Cross-Country titles. In the AAA 10 000 m, held at Portsmouth prior to the main Championships, he had won by over 52 sec, the biggest margin ever in the AAA race, in a European record of 27 min 47 sec.

He started the 5000 m at a pace that put him 4 sec up on Clarke's schedule at 1000 m and 1.8 sec up at 2000 m. At 3000 m, he was 1.8 sec down — then, sensationally, about 150 m later he pulled up. While the press besieged him for a statement, the rest of the field completed the last five laps. Mike Baxter's victory was politely applauded, but so crushing was the anticlimax that his time of 13 min 39.6 sec goes down as the least appreciated Championship record. Bedford, it was learned, had felt a sharp pain in his right leg, assumed at the time to be cramp. In later years his running was bedevilled by recurrences of the trouble.

Meanwhile in the centre, Les Mills (NZ) notched an impressive double in the shot, with 19.27 m/63 ft $2\frac{3}{4}$ in, a Championship best, and the discus, 58.62 m/192 ft 4 in. Another New Zealander, Tony Polhill, surprised the best of Britain's 1500 m talent, including Brendan Foster and the Stewart brothers, with a new Championship record of 3 min 40.3 sec.

The main international interest that season was in the European Championships in Helsinki. Britain had just one winner, 19-year-old David Jenkins, who took the 400 m in 45.5 sec. If it had not been noted already, it was made clear in Helsinki that most medals were won by nations who invested heavily in sport for national prestige. The competition was intense, with super-athletes like Borzov (USSR) and Stecher (GDR) looking good for the 1972 Olympics.

### 1972 — RECORDS GALORE

Britain went into Olympic year in a more buoyant mood than had seemed possible a year before. The AAA was solvent. Moreover it was being backed by a major sponsor. By supporting the Championships from 1972 onwards, the Nationwide Building Society began a generous and productive association with athletics which continues. The strong relationship with Nationwide — its Chairman, Sir Herbert Ashworth, is a Vice-Patron of the AAA — freed the Association from its earlier financial worries and provided a firm base on which to plan for the future.

With places in the Olympic team at stake, and Dave Bedford hungry for records, a near-capacity crowd came to the Crystal Palace. This year Bedford handsomely compensated for the disappointment of 1971. On the Friday he made a last-minute decision to run the 5000 m and almost fell over dashing into the lead. From the first lap

**Olympic champion David Hemery beats challenger John Akii-Bua (Uganda) in the 1972 AAA 440 yd hurdles, but Akii-Bua went on to win the Olympic gold in Munich. Between them is John Sherwood. (All Sport/Tony Duffy)**

The 1969 AAA Junior high hurdles champion, Berwyn Price, has dominated the senior event in recent years. (All Sport/Don Morley)

on, he kept inside the times Ron Clarke had logged in his 1966 world record of 13 min 16.6 sec. Nobody would risk staying with him for more than five laps. At 4000 m, he was still 1.4 sec inside Clarke's time. He passed the 3 mile mark in 12 min 52 sec — better than the Australian's epic Championship best of 1965 — and reached the line in 13 min 17.2 sec, a split-second from making history. Brash and opinionated as he often appeared from press interviews, Bedford had the courage and ability to put words into action. Who else but he, the day after that astonishing run, would set out in blistering heat to chase the world record for 10 000 m? With a time of 27 min 52.8 sec, he not only ran faster than anyone in the world save Clarke and himself, but won by 46 sec. Ron Clarke himself described Bedford's double as the greatest ever. Perversely, it probably blighted Britain's chances in the Olympics, for three of the fancied candidates for Munich, Mike Tagg, Jack Lane and Tony Simmons, were burned off by the pace and heat, and failed to make the team. Bedford, bidding for the Olympic double, succumbed in Munich to the strain of four distance runs of top quality within ten days.

All told, these were the best AAA Championships to date. New best performances were set in every track event but the 800 m. For the second year, Alan Pascoe had a double victory in the 110 m hurdles (13.9 sec) and the 200 m (20.9 sec). David Jenkins, with 45.4 sec in the 400 m, looked sharp, but confessed to disappointment. Peter Stewart won the 1500 m in 3 min 38.2 sec — a UK record. Steve Hollings cut the steeplechase best to 8 min 31.2 sec. And David Hemery, trying a new stride pattern in his bid to defend the Olympic 400 m hurdles title, clocked 49.7 sec, but John Akii-Bua (Uganda) ominously caught him at the finish to share the same time. There was a spectacular pole vault of 5.21 m/17 ft 1 in, which gave Mike Bull a UK National record, and displaced John Pennel's 1963 Championship record. With wind assistance, Alan Lerwill long jumped 8.15 m/26 ft 9 in, while Championship

Note the remarkable bow in the fibre glass pole as Mike Bull sets a new National record to win the 1972 AAA title. (ED Lacey)

records were restored to Britain by Geoff Capes, with a shot put of 19.47 m/63 ft 10½ in, and Bill Tancred, who threw the discus 61.06 m/200 ft 4 in. In the hammer, Barry Williams set an AAA National record of 67.24 m/220 ft 7 in.

So there was optimism, if not confidence, over the Olympic Games. Yet for the fourth time since the war Britain was limited to one gold medal, although it seemed to have the worth of several as the nation lived through the five events of the pentathlon with Mary Peters, who showed that even in the modern Olympic Games there can be joy in taking part. Silver medals went to the 4 × 400 m team — Martin Reynolds, Alan Pascoe, David Hemery and David Jenkins — with a thrilling final leg so reminiscent of Brightwell's in 1964. In the 400 m hurdles Hemery led gallantly to the last turn, when Akii-Bua went by; at the line, Ralph Mann (USA) edged past for the silver medal. Bronze, too, for Ian Stewart in the 5000 m, won in a time 9 sec slower than Bedford's at Crystal Palace. Bedford himself was sixth in the 10 000 m and twelfth in the 5000 m.

There was renewed pressure after the Games to implement one of the main proposals in the Byers Report. Four previous captains of the Great Britain team, David Hemery, Alan Pascoe, Lynn Davies and Les Piggott, published an open letter urging the appointment of a Director of British Athletics, 'a relatively young, full-time professional administrator with overall responsibility for the planning and direction of all areas of the sport', and a second professional administrator to organize and co-ordinate British international athletics. The idea of professional administrators was not, in fact, opposed by the BAAB or the AAA. In June, 1970, the Board had invited Arthur Gold, its Hon Secretary since 1965, to accept a salaried appointment, but he had declined because 'among other considerations, the AAA suddenly had financial problems and I deemed it inopportune to take a salaried appointment with the Board when one of its constituent members was having to dismiss employed staff'. Gold had used his influence as an elected official to secure solid progress towards the restructuring of the BAAB as a confederation of the various men's and women's Associations, which was the most fundamental of the Byers recommendations. Coaching was now on a UK footing, and the AAA was ready to relinquish other functions, including the training of officials and consultation with schools. Progress by consensus was less spectacular than the remedy suggested in the team captains' letter, but those on the inside judged it more likely to succeed.

### 1973 — BEDFORD'S WORLD RECORD

A development of practical importance was the move in 1973 of the BAAB, the AAA, the Southern Counties AAA and the Women's AAA to premises on the same site at 70 Brompton Road, London SW3, made available to the Sports Council. The AAA now appointed a full-time National Administrator, John Martell, who as

**The first seventeen-foot pole vault in Championship history — Mike Bull in 1972. (All Sport/Tony Duffy)**

**Andy Carter jubilant as he wins the second of three AAA 800 metres titles (1972). (All Sport/Tony Duffy)**

Hon Treasurer had piloted the AAA safely through its worst crisis.

For the third successive year, the Championships were dominated by Dave Bedford. Troubled all season by the hamstring injury, he had made only two appearances, yet from the gun in the 10 000 m he attacked Lasse Viren's world record. For a time, Tony Simmons stayed with the pace, and actually led for $1\frac{1}{2}$ laps towards the halfway mark, covered by Bedford in 13 min 39.4 sec — which would have won the AAA 5000 m each year up to 1971. Steadily, though, Bedford's steam-hammer rhythm took him into regions where the only rival was the clock. With a 60.8 sec final 400 m he cut the world record by 7.8 sec, to 27 min 30.8 sec. It was a truly historic run, no 'soft' record, but a Championship win over a standard Olympic distance. Bedford celebrated by blowing kisses to the grandstand in a ritual that was to become familiar after famous victories at the Crystal Palace.

He gratified the packed stadium next afternoon

Geoff Capes, whose strength and speed in the 7 ft circle made shot-putting a spectacular event at the Crystal Palace. (All Sport/Tony Duffy)

by turning out for the 5000 m, but it had to be a token run, and he finished sixth. The winner was the man destined to succeed Bedford as the King of the Crystal Palace. Brendan Foster, the European and Commonwealth bronze medallist over 1500 m, here challenged the distance men and ran clean away from them in the final 1000 m to win in 13 min 23.8 sec. In the 800 m Andy Carter beat the swift South African, Danie Malan, in an all-comers' record of 1 min 45.1 sec. Sixth was a 17-year-old named Steve Ovett, who set a world best for his age, 1 min 47.3 sec. Geoff Capes and Bill Tancred improved on their respective bests in shot and discus, but the doughtiest performer in the field was Howard Payne, winner of the hammer for the fifth time. Now 42, he had not missed an AAA final since 1958. By contrast, the AAA marathon, held in October, was won in story-book style by a novice to the event, Ian Thompson. His time of 2 hr 12 min 40 sec was the fastest ever for a marathon

*Right:* Ian Thompson, who achieved the marathon-runner's dream of winning his first race at the distance, the 1973 AAA Championship, and in 1974 won the Commonwealth and European titles. (All Sport/Tony Duffy)

US
27
21
17

*Left:* Three 5000 metres stars in the 1975 AAA race — Ian Stewart (21), America's Marty Liquori (27), the eventual winner, and Nick Rose (17). (ED Lacey)

*Above:* New Zealand's Rod Dixon (9) has won the AAA 1500 metres twice, in 1973, and, here, in 1976, from David Moorcroft (24) and bearded Frank Clement. Future Olympic 5000 metres silver medallist Dick Quax (40) trails. (All Sport/Tony Duffy)

*Right:* Bill Hartley winning the 1975 400 metres hurdles title. (All Sport/Tony Duffy)

debut — and he had only been persuaded to enter to make up his club team.

The fixture-list in the seventies provided major international games each year. In 1973 Great Britain made its first impact in the European Cup Final, in which the men's team had competed at its inauguration in 1965, but failed to win a single event. This time AAA champions Chris Monk (200 m), Andy Carter (800 m), Brendan Foster (5000 m) and Alan Pascoe (400 m hurdles) all won, and Frank Clement, second to Rod Dixon (NZ) in the Championships, made it five for Britain in the Edinburgh Final. A knock-out competition was introduced the same year in domestic athletics as the British Athletics Cup and won by Wolverhampton and Bilston AC; from 1974–6 it was for the Pye Gold Cup; since 1977 it has been for the GRE Gold Cup.

**1974 — ANOTHER AMERICAN INVASION**

If Britain's successes in Europe were mainly on the track, equilibrium was preserved by the Commonwealth Games, in which the field event specialists came into their own. In Christchurch, New Zealand, in January, 1974, Geoff Capes gave his own meaning to the term police force by putting the shot 20.74 m/68 ft 0½ in, over a metre beyond his rivals. Alan Lerwill, with 7.94 m/26 ft 0¾ in, won the long jump, and Charles Clover, with a world junior record of 84.92 m/278 ft 7 in, the javelin. In the hammer, Ian Chipchase, with 69.56 m/228 ft 2 in, deprived Howard Payne of an unprecedented fourth consecutive victory. Alan Pascoe was the only male UK track champion, with 48.83 sec for 400 m hurdles, but the gentlemen of the roads, John Warhurst (20 mile walk) and Ian Thompson (marathon), still living his dream, upheld Britain's strong tradition in their events. The English women's team took the 100 m hurdles (Judy Vernon), the high jump (Barbara Lawton) and the 4 × 400 m. For Northern Ireland, Mike Bull (decathlon) and Mary Peters (pentathlon) scored a notable double.

That summer a strong US contingent won eight AAA titles, as many as the American invaders who caused such a sensation in 1900. But unlike the Championships 74 years before, these were held in cold, wet conditions that limited the visitors to two British all-comers' records. Jim

**The form that enabled long jumper Alan Lerwill to succeed Lynn Davies as AAA Championship record-holder. (All Sport/Tony Duffy)**

**Steve Ovett (18) wins his first AAA title in the 1974 800 metres. After him, in finishing order, came Andy Carter (1), Byron Dyce (Jamaica) (28), Mark Winzenreid (USA) (26), Colin Campbell (5), Peter Browne (4) and David McMeekin (6). (Keystone Press Agency Ltd)**

Bolding ran 400 m hurdles in 49.1 sec, and Al Feuerbach produced the first 70 ft shot put in Britain, with 21.37 m/70 ft $1\frac{1}{2}$ in. Best Championship performances were recorded by Steve Williams, winner of the 100 m in 10.2 sec, for which he received the Prince Hassan cup from Harold Abrahams, who had won it exactly half a century before; by Mark Lutz, with 20.9 sec in the 200 m; Dwight Stones, with the first high jump over 7 ft — actually 2.14 m/7 ft $0\frac{1}{4}$ in — in Championship history; discus thrower John Powell, with 62.06 m/203 ft 7 in; South African Adam Barnard in the hammer, 70.62 m/231 ft 8 in; and Toshiaki Inoue (Japan) in the triple jump, 16.12 m/52 ft $10\frac{3}{4}$ in. The first athlete in each event eligible to represent the UK received a special BAAB gold medal as official UK champion (this had been instituted in 1972), but the ten foreign wins still led to demands for a UK closed Championship meeting. Of the nine home athletes who were successful, Dave Bedford won the 10 000 m for the fifth year in, for him, a remarkable manner, letting others make the pace throughout — 'Hunted turned hunter,' he commented afterwards; John Davies set a Championship record, 8 min 26.8 sec, in the steeplechase; and Steve Ovett, 18, dashed through a talented 800 m field in the home stretch to win in 1 min 46.9 sec.

But the most significant performance in those Championships was Brendan Foster's 5000 m, not for its time, but the manner in which he won it. Just after the halfway mark, he ran a lap in 59.2 sec, as if some mysterious reflex had made him once again into a 1500 m runner. It transpired that this was Brendan's new way of destroying the opposition. It succeeded; he won by over 25 sec.

He repeated the tactics against more illustrious opposition in the European Championships in Rome that year, with the same devastating result. He won decisively in 13 min 17.2 sec. And Britain almost had the winner of the other distance Championship, the 10 000 m, for Tony Simmons raised a last lap sprint that gave him the same time as the winner, Kuschmann (GDR). In the longest race of all, Ian Thompson won his second gold medal of 1974 and still seemed bemused by this newfound talent. Alan Pascoe, too, repeated his Commonwealth success — to within one-hundredth of a second — with a 48.82 sec victory. To round off these successful Championships,

*Above:* Flopper Extraordinary — Dwight Stones (USA), world-record holder in the high jump, won the 1974 AAA title with a Championship best. (All Sport/Tony Duffy)

*Left:* Geoff Capes dominated British shot putting in the seventies. (All Sport/Tony Duffy)

*Right:* Prolific world record breaker Henry Rono (Kenya) on his way to the 1978 AAA 5000 metres title. (All Sport/Tony Duffy)

Nationwide
38
38
42
33

David Jenkins in action in the 1975 Championships. His string of six AAA 400 metres wins (1971–76) is unmatched in the history of the event. (All Sport/Tony Duffy)

Britain's team of Glen Cohen, Bill Hartley, Pascoe and David Jenkins won the 4 × 400 m.

### 1975 — ONE HUNDRED UP

The 1975 Championships were the 100th since the AAC started it all in 1866. What the Victorian gentlemen-amateurs would have made of a modern athletics meeting is debatable. It must be doubted whether they would have recognized the sponsored, metricated, electronically recorded and televised Championships as the sports meeting they started at Beaufort House. Certainly the pressures of modern top-class athletics would have baffled them. 'I'm not really running well,' said Steve Ovett after winning the 800 m in 1 min 46.1 sec, '— only just the best in Britain.' In 1975 the strains of training and all-year-round competition were more conspicuous than usual. Injuries prevented two of the biggest stars, Bedford and Pascoe, from competing at the Championships. Another, Brendan Foster, disappointed by a recent defeat at Gateshead, was taking a holiday and reflecting on his approach to running: 'I realised what the events of recent months had been telling me,' he wrote in his book, *Brendan Foster*: 'that I was not a robot, programmed to run certain times irrespective of other considerations . . . I was becoming too regimented.' Standards had risen so high in some events, the 5000 m, pole vault and shot, that British entries were in single figures. In the 5000 m, Ian Stewart, the European indoor 3000 m champion, stopped running in the seventh lap. Injury was not the problem; his legs felt heavy. 'I knew there was no way I could pick it up, no way I could get around twelve laps,' he told Melvyn Watman, Editor of *Athletics Weekly*. Paul Nihill, 35-year-old winner of the 3000 m walk, revealed that he hoped to compete in the 1976 Olympic Games, but admitted, 'I seem to have lost the will to train really hard.' Others, like David Jenkins, winner of the 400 m in 45.87 sec, had their sights on the European Cup Final, for which Great Britain had qualified.

Perhaps it was not surprising, then, that South African athletes, their possibilites of competition limited, won five AAA titles, breaking three Championship records. Danie Malan, with a 1500 m run of 3 min 38.1 sec, won by over 2 sec, the longest margin since Bannister 21 years before. Adam Barnard threw the hammer 73.58 m/241 ft 5 in. And in a thrilling discus competition, John Van Reenen with his last throw beat Britain's Bill Tancred by 4 cm, with 62.26 m/204 ft 3 in. But the Harvey Cup for the best AAA champion was awarded to Dave Black, winner of the 10 000 m in 27 min 54.2 sec, which only Dave Bedford had ever beaten in the meeting.

In Nice that summer Britain had its best result to date in the European Cup Final, finishing fourth, with six first places, more than any other nation, thanks to David Jenkins (400 m), Steve Ovett (800 m), Brendan Foster (5000 m), Alan Pascoe (400 m hurdles), Geoff Capes (shot) and the 4 × 400 m squad of Glen Cohen, Jim Aukett, Bill Hartley and David Jenkins. Going into 1976, even after the disappointments of Munich, there was guarded optimism about Britain's prospects for the Montreal Olympics.

### 1976 — YEAR OF THE YOUNG MEN

The Games proved notable for Britain only because the tally of medal-winners was our lowest in the history of the modern Olympics. Brendan Foster was a brave third in the 10 000 m and that was the extent of it. Injuries, illness and loss of form more than reasonably weakened and subdued the team, but in many events the winners — men like Alberto Juantorena, Lasse Viren and Ed Moses — performed like supermen. Montreal presented Britain with an ultimatum: recognize

The powerful action of 1975 double sprint champion, Steve Riddick (USA). (ED Lacey)

Olympic champion Don Quarrie (Jamaica) wins his second AAA 200 metres title, in 1978. (All Sport/Tony Duffy)

**Quarrie also won the 1976 AAA 100 metres from Allan Wells (25). (Keystone Press Agency Ltd)**

and develop an élite among athletes, or lower your aspirations in future Olympics to appearing in the heats.

The 1976 Championships, held after the Games, reinforced the point by revealing abundant young talent capable of being nurtured into brilliance. Mike McFarlane, 16, finished third to Don Quarrie (Jamaica) and Allan Wells in the 100 m; Milton Palmer, 17, won the high jump at 2.06 m/6 ft 9 in, with Ross Hepburn, only 14 years 10 months — almost certainly the youngest competitor ever in the Championships (his standard was so good that the AAA did not check his age) — fourth with 2.03 m/6 ft 8 in; Daley Thompson, 18, was second in the long jump; and Keith Connor, 18, second in the triple jump. Steve Ovett, still 20, handed a precocious defeat to Olympic 1500 m champion, John Walker (NZ), in the 800 m, with three teenagers finishing in the first seven. And Sebastian Coe, 19, was fourth in the 1500 m, won by Rod Dixon (NZ) in 3 min 41.2 sec. Just to indicate the gulf between the good and the excellent, Don Quarrie zipped through his gold medal event, the 200 m, in 20.35 sec, six metres clear of anyone else. It was a Championship best and with his 100 m victory it earned him the Harvey Cup.

On 6 November 1976, at the AAA AGM, the Marquess of Exeter retired from the office of President after 40 years' service. In his place was elected Harold Abrahams, who became the sixth President in 96 years. A third great athlete of the twenties, Douglas Lowe, made the presentation to Lord Exeter. In his farewell address, Lord Exeter stressed the importance to the sport of the ordinary club athlete, and of the officials who put something back for future generations. Mindful of the future, he warned that there were three enemies of his concept of athletics, and they were commercialism, super-nationalism and interference by governments in sport.

## 1977 — THE JUBILEE CHAMPIONSHIPS

One of the new President's duties in 1977 was drafting the Loyal Message from the AAA to its Patron, Her Majesty the Queen, in the year of the Silver Jubilee of her accession to the throne. A reception was held in the very room in the Prince of Wales Hotel at Southport where the Northern Counties AA had been formed in 1879. From there the message was carried to Buckingham Palace by a relay of runners from all four areas of the AAA. One of the change points was the Randolph Hotel, Oxford, where the Association

**Alan Pascoe (1), won a total of thirteen AAA titles in the outdoor and indoor Championships, but in this 1977 400 metres hurdles final came second to Richard Graybehl (7) of the USA. (George Herringshaw)**

itself had been founded.

Her Majesty's reply was carried by another relay of runners and borne into the Crystal Palace as the AAA Championships were taking place by Ian Thompson, the Commonwealth and European marathon champion. Harold Abrahams then read aloud to the 14 000 spectators the Queen's acknowledgement of the message: 'Please convey to all the athletes and officials of the Amateur Athletic Association the warm thanks of The Queen for their kind and loyal message of Silver Jubilee greetings which Her Majesty much appreciates. As Patron of the Association, The Queen sends her best wishes for the success of the 1977 Nationwide Building Society Silver Jubilee AAA Championships to all those taking part in them.' The occasion was to have a further significance, because for most of those present this was the last opportunity to hear in public the distinctive voice of Harold Abrahams, so familiar from over 50 years of broadcasting on athletics.

Two best Championship performances were equalled that afternoon: 3000 m walker, Roger Mills, won his sixth AAA title in 12 min 8.4 sec; and Alan Dainton's high jump of 2.14 m/7 ft $0\frac{1}{4}$ in matched the 1974 winning jump of world record holder, Dwight Stones. It also equalled the AAA National record, and was the first 7 ft/2.13 m clearance by a British athlete in the Championships, 101 years since Marshall Brooks was the first over 6 ft/1.83 m. On the track, the 10 000 m again inspired a world class performance, with Brendan Foster recording 27 min 45.7 sec. In the 400 m David Jenkins, attempting a seventh successive win, had to yield to Tom Andrews (USA), but finished well ahead of the British opposition.

The same summer, two new meetings were slotted into the athletic calendar. The BAAB, against the advice of the AAA members of the Board, instituted the UK National Championships, open only to men and women eligible to represent the UK, at Cwmbran on 10–12 June.

And at Düsseldorf in September, the IAAF held the first World Cup competition. The proliferation of first-class fixtures faced leading athletes with exacting choices. Steve Ovett, who missed the AAA Championships, won the Jackson cup as the outstanding UK athlete of the year; his achievements included UK National records in the mile, 3 min 54.7 sec, and 1500 m, 3 min 34.5 sec, and crushing victories in the European and the World Cup Finals. A second British winner in the European Cup Final was Nick Rose, who ran away from the field in the 5000 m.

**1978 — THE PURSUIT OF EXCELLENCE**

The first news of 1978 was that the BAAB had appointed a professional General Secretary. David Shaw, 41, a former Scottish champion in the steeplechase (1957), who had represented Great Britain and later became team manager for RAF athletics, took up his duties in April. The Hon Secretary of the Board from 1965 to 1977, Arthur Gold, who had devoted himself to the sport since his days as an international high jumper (1937), and as coach and administrator had played a major role in shaping the structure of British athletics, was now President of the European Athletic Association. Ever since Baron Pierre de Coubertin in 1894 sought the help of Charles Herbert for his Olympic idea, British experience has informed and often led the international organizations.

With the Commonwealth Games and European Championships to follow, the 1978 AAA Championships drew a strong entry from Britain and overseas. As so often before, Friday evening's events captured the headlines. Undeterred by heavy rain, Brendan Foster for the second year excelled in the 10 000 m. Soon drawing clear, splashing through puddles and past lapped runners at a beautifully controlled pace, he eventually reached the line in 27 min 30.3 sec, which was a fifth of a second better than the officially listed world record, although Henry Rono (Kenya) had posted a time 7.8 sec faster that was, as yet, unratified. So Dave Bedford's Championship best was beaten after 5 years. Another record-breaker that night was triple jumper Aston Moore, who stretched out to 16.68 m/54 ft 8¾ in, a UK National record. The next day's events were anti-climactic, even a 5000 m including world record-holders Henry Rono, Filbert Bayi (Tanzania) and Samson Kimobwa (Kenya), for canny tactics and a troublesome wind kept the phenomenal record-chaser Rono down to 13 min 20.8 sec. However, three high jumpers, including Brian Burgess (GB), beat the previous best in the Championships, with Franklin Jacobs (USA) taking the title on countback from 18-year-old Gail Olson (USA), at 2.20 m/7 ft 2½ in, while in the pole vault, Bob Pullard (USA) raised the meeting best to 5.40 m/17 ft 8¾ in.

A minor sensation at the Championships was the disqualification of Colin Sutherland, the athlete placed first in the discus, after he declined to take a test for drugs. This was the first time competitors had been asked to submit to tests, but the AAA in common with other national and international governing bodies was committed to taking measures to eliminate the use of drugs. The problem was not new; as early as 1905, Charles Lucas, the trainer of the 1904 Olympic marathon champion, Thomas Hicks (USA), admitted in a book that twice during the race he injected Hicks with small amounts of strychnine. A less dangerous stimulant, oxygen, was used in experiments in England in 1908 to determine the assistance it would give runners if administered immediately before a race; the AAA 880 yd champion, Theodore Just, was said to have improved his personal best time by 3 sec in a test. In 1909 the AAA gave a ruling that they were 'strongly against such practice'. Since 1908 the rules for marathon running have prohibited the use of drugs, but comprehensive anti-doping legislation is much more recent in origin. It was adopted by the IAAF in 1971 and incorporated in the AAA Rules for Competition in 1975.

In Edmonton, Canada, in 1978, England scooped a record total of 16 Commonwealth Games gold medals; in fact, on the closing day the United Kingdom countries won seven of the nine finals. In a sense, victory is an ultimate, but if one performance merited additional credit, it was Daley Thompson's in the decathlon. His zest for competition and his rapport with the crowd throughout the ten technically demanding events inspired him to the third highest score in history, 8467 points. England's other winners were David Moorcroft (1500 m), Brendan Foster (10 000 m), Olly Flynn (30 km walk), Roy Mitchell (long jump), Keith Connor (triple jump), Geoff Capes (shot), and, in women's events, Sonia Lannaman (100 m), Donna Hartley (400 m), Mary Stewart (1500 m), Paula Fudge (3000 m), Lorna Boothe (100 m hurdles), Sue Reeve (long jump), Tessa Sanderson (javelin) and the teams in the 4 × 100 m and 4 × 400 m. For Scotland, Allan Wells won the 200 m and the sprint relay team won the men's 4 × 100 m. Wales earned one gold medal through Berwyn Price (110 m hurdles).

The European Championships the following month supplied a sharp corrective to complacency, for Great Britain won just one event.

Steve Ovett, following a hat-trick of AAA 800 metres titles, became the world's top miler. (ED Lacey)

Ovett — King of the Crystal Palace. (All Sport/Tony Duffy)

Steve Ovett had limited his races through the season, missing the Commonwealth Games, and trained for Prague. He won the 1500 m with sufficient ease to include his characteristic wave, and took a silver medal in the 800 m. Britain's least successful European Championships reaffirmed the lesson of Montreal.

The implications were swiftly taken up by BAAB General Secretary David Shaw. In October, he announced that the BAAB had approved in principle a £160 000 plan to help Britain's top athletes prepare for the 1980 Olympic Games. Potential medallists would be backed by grants of up to £4000 each towards a programme of physiological testing, competition and training in Britain and abroad; potential finalists would qualify for up to £2000 in support. The grants would be additional to any sponsored scholarships or awards received by the athletes. In early 1979 the original sponsors of this plan dropped out due to the unwillingness of a few top athletes to join the scheme because of conflicts of sponsorship or a reluctance to be beholden to sponsors. However, the Sports Aid Foundation took up the idea and made available similar funds to potential Olympic medallists. So the Board proclaimed its willingness to invest in an élite group of athletes to keep Britain competitive at the highest international level as part of its 'Action Plan for Moscow', which promised better management and more enlightened selection policies.

So many developments have taken place in the 100 years of the Association's history that it is curious to find a modern parallel with Victorian athletics. The leading amateur athletes of the 1870s and earlier were a privileged group with the time and means to indulge in athletics. 1980 standards require the best performers to devote so much time to the sport they they, too, have to find jobs that allow them the freedom to train; or, like the nineteenth-century gentlemen of independent means, they have no jobs at all. In 1978, Steve Ovett and Daley Thompson shared the CN Jackson cup as the outstanding UK athletes of the year; both were full-time athletes, Ovett supported by his parents, Thompson by sponsorship. The BAAB plan recognized the commitment necessary to excel and created a modern élite, based not on social class, but physical ability.

## 1979 — SEB JOINS THE GIANTS

The 1979 season began with more talk than track, as controversies dominated domestic athletics. Inquiries were reported to be taking place into the alleged payment of appearance money to star athletes from both home and abroad who had competed in a major invitational meeting in Scotland in 1978. Then another familiar issue surfaced, when the severity of judges of race walking was criticized after a number of the best-known British walkers were disqualified in an RWA Championship event. By midsummer the hottest topic was the insistence of the governing body that athletes should not compete abroad without authority. These were fundamental and important issues that deserved to be discussed.

But it was still a relief early in July to see running itself restored to the headlines.

On 5 July in Oslo, Sebastian Coe improved the world record for 800 m by more than a full second, to 1 min 42.33 sec. Twelve days later on the same track, he won the Dubai Golden Mile in the world record time of 3 min 48.95 sec. At 22, he had achieved more in record-breaking than any British middle-distance runner since Sydney Wooderson. Always an athlete of outstanding promise — at 16 he had won the AAA Youth 1500 m and at 18 the Junior title — Coe demonstrated what many had believed was impossible: that a lightweight no heavier and not much taller than Wooderson could beat records set by such powerfully built runners as the giant-striding Cuban, Alberto Juantorena, and the master miler from New Zealand, John Walker. Moreover, Coe achieved his records in strong competitive races; his aim had been to win, and the times surprised him.

With three other British milers, John Robson, Graham Williamson and David Moorcroft, finishing inside 3 min 55 sec in the Oslo race, and the European 1500 m champion, Steve Ovett, who did not compete, still running with enough authority to seem unassailable, prospects for middle distance in the eighties looked outstanding.

Ovett won the AAA 1500 m as he liked in 3 min 39.1 sec, with backward glances at the opposition most of the way up the straight to calculate how finely he could judge the race. Coe entered for the 400 m, to build more speed into his running. He set a personal best, but was outpaced by the Champion of Africa, El Kasheef Hassan (Sudan). A capacity crowd for the Championships saw several more of its heroes eclipsed. Berwyn Price, bidding to emulate the late Don Finlay with a seventh straight win in the high hurdles, was never among the leaders; Brendan Foster had an unlucky fall in the 5000 m, and was sixth; and the man who had dominated the discus event in four Olympic Games, Al Oerter (USA), 42, was beaten by his countryman, John Powell. There was compensation in the competitive thrills of the two distance events, each won by an Irishman. Eamonn Coghlan took the 5000 m from Mike McLeod, Rod Dixon (NZ) and the world record holder, Henry Rono; and the 10 000 m was won by the world cross-country champion, John Treacy. AAA Championship records were set by the peerless 400 m hurdler, Ed Moses (48.58 sec), steeplechaser. Hilary Tuwei (Kenya) (8 min 23.7 sec), and pole vaulter Mike Tully (USA) (5.45 m/17 ft 10½ in).

Five continents — Africa, America, Asia, Australasia and Europe — were represented among the 1979 Championship winners. Organized athletics, not only for athletes of championship class, but for people of all levels of ability, was truly world wide. The meeting that formed the AAA 100 years ago laid the foundations. By supplying facilities, training coaches and officials, fostering clubs and associations and maintaining rules, the AAA has touched the lives of millions. This history has concentrated on the events and deeds that have made news, but the Association's greatest achievement is not sensational. It is that athletics is so universally practised and enjoyed.

**Sebastian Coe setting his world record for 1 mile of 3 min 48.95 sec in Oslo within 12 days of also breaking the record for 800 metres in July 1979. (The Associated Press Limited)**

# AAA 1

**'He always seems to have complete control of his nerves, and has the happy gift of being able to talk and joke about any subject under the sun, the farther removed from athletics the better,' wrote Bob Tisdall, the Olympic 400 m hurdles champion, remembering Lord Burghley at the start of the 1932 final.**

Two Olympic champions who went on to give outstanding service to the sport. Douglas Lowe (left) makes a presentation to the Marquess of Exeter on his retirement as AAA President in 1976. (ED Lacey)

David George Brownlow Cecil, Lord Burghley, since 1956 the 6th Marquess of Exeter, served as AAA President from 1936 to 1976, when the title of President Emeritus was conferred on him for life. In his long association with the AAA, Lord Exeter has maintained and demonstrated that athletics may be competitive, but is also a source of enjoyment and friendship.

He is a direct descendant of the statesman William Cecil, whom Queen Elizabeth I created the first Lord Burghley. He resides in one of the great English stately homes, Burghley House, in Lincolnshire. But when athletes go to their marks, blue blood is of no assistance. In fact, Lord Burghley started with a slight disadvantage, a childhood injury that prevented him completely straightening his leading leg in the orthodox hurdling style. He still succeeded in becoming the first British athlete to beat 15 sec for the 120 yd hurdles, in 1927, on grass, over barriers it was unwise to skim.

In this event he made his Olympic debut at 19, and won three AAA titles (1929–31). Without ever giving up the high hurdles, he earned immortality in the 400 m hurdles by winning the Olympic title in 1928. On his return to England, he was mobbed on arrival in London at Liverpool Street Station, lifted shoulder-high until station staff, fearing for his safety, escorted him away. 'What a reception!' he was reported as saying. 'I would rather face a hundred champions than a crowd like that.' He continued to compete until 1933, collecting a total of five AAA 440 yd hurdle titles, one in world record time. In 1930 he achieved a unique 120/440 yd hurdles double, and repeated the feat in the first British Empire Games, in which he gained a third gold medal in the 4 × 440 yd. He captained Britain's team in the 1932 Olympics, reached the finals of both hurdles events, set a British record of 52.2 sec finishing fourth in the longer race, and won a silver medal in the 4 × 400 m. At about this time a poll was held by a national newspaper to find the ten most popular young men in Britain. Lord Burghley was top of the list, Jim Mollison, the pilot, second, Noel Coward, third.

Lord Burghley was 31 and the MP for Peterborough when he became the youngest-ever AAA President in 1936. He went to Berlin with the British team and saw the Olympic 400 m hurdles won in a time slower than his of 1932. In the late thirties he made such a strong impression in the National Fitness Council that there was talk of his becoming Britain's first Minister of Sport. War intervened. In the army he rose to the rank of Lieutenant Colonel, and became Controller of Aircraft Repairs and Supplies. Churchill in 1943 appointed him Governor and Commander-in-Chief of Bermuda, then a vital strategic naval and air base. He returned to Britain in 1945 and was soon deeply involved again in service to sport. The IAAF elected him President in 1946, a post he held for 30 years. He was immediately faced with a crisis; a Soviet Union team arrived in Oslo for the European Championships, but the Russians had not yet affiliated to the IAAF. He advised the Council that it was in the interest of international sport to allow them to compete. A Finnish member drily commented, 'So now Britannia waives the rules.' In the same year the decision was made to hold the 1948 Olympic Games in London, and, since Lord Burghley was the prime mover, he found himself Chairman of the Organizing Committee. His high spirits, energy and managerial skill never had a more formidable challenge. The Games were memorable, successful and actually showed a profit — the last time in Olympic history.

The handicap of chronically arthritic hips has not stopped him from active participation in the management of sport. In 1964 he stood for election as President of the International Olympic Committee, on which he had served since 1933, and lost to Avery Brundage by a handful of votes. He was Chairman of the British Olympic Association from 1936 to 1966 and President from 1966 to 1976.

In 1976 Lord Exeter retired from the Presidency of the AAA. Uniquely, the title of President Emeritus was conferred on him for life, in order to keep him as an officer of the Association and as a token of respect and gratitude for his contribution to athletics. His successor, Harold Abrahams, quipped that as incoming President he claimed the registration plate AAA 1 that the Marquess had on his Rolls Royce, but if it was difficult to unfix he was prepared to take delivery of what was attached to it.

The third member of the famous Cambridge trio of gold medallists, Douglas Lowe, who had been AAA Hon Secretary in 1936 when Lord Exeter became President, made a presentation on behalf of the Association, and expressed the gratitude of generations of athletes with the words, 'He has rendered to us a tremendous service over forty years.'

For all his fame as Olympic champion and world record-breaker, the Marquess of Exeter is remembered at his University for another athletic feat. In his last term at Cambridge in 1927 he succeeded in running completely round the Great Court of Trinity College (370 yd/338 m on the Flagstone path) in a dinner jacket while the clock was striking twelve. Many had tried to beat the clock (44.9 sec), but he was the first to succeed in this century. Whether the contest conformed to AAA Laws it is too late to inquire . . .

# The Confidence of the Long Distance Runner

**When Brendan Foster wins at the Crystal Palace and salutes the grandstand with raised arms the response is immediate. British crowds love a great distance runner. In 1971, after years of diminishing attendances at the White City, they flocked to the Crystal Palace to see Dave Bedford attack the 5000 m world record in the AAA Championships.**

Foster and Bedford are not much alike, but they have one thing in common that makes them great champions. Gordon Pirie in the fifties had it. So did Alfred Shrubb, back in Edwardian days. And the Victorian champion, Walter George. They dared to go out alone and test themselves beyond their known limits. Front running in the distance events demands a commitment different from sprinting, jumping or throwing. When Foster puts in a 60 sec lap midway through a 5000 m, he stakes everything on his ability to finish the race. He has to be confident.

The confidence is built on thousands of miles' training, on the tracks, roads and across country. The cross-country season has been a keenly competitive feature of British athletics for over 100 years, and certainly helps to account for the nation's strength in depth at distance running. It was not by chance that Walter George, the first outstanding champion, came to prominence in the years when cross-country was established on a national basis.

The modern cross-country race is a fusion of several traditions. Professional runners in the eighteenth century kept race-fit by following the hounds on foot. In the 1820s, foot steeplechases, usually between local landmarks, were staged in the Scottish Lowlands and soon spread to the English North and Midlands. By 1834 the sport was known in the public schools, with hare and hounds, a form of paperchase, adding an extra dimension. The credit for initiating cross-country at club level is given to Walter Rye, the waspish correspondent of the *Sporting Gazette*. He organized a run in 1867 for Thames Rowing Club, which led, the following year, to the founding of Thames Hare and Hounds. After that, clubs proliferated, and their names — Hare and Hounds, Harriers, Beagles, even Tally Ho! — preserved the connection with hunting. On 24 February 1877, Rye laid a paper trail for what is regarded as the first Championship. It was won by Percy (he preferred to be known as Peter) Stenning (1854–92), who successfully defended his title for the next 3 years.

**Walter George, distance-running champion and record-breaker of the 1880s. With shorts like that he *had* to be good!**

Cross-country was represented at the formation of the AAA in 1880 by four delegates, but it was still considered appropriate to form a National Cross-Country Union — known since 1937 as the English CCU — on 18 August 1883. Predictably, Walter Rye balked at the notion of a Union open to all; in his absence he was unanimously 'selected' as President, but he declined the office.

The celebrated Walter G. George won the inaugural Midland Cross-Country Championship in 1879, at the age of 20, and took it again in 1882 and 1884. In the latter 2 years he also won the National. His slender physique and long stride were really better suited to track running, in which he repeatedly set world records at all distances from 1 to 10 miles. He and his Moseley

**Alf Shrubb (centre) in the 1903 AAA 1 mile, in which he beat the holder, Joe Binks (1) and Edmund Gay-Roberts (leading), the Universities champion.**

Harriers companion, Bill Snook, the man more than once in trouble with the AAA, dominated distance running between 1879 and 1885 so totally that they won 20 Championship titles, this despite George's variable health and Snook's suspensions. It was nothing extraordinary for one of them to win the 880 yd, 1 mile and 4 miles in an afternoon and come back two days later to take the 10 miles. Of the two at their best, George had the edge. He beat Snook decisively in 1884 to take the mile title in 4 min 18.4 sec, a world best performance. As a professional 2 years later, he improved to 4 min 12¾ sec, the best achieved in his century. But he always regarded himself as better over longer distances, where his fearless, but thoughtfully planned front running strikingly altered men's conceptions of what was possible.

With the knowledge that a mile can be run more than 20 sec faster than George's record, and that in a 10 000 m race Brendan Foster would theoretically beat him by 3½ laps, we can appreciate the improvements made possible by modern training techniques. Yet it is arguable that confidence — the knowledge that the distances *can* be covered in faster time — has something to do with it. It took some 20 years for another runner of Walter George's trail-blazing temperament to appear. He was a bricklayer by trade, whose powers of endurance were discovered in 1898, when he ran across country to a fire in a village 3 miles from his native Slinfold, in Sussex. Alfred Shrubb was persuaded to join the local Harriers, and the same year won county championships at 1, 3 and 4 miles. He had an uncomplicated attitude to tactics: 'Set your mind on getting in front as soon as you can, and staying in that position for as long as you can manage . . . It's the best place to be in, you know.' In his first AAA Championships in 1900, he sped away and made the pace in the 4 miles, but was overhauled by Jack Rimmer and Charles Bennett, each of whom won an Olympic gold medal the same year. But by the next year Shrubb was literally out on his own, and remained so for 4 years. Between 1901 and 1904 he won each Southern and National Cross-Country title and ten AAA titles, two at 1 mile and four each at 4 and 10 miles. In 1903 he won the inaugural International Cross-Country Championship by over half a minute and defended it successfully in 1904. Like Walter George, he took up professional running at the age of 26, and in 1915 he was appointed professional coach to Oxford University AC. In this he was a disappointment. Oxford athletes of the period remember him starting a training session with the words, 'Now, gentlemen, we'll just warm up with a few turns,' and then, past 40, scudding off round the track, oblivious of who followed. He rarely said much. Running, for Shrubb, was the pursuit of solitude.

When the IAAF issued its first list of official world records in 1921, Alf Shrubb was declared holder of every record over the linear distances from 2 to 10 miles. The next United Kingdom athlete to set a world record in a standard distance event was Gordon Pirie, 49 years after fellow South London Harrier, Shrubb, with 28 min 19.4 sec for 6 miles, in the 1953 AAA Championships. Half a century of British distance running had not been altogether devoid of success, but Pirie was the first in Shrubb's mould, a runner resolved to be alone. In a period of 2 years he lifted British distance running from mediocrity to world class. He lopped 19 sec off the British 3 miles record, 74 sec off the 6 miles. His single-mindedness, ruthless training and blunt statements to the press were strong stuff in post-war Britain, still clinging to the ethic that a sportsman should succeed by dint of sheer talent, and then disclaim it. Pirie's candour was perfect copy for the press: win or lose, he made headlines. He was a celebrity. Soon after him came other British world record-breakers. Fred Green and Chris Chataway shared the 3 miles record in 1954, and Chataway set records all his own at 5000 m in 1954 and 3 miles in 1955. But neither was a committed front runner like Pirie in the early years of his career. Later, he profited from the pacemaking of other top international athletes when he set world records for 3000 m and 5000 m in 1956. In Melbourne at the end of that year, chasing the 10 000 m/5000 m double for the second time in an Olympic Games, Pirie was put on the rack by a greater master of pace, the Russian, Vladimir Kuts. 'Up till now,' wrote Kuts, 'I was only able to guess his condition by the way his spikes struck the ground and the

**Champions of the 1950s, Gordon Pirie (1) and Ken Norris (2) achieved a rare distinction in this 1955 London v Prague 10 000 metres by defeating the legendary Emil Zatopek (Czechoslovakia). (The Sport and General Press Agency Ltd)**

way he breathed behind me.' In the twentieth lap, he waved Pirie ahead. 'For the first time I was able to get a good look at the tired, limp figure . . . Fatigue was spelt over the whole of Gordon's face. I realized that this was the moment for the decisive spurt.' Pirie continued in athletics for another 5 years, but he was never so good again.

After the first four minute mile was achieved in 1954, the four-lap race lost some of its glamour. There was a shift of interest to the longer distances. The dramatic improvement in standards meant that a 3 miles or a 5000 m was no longer a test of attrition, but a fiercely competitive event with intriguing tactical possibilities. Soon this was equally true of the 10 000 m. Distance running became emphatically more popular with competitors. The field for the National Cross-Country Championship first topped 500 in 1955, when Pirie won for the third year; by 1969 it was over 1000 and by 1978, 1500. An associated development had been the formation of the Road Runners Club in 1952. The AAA National Road Relay Championship, started in 1967, was another outcome of the distance running boom.

On the track, Britain kept up with the quickening pace, thanks to runners of the quality of Stan Eldon, John Merriman and Bruce Tulloh. Then in the mid-sixties the phenomenal Australian, Ron Clarke, set a series of records that left the UK bests lagging by up to 73 sec in the 10 000 m. Dick Taylor, Ian Stewart, Jim Hogan and Mike Freary improved standards by degrees, but it required someone in the tradition of George, Shrubb and Pirie to go after Clarke's records.

He was Dave Bedford. Like Pirie, he was a natural newsmaker, as dramatic in failure as in success. He was 19 when he set his first UK record at 10 000 m in 1969. At 20, he won the first of five AAA Championships in the event, leading from gun to tape. The next year he won the National and International Cross-Country Championships and set UK records in the 5000 m, 10 000 m and — fulfilling a boast — the 3000 m steeplechase! In 1972 he accomplished a double in the AAA 5000 and 10 000 m, a feat previously achieved only by Pirie and Eldon in the 3 and 6 mile events. His world record in the 10 000 m Championship of 1973 was a stunning run, over 7 sec inside Viren's time. Prosaically, he compared it to running after a bus: 'I found it difficult to catch in the last eight laps.'

**In 1952 Alf Shrubb, then 73, met Gordon Pirie at the South London Harriers' Dinner. (The Associated Press Ltd)**

*Left:* 'It was like running after a bus,' commented Dave Bedford after this world record performance of 27 min 30.8 sec in the 1973 AAA 10 000 metres. (ED Lacey)

*Right:* Brendan Foster leads Nick Rose in the 1976 AAA 5000 metres, won by Foster. (All Sport/Tony Duffy)

*Below:* A common sight at Crystal Palace in the 1970s — 'Big Bren' salutes his fans after a winning run. (All Sport/Don Morley)

When Nurmi, the Flying Finn, was champion in the twenties, distance running had become mysterious and romantic. Gunder Hägg, the man who came from Swedish pine forests to set numerous records in the forties, strengthened the legend. Zatopek, the Human Locomotive, introduced an element of suffering. Kuts, the Soviet Iron Man, made it heroic. And Bedford? He exploded the myths. With his hippie hairstyle and red socks he flouted convention, and with his words — there were plenty — he pulled the plug on romance. 'What I did tonight is a chicken way of running a race, but it's effective,' he commented after his 1974 AAA 10 000 m. 'It got me results.' Yet the results did not come in the major international championships. Trying for a double in the 1972 Olympics, he finished sixth in the 10 000 m and twelfth in the 5000 m. His career disintegrated after 1974. He was still only 24, reduced by a persistent leg injury to counting the consultants he had seen, but big enough in spirit to join the pack of plodding club runners. He had never pretended that running was glamorous.

Brendan Foster, who replaced Bedford as British record-holder for 5000 m and 10 000 m, was actually 2 years his senior. After three seasons as an international 1500 m runner and bronze medals in the 1970 Commonwealth Games and 1971 European Championships, he took up the longer distances in 1973 and established himself as a distance man of exceptional talent, invention and courage. 'Big Bren' broke world records — for 2 miles (1973) and 3000 m (1974) — *and* had the competitive flair to win international titles: the European Cup Final 5000 m in 1973 and 1975; the European Championship 5000 m in 1974; and the Commonwealth 10 000 m in 1978. He brought a new dimension to front running with his sub-60 sec kick for a whole lap midway through a race. When he added the 10 000 m to his repertoire in 1975, he ran a world class time on his debut. In the 1976 Olympic Games he took a bronze medal in this event, and might have done better but for an untimely stomach upset.

Foster's unique contribution to British athletics has been his success in turning public support into active involvement in the sport. It started in Gateshead, where a whole community was caught up in his endeavours as runner and Sports and Recreation Officer. A £140 000 track was built and top-class events staged there and televised. The local club, Gateshead Harriers, recruited on a grand scale. In 1973 they won the National Cross-Country Championship and they have won it four times since. When jogging became popular, Brendan Foster was among the first to organize mass 'fun-runs'. He had recognized that people were ready to participate in running. After a win at Gateshead or the Crystal Palace he stood before his public with open arms, and the response was as rapturous as the last night of the Proms. Brendan Foster was the man who gave the lie to the loneliness of the long-distance runner.

# Over to Harold Abrahams

**His voice was known to millions. Harold Abrahams made his first radio broadcast on athletics in 1925. He was already a celebrity, the sprinter who had won the Olympic 100 m the year before in Paris. The best sportsmen are not necessarily the best speakers on sport, but in this case the voice, like the man, was a winner. He had the approved BBC accent without the sanctimoniousness of so much broadcasting of the period. For some 40 years, Harold Abrahams regularly presented athletics with a warmth and sense of proportion that made it one of the most popular sports on radio.**

After the war, his articulateness combined with his involvement in the organization of athletics made it inevitable that he became a spokesman for the sport. For some 20 years he and Jack Crump — a very different, but no less confident speaker and broadcaster — were the public voices of the athletics administration. This had definite advantages. Athletics was publicly represented with an advocate's skill. In the councils of sport it earned respect. It attracted better sponsorship than most other sports. But there were disadvantages as well. There was the danger that others within the sport and outside it would gain the impression that it was controlled by its two spokesmen. When there was criticism, it became personal; the failings of athletics were represented as the failings of Harold Abrahams and Jack Crump. Increasingly they were open to the charge that they were elderly officials managing a young men's sport.

Harold Abrahams began his service as an AAA official literally by accident. In May, 1925, he was still only 25. He was Olympic sprint champion.

Harold Abrahams presents the cup to the winner of the 1974 AAA 100 metres, Steve Williams (USA), 50 years after his own victory. (ED Lacey)

He held the English record for the long jump. He had accumulated more wins in the Oxford and Cambridge sports than any other man. He was the reigning AAA champion for the 100 yd and the long jump. It was his ambition to jump over 25 ft/7.62 m. Trying for a big one at Stamford Bridge, he missed his footing at take-off and crashed with full force on his right leg. 'I heard a noise rather like Smee tearing cloth in Peter Pan.' The bone had snapped, irreparably damaging the muscles. He was finished as an athlete. Ten weeks after the accident, he limped out to the centre at Stamford Bridge to officiate as a field event judge at the Championships.

He channelled his zest for the sport into a torrent of activities. In 6 years he wrote three technical books on athletics; edited the 1928 Olympic Report; and in co-authorship produced two monumental volumes recording the results of all Oxford and Cambridge sports, and the AAA Championships. He wrote regularly for the *Sunday Times*, *Daily Sketch*, *Sunday Graphic* and *Athletic News*, and his journalism was stylish, informative and scrupulously fair. He began broadcasting regularly; captained the British team in the 1928 Olympic Games; became Hon Treasurer of the Middlesex AAA; served on the Southern Committee and, from 1926, the General Committee of the AAA. Not one of these enterprises was skimped. He worked at them as he had worked at winning a gold medal.

He also pursued his career as a barrister; he had been called to the bar of the Inner Temple in 1924. His ability to present a case persuasively came to the rescue of British athletics in 1931. With another able lawyer, Douglas Lowe, he resolved the crisis over the United Kingdom representation on the IAAF by negotiating the formation of the International Board, known later as the BAAB. He was an active member of the Board for 44 years. He served as Hon Treasurer from 1946 to 1969 and Chairman from 1969 to 1975. In the AAA he helped out for a few months in 1938 as acting Hon Secretary, but generally participated as a member of General Committee and by serving on sub-committees rather than through executive office. He was elected a Vice-President of the Association in 1948 and a Life Vice-President in 1958.

He was no less active in international athletics administration. He attended each IAAF Congress from 1934 to the end of his life. When the initiative in making laws passed from the AAA to the IAAF, he joined the IAAF Technical Committee, where he was soon recognized as the key member, and later its Chairman. He has been described as the architect of the modern laws of athletics.

The facts are impressive enough, but they are less than the man. His achievement was lasting because he earned the affection of practically everyone he met. He cared about people, and was infinitely thoughtful in the kindnesses of human contact. Loyalty was the guiding principle of his life. But it was loyalty to people rather than abstractions. In debate he could be a formidable adversary, more formidable, probably, than he realized. In personal contact he was disarming, inclined to laugh at himself, prepared to be persuaded of an alternative view if it was reasonable.

The biographical landmarks in Harold Abrahams' life give the clear impression of an establishment figure: Repton, Cambridge, the Inner Temple, the BBC, the Garrick Club and the Civil Service (he received the CBE for his 13 years in the National Parks Commission). In athletics he was often obliged to represent the establishment view. It would be misleading to suggest that he was at odds with the policies of the AAA or the BAAB, but it is equally erroneous to cast him as a diehard, clinging to a nineteenth-century concept of amateurism.

The truth is that he was one of the first to challenge the old ideals. In 1929, when the entire athletics establishment, the British Olympic Association and the governing bodies of practically all amateur sports were campaigning against a proposal that amateur sportsmen should be compensated for 'broken time' from their employment, he wrote a series of articles in the *Sunday Times* defending the idea. 'In truth the attempt to draw a clear-cut line between amateurs and professionals grows more and more complicated every day, and the sooner we admit that there is but little place for the old time casual amateur in this modern world of specialisation and international encounter, the better we will be able to face in a logical manner the bogy of "broken time".' Through the years he consistently challenged the concept of amateurism. 'I would, for example, omit the word "amateur" from the rules,' he wrote in *XVII Olympiad, 1960*. 'What the Bodies governing a particular sport ought to be concerned with is to draft a code of rules to control competition in the sport. They should not concern themselves with theoretical principles, principles first expounded well-nigh one hundred years ago.'

For his service to athletics totalling almost 60 years, Harold Abrahams received no public honours, but in November, 1976, the sport awarded him its highest accolade by electing him President of the AAA. Sadly he did not live to see the Centenary for which he was already initiating plans. When he died, in January, 1978, many moving tributes were paid, some of the warmest from his critics in Fleet Street. Chris Brasher wrote in *The Observer*, '. . . he would always listen to an opponent's views and if he thought there was merit in them he would throw his influence behind an attempt to right a wrong'. Above this notice were the words 'A heart of gold'.

In 1930, when the famous distance-runner, Paavo Nurmi, visited England, he was seated next to Harold Abrahams at a dinner party. Nurmi's uncertain command of English made conversation difficult, but Harold succeeded in conveying how much he had admired the Finn's brilliant running at the Paris Olympic Games in 1924. 'Ah!' said Nurmi, 'But you were the black horse at the Games!'

**'The Amateur Athletic Association ought to be told about this.' (*Punch*)**

# Principal Officers of the AAA

Patron: HER MAJESTY THE QUEEN
President Emeritus: Most Hon The Marquess of Exeter, KCMG
President: Squire S. Yarrow
Hon Treasurer: Raymond L. Stroud
Hon Secretary: Barry E. Willis
National Administrator: F. John Martell

**Vice-Patrons**

Right Hon The Lord Luke of Pavenham, KCVO, TD
Right Hon Lord Byers, PC, OBE
Right Hon Lord Noel-Baker, PC
Lord Porritt, GCMG, GCVO, CBE
Sir Herbert Ashworth
Edward Courage, CBE
Percy B. Lucas, DSO, DFC
Captain DML Neame, DSO RN (RTD)
Donald TP Pain, MBE
Leslie Swabey

**Past Presidents**

1880–1890 Right Hon The Earl of Jersey
1891–1915 Right Hon The Viscount Alverstone, GCMG, PC
1916–1930 Right Hon Sir Montague Shearman, PC
1930–1936 Right Hon Lord Desborough, KG, GCVO
1936–1976 Most Hon The Marquess of Exeter, KCMG
1976–1978 Harold M. Abrahams, CBE

**Past Hon Treasurers**

1880–1910 Clement N. Jackson
1910–1932 William M. Barnard
1932–1938 Ernest JH Holt, CMG, CBE
1938–1947 Claude WF Pearce
1947–1957 Walter C. Jewell
1957–1960 Arthur D. Thwaites
1960–1966 Philip S. Gale
1966–1967 George B. Cooper
1967–1970 Frank JB Read
1970–1974 F. John Martell

**Past Hon Secretaries**

1880–1883 Right Hon Sir Montague Shearman, PC
1883–1906 Charles Herbert
1906–1915 Percy L. Fisher
1915–1931 Sir Harry Barclay
1931–1938 Douglas GA Lowe
1938–1947 Ernest JH Holt, CMG, CBE
1947–1965 Ernest HL Clynes, OBE

**Squire Yarrow (second from left), who became the seventh AAA President in 1978, pictured with John Martell (right), AAA Hon Treasurer 1970–74, and now the Association's National Administrator, and Don Shelley (on left), the National Marathon Organizer since 1978. They are holding the AAA marathon trophy presented by the late Tony Fattorini in 1927, and won by Squire Yarrow in 1946.**

# AAA Championship Results

## 100 YARDS

| | | sec |
|---|---|---|
| 1880 | William Phillips | 10.2 |
| 1881 | William Phillips | 10.2 |
| 1882 | William Phillips | 10.2 |
| 1883 | James Cowie | 10.2 |
| 1884 | James Cowie | 10.2 |
| 1885 | James Cowie | 10.2 |
| 1886 | Arthur Wharton | 10.0 |
| 1887 | Arthur Wharton | 10.1 |
| 1888 | Frederick Westing (USA) | 10.2 |
| 1889 | Ernest Pelling | 10.4 |
| 1890 | Norman Morgan (Ireland) | 10.4 |
| 1891 | Luther Cary (USA) | 10.2 |
| 1892 | Charles Bradley | 10.2 |
| 1893 | Charles Bradley | 10.0* |
| 1894 | Charles Bradley | 10.2 |
| 1895 | Charles Bradley | 10.0 |
| 1896 | Norman Morgan (Ireland) | 10.4 |
| 1897 | JH Palmer | 10.8 |
| 1898 | Fred Cooper | 10.0 |
| 1899 | Reg Wadsley | 10.2 |
| 1900 | Arthur Duffey (USA) | 10.0 |
| 1901 | Arthur Duffey (USA) | 10.0 |
| 1902 | Arthur Duffey (USA) | 10.0 |
| 1903 | Arthur Duffey (USA) | 10.0 |
| 1904 | John Morton | 10.0 |
| 1905 | John Morton | 10.2 |
| 1906 | John Morton | 10.4 |
| 1907 | John Morton | 10.8 |
| 1908 | Robert Kerr (Canada) | 10.0 |
| 1909 | Reginald Walker (S. Africa) | 10.0 |
| 1910 | Fred Ramsdell (USA) | 10.2 |
| 1911 | Fred Ramsdell (USA) | 10.4 |
| 1912 | George Patching (S. Africa) | 9.8 |
| 1913 | William Applegarth | 10.0 |
| 1914 | William Applegarth | 10.0 |
| 1919 | William Hill | 10.0 |
| 1920 | Harry Edward | 10.0 |
| 1921 | Harry Edward | 10.2 |
| 1922 | Harry Edward | 10.0 |
| 1923 | Eric Liddell | 9.7 |
| 1924 | Harold Abrahams | 9.9 |
| 1925 | Loren Murchison (USA) | 9.9 |
| 1926 | Richard Corts (Germany) | 10.0 |
| 1927 | Helmut Kornig (Germany) | 10.1 |
| 1928 | Wilfred Legg (S. Africa) | 9.9 |
| 1929 | Jack London | 10.0 |
| 1930 | Christiaan Berger (Netherlands) | 9.9 |
| 1931 | Ernest Page | 10.0 |
| 1932 | Frederick Reid | 9.9 |
| 1933 | George Saunders | 9.9 |
| 1934 | József Sir (Hungary) | 9.9 |
| 1935 | Arthur Sweeney | 10.2 |
| 1936 | Martinus Osendarp (Netherlands) | 9.8 |
| 1937 | Cyril Holmes | 9.9 |
| 1938 | Martinus Osendarp (Netherlands) | 9.8 |
| 1939 | Arthur W. Sweeney | 9.9 |
| 1946 | McDonald Bailey | 9.8 |
| 1947 | McDonald Bailey | 9.7 |
| 1948 | John Treloar (Australia) | 9.8 |
| 1949 | McDonald Bailey | 9.7 |
| 1950 | McDonald Bailey | 9.9 |
| 1951 | McDonald Bailey | 9.6 |
| 1952 | McDonald Bailey | 9.6 |
| 1953 | McDonald Bailey | 9.8 |
| 1954 | George Ellis | 9.9 |
| 1955 | Roy Sandstrom | 10.0 |
| 1956 | John Young | 9.9 |
| 1957 | Kenneth Box | 10.0 |
| 1958 | James Omagbemi (Nigeria) | 9.9 |
| 1959 | Peter Radford | 9.7 |
| 1960 | Peter Radford | 9.7 |
| 1961 | Harry Jerome (Canada) | 9.6 |
| 1962 | Seraphino Antao (Kenya) | 9.8 |
| 1963 | Berwyn Jones | 9.7 |
| 1964 | Enrique Figuerola (Cuba) | 9.4 |
| 1965 | Enrique Figuerola (Cuba) | 9.6 |
| 1966 | Paul Nash (S. Africa) | 9.6 |
| 1967 | Barrie Kelly | 9.9 |
| 1968 | Paul Nash (S. Africa) | 9.9 |

*Up-hill

## 100 METRES

| | | sec |
|---|---|---|
| 1969 | Ronald Jones | 10.7 |
| 1970 | Gary 'Rocky' Symonds (Bermuda) | 10.3 |
| 1971 | Brian Green | 10.6 |
| 1972 | Vassilios Papageorgopoulos (Greece) | 10.2 |
| 1973 | Donald Halliday | 10.6 |
| 1974 | Steve Williams (USA) | 10.2 |
| 1975 | Steve Riddick (USA) | 10.39 |
| 1976 | Donald Quarrie (Jamaica) | 10.42 |
| 1977 | Clancy Edwards (USA) | 10.48 |
| 1978 | James Sanford (USA) | 10.42 |
| 1979 | Clancy Edwards (USA) | 10.35 |

## 220 YARDS

| | | sec |
|---|---|---|
| 1902 | Reg Wadsley | 22.4 |
| 1903 | George Brewill | 23.0 |
| 1904 | Claude Jupp | 22.8 |
| 1905 | Harry Hyman (USA) | 22.4 |
| 1906 | Claude Jupp | 22.6 |
| 1907 | Jack George | 22.8 |
| 1908 | Robert Kerr (Canada) | 22.4 |
| 1909 | Nathaniel Cartmell (USA) | 22.0 |
| 1910 | Fred Ramsdell (USA) | 22.4 |
| 1911 | Fred Ramsdell (USA) | 22.2 |
| 1912 | William Applegarth | 22.0 |
| 1913 | William Applegarth | 21.6 |
| 1914 | William Applegarth | 21.2 |
| 1919 | William Hill | 22.6 |
| 1920 | Harry Edward | 21.6 |
| 1921 | Harry Edward | 22.2 |
| 1922 | Harry Edward | 22.0 |
| 1923 | Eric Liddell | 21.6 |
| 1924 | Howard Kinsman (S. Africa) | 21.7 |
| 1925 | Loren Murchison (USA) | 21.6 |
| 1926 | Guy Butler | 21.9 |
| 1927 | Hubert Houben (Germany) | 21.8 |
| 1928 | Friedrich Wichmann (Germany) | 21.7 |
| 1929 | John Hanlon | 21.9 |
| 1930 | Stanley Englehart | 22.0 |

| | | |
|---|---|---|
| 1931 | Robin Murdoch | 22.5 |
| 1932 | Frederick Reid | 22.0 |
| 1933 | Christiaan Berger (Netherlands) | 22.0 |
| 1934 | Robin Murdoch | 22.1 |
| 1935 | Martinus Osendarp (Netherlands) | 22.2 |
| 1936 | Arthur Sweeney | 21.9 |
| 1937 | Arthur Sweeney | 21.9 |
| 1938 | Wijnand van Beveren (Netherlands) | 22.1 |
| 1939 | Cyril Holmes | 21.9 |
| 1946 | McDonald Bailey | 22.3 |
| 1947 | McDonald Bailey | 21.7 |
| 1948 | Alistair McCorquodale | 22.2 |
| 1949 | McDonald Bailey | 21.7 |
| 1950 | McDonald Bailey | 21.8 |
| 1951 | McDonald Bailey | 21.4 |
| 1952 | McDonald Bailey | 21.4 |
| 1953 | McDonald Bailey | 21.4 |
| 1954 | Brian Shenton | 21.5 |
| 1955 | George Ellis | 22.0 |
| 1956 | Brian Shenton | 21.8 |
| 1957 | David Segal | 21.9 |
| 1958 | David Segal | 21.4 |
| 1959 | David Jones | 21.7 |
| 1960 | David Jones | 21.3 |
| 1961 | David Jones | 21.4 |
| 1962 | Seraphino Antao (Kenya) | 21.1 |
| 1963 | David Jones | 21.3 |
| 1964 | Menzies Campbell | 21.1 |
| 1965 | Patrick Morrison | 21.8 |
| 1966 | Paul Nash (S. Africa) | 21.2 |
| 1967 | Menzies Campbell | 21.4 |
| 1968 | Paul Nash (S. Africa) | 21.2 |

## 200 METRES

| | | sec |
|---|---|---|
| 1969 | David Dear | 21.4 |
| 1970 | Martin Reynolds | 21.0 |
| 1971 | Alan Pascoe | 21.1 |
| 1972 | Alan Pascoe | 20.9 |
| 1973 | Christopher Monk | 21.1 |
| 1974 | Mark Lutz (USA) | 20.9 |
| 1975 | Steve Riddick (USA) | 20.81 |
| 1976 | Donald Quarrie (Jamaica) | 20.35 |
| 1977 | Clancy Edwards (USA) | 21.05 |
| 1978 | Donald Quarrie (Jamaica) | 20.79 |
| 1979 | Clancy Edwards (USA) | 20.77 |

## 440 YARDS

| | | sec |
|---|---|---|
| 1880 | Montague Shearman | 52.2 |
| 1881 | Lawrence Myers (USA) | 48.6 |
| 1882 | Henry Ball | 50.2 |
| 1883 | James Cowie | 51.0 |
| 1884 | James Cowie | 50.4 |
| 1885 | Lawrence Myers (USA) | 52.4 |
| 1886 | Charles Wood | 49.8 |
| 1887 | Charles Wood | 51.0 |
| 1888 | Lenox Tindall | 51.4 |
| 1889 | Lenox Tindall | 48.5 |
| 1890 | Tom Nicholas | 51.8 |
| 1891 | Mortimer Remington (USA) | 51.0 |
| 1892 | Cyril Dickinson (Ireland) | 50.4 |
| 1893 | Edgar Bredin | 49.2 |
| 1894 | Edgar Bredin | 50.0 |
| 1895 | William Fitzherbert | 49.6 |
| 1896 | James Meredith (Ireland) | 52.0 |
| 1897 | Sam Elliott | 53.2 |
| 1898 | William Fitzherbert | 50.0 |
| 1899 | Reg Wadsley | 54.6 |
| 1900 | Maxey Long (USA) | 49.8 |
| 1901 | Reg Wadsley | 49.8 |
| 1902 | George White | 50.2 |
| 1903 | Charles McLachlan | 52.2 |
| 1904 | RL Watson | 51.8 |
| 1905 | Wyndham Halswelle | 50.8 |
| 1906 | Wyndham Halswelle | 48.8 |
| 1907 | Edwin Montague | 52.6 |
| 1908 | Wyndham Halswelle | 49.4 |
| 1909 | Alan Patterson | 51.2 |
| 1910 | Lionel Reed | 51.0 |
| 1911 | Frank Halbhaus (Canada) | 50.8 |
| 1912 | Cyril Seedhouse | 49.8 |
| 1913 | George Nicol | 49.4 |
| 1914 | Cyril Seedhouse | 50.0 |
| 1919 | Guy Butler | 49.2 |
| 1920 | Bevil Rudd (S. Africa) | 49.2 |
| 1921 | Robert Lindsay | 50.4 |
| 1922 | Harry Edward | 50.4 |
| 1923 | William Stevenson (USA) | 49.6 |
| 1924 | Eric Liddell | 49.6 |
| 1925 | Hyla Stallard | 50.0 |
| 1926 | John Rinkel | 49.8 |
| 1927 | Douglas Lowe | 48.8 |
| 1928 | Douglas Lowe | 50.0 |
| 1929 | John Hanlon | 49.1 |
| 1930 | Kenneth Brangwin | 49.8 |
| 1931 | Godfrey Rampling | 48.6 |
| 1932 | Crew Stoneley | 49.8 |
| 1933 | Frederick Wolff | 49.0 |
| 1934 | Godfrey Rampling | 49.6 |
| 1935 | William Roberts | 49.0 |
| 1936 | Godfrey Brown | 48.6 |
| 1937 | William Roberts | 48.2 |
| 1938 | Godfrey Brown | 49.2 |
| 1939 | Alan Pennington | 48.8 |
| 1946 | Arthur Wint (Jamaica) | 48.4 |
| 1947 | Jimmy Reardon (Ireland) | 48.3 |
| 1948 | Maurice Curotta (Australia) | 48.2 |
| 1949 | Derek Pugh | 48.5 |
| 1950 | Leslie Lewis | 48.2 |
| 1951 | Derek Pugh | 47.9 |
| 1952 | Arthur Wint (Jamaica) | 48.1 |
| 1953 | Peter Fryer | 48.9 |
| 1954 | Peter Fryer | 48.4 |
| 1955 | Peter Fryer | 47.7 |
| 1956 | Michael Wheeler | 47.7 |
| 1957 | Peter Higgins | 47.6 |
| 1958 | John Salisbury | 47.2 |
| 1959 | John Wrighton | 47.5 |
| 1960 | Milkha Singh (India) | 46.5 |
| 1961 | Adrian Metcalfe | 47.6 |
| 1962 | Robbie Brightwell | 45.9 |
| 1963 | Adrian Metcalfe | 47.3 |
| 1964 | Robbie Brightwell | 47.5 |
| 1965 | Michael Larrabee (USA) | 47.6 |
| 1966 | Wendell Mottley (Trinidad) | 45.9 |
| 1967 | Timothy Graham | 46.6 |
| 1968 | Martin Winbolt Lewis | 46.9 |

## 400 METRES

| | | sec |
|---|---|---|
| 1969 | Gwynne Griffiths | 46.8 |
| 1970 | Martin Bilham | 46.6 |
| 1971 | David Jenkins | 47.1 |
| 1972 | David Jenkins | 45.4 |
| 1973 | David Jenkins | 46.4 |
| 1974 | David Jenkins | 46.1 |
| 1975 | David Jenkins | 45.87 |
| 1976 | David Jenkins | 45.86 |
| 1977 | Tom Andrews (USA) | 46.00 |
| 1978 | Maurice Peoples (USA) | 45.78 |
| 1979 | El Kasheef Hassan (Sudan) | 45.82 |

## 880 YARDS

| | | min | sec |
|---|---|---|---|
| 1880 | Samuel Holman | 2 | 00.4 |
| 1881 | Sidney Baker | 2 | 02.2 |
| 1882 | Walter George | 1 | 58.2 |
| 1883 | William Birkett | 1 | 58.0 |
| 1884 | Walter George | 2 | 02.2 |
| 1885 | Lawrence Myers (USA) | 2 | 01.0 |
| 1886 | ED Robinson | 1 | 59.0 |
| 1887 | Francis Cross | 1 | 59.0 |
| 1888 | Alfred Le Maitre | 2 | 00.2 |
| 1889 | Lenox Tindall | 1 | 56.4 |
| 1890 | TT Pitman | 1 | 58.4 |
| 1891 | WJ Holmes | 2 | 00.8 |
| 1892 | WJ Holmes | 2 | 00.0 |
| 1893 | Edgar Bredin | 1 | 55.3 |
| 1894 | Edgar Bredin | 1 | 56.8 |
| 1895 | Edgar Bredin | 1 | 55.8 |
| 1896 | AW de C. King | 2 | 01.4 |
| 1897 | Albert Relf | 1 | 56.2 |

1898 Alfred Tysoe 1 58.6
1899 Alfred Tysoe 1 58.6
1900 Alfred Tysoe 1 57.8
1901 Ray Cleave 1 59.6
1902 AB Manning 1 59.8
1903 Bert Blunden 1 58.8
1904 Herbert Workman 1 59.4
1905 Bert Blunden 2 02.0
1906 Arthur Astley 1 57.8
1907 Ian Fairbairn-Crawford 1 59.6
1908 Theodore Just 1 58.2
1909 Hans Braun (Germany) 1 57.6
1910 Jim Hill 2 01.4
1911 Hans Braun (Germany) 1 59.8
1912 Hans Braun (Germany) 1 58.2
1913 Edvin Wide (Sweden) 2 00.6
1914 Homer Baker (USA) 1 54.4
1919 Albert Hill 1 55.2
1920 Bevil Rudd (S. Africa) 1 55.8
1921 Edgar Mountain 1 56.8
1922 Edgar Mountain 1 55.6
1923 Cecil Griffiths 1 56.6
1924 Hyla Stallard 1 54.6
1925 Cecil Griffiths 1 57.2
1926 Otto Peltzer (Germany) 1 51.6
1927 Douglas Lowe 1 54.6
1928 Douglas Lowe 1 56.6
1929 Cyril Ellis 1 54.6
1930 Thomas Hampson 1 53.2
1931 Thomas Hampson 1 54.8
1932 Thomas Hampson 1 56.4
1933 Cliff Whitehead 1 54.0
1934 Jack Cooper 1 56.6
1935 James Stothard 1 53.3
1936 John Powell 1 54.7
1937 Arthur Collyer 1 53.3
1938 Arthur Collyer 1 53.7
1939 Godfrey Brown 1 55.1
1946 Arthur Wint (Jamaica) 1 54.8
1947 Thomas White 1 53.8
1948 John Parlett 1 52.2
1949 John Parlett 1 53.7
1950 Arthur Wint (Jamaica) 1 51.6
1951 Arthur Wint (Jamaica) 1 49.6
1952 Roger Bannister 1 51.5
1953 Brian Hewson 1 54.2
1954 Brian Hewson 1 52.2
1955 Derek Johnson 1 51.4
1956 Michael Rawson 1 51.3
1957 Ron Delany (Ireland) 1 49.6
1958 Brian Hewson 1 48.3
1959 Brian Hewson 1 52.0
1960 Thomas Farrell 1 49.3
1961 George Kerr (Jamaica) 1 51.5
1962 Cary Weisiger (USA) 1 50.1
1963 Noel Carroll (Ireland) 1 50.3
1964 William Crothers (Canada) 1 50.1
1965 Thomas Farrell (USA) 1 49.5
1966 Noel Carroll (Ireland) 1 48.0
1967 John Boulter 1 47.3
1968 Noel Carroll (Ireland) 1 50.0

## 800 METRES

min sec
1969 David Cropper 1 49.0
1970 Andrew Carter 1 49.6
1971 Peter Browne 1 47.5
1972 Andrew Carter 1 48.2
1973 Andrew Carter 1 45.1
1974 Steven Ovett 1 46.8
1975 Steven Ovett 1 46.1
1976 Steven Ovett 1 47.3
1977 Milovan Savic (Yugoslavia) 1 46.3
1978 Tom McLean (USA) 1 48.5
1979 Steve Scott (USA) 1 47.3

## MILE

min sec
1880 Walter George 4 28.6
1881 Bernhard Wise (Australia) 4 24.4
1882 Walter George 4 32.8
1883 William Snook 4 25.8
1884 Walter George 4 18.4
1885 William Snook 4 44.0
1886 Thomas Nalder 4 25.8
1887 Francis Cross 4 25.4
1888 Thomas Conneff (USA) 4 31.6
1889 James Kibblewhite 4 29.8
1890 James Kibblewhite 4 23.2
1891 James Kibblewhite 4 28.6
1892 Harold Wade 4 19.2
1893 Frederick Bacon 4 22.2
1894 Frederick Bacon 4 25.8
1895 Frederick Bacon 4 17.0
1896 Benson Lawford 4 31.4
1897 Alfred Tysoe 4 27.0
1898 Hugh Welsh 4 17.2
1899 Hugh Welsh 4 25.0
1900 Charles Bennett 4 28.2
1901 Francis Cockshott 4 21.4
1902 Joseph Binks 4 16.8
1903 Alfred Shrubb 4 24.0
1904 Alfred Shrubb 4 22.0
1905 George Butterfield 4 25.2
1906 George Butterfield 4 18.4
1907 George Butterfield 4 22.4
1908 Harold Wilson 4 20.2
1909 Edward Owen 4 23.0
1910 Emil Voigt 4 26.2
1911 Douglas McNicol 4 22.2
1912 Edward Owen 4 21.4
1913 John Zander (Sweden) 4 25.8
1914 George Hutson 4 22.0
1919 Albert Hill 4 21.2
1920 Armand Burtin (France) 4 23.0
1921 Albert Hill 4 13.8
1922 Duncan McPhee 4 27.4
1923 Hyla Stallard 4 21.6
1924 William Seagrove 4 21.2
1925 Bernard McDonald 4 18.0
1926 Georges Baraton (France) 4 17.4
1927 Cyril Ellis 4 17.0
1928 Cyril Ellis 4 20.8
1929 Cyril Ellis 4 22.0
1930 Reginald Thomas 4 15.2
1931 Reginald Thomas 4 16.4
1932 'Jerry' Cornes 4 14.2
1933 Reginald Thomas 4 14.2
1934 Jack Lovelock (New Zealand) 4 26.6
1935 Sydney Wooderson 4 17.2
1936 Sydney Wooderson 4 15.0
1937 Sydney Wooderson 4 12.2
1938 Sydney Wooderson 4 13.4
1939 Sydney Wooderson 4 11.8
1946 Douglas Wilson 4 17.4
1947 Sandor Garay (Hungary) 4 10.6
1948 William Nankeville 4 14.2
1949 William Nankeville 4 08.8
1950 William Nankeville 4 12.2
1951 Roger Bannister 4 07.8
1952 William Nankeville 4 09.8
1953 Roger Bannister 4 05.2
1954 Roger Bannister 4 07.6
1955 Brian Hewson 4 05.4
1956 Kenneth Wood 4 06.8
1957 Brian Hewson 4 06.7
1958 Graham Everett 4 06.4
1959 Kenneth Wood 4 08.1
1960 László Tabori (Hungary/USA) 4 01.0
1961 Michel Bernard (France) 4 05.8
1962 Stanley Taylor 4 04.8
1963 Alan Simpson 4 04.9
1964 Alan Simpson 4 01.1
1965 Alan Simpson 4 01.9
1966 John Camien (USA) 4 01.1
1967 Andrew Green 4 00.6
1968 John Whetton 4 06.0

## 1500 METRES

min sec
1969 Frank Murphy (Ireland) 3 40.9
1970 Walter Wilkinson 3 45.3
1971 Anthony Polhill (New Zealand) 3 40.3
1972 Peter Stewart 3 38.2

| | | |
|---|---|---|
| 1973 | Rod Dixon (New Zealand) | 3 39.0 |
| 1974 | Anthony Waldrop (USA) | 3 41.9 |
| 1975 | Daniel Malan (S. Africa) | 3 38.1 |
| 1976 | Rod Dixon (New Zealand) | 3 41.4 |
| 1977 | Eamonn Coghlan (Ireland) | 3 43.0 |
| 1978 | David Moorcroft | 3 42.9 |
| 1979 | Steve Ovett | 3 39.1 |

### 3 MILES

| | | min sec |
|---|---|---|
| 1932 | Walter Beavers | 14 23.2 |
| 1933 | Lauri Lehtinen (Finland) | 14 09.2 |
| 1934 | Janusz Kusocinski (Poland) | 14 13.6 |
| 1935 | Aubrey Reeve | 14 38.0 |
| 1936 | Peter Ward | 14 15.8 |
| 1937 | Peter Ward | 14 19.8 |
| 1938 | John Emery | 14 21.0 |
| 1939 | John Emery | 14 08.0 |
| 1946 | Sydney Wooderson | 13 53.2 |
| 1947 | Jeff Lataster (Netherlands) | 14 20.0 |
| 1948 | Willem Slijkhuis (Netherlands) | 14 07.0 |
| 1949 | John Joe Barry (Ireland) | 14 11.0 |
| 1950 | Lucien Theys (Belgium) | 14 09.0 |
| 1951 | Roy Beckett | 14 02.6 |
| 1952 | Christopher Chataway | 13 59.6 |
| 1953 | Gordon Pirie | 13 43.4 |
| 1954 | Frederick Green | 13 32.2 |
| 1955 | Christopher Chataway | 13 33.6 |
| 1956 | Derek Ibbotson | 13 32.6 |
| 1957 | Derek Ibbotson | 13 20.8 |
| 1958 | Stanley Eldon | 13 22.4 |
| 1959 | Bruce Tulloh | 13 31.2 |
| 1960 | Frank Salvat | 13 33.0 |
| 1961 | Gordon Pirie | 13 31.2 |
| 1962 | Bruce Tulloh | 13 16.0 |
| 1963 | Bruce Tulloh | 13 23.8 |
| 1964 | Lech Boguszewicz (Poland) | 13 24.4 |
| 1965 | Ronald Clarke (Australia) | 12 52.4 |
| 1966 | Ronald Clarke (Australia) | 12 58.2 |
| 1967 | Ronald Clarke (Australia) | 12 59.6 |
| 1968 | Lachie Stewart | 13 28.4 |

### 5000 METRES

| | | min sec |
|---|---|---|
| 1969 | Ian Stewart | 13 39.8 |
| 1970 | Christopher Stewart | 13 49.6 |
| 1971 | Michael Baxter | 13 39.6 |
| 1972 | David Bedford | 13 17.2 |
| 1973 | Brendan Foster | 13 23.8 |
| 1974 | Brendan Foster | 13 27.4 |
| 1975 | Marty Liquori (USA) | 13 32.6 |
| 1976 | Brendan Foster | 13 33.0 |
| 1977 | David Black | 13 33.2 |
| 1978 | Henry Rono (Kenya) | 13 20.8 |
| 1979 | Eamonn Coghlan (Ireland) | 13 23.6 |

### 4 MILES

| | | min sec |
|---|---|---|
| 1880 | Walter George | 20 45.8 |
| 1881 | George Nehan | 20 26.2 |
| 1882 | Walter George | ran-over |
| 1883 | William Snook | 20 37.0 |
| 1884 | Walter George | 20 12.8 |
| 1885 | William Snook | 20 51.8 |
| 1886 | C. Rogers | 21 01.8 |
| 1887 | Edward Carter | 21 10.0 |
| 1888 | Edward Parry | 20 22.2 |
| 1889 | Sidney Thomas | 20 31.8 |
| 1890 | James Kibblewhite | 20 16.4 |
| 1891 | William Morton | 20 53.6 |
| 1892 | James Kibblewhite | 19 50.6 |
| 1893 | Charles Pearce | 20 12.6 |
| 1894 | Frederick Bacon | 19 48.8 |
| 1895 | Henry Munro | 19 49.4 |
| 1896 | Henry Harrison | 20 27.4 |
| 1897 | Charles Bennett | 20 52.6 |
| 1898 | Charles Bennett | 20 14.4 |
| 1899 | Charles Bennett | 20 49.6 |
| 1900 | John Rimmer | 20 11.0 |
| 1901 | Alfred Shrubb | 20 01.8 |
| 1902 | Alfred Shrubb | 20 01.4 |
| 1903 | Alfred Shrubb | 20 06.0 |
| 1904 | Alfred Shrubb | 19 56.8 |
| 1905 | J. Smith | 21 08.8 |
| 1906 | Frederick Hulford | 20 27.4 |
| 1907 | Alex Duncan | 19 51.4 |
| 1908 | Emil Voigt | 19 47.4 |
| 1909 | Emil Voigt | 19 57.6 |
| 1910 | Albert Hill | 20 00.6 |
| 1911 | Hannes Kolehmainen (Finland) | 20 03.6 |
| 1912 | George Hutson | 20 10.8 |
| 1913 | George Hutson | 19 32.0 |
| 1914 | George Hutson | 19 41.4 |
| 1919 | Erik Backman (Sweden) | 19 56.4 |
| 1920 | Charles Blewitt | 20 10.8 |
| 1921 | Wal Monk | 19 59.2 |
| 1922 | Paavo Nurmi (Finland) | 19 52.2 |
| 1923 | Charles Blewitt | 19 56.6 |
| 1924 | William Cotterell | 19 45.6 |
| 1925 | Charles Blewitt | 19 54.6 |
| 1926 | Jack Webster | 19 49.6 |
| 1927 | Bror Ohrn (Sweden) | 19 40.8 |
| 1928 | Walter Beavers | 19 41.6 |
| 1929 | Walter Beavers | 19 49.4 |
| 1930 | Lauri Virtanen (Finland) | 19 36.2 |
| 1931 | Alec Burns | 19 49.4 |

### 6 MILES

| | | min sec |
|---|---|---|
| 1932 | John Potts | 30 23.2 |
| 1933 | Jack Holden | 30 32.2 |
| 1934 | Jack Holden | 30 43.8 |
| 1935 | Jack Holden | 30 50.6 |
| 1936 | Józef Noji (Poland) | 29 43.4 |
| 1937 | János Kelen (Hungary) | 30 07.8 |
| 1938 | Giuseppe Beviacqua (Italy) | 30 06.0 |
| 1939 | Sam Palmer | 30 06.4 |
| 1946 | James Peters | 30 50.4 |
| 1947 | Anthony Chivers | 30 31.4 |
| 1948 | Stanley Cox | 30 08.4 |
| 1949 | Valdu Lillakas (ex-Estonia) | 30 15.0 |
| 1950 | Frank Aaron | 29 33.6 |
| 1951 | Gordon Pirie | 29 32.0 |
| 1952 | Gordon Pirie | 28 55.6 |
| 1953 | Gordon Pirie | 28 19.4 |
| 1954 | Peter Driver | 28 34.8 |
| 1955 | Kenneth Norris | 29 00.6 |
| 1956 | Kenneth Norris | 28 13.6 |
| 1957 | George Knight | 28 50.4 |
| 1958 | Stanley Eldon | 28 05.0 |
| 1959 | Stanley Eldon | 28 12.4 |
| 1960 | Gordon Pirie | 28 09.6 |
| 1961 | David Power (Australia) | 27 57.8 |
| 1962 | Roy Fowler | 27 49.8 |
| 1963 | Ronald Hill | 27 49.8 |
| 1964 | Michael Bullivant | 27 26.6 |
| 1965 | Muhamed Gammoudi (Tunisia) | 27 38.2 |
| 1966 | Muhamed Gammoudi (Tunisia) | 27 23.4 |
| 1967 | Jurgen Haase (E. Germany) | 27 33.2 |
| 1968 | Timothy Johnston | 27 22.2 |

### 10 000 METRES

| | | min sec |
|---|---|---|
| 1969 | Richard Taylor | 28 27.6 |
| 1970 | David Bedford | 28 26.4 |
| 1971 | David Bedford | 27 47.0 |
| 1972 | David Bedford | 27 52.8 |
| 1973 | David Bedford | 27 30.8 |
| 1974 | David Bedford | 28 14.8 |
| 1975 | David Black | 27 54.2 |
| 1976 | Gerard Tebroke (Netherlands) | 28 04.0 |
| 1977 | Brendan Foster | 27 45.7 |
| 1978 | Brendan Foster | 27 30.3 |
| 1979 | John Treacy (Ireland) | 28 12.1 |

### 10 MILES

|  |  | min sec |
|---|---|---|
| 1880 | Charles Mason | 56 07.0 |
| 1881 | George Dunning | 54 34.0 |
| 1882 | Walter George | 54 41.0 |
| 1883 | William Snook | 57 41.0 |
| 1884 | Walter George | 54 02.0 |
| 1885 | William Snook | 53 25.2 |
| 1886 | William Coad | 55 44.2 |
| 1887 | Edward Carter | 55 09.0 |
| 1888 | Edward Parry | 53 43.4 |
| 1889 | Sidney Thomas | 51 31.4 |
| 1890 | James Kibblewhite | 53 49.0 |
| 1891 | William Morton | 52 33.8 |
| 1892 | Sidney Thomas | 53 25.2 |
| 1893 | Sidney Thomas | 52 41.4 |
| 1894 | Sidney Thomas | 51 37.0 |
| 1895 | Frederick Bacon | 52 43.8 |
| 1896 | George Crossland | 52 05.0 |
| 1897 | Alfred Tysoe | 55 59.6 |
| 1898 | Sidney Robinson | 53 12.0 |
| 1899 | Charles Bennett | 54 18.4 |
| 1900 | Sidney Robinson | 53 14.4 |
| 1901 | Alfred Shrubb | 53 32.0 |
| 1902 | Alfred Shrubb | 52 25.4 |
| 1903 | Alfred Shrubb | 51 55.8 |
| 1904 | Alfred Shrubb | 54 30.4 |
| 1905 | Albert Aldridge | 51 49.0 |
| 1906 | Albert Aldridge | 54 07.2 |
| 1907 | A. Underwood | 54 03.0 |
| 1908 | Alex Duncan | 53 40.4 |
| 1909 | Edward Wood | 52 40.0 |
| 1910 | Francis O'Neill (Ireland) | 52 41.4 |
| 1911 | Walter Scott | 52 26.4 |
| 1912 | Walter Scott | 52 35.0 |
| 1913 | Ernest Glover | 51 56.8 |
| 1914 | Tom Fennah | 53 33.4 |
| 1919 | Charles Blewitt | 53 45.6 |
| 1920 | Charles Clibbon | 53 53.4 |
| 1921 | Halland Britton | 54 58.2 |
| 1922 | Halland Britton | 53 24.2 |
| 1923 | Ernest Harper | 53 34.6 |
| 1924 | Halland Britton | 52 48.8 |
| 1925 | Jack Webster | 52 32.6 |
| 1926 | Ernest Harper | 52 04.0 |
| 1927 | Ernest Harper | 52 21.2 |
| 1928 | Jack Webster | 52 16.2 |
| 1929 | Ernest Harper | 52 15.8 |
| 1930 | Jack Winfield | 53 05.4 |
| 1931 | Jack Winfield | 54 34.4 |
| 1932 | Jimmy Wood | 52 00.2 |
| 1933 | George Bailey | 50 51.0 |
| 1934 | Jack Holden | 52 21.4 |
| 1935 | Frank Marsland | 54 38.6 |
| 1936 | William Eaton | 50 30.8 |
| 1937 | Reg Walker | 52 33.8 |
| 1938 | Reg Draper | 52 40.6 |
| 1939 | Jean Chapelle (Belgium) | 51 56.0 |
| 1947 | James Peters | 53 21.0 |
| 1958 | Frederick Norris | 49 39.0 |
| 1959 | Frederick Norris | 48 32.4 |
| 1960 | Basil Heatley | 48 18.4 |
| 1961 | Basil Heatley | 47 47.0 |
| 1962 | Leonard Edelen (USA) | 48 31.8 |
| 1963 | Melvyn Batty | 48 13.4 |
| 1964 | Melvyn Batty | 47 26.8 |
| 1965 | Ronald Hill | 48 56.0 |
| 1966 | Ronald Hill | 50 04.0 |
| 1967 | Ronald Hill | 47 38.6 |
| 1968 | Ronald Hill | 47 02.2 |
| 1969 | Ronald Hill | 47 27.0 |
| 1970 | Trevor Wright | 47 20.2 |
| 1971 | Trevor Wright | 46 51.6 |
| 1972 | Bernard Plain | 48 25.8 |

### MARATHON

|  |  | hr min sec |
|---|---|---|
| 1925 | Samuel Ferris | 2 35 58.2 |
| 1926 | Samuel Ferris | 2 42 24.2 |
| 1927 | Samuel Ferris | 2 40 32.2 |
| 1928 | Harry Payne | 2 34 34.0 |
| 1929 | Harry Payne | 2 30 57.6 |
| 1930 | Duncan McLeod Wright | 2 38 29.4 |
| 1931 | Duncan McLeod Wright | 2 49 54.2 |
| 1932 | Donald McNab Robertson | 2 34 32.6 |
| 1933 | Donald McNab Robertson | 2 43 13.6 |
| 1934 | Donald McNab Robertson | 2 41 55.0 |
| 1935 | Arthur Norris | 3 02 57.8 |
| 1936 | Donald McNab Robertson | 2 35 02.4 |
| 1937 | Donald McNab Robertson | 2 37 19.2 |
| 1938 | Jack Beman | 2 36 39.6 |
| 1939 | Donald McNab Robertson | 2 35 37.0 |
| 1946 | Squire Yarrow | 2 43 14.4 |
| 1947 | Jack Holden | 2 33 20.2 |
| 1948 | Jack Holden | 2 36 44.6 |
| 1949 | Jack Holden | 2 34 10.6 |
| 1950 | Jack Holden | 2 31 03.4 |
| 1951 | James Peters | 2 31 42.6 |
| 1952 | James Peters | 2 20 42.2 |
| 1953 | James Peters | 2 22 29.0 |
| 1954 | James Peters | 2 17 39.4 |
| 1955 | Robert McMinnis | 2 39 35.0 |
| 1956 | Harry Hicks | 2 26 15.0 |
| 1957 | Edward Kirkup | 2 22 27.8 |
| 1958 | Colin Kemball | 2 22 27.4 |
| 1959 | Christopher Fleming-Smith | 2 30 11.6 |
| 1960 | Brian Kilby | 2 22 48.8 |
| 1961 | Brian Kilby | 2 24 37.0 |
| 1962 | Brian Kilby | 2 26 15.0 |
| 1963 | Brian Kilby | 2 16 45.0 |
| 1964 | Brian Kilby | 2 23 01.0 |
| 1965 | William Adcocks | 2 16 50.0 |
| 1966 | Graham Taylor | 2 19 04.0 |
| 1967 | James Alder | 2 16 08.0 |
| 1968 | Timothy Johnston | 2 15 26.0 |
| 1969 | Ronald Hill | 2 13 42.0 |
| 1970 | Donald Faircloth | 2 18 15.0 |
| 1971 | Ronald Hill | 2 12 39.0 |
| 1972 | Lutz Philipp (W. Germany) | 2 12 50.0 |
| 1973 | Ian Thompson | 2 12 40.0 |
| 1974 | Akio Usami (Japan) | 2 15 16.0 |
| 1975 | Jeffrey Norman | 2 15 50.0 |
| 1976 | Barry Watson | 2 15 08.0 |
| 1977 | David Cannon | 2 15 02.0 |
| 1978 | Anthony Simmons | 2 12 33.0 |
| 1979 | Gregory Hannon | 2 13 06.0 |

### STEEPLECHASE (DISTANCE VARIED)

|  |  |
|---|---|
| 1880 | James Concannon |
| 1881 | John Ogden |
| 1882 | Thomas Crellin |
| 1883 | Thomas Thornton |
| 1884 | William Snook |
| 1885 | William Snook |
| 1886 | MA Harrison |
| 1887 | MA Harrison |
| 1888 | JC Cope |
| 1889 | Tom White |
| 1890 | William Parry |
| 1891 | William Parry |
| 1892 | WH Smith |
| 1893 | George Martin |
| 1894 | Alfred George |
| 1895 | Edwin Wilkins |
| 1896 | Sidney Robinson |
| 1897 | George Lee |
| 1898 | George Orton (Canada/USA) |
| 1899 | W. Stokes |
| 1900 | Sidney Robinson |
| 1901 | Sidney Robinson |
| 1902 | George Martin |
| 1903 | Sidney Robinson |
| 1904 | Arthur Russell |
| 1905 | Arthur Russell |
| 1906 | Arthur Russell |
| 1907 | Joseph English |
| 1908 | Reginald Noakes |
| 1909 | Reginald Noakes |
| 1910 | Joseph English |

| | | |
|---|---|---|
| 1911 | Reginald Noakes | |
| 1912 | Sydney Frost | |

## 2 MILES STEEPLECHASE

| | | min sec |
|---|---|---|
| 1913 | Charles Ruffell | 11 03.6 |
| 1914 | Sydney Frost | 11 10.6 |
| 1919 | Percy Hodge | 11 53.6 |
| 1920 | Percy Hodge | 11 22.8 |
| 1921 | Percy Hodge | 10 57.2 |
| 1922 | Paavo Nurmi (Finland) | 11 11.2 |
| 1923 | Percy Hodge | 11 13.6 |
| 1924 | Charles Blewitt | 11 02.0 |
| 1925 | Jack Webster | 11 01.4 |
| 1926 | Jack Webster | 10 34.2 |
| 1927 | Jack Webster | 11 06.0 |
| 1928 | Jack Webster | 10 44.8 |
| 1929 | Horace Oliver | 10 53.2 |
| 1930 | George Bailey | 10 55.4 |
| 1931 | Thomas Evenson | 10 36.4 |
| 1932 | Thomas Evenson | 10 13.8 |
| 1933 | Volmari Iso-Hollo (Finland) | 10 06.6 |
| 1934 | Stanley Scarsbrook | 10 48.4 |
| 1935 | George Bailey | 10 20.4 |
| 1936 | Thomas Evenson | 10 24.8 |
| 1937 | William Wylie | 10 27.0 |
| 1938 | John Potts | 10 39.2 |
| 1939 | Jean Chapelle (Belgium) | 10 22.4 |
| 1946 | Marcel Vandewattyne (Belgium) | 10 27.6 |
| 1947 | Laszló Hires (Hungary) | 10 39.3 |
| 1948 | Thomas Curry | 10 31.8 |
| 1949 | Frederick Holt | 10 29.0 |
| 1950 | Petar Segedin (Yugoslavia) | 10 02.4 |
| 1951 | Petar Segedin (Yugoslavia) | 9 58.6 |
| 1952 | John Disley | 9 44.0 |
| 1953 | Edward Ellis | 10 02.8 |

## 3000 METRES STEEPLECHASE

| | | min sec |
|---|---|---|
| 1954 | Kenneth Johnson | 9 00.8 |
| 1955 | John Disley | 8 56.6 |
| 1956 | Eric Shirley | 8 51.6 |
| 1957 | John Disley | 8 56.8 |
| 1958 | Eric Shirley | 8 51.0 |
| 1959 | Maurice Herriott | 8 52.8 |
| 1960 | Eric Shirley | 8 51.0 |
| 1961 | Maurice Herriott | 8 53.6 |
| 1962 | Maurice Herriott | 8 43.8 |
| 1963 | Maurice Herriott | 8 47.8 |
| 1964 | Maurice Herriott | 8 40.0 |
| 1965 | Maurice Herriott | 8 41.0 |
| 1966 | Maurice Herriott | 8 37.0 |
| 1967 | Maurice Herriott | 8 33.8 |
| 1968 | Gareth Bryan-Jones | 8 36.2 |
| 1969 | John Jackson | 8 35.0 |
| 1970 | Andrew Holden | 8 38.0 |
| 1971 | Andrew Holden | 8 38.0 |
| 1972 | Stephen Hollings | 8 31.2 |
| 1973 | Stephen Hollings | 8 30.8 |
| 1974 | John Davies | 8 26.8 |
| 1975 | Anthony Staynings | 8 30.0 |
| 1976 | Anthony Staynings | 8 34.6 |
| 1977 | Dennis Coates | 8 28.3 |
| 1978 | Dennis Coates | 8 34.4 |
| 1979 | Hilary Tuwei (Kenya) | 8 23.7 |

## 120 YARDS HURDLES

| | | sec |
|---|---|---|
| 1880 | George Lawrence | 16.4 |
| 1881 | George Lawrence | 16.2 |
| 1882 | Samuel Palmer | 16.6 |
| 1883 | Samuel Palmer | 16.2 |
| 1884 | CW Gowthorpe | 16.6 |
| 1885 | Charles Daft | 16.6 |
| 1886 | Charles Daft | 16.0 |
| 1887 | John Le Fleming | 16.2 |
| 1888 | Sherard Joyce | 16.0 |
| 1889 | CW Haward | 16.4 |
| 1890 | Charles Daft | 16.8 |
| 1891 | Daniel Bulger (Ireland) | 16.6 |
| 1892 | Daniel Bulger (Ireland) | 16.0 |
| 1893 | Godfrey Shaw | 16.4 |
| 1894 | Godfrey Shaw | 16.6 |
| 1895 | Godfrey Shaw | 15.8 |
| 1896 | Godfrey Shaw | 15.6 |
| 1897 | Alfred Trafford | 17.4 |
| 1898 | HR Parkes | 16.4 |
| 1899 | William Paget-Tomlinson | 16.4 |
| 1900 | Alvin Kraenzlein (USA) | 15.4 |
| 1901 | Alvin Kraenzlein (USA) | 15.6 |
| 1902 | George Smith (New Zealand) | 16.0 |
| 1903 | George Garnier | 15.8 |
| 1904 | Robert Stronach | 16.0 |
| 1905 | Robert Stronach | 16.8 |
| 1906 | Robert Stronach | 16.6 |
| 1907 | Oswald Groenings | 16.8 |
| 1908 | Vincent Duncker (S. Africa) | 16.2 |
| 1909 | AH Healey | 15.8 |
| 1910 | Gerard Anderson | 16.0 |
| 1911 | Percy Phillips | 16.2 |
| 1912 | Gerard Anderson | 15.6 |
| 1913 | George Gray | 16.0 |
| 1914 | George Gray | 15.8 |
| 1919 | Harry Wilson (New Zealand) | 15.8 |
| 1920 | George Trowbridge (USA) | 15.4 |
| 1921 | Henri Bernard (France) | 15.8 |
| 1922 | Frederick Gaby | 15.6 |
| 1923 | Frederick Gaby | 15.2 |
| 1924 | Sydney Atkinson (S. Africa) | 15.1 |
| 1925 | Frederick Gaby | 15.2 |
| 1926 | Frederick Gaby | 15.1 |
| 1927 | Frederick Gaby | 14.9 |
| 1928 | Sydney Atkinson (S. Africa) | 14.7 |
| 1929 | Lord Burghley | 15.4 |
| 1930 | Lord Burghley | 15.2 |
| 1931 | Lord Burghley | 14.8 |
| 1932 | Donald Finlay | 14.9 |
| 1933 | Donald Finlay | 15.0 |
| 1934 | Donald Finlay | 14.8 |
| 1935 | Donald Finlay | 15.0 |
| 1936 | Donald Finlay | 14.6 |
| 1937 | Donald Finlay | 14.5 |
| 1938 | Donald Finlay | 14.4 |
| 1939 | Reindert Jan Brasser (Netherlands) | 14.7 |
| 1946 | 'Pol' Braekman (Belgium) | 14.9 |
| 1947 | 'Pol' Braekman (Belgium) | 14.9 |
| 1948 | Joseph Birrell | 15.1 |
| 1949 | Donald Finlay | 14.6 |
| 1950 | Peter Hildreth | 15.2 |
| 1951 | John Parker | 14.8 |
| 1952 | Ray Weinberg (Australia) | 14.4 |
| 1953 | Peter Hildreth | 14.6 |
| 1954 | John Parker | 14.7 |
| 1955 | John Parker | 14.6 |
| 1956 | Peter Hildreth | 14.5 |
| 1957 | Eamonn Kinsella (Ireland) | 14.7 |
| 1958 | Keith Gardner (Jamaica) | 14.1 |
| 1959 | Victor Matthews | 14.5 |
| 1960 | Ghulam Raziq (Pakistan) | 14.6 |
| 1961 | Nereo Svara (Italy) | 14.4 |
| 1962 | Blaine Lindgren (USA) | 14.2 |
| 1963 | Laurence Taitt | 14.1 |
| 1964 | Michael Parker | 14.2 |
| 1965 | Laurence Taitt | 14.3 |
| 1966 | David Hemery | 14.0 |
| 1967 | Eddy Ottoz (Italy) | 14.0 |
| 1968 | Alan Pascoe | 14.1 |

## 110 METRES HURDLES

| | | sec |
|---|---|---|
| 1969 | Willem Coetzee (S. Africa) | 14.0 |
| 1970 | David Hemery | 13.9 |
| 1971 | Alan Pascoe | 14.5 |
| 1972 | Alan Pascoe | 13.9 |
| 1973 | Berwyn Price | 14.1 |
| 1974 | Berwyn Price | 13.9 |
| 1975 | Berwyn Price | 13.94 |
| 1976 | Berwyn Price | 13.80 |
| 1977 | Berwyn Price | 14.17 |
| 1978 | Berwyn Price | 14.14 |
| 1979 | Mark Holtom | 13.78 |

## 220 YARDS HURDLES

| | | sec |
|---|---|---|
| 1952 | Peter Hildreth | 24.6 |
| 1953 | Harry Whittle | 24.2 |
| 1954 | Peter Hildreth | 24.6 |
| 1955 | Paul Vine | 23.7 |
| 1956 | Paul Vine | 24.5 |
| 1957 | John Scott-Oldfield | 24.2 |
| 1958 | Kenneth Wilmshurst | 24.3 |
| 1959 | John Metcalf | 23.8 |
| 1960 | Christopher Surety | 24.9 |
| 1961 | Salvatore Morale (Italy) | 23.9 |
| 1962 | Blaine Lindgren (USA) | 23.9 |

## 440 YARDS HURDLES

| | | sec |
|---|---|---|
| 1914 | Joseph English | 59.8 |
| 1919 | George Gray | 59.8 |
| 1920 | EW Wheller | 57.4 |
| 1921 | Carl-Axel Christiernsson (Sweden) | 55.4 |
| 1922 | Wilfred Kent-Hughes | 59.0 |
| 1923 | LH Phillips | 58.0 |
| 1924 | Wilfred Tatham | 57.6 |
| 1925 | Ivan Riley (USA) | 57.8 |
| 1926 | Lord Burghley | 55.0 |
| 1927 | Lord Burghley | 54.2 |
| 1928 | Lord Burghley | 54.0 |
| 1929 | Luigi Facelli (Italy) | 53.4 |
| 1930 | Lord Burghley | 53.8 |
| 1931 | Luigi Facelli (Italy) | 54.6 |
| 1932 | Lord Burghley | 54.4 |
| 1933 | Luigi Facelli (Italy) | 55.6 |
| 1934 | Ralph Brown | 55.4 |
| 1935 | Alan Hunter | 55.3 |
| 1936 | John Sheffield | 55.6 |
| 1937 | Jules Bosmans (Belgium) | 55.0 |
| 1938 | Jules Bosmans (Belgium) | 54.1 |
| 1939 | Jules Bosmans (Belgium) | 54.9 |
| 1946 | Ronald Ede | 57.0 |
| 1947 | Harry Whittle | 55.0 |
| 1948 | Harry Whittle | 54.9 |
| 1949 | Harry Whittle | 54.9 |
| 1950 | Harry Whittle | 55.2 |
| 1951 | Harry Whittle | 54.2 |
| 1952 | Harry Whittle | 53.3 |
| 1953 | Harry Whittle | 52.7 |
| 1954 | Harry Kane | 53.4 |
| 1955 | Robert Shaw | 52.2 |
| 1956 | Ilie Savel (Rumania) | 52.2 |
| 1957 | Thomas Farrell | 52.1 |
| 1958 | David Lean (Australia) | 51.2 |
| 1959 | Christopher Goudge | 52.7 |
| 1960 | Maxwell Boyes | 52.2 |
| 1961 | Jussi Rintamaki (Finland) | 51.5 |
| 1962 | Russ Rogers (USA) | 51.0 |
| 1963 | Willie Atterberry (USA) | 51.2 |
| 1964 | John Cooper | 51.1 |
| 1965 | 'Rex' Cawley (USA) | 50.9 |
| 1966 | John Sherwood | 51.1 |
| 1967 | John Sherwood | 50.9 |
| 1968 | David Hemery | 50.2 |

## 400 METRES HURDLES

| | | sec |
|---|---|---|
| 1969 | John Sherwood | 50.1 |
| 1970 | Robert Roberts | 52.4 |
| 1971 | John Sherwood | 51.4 |
| 1972 | David Hemery | 49.7 |
| 1973 | Alan Pascoe | 49.8 |
| 1974 | James Bolding (USA) | 49.1 |
| 1975 | William Hartley | 49.65 |
| 1976 | Alan Pascoe | 49.57 |
| 1977 | Richard Graybehl (USA) | 49.96 |
| 1978 | Alan Pascoe | 50.34 |
| 1979 | Edwin Moses (USA) | 48.58 |

## HIGH JUMP

| | | metres |
|---|---|---|
| 1880 | John Parsons | 1.77 |
| 1881 | Patrick Davin (Ireland) | 1.84 |
| 1882 | RF Houghton | 1.71 |
| 1883 | John Parsons | 1.83 |
| 1884 | Thomas Ray | 1.70 |
| 1885 | Patrick Kelly (Ireland) | 1.80 |
| 1886 | George Rowdon | 1.81 |
| 1887 | George Rowdon and William Byrd Page (USA) | 1.83 |
| 1888 | George Rowdon | 1.72 |
| 1889 | Thomas Jennings | 1.74 |
| 1890 | CW Haward | 1.74 |
| 1891 | Thomas Jennings | 1.76 |
| 1892 | Arthur Watkinson | 1.74 |
| 1893 | James Ryan (Ireland) | 1.89 |
| 1894 | Reg Williams | 1.76 |
| 1895 | James Ryan (Ireland) | 1.81 |
| 1896 | Murty O'Brien (Ireland) | 1.80 |
| 1897 | CEH Leggatt | 1.75 |
| 1898 | Patrick Leahy (Ireland) | 1.82 |
| 1899 | Patrick Leahy (Ireland) | 1.78 |
| 1900 | Irving Baxter (USA) | 1.88 |
| 1901 | Irving Baxter (USA) | 1.80 |
| 1902 | Samuel Jones (USA) | 1.90 |
| 1903 | Peter O'Connor (Ireland) | 1.72 |
| 1904 | Peter O'Connor (Ireland), RG Murray and John Milne | 1.76 |
| 1905 | Con Leahy (Ireland) | 1.78 |
| 1906 | Con Leahy (Ireland) | 1.83 |
| 1907 | Con Leahy (Ireland) | 1.83 |
| 1908 | Con Leahy (Ireland) | 1.80 |
| 1909 | JH Banks | 1.75 |
| 1910 | Howard Baker | 1.74 |
| 1911 | Robert Pasemann (Germany) | 1.83 |
| 1912 | Howard Baker | 1.83 |
| 1913 | Howard Baker | 1.83 |
| 1914 | Wesley Oler (USA) | 1.89 |
| 1919 | Howard Baker | 1.80 |
| 1920 | Howard Baker | 1.92 |
| 1921 | Howard Baker | 1.88 |
| 1922 | Pierre Lewden (France) | 1.80 |
| 1923 | Pierre Lewden (France) | 1.93 |
| 1924 | Larry Stanley (Ireland) | 1.86 |
| 1925 | Harold Osborn (USA) | 1.93 |
| 1926 | Carl van Geyzel | 1.85 |
| 1927 | Herbert Adolfsson (Sweden) | 1.83 |
| 1928 | Claude Ménard (France) | 1.90 |
| 1929 | Kalman Kesmarki (Hungary) | 1.90 |
| 1930 | Colin Gordon | 1.85 |
| 1931 | Arthur Gray | 1.83 |
| 1932 | William Land | 1.85 |
| 1933 | Mihály Bodosi (Hungary) | 1.90 |
| 1934 | Mihály Bodosi (Hungary) | 1.90 |
| 1935 | Stanley West | 1.90 |
| 1936 | John Metcalfe (Australia) | 1.85 |
| 1937 | John Newman | 1.88 |
| 1938 | Richard O'Rafferty (Ireland) | 1.85 |
| 1939 | John Newman | 1.88 |
| 1946 | Alan Paterson | 1.88 |
| 1947 | Prince Adegboyega Adedoyin (Nigeria) | 1.93 |
| 1948 | John Winter (Australia) | 1.93 |
| 1949 | Alan Paterson | 1.93 |
| 1950 | Alan Paterson | 1.93 |
| 1951 | Ronald Pavitt | 1.95 |
| 1952 | Ronald Pavitt | 1.93 |
| 1953 | Derek Cox | 1.90 |
| 1954 | Brendan O'Reilly (Ireland) | 1.95 |
| 1955 | William Piper | 1.90 |
| 1956 | Ion Sòter (Rumania) | 1.93 |
| 1957 | Oladipo Okuwobi (Nigeria) | 1.95 |
| 1958 | Patrick Etolu (Uganda) | 2.03 |
| 1959 | Crawford Fairbrother | 2.00 |
| 1960 | Richard Kotei (Ghana) | 2.08 |
| 1961 | Crawford Fairbrother | 2.05 |
| 1962 | Kuniyoshi Sugioka (Japan) | 2.09 |
| 1963 | Kuniyoshi Sugioka (Japan) | 2.03 |
| 1964 | Crawford Fairbrother | 2.03 |
| 1965 | Kjell-Åke Nilsson (Sweden) | 2.03 |
| 1966 | Joseph Kadiri (Nigeria) | 1.98 |
| 1967 | Elridge Lansdell (S. Africa) | 2.00 |
| 1968 | Dan Mendenhall (USA) | 2.08 |
| 1969 | Kenneth Lundmark (Sweden) | 2.10 |
| 1970 | Hidehiko Tomizawa (Japan) | 2.08 |
| 1971 | Michael Campbell | 2.04 |
| 1972 | Milan Jarmrich (West Germany) | 2.08 |

| | | |
|---|---|---|
| 1973 | Chris Dunn (USA) | 2.06 |
| 1974 | Dwight Stones (USA) | 2.14 |
| 1975 | Reinhard Schiel (S. Africa) | 2.10 |
| 1976 | Milton Palmer | 2.06 |
| 1977 | Alan Dainton | 2.14 |
| 1978 | Franklin Jacobs (USA) | 2.20 |
| 1979 | Takao Sakamoto (Japan) | 2.15 |

### POLE VAULT

| | | metres |
|---|---|---|
| 1880 | Edward Strachan | 3.15 |
| 1881 | Thomas Ray | 3.43 |
| 1882 | Thomas Ray | 3.20 |
| 1883 | HJ Cobbold | 2.89 |
| 1884 | Thomas Ray | 3.15 |
| 1885 | Thomas Ray | 3.05 |
| 1886 | Thomas Ray | 3.34 |
| 1887 | Thomas Ray | 3.38 |
| 1888 | Lat Stones and Thomas Ray | 3.36 |
| 1889 | Lat Stones | 3.39 |
| 1890 | Richard Dickinson | 3.35 |
| 1891 | R. Watson | 3.43 |
| 1892 | R. Watson and Richard Dickinson | 3.35 |
| 1893 | Richard Dickinson | 3.40 |
| 1894 | Richard Dickinson | 3.32 |
| 1895 | Richard Dickinson | 3.05 |
| 1896 | RE Foreshaw | 3.05 |
| 1897 | James Poole | 3.01 |
| 1898 | James Poole | 3.12 |
| 1899 | EC Pritchard | 2.77 |
| 1900 | Bascom Johnson (USA) | 3.45 |
| 1901 | Irving Baxter (USA) and WH Hodgson | 2.99 |
| 1902 | Jakab Kauser (Hungary) | 3.25 |
| 1903 | S. Morriss (Germany) | 2.59 |
| 1904 | André Puységur (France) | 3.20 |
| 1905 | Fernand Gonder (France) | 3.10 |
| 1906 | AEA Harragin (Trinidad) | 3.15 |
| 1907 | Bruno Soderstrom (Sweden) | 3.20 |
| 1908 | Ed Archibald (Canada) | 3.66 |
| 1909 | Alfred Flaxman | 2.93 |
| 1910 | Kalman Szathmary (Hungary) | 3.54 |
| 1911 | Robert Pasemann (Germany) | 3.66 |
| 1912 | Owen Conquest | 2.91 |
| 1913 | Claes Gille (Sweden) | 3.68 |
| 1914 | Richard Sjöberg (Sweden) | 3.40 |
| 1919 | Georg Högström (Sweden) | 3.35 |
| 1920 | André Franquenelle (France) | 3.20 |
| 1921 | Ernfrid Rydberg (Sweden) | 3.72 |
| 1922 | Charles Hoff (Norway) | 3.66 |
| 1923 | Pierre Lewden (France) | jump-over |
| 1924 | DJR Sumner (Australia) | 3.12 |
| 1925 | PW Jones (USA) | 3.50 |
| 1926 | FJ Kelley (USA) | 3.66 |
| 1927 | Henry Lindblad (Sweden) | 3.81 |
| 1928 | FJ Kelley (USA) | 3.83 |
| 1929 | Howard Ford | 3.58 |
| 1930 | Henry Lindblad (Sweden) and A. Van De Zee (Netherlands) | 3.66 |
| 1931 | Henry Lindblad (Sweden) and A. Van De Zee (Netherlands) | 3.81 |
| 1932 | Patrick Ogilvie | 3.66 |
| 1933 | Danilo Innocenti (Italy) | 3.81 |
| 1934 | Frank Phillipson | 3.73 |
| 1935 | Keith Brown (USA) | 4.21 |
| 1936 | Richard Webster | 3.88 |
| 1937 | John Dodd | 3.66 |
| 1938 | Mario Romeo (Italy) | 3.96 |
| 1939 | Richard Webster | 3.73 |
| 1946 | Cor Lamoree (Netherlands) | 3.91 |
| 1947 | Zaltán Zitvay (Hungary) | 3.81 |
| 1948 | Richard Webster | 3.73 |
| 1949 | Paul Harwood (USA) | 3.81 |
| 1950 | Rudy Stjernild (Denmark) | 3.81 |
| 1951 | Turfi Bryngeirsson (Iceland) | 4.04 |
| 1952 | Geoffrey Elliott | 3.96 |
| 1953 | Geoffrey Elliott | 4.11 |
| 1954 | Tämás Homonnay (Hungary) | 4.26 |
| 1955 | Geoffrey Elliott | 4.11 |
| 1956 | Ian Ward | 3.96 |
| 1957 | Ian Ward | 4.09 |
| 1958 | Mervyn Richards (New Zealand) | 4.11 |
| 1959 | Allah Ditta (Pakistan) | 4.11 |
| 1960 | Rex Porter | 4.11 |
| 1961 | Risto Ankio (Finland) | 4.42 |
| 1962 | Pentti Nikula (Finland) | 4.65 |
| 1963 | John Pennel (USA) | 5.10 |
| 1964 | Fred Hansen (USA) | 4.57 |
| 1965 | Paul Wilson (USA) | 4.72 |
| 1966 | Michael Bull | 4.57 |
| 1967 | Michael Bull | 4.57 |
| 1968 | Renato Dionisi (Italy) | 5.03 |
| 1969 | Michael Bull | 4.73 |
| 1970 | Kiyoshi Niwa (Japan) | 5.00 |
| 1971 | Michael Bull | 5.05 |
| 1972 | Michael Bull | 5.21 |
| 1973 | Brian Hooper | 5.16 |
| 1974 | Casey Carrigan (USA) | 5.10 |
| 1975 | Raymond Boyd (Australia) | 5.00 |
| 1976 | Mike Tully (USA) | 5.33 |
| 1977 | Larry Jessee (USA) | 5.30 |
| 1978 | Robert Pullard (USA) | 5.40 |
| 1979 | Mike Tully (USA) | 5.45 |

### LONG JUMP

| | | metres |
|---|---|---|
| 1880 | Charles Lockton | 6.75 |
| 1881 | Patrick Davin (Ireland) | 6.98 |
| 1882 | Thomas Malone (Ireland) | 6.64 |
| 1883 | John Parsons | 7.01 |
| 1884 | Ernest Horwood | 6.63 |
| 1885 | John Purcell (Ireland) | 6.67 |
| 1886 | John Purcell (Ireland) | 6.81 |
| 1887 | Francis Roberts | 6.81 |
| 1888 | Alexander Jordan (USA) | 6.62 |
| 1889 | Daniel Bulger (Ireland) | 6.55 |
| 1890 | RG Hogarth | 6.09 |
| 1891 | Daniel Bulger (Ireland) and Malcolm Ford (USA) | 6.20 |
| 1892 | Daniel Bulger (Ireland) | 6.51 |
| 1893 | Terence Donovan (Ireland) | 6.68 |
| 1894 | Terence Donovan (Ireland) | 6.30 |
| 1895 | William Oakley | 6.56 |
| 1896 | CEH Leggatt | 7.03 |
| 1897 | CEH Leggatt | 6.50 |
| 1898 | Walter Newburn (Ireland) | 7.19 |
| 1899 | Walter Newburn (Ireland) | 6.75 |
| 1900 | Alvin Kraenzlein (USA) | 6.96 |
| 1901 | Peter O'Connor (Ireland) | 7.22 |
| 1902 | Peter O'Connor (Ireland) | 7.20 |
| 1903 | Peter O'Connor (Ireland) | 6.95 |
| 1904 | Peter O'Connor (Ireland) | 7.07 |
| 1905 | Peter O'Connor (Ireland) | 7.25 |
| 1906 | Peter O'Connor (Ireland) | 7.15 |
| 1907 | Denis Murray (Ireland) | 6.70 |
| 1908 | Wilfred Bleaden | 6.79 |
| 1909 | Timothy Ahearne (Ireland) | 6.81 |
| 1910 | Percy Kirwan (Ireland) | 6.72 |
| 1911 | Percy Kirwan (Ireland) | 7.15 |
| 1912 | Percy Kirwan (Ireland) | 7.07 |
| 1913 | Sidney Abrahams | 6.86 |
| 1914 | Philip Kingsford | 7.09 |
| 1919 | Wilhelm Bjornemann (Sweden) | 7.18 |
| 1920 | Donald Lowrie (USA) | 6.81 |
| 1921 | HC Taylor (USA) | 6.73 |
| 1922 | Charles Hoff (Norway) | 7.08 |
| 1923 | Harold Abrahams | 7.23 |
| 1924 | Harold Abrahams | 6.92 |
| 1925 | Richard St J. Honner (Australia) | 7.30 |
| 1926 | Richard St J. Honner (Australia) | 7.21 |
| 1927 | Rudolf Dobermann (Germany) | 7.31 |
| 1928 | Hannes De Boer (Netherlands) | 7.37 |
| 1929 | James Cohen | 6.88 |
| 1930 | Olle Hallberg (Sweden) | 7.36 |
| 1931 | Hannes De Boer (Netherlands) | 7.21 |
| 1932 | Robert Evans (S. Africa) | 7.06 |
| 1933 | Lajos Balogh (Hungary) | 7.07 |
| 1934 | Robert Paul (France) | 7.03 |
| 1935 | Robert Paul (France) | 7.28 |
| 1936 | George Traynor | 7.07 |
| 1937 | Luz Long (Germany) | 7.48 |
| 1938 | Arturo Maffei (Italy) | 7.52 |
| 1939 | William Breach | 7.21 |

| | | |
|---|---|---|
| 1946 | Denis Watts | 7.11 |
| 1947 | Harry Whittle | 7.25 |
| 1948 | Theo Bruce (Australia) | 7.25 |
| 1949 | Harry Whittle | 7.15 |
| 1950 | Harry Askew | 7.07 |
| 1951 | Sylvanus Williams (Nigeria) | 7.05 |
| 1952 | Sylvanus Williams (Nigeria) | 7.32 |
| 1953 | Karim Olowu (Nigeria) | 7.15 |
| 1954 | Ödon Földessy (Hungary) | 7.48 |
| 1955 | Karim Olowu (Nigeria) | 7.36 |
| 1956 | Roy Cruttenden | 7.25 |
| 1957 | Roy Cruttenden | 7.26 |
| 1958 | Karim Olowu (Nigeria) | 7.28 |
| 1959 | David Whyte | 7.24 |
| 1960 | Frederick Alsop | 7.19 |
| 1961 | John Oladitan (Nigeria) | 7.41 |
| 1962 | Jorma Valkama (Finland) | 7.65 |
| 1963 | Frederick Alsop | 7.52 |
| 1964 | Lynn Davies | 7.95 |
| 1965 | Frederick Alsop | 7.38 |
| 1966 | Lynn Davies | 8.06 |
| 1967 | Lynn Davies | 7.93 |
| 1968 | Lynn Davies | 7.94 |
| 1969 | Lynn Davies | 7.62 |
| 1970 | Alan Lerwill | 7.64 |
| 1971 | Henry Hines (USA) | 8.01 |
| 1972 | Alan Lerwill | 8.15 |
| 1973 | Geoffrey Hignett | 7.37 |
| 1974 | Alan Lerwill | 7.77 |
| 1975 | Alan Lerwill | 7.77 |
| 1976 | Roy Mitchell | 7.93 |
| 1977 | Daley Thompson | 7.52 |
| 1978 | Roy Mitchell | 7.76 |
| 1979 | Ronald Desruelles (Belgium) | 7.95 |

## TRIPLE JUMP

| | | metres |
|---|---|---|
| 1914 | Ivar Sahlin (Sweden) | 14.03 |
| 1920 | Charles Lively | 14.11 |
| 1921 | Folke Jansson (Sweden) | 14.19 |
| 1922 | Vilho Tuulos (Finland) | 14.27 |
| 1923 | John Odde | 14.13 |
| 1924 | Jack Higginson | 13.99 |
| 1925 | Ellmer Somfay (Hungary) | 14.29 |
| 1926 | Jack Higginson | 13.87 |
| 1927 | Willem Peters (Netherlands) | 15.47 |
| 1928 | Willem Peters (Netherlands) | 14.91 |
| 1929 | Willem Peters (Netherlands) | 14.22 |
| 1930 | Willem Peters (Netherlands) | 15.10 |
| 1931 | Jan Blankers (Netherlands) | 14.22 |
| 1932 | Arthur Gray | 13.82 |
| 1933 | Jan Blankers (Netherlands) | 14.69 |
| 1934 | Edmond Boyce | 14.55 |
| 1935 | Willem Peters (Netherlands) | 14.29 |
| 1936 | John Metcalfe (Australia) | 15.07 |
| 1937 | Willem Peters (Netherlands) | 14.32 |
| 1938 | Edward Boyce | 14.06 |
| 1939 | Ioannis Palamiotis (Greece) | 15.03 |
| 1946 | Denis Watts | 14.29 |
| 1947 | Denis Watts | 14.25 |
| 1948 | George Avery (Australia) | 14.15 |
| 1949 | Henk Van Egmond (Netherlands) | 14.32 |
| 1950 | Sidney Cross | 14.26 |
| 1951 | Sidney Cross | 14.32 |
| 1952 | Willi Burgard (Saar) | 14.59 |
| 1953 | Kenneth Wilmshurst | 14.36 |
| 1954 | Kenneth Wilmshurst | 14.87 |
| 1955 | Kenneth Wilmshurst | 15.17 |
| 1956 | Kenneth Wilmshurst | 15.16 |
| 1957 | Kenneth Wilmshurst | 14.86 |
| 1958 | David Norris (New Zealand) | 15.64 |
| 1959 | John Whall | 15.00 |
| 1960 | Frederick Alsop | 15.44 |
| 1961 | Frederick Alsop | 15.37 |
| 1962 | Tomio Ota (Japan) | 15.66 |
| 1963 | Koji Sakurai (Japan) | 15.63 |
| 1964 | Frederick Alsop | 15.92 |
| 1965 | Frederick Alsop | 15.88 |
| 1966 | Józef Szmidt (Poland) | 15.99 |
| 1967 | Frederick Alsop | 15.67 |
| 1968 | Serban Ciochina (Rumania) | 16.03 |
| 1969 | Anthony Wadhams | 15.66 |
| 1970 | Masato Muraki (Japan) | 15.91 |
| 1971 | Anthony Wadhams | 15.16 |
| 1972 | David Johnson | 15.80 |
| 1973 | Anthony Wadhams | 15.76 |
| 1974 | Toshiaki Inoue (Japan) | 16.12 |
| 1975 | Michael McGrath (Australia) | 16.12 |
| 1976 | Aston Moore | 16.30 |
| 1977 | David Johnson | 16.07 |
| 1978 | Aston Moore | 16.68 |
| 1979 | Keith Connor | 15.87 |

## SHOT

| | | metres |
|---|---|---|
| 1880 | William Winthrop | 11.35 |
| 1881 | Maurice Davin (Ireland) | 12.05 |
| 1882 | George Ross | 12.90 |
| 1883 | Owen Harte (Ireland) | 12.52 |
| 1884 | Owen Harte (Ireland) | 12.14 |
| 1885 | Donald Mackinnon | 13.12 |
| 1886 | James Mitchell (Ireland) | 11.61 |
| 1887 | James Mitchell (Ireland) | 11.92 |
| 1888 | George Gray (Canada) | 13.28 |
| 1889 | William Barry (Ireland) and RA Greene | 12.09 |
| 1890 | RA Greene | 11.48 |
| 1891 | William Barry (Ireland) | 12.39 |
| 1892 | William Barry (Ireland) | 13.07 |
| 1893 | Denis Horgan (Ireland) | 13.03 |
| 1894 | Denis Horgan (Ireland) | 12.90 |
| 1895 | Denis Horgan (Ireland) | 13.50 |
| 1896 | Denis Horgan (Ireland) | 13.24 |
| 1897 | Denis Horgan (Ireland) | 13.82 |
| 1898 | Denis Horgan (Ireland) | 13.71 |
| 1899 | Denis Horgan (Ireland) | 14.03 |
| 1900 | Richard Sheldon (USA) | 13.98 |
| 1901 | Wesley Coe (USA) | 13.85 |
| 1902 | Wesley Coe (USA) | 13.07 |
| 1903 | Thomas Nicolson | 12.38 |
| 1904 | Denis Horgan (Ireland) | 13.76 |
| 1905 | Denis Horgan (Ireland) | 13.55 |
| 1906 | Tom Kirkwood | 13.83 |
| 1907 | Tom Kirkwood | 13.46 |
| 1908 | Denis Horgan (Ireland) | 13.59 |
| 1909 | Denis Horgan (Ireland) | 13.43 |
| 1910 | Denis Horgan (Ireland) | 13.03 |
| 1911 | John Barrett (Ireland) | 13.23 |
| 1912 | Denis Horgan (Ireland) | 13.66 |
| 1913 | Einar Nilsson (Sweden) | 14.44 |
| 1914 | Armas Taipale (Finland) | 13.60 |
| 1919 | Bertil Jansson (Sweden) | 12.98 |
| 1920 | Simon Paoli (France) | 13.36 |
| 1921 | Bertil Jansson (Sweden) | 14.08 |
| 1922 | Ville Pörhölä (Finland) | 14.58 |
| 1923 | John Barrett (Ireland) | 11.95 |
| 1924 | 'Rex' Salisbury Woods | 13.36 |
| 1925 | Herb Schwarze (USA) | 14.40 |
| 1926 | 'Rex' Salisbury Woods | 13.69 |
| 1927 | Georg Brechenmacher (Germany) | 14.18 |
| 1928 | Edouard Duhour (France) | 14.45 |
| 1929 | József Daranyi (Hungary) | 14.20 |
| 1930 | Jules Noel (France) | 13.76 |
| 1931 | József Daranyi (Hungary) | 15.23 |
| 1932 | Harry Hart (S. Africa) | 14.77 |
| 1933 | Zygmunt Heljasz (Poland) | 15.75 |
| 1934 | Zygmunt Heljasz (Poland) | 14.89 |
| 1935 | Aad De Bruyn (Netherlands) | 14.88 |
| 1936 | Aad De Bruyn (Netherlands) | 14.08 |
| 1937 | Hans Wöllke (Germany) | 15.39 |
| 1938 | Angiolo Profeti (Italy) | 14.06 |
| 1939 | Aad De Bruyn (Netherlands) | 14.79 |
| 1946 | Aad De Bruyn (Netherlands) | 13.31 |
| 1947 | David Guiney (Ireland) | 14.48 |
| 1948 | David Guiney (Ireland) | 14.41 |
| 1949 | John Giles | 14.13 |
| 1950 | Petar Sarcević (Yugoslavia) | 15.23 |
| 1951 | Gunnar Huseby (Iceland) | 15.87 |
| 1952 | John Savidge | 16.50 |
| 1953 | John Savidge | 16.17 |
| 1954 | John Savidge | 15.54 |
| 1955 | Barclay Palmer | 15.11 |
| 1956 | Barclay Palmer | 16.51 |
| 1957 | Arthur Rowe | 16.38 |
| 1958 | Arthur Rowe | 17.30 |
| 1959 | Arthur Rowe | 17.95 |

| | | |
|---|---|---|
| 1960 | Arthur Rowe | 18.04 |
| 1961 | Arthur Rowe | 18.58 |
| 1962 | Jay Silvester (USA) | 18.18 |
| 1963 | Michael Lindsay | 17.64 |
| 1964 | Vilmos Varju (Hungary) | 18.84 |
| 1965 | Vilmos Varju (Hungary) | 19.02 |
| 1966 | Johannes Botha (S. Africa) | 17.14 |
| 1967 | David Booysen (S. Africa) | 17.79 |
| 1968 | Jeffrey Teale | 17.74 |
| 1969 | Jeffrey Teale | 18.32 |
| 1970 | Leslie Mills (New Zealand) | 18.66 |
| 1971 | Leslie Mills (New Zealand) | 19.27 |
| 1972 | Geoffrey Capes | 19.47 |
| 1973 | Geoffrey Capes | 20.27 |
| 1974 | Al Feuerbach (USA) | 21.37 |
| 1975 | Geoffrey Capes | 20.20 |
| 1976 | Geoffrey Capes | 20.92 |
| 1977 | Geoffrey Capes | 20.70 |
| 1978 | Geoffrey Capes | 19.94 |
| 1979 | Geoffrey Capes | 19.39 |

## DISCUS

| | | metres |
|---|---|---|
| 1914 | Armas Taipale (Finland) | 44.04 |
| 1920 | Patrick Quinn (Ireland) | 37.62 |
| 1921 | Oscar Zallhagen (Sweden) | 41.00 |
| 1922 | Vilho Nittyman (Finland) | 41.64 |
| 1923 | GT Mitchell | 33.60 |
| 1924 | Patrick Bermingham (Ireland) | 41.18 |
| 1925 | Patrick Bermingham (Ireland) | 42.24 |
| 1926 | Patrick Bermingham (Ireland) | 43.38 |
| 1927 | Kalman Marvalits (Hungary) | 44.40 |
| 1928 | Ernst Paulus (Germany) | 44.80 |
| 1929 | Harald Stenerud (Norway) | 43.54 |
| 1930 | Jules Noel (France) | 44.66 |
| 1931 | Endre Madarasz (Hungary) | 43.10 |
| 1932 | Patrick Bermingham (Ireland) | 42.44 |
| 1933 | Endre Madarasz (Hungary) | 44.18 |
| 1934 | Patrick Bermingham (Ireland) | 41.28 |
| 1935 | Harald Andersson (Sweden) | 51.82 |
| 1936 | Bernar Prendergast (Jamaica) | 43.10 |
| 1937 | Nicolaus Syllas (Greece) | 49.18 |
| 1938 | Adolfo Consolini (Italy) | 43.60 |
| 1939 | Nicolaus Syllas (Greece) | 49.12 |
| 1946 | Jan Brasser (Netherlands) | 43.58 |
| 1947 | Jan Brasser (Netherlands) | 43.76 |
| 1948 | Cummin Clancy (Ireland) | 42.22 |
| 1949 | Ferenc Klics (Hungary) | 47.66 |
| 1950 | Raymond Kintziger (Belgium) | 46.74 |
| 1951 | Giuseppe Tosi (Italy) | 53.58 |
| 1952 | Mark Pharaoh | 44.70 |
| 1953 | Mark Pharaoh | 47.66 |
| 1954 | Ferenc Klics (Hungary) | 51.34 |
| 1955 | Mark Pharaoh | 47.72 |
| 1956 | Mark Pharaoh | 50.02 |
| 1957 | Michael Lindsay | 50.76 |
| 1958 | Stephanus du Plessis (S. Africa) | 52.22 |
| 1959 | Michael Lindsay | 53.54 |
| 1960 | Michael Lindsay | 52.62 |
| 1961 | Elfranco Malan (S. Africa) | 56.04 |
| 1962 | Jay Silvester (USA) | 60.84 |
| 1963 | David Weill (USA) | 53.90 |
| 1964 | Roy Hollingsworth (Trinidad) | 54.82 |
| 1965 | Lars Haglund (Sweden) | 53.94 |
| 1966 | William Tancred | 51.76 |
| 1967 | William Tancred | 51.74 |
| 1968 | William Tancred | 53.06 |
| 1969 | William Tancred | 53.08 |
| 1970 | William Tancred | 53.88 |
| 1971 | Leslie Mills (New Zealand) | 58.62 |
| 1972 | William Tancred | 61.06 |
| 1973 | William Tancred | 61.22 |
| 1974 | John Powell (USA) | 62.06 |
| 1975 | John van Reenen (S. Africa) | 62.26 |
| 1976 | John Powell (USA) | 65.52 |
| 1977 | Peter Tancred | 57.58 |
| 1978 | Peter Tancred | 55.78 |
| 1979 | John Powell (USA) | 61.50 |

## HAMMER

| | | metres |
|---|---|---|
| 1880 | Walter Lawrence | 29.26 |
| 1881 | Maurice Davin (Ireland) | 30.12 |
| 1882 | Edmund Baddeley | 29.36 |
| 1883 | John Gruer | 30.84 |
| 1884 | Owen Harte (Ireland) | 25.42 |
| 1885 | William Barry (Ireland) | 33.18 |
| 1886 | James Mitchell (Ireland) | 33.64 |
| 1887 | James Mitchell (Ireland) | 37.80 |
| 1888 | James Mitchell (Ireland) | 38.00 |
| 1889 | William Barry (Ireland) | 39.62 |
| 1890 | R. Lindsay | 31.14 |
| 1891 | Charles Queckberner (USA) | 39.58 |
| 1892 | William Barry (Ireland) | 40.62 |
| 1893 | Denis Carey (Ireland) | 37.60 |
| 1894 | William Barry (Ireland) | 38.62 |
| 1895 | William Barry (Ireland) | 40.52 |
| 1896 | John Flanagan (USA) | 40.22 |
| 1897 | Thomas Kiely (Ireland) | 43.42 |
| 1898 | Thomas Kiely (Ireland) | 42.70 |
| 1899 | Thomas Kiely (Ireland) | 41.56 |
| 1900 | John Flanagan (USA) | 49.78 |
| 1901 | Thomas Kiely (Ireland) | 45.28 |
| 1902 | Thomas Kiely (Ireland) | 43.52 |
| 1903 | Thomas Nicolson | 43.46 |
| 1904 | Thomas Nicolson | 47.98 |
| 1905 | Thomas Nicolson | 47.50 |
| 1906 | Henry Leeke | 37.52 |
| 1907 | Thomas Nicolson | 48.38 |
| 1908 | Simon Gillis (USA) | 50.12 |
| 1909 | Thomas Nicolson | 50.20 |
| 1910 | Alfred Flaxman | 35.80 |
| 1911 | George Putnam (USA) | 45.00 |
| 1912 | Thomas Nicolson | 49.44 |
| 1913 | Carl-Johan Lind (Sweden) | 47.42 |
| 1914 | Carl-Johan Lind (Sweden) | 49.76 |
| 1919 | Einar Midtgaard (Denmark) | 44.00 |
| 1920 | T. Speers (USA) | 42.80 |
| 1921 | Carl-Johan Lind (Sweden) | 49.36 |
| 1922 | Carl-Johan Lind (Sweden) | 52.50 |
| 1923 | Malcolm Nokes | 49.18 |
| 1924 | Malcolm Nokes | 51.12 |
| 1925 | Malcolm Nokes | 46.04 |
| 1926 | Malcolm Nokes | 48.62 |
| 1927 | Ossian Skiöld (Sweden) | 50.30 |
| 1928 | William Britton | 46.62 |
| 1929 | William Britton | 47.60 |
| 1930 | Ossian Skiöld (Sweden) | 51.14 |
| 1931 | Ossian Skiöld (Sweden) | 51.36 |
| 1932 | George Walsh (Ireland) | 43.16 |
| 1933 | William Britton | 44.96 |
| 1934 | Patrick O'Callaghan (Ireland) | 51.44 |
| 1935 | Fred Warngård (Sweden) | 44.58 |
| 1936 | Norman Drake | 46.26 |
| 1937 | Karl Hein (Germany) | 55.86 |
| 1938 | Bert Healion (Ireland) | 52.46 |
| 1939 | Bert Healion (Ireland) | 49.28 |
| 1946 | Hans Houtzager (Netherlands) | 48.48 |
| 1947 | Imre Németh (Hungary) | 53.34 |
| 1948 | Norman Drake | 49.24 |
| 1949 | Imre Németh (Hungary) | 55.60 |
| 1950 | Duncan Clark | 54.36 |
| 1951 | Teseo Taddia (Italy) | 54.00 |
| 1952 | Duncan Clark | 53.02 |
| 1953 | Donald Anthony | 53.24 |
| 1954 | József Csermák (Hungary) | 59.42 |
| 1955 | Ewan Douglas | 56.52 |
| 1956 | Peter Allday | 57.28 |
| 1957 | Michael Ellis | 60.28 |
| 1958 | Michael Ellis | 61.92 |
| 1959 | Michael Ellis | 61.28 |
| 1960 | Michael Ellis | 64.18 |
| 1961 | John Lawlor (Ireland) | 64.12 |
| 1962 | Noboru Okamoto (Japan) | 62.18 |
| 1963 | Takeo Sugawara (Japan) | 65.56 |
| 1964 | Howard Payne | 59.88 |
| 1965 | Gyula Zsivótzky (Hungary) | 68.14 |
| 1966 | Gyula Zsivótzky (Hungary) | 66.04 |
| 1967 | Edward Burke (USA) | 67.60 |
| 1968 | Lázár Lovász (Hungary) | 66.20 |
| 1969 | Howard Payne | 66.80 |
| 1970 | Howard Payne | 67.66 |
| 1971 | Howard Payne | 66.44 |

| | | |
|---|---|---|
| 1972 | Barry Williams | 67.24 |
| 1973 | Howard Payne | 67.98 |
| 1974 | Adam Barnard (S. Africa) | 70.62 |
| 1975 | Adam Barnard (S. Africa) | 73.58 |
| 1976 | Christopher Black | 72.64 |
| 1977 | Christopher Black | 69.50 |
| 1978 | Peter Farmer (Australia) | 70.72 |
| 1979 | Peter Farmer (Australia) | 70.16 |

## JAVELIN

| | | metres |
|---|---|---|
| 1914 | Mor Koczan (Hungary) | 59.72 |
| 1920 | FL Murrey (USA) | 45.64 |
| 1921 | Gunnar Lindström (Sweden) | 62.48 |
| 1922 | P. Johansson (Finland) | 61.08 |
| 1923 | 'Jock' Dalrymple | 45.34 |
| 1924 | Edward Sutherland (S. Africa) | 53.02 |
| 1925 | Béla Szepes (Hungary) | 53.92 |
| 1926 | Olav Sunde (Norway) | 61.34 |
| 1927 | Béla Szepes (Hungary) | 64.80 |
| 1928 | Stanley Lay (New Zealand) | 67.90 |
| 1929 | Béla Szepes (Hungary) | 66.70 |
| 1930 | Alberto Dominutti (Italy) | 61.60 |
| 1931 | Olav Sunde (Norway) | 60.76 |
| 1932 | Otto Jürgis (Latvia) | 64.52 |
| 1933 | WP Abell | 51.54 |
| 1934 | CG Bowen | 51.74 |
| 1935 | Lennart Atterwall (Sweden) | 65.70 |
| 1936 | JF Van Der Poll (Netherlands) | 57.66 |
| 1937 | Stanley Wilson | 59.18 |
| 1938 | Ralph Blakeway (S. Africa) | 60.08 |
| 1939 | James MacKillop | 56.88 |
| 1946 | Nico Lutkeveld (Netherlands) | 56.60 |
| 1947 | Janis Stendzenieks (ex-Latvia) | 64.20 |
| 1948 | Janis Stendzenieks (ex-Latvia) | 66.68 |
| 1949 | Antony Hignell | 56.32 |
| 1950 | Michael Denley | 58.52 |
| 1951 | Amos Metteucci (Italy) | 61.08 |
| 1952 | Michael Denley | 65.86 |
| 1953 | Michael Denley | 63.58 |
| 1954 | Maurice Morrell | 60.36 |
| 1955 | Dumitru Zamfir (Rumania) | 67.90 |
| 1956 | Peter Cullen | 65.28 |
| 1957 | Peter Cullen | 72.12 |
| 1958 | Colin Smith | 66.48 |
| 1959 | Colin Smith | 69.90 |
| 1960 | Mohammed Nawaz (Pakistan) | 76.38 |
| 1961 | Michel Macquet (France) | 77.12 |
| 1962 | John McSorley | 79.26 |
| 1963 | Colin Smith | 72.46 |
| 1964 | John FitzSimons | 74.10 |
| 1965 | David Travis | 73.76 |
| 1966 | Jorma Kinnunen (Finland) | 83.22 |
| 1967 | Barry Sanderson | 73.44 |
| 1968 | David Travis | 72.16 |
| 1969 | Wladyslaw Nikiciuk (Poland) | 85.08 |
| 1970 | David Travis | 76.90 |
| 1971 | David Travis | 77.00 |
| 1972 | David Travis | 79.62 |
| 1973 | David Travis | 73.58 |
| 1974 | David Travis | 75.20 |
| 1975 | Herman Potgieter (S. Africa) | 78.14 |
| 1976 | Peter Maync (Switzerland) | 75.16 |
| 1977 | David Ottley | 77.78 |
| 1978 | Peter Yates | 80.10 |
| 1979 | Simon Osborne | 81.68 |

## 56 lb WEIGHT

| | | metres |
|---|---|---|
| 1920 | Wesley Coe (USA) | 7.21 |

(discontinued)

## DECATHLON

| | | pts |
|---|---|---|
| 1928 | Harry Hart (S. Africa) | 6016* |
| 1937 | Jim Miggins (Ireland) | 4647* |
| 1938 | Thomas Langton-Lockton | 5513* |
| 1947 | Hans Moesgaard-Kjeldsen (Denmark) | 5965* |
| 1948 | Hans Moesgaard-Kjeldsen (Denmark) | 5794* |
| 1949 | Hans Moesgaard-Kjeldsen (Denmark) | 6138* |
| 1950 | Harry Whittle | 6087* |
| 1951 | Leslie Pinder | 5089† |
| 1952 | Leslie Pinder | 5504† |
| 1953 | Leslie Pinder | 5321† |
| 1954 | Leslie Pinder | 5415† |
| 1955 | M. Dodds | 4690† |
| 1956 | Gerald Brown (Rhodesia) | 4934† |
| 1957 | Hywel Williams | 5370† |
| 1958 | Colin Andrews | 5113† |
| 1959 | Colin Andrews | 5517† |
| 1960 | Colin Andrews | 6176† |
| 1961 | Daniel Burger (Rhodesia) | 6343† |
| 1962 | Zlatko Sumich (Australia) | 6237† |
| 1963 | Zlatko Sumich (Australia) | 6538† |
| 1964 | Derek Clarke | 6084† |
| 1965 | Norman Foster | 6840 |
| 1966 | Derek Clarke | 7001 |
| 1967 | Peter Gabbett | 6533 |
| 1968 | Peter Gabbett | 7247 |
| 1969 | Peter de Villiers (S. Africa) | 6960 |
| 1970 | Peter Gabbett | 7331 |
| 1971 | David Kidner | 6691 |
| 1972 | Barry King | 7346 |
| 1973 | David Kidner | 6969 |
| 1974 | Michael Corden | 7035 |
| 1975 | Panayiotis Zeniou | 6931 |
| 1976 | Daley Thompson | 7684 |
| 1977 | Panayiotis Zeniou | 7087 |
| 1978 | Alan Drayton | 7424 |
| 1979 | Brad McStravick | 7569 |

*Scored on 1934 Tables.
†Scored on 1950 Tables.

Note: Daley Thompson won 1975 Junior title, held in conjunction with senior, with 7008 pts.

## 2 MILES WALK

| | | min sec |
|---|---|---|
| 1901 | G. Deyermond (Ireland) | 14 17.4 |
| 1902 | William Sturgess | 14 46.6 |
| 1903 | EJ Negus | 14 34.4 |
| 1904 | George Larner | 13 57.6 |
| 1905 | George Larner | 13 50.0 |
| 1906 | Albert Yeomans | 14 20.4 |
| 1907 | Richard Harrison | 14 01.8 |
| 1908 | George Larner | 13 58.4 |
| 1909 | Ernest Webb | 13 56.4 |
| 1910 | Ernest Webb | 13 54.4 |
| 1911 | Harold Ross | 13 55.4 |
| 1912 | Robert Bridge | 13 55.4 |
| 1913 | Robert Bridge | 13 51.8 |
| 1914 | Robert Bridge | 13 57.2 |
| 1919 | Robert Bridge | 14 18.4 |
| 1920 | Charles Dowson | 14 32.0 |
| 1921 | John Evans | 14 40.2 |
| 1922 | Ugo Frigerio (Italy) | 14 30.0 |
| 1923 | Gordon Watts | 14 24.0 |
| 1924 | Reginald Goodwin | 14 11.2 |
| 1925 | Reginald Goodwin | 14 07.4 |
| 1926 | William Cowley | 14 32.4 |
| 1927 | Alfred Pope | 14 21.6 |
| 1928 | Alfred Pope | 14 04.8 |
| 1929 | Alfred Pope | 13 57.6 |
| 1930 | Cecil Hyde | 13 56.4 |
| 1931 | Alfred Pope | 13 52.6 |
| 1932 | Albert Cooper | 13 44.6 |
| 1933 | Albert Cooper | 13 39.8 |
| 1934 | Albert Cooper | 13 41.0 |
| 1935 | Albert Cooper | 13 46.6 |
| 1936 | Albert Cooper | 13 50.0 |
| 1937 | Albert Cooper | 13 58.2 |
| 1938 | Albert Cooper | 14 02.2 |
| 1939 | Harry Churcher | 13 50.0 |
| 1946 | Lars Hindmar (Sweden) | 13 59.0 |
| 1947 | Lars Hindmar (Sweden) | 13 54.4 |
| 1948 | Harry Churcher | 13 49.8 |
| 1949 | Arne Borjesson (Sweden) | 14 06.6 |
| 1950 | Roland Hardy | 13 46.8 |

| | | |
|---|---|---|
| 1951 | Roland Hardy | 13 43.2 |
| 1952 | Roland Hardy | 13 27.8 |
| 1953 | George Coleman | 14 02.2 |
| 1954 | George Coleman | 13 52.0 |
| 1955 | George Coleman | 14 01.0 |
| 1956 | Robert Goodall | 14 20.8 |
| 1957 | Stanley Vickers | 14 05.6 |
| 1958 | Stanley Vickers | 13 33.4 |
| 1959 | Kenneth Matthews | 13 19.4 |
| 1960 | Stanley Vickers | 13 02.4 |
| 1961 | Kenneth Matthews | 13 24.6 |
| 1962 | Kenneth Matthews | 13 59.0 |
| 1963 | Kenneth Matthews | 13 18.2 |
| 1964 | Kenneth Matthews | 13 22.4 |
| 1965 | Paul Nihill | 13 20.0 |
| 1966 | Ronald Wallwork | 13 35.0 |
| 1967 | Ronald Wallwork | 13 44.8 |
| 1968 | Arthur Jones | 13 35.6 |

### 3000 METRES WALK

| | | min sec |
|---|---|---|
| 1969 | Roger Mills | 12 57.0 |
| 1970 | Paul Nihill | 12 13.8 |
| 1971 | Paul Nihill | 12 08.4 |
| 1972 | Roger Mills | 12 31.6 |
| 1973 | Roger Mills | 12 16.8 |
| 1974 | Roger Mills | 12 27.0 |
| 1975 | Paul Nihill | 12 43.2 |
| 1976 | Roger Mills | 12 22.6 |
| 1977 | Roger Mills | 12 08.4 |
| 1978 | Roger Mills | 12 05.8 |
| 1979 | Roger Mills | 12 09.1 |

### 4 MILES WALK

| | | min sec |
|---|---|---|
| 1894 | Harry Curtis | 30 05.8 |
| 1895 | William Sturgess | 30 17.4 |
| 1896 | William Sturgess | 28 57.6 |
| 1897 | William Sturgess | 28 24.8 |
| 1898 | William Sturgess | 29 10.0 |
| 1899 | William Sturgess | 29 20.6 |
| 1900 | William Sturgess | 30 20.8 |

### 7 MILES WALK

| | | min sec |
|---|---|---|
| 1880 | George Beckley | 56 40.0 |
| 1881 | James Raby | 54 48.2 |
| 1882 | Henry Whyatt | 55 56.5 |
| 1883 | Henry Whyatt | 59 15.0 |
| 1884 | Henry Meek (USA) | 54 27.0 |
| 1885 | James Jervis | 56 10.6 |
| 1886 | Joseph Jullie | 56 30.2 |
| 1887 | CWV Clarke | 56 59.8 |
| 1888 | CWV Clarke | 57 08.6 |
| 1889 | William Wheeler | 56 29.4 |
| 1890 | Harry Curtis | 52 28.4 |
| 1891 | Harry Curtis | 54 00.2 |
| 1892 | Harry Curtis | 55 56.2 |
| 1893 | Harry Curtis | 56 37.2 |
| 1901 | Jack Butler | 54 37.0 |
| 1902 | William Sturgess | 52 49.4 |
| 1903 | Jack Butler | 56 17.2 |
| 1904 | George Larner | 52 57.4 |
| 1905 | George Larner | 52 34.0 |
| 1906 | Frank Carter | 53 20.2 |
| 1907 | Frederick Thompson | 52 46.6 |
| 1908 | Ernest Webb | 53 02.6 |
| 1909 | Ernest Webb | 52 37.0 |
| 1910 | Ernest Webb | 51 37.0 |
| 1911 | George Larner | 52 08.0 |
| 1912 | Robert Bridge | 52 45.6 |
| 1913 | Robert Bridge and Harold Ross | 52 08.4 |
| 1914 | Robert Bridge | 52 32.0 |
| 1919 | William Hehir | 53 23.6 |
| 1920 | Charles Dowson | 53 50.0 |
| 1921 | Harold Ross | 55 48.6 |
| 1922 | Gordon Watts | 53 24.2 |
| 1923 | Gordon Watts | 54 35.4 |
| 1924 | Reginald Goodwin | 52 00.6 |
| 1925 | Gordon Watts | 52 53.8 |
| 1926 | Reginald Goodwin | 53 56.0 |
| 1927 | William Cowley | 55 46.4 |
| 1928 | Cecil Hyde | 55 46.2 |
| 1929 | Cecil Hyde | 53 38.6 |
| 1930 | Cecil Hyde | 53 32.4 |
| 1931 | Ugo Frigerio (Italy) | 54 09.0 |
| 1932 | Alfred Pope | 51 25.4 |
| 1933 | Johnny Johnson | 52 01.6 |
| 1934 | Johnny Johnson | 52 10.4 |
| 1935 | Henry Hake | 53 48.0 |
| 1936 | Victor Stone | 52 21.2 |
| 1937 | John Mikaelsson (Sweden) | 50 19.2 |
| 1938 | John Mikaelsson (Sweden) | 51 48.2 |
| 1939 | Harry Churcher | 52 37.0 |
| 1946 | Lars Hindmar (Sweden) | 52 30.0 |
| 1947 | Harry Churcher | 52 48.4 |
| 1948 | Harry Churcher | 52 32.8 |
| 1949 | Harry Churcher | 52 41.8 |
| 1950 | Roland Hardy | 50 11.6 |
| 1951 | Roland Hardy | 51 14.6 |
| 1952 | Roland Hardy | 50 05.6 |
| 1953 | Roland Hardy | 51 47.0 |
| 1954 | George Coleman | 51 22.8 |
| 1955 | Roland Hardy | 53 04.6 |
| 1956 | George Coleman | 50 19.0 |
| 1957 | Stanley Vickers | 51 34.4 |
| 1958 | Stanley Vickers | 51 10.2 |
| 1959 | Kenneth Matthews | 50 28.8 |
| 1960 | Kenneth Matthews | 49 42.6 |
| 1961 | Kenneth Matthews | 49 43.6 |
| 1962 | Colin Williams | 52 15.0 |
| 1963 | Kenneth Matthews | 49 52.8 |
| 1964 | Kenneth Matthews | 48 23.0 |
| 1965 | Paul Nihill | 51 54.4 |
| 1966 | Paul Nihill | 50 52.0 |
| 1967 | Malcolm Tolley | 52 32.4 |
| 1968 | Paul Nihill | 51 10.4 |

### 10 000 METRES WALK

| | | min sec |
|---|---|---|
| 1969 | Paul Nihill | 44 07.0 |
| 1970 | William Sutherland | 45 16.8 |
| 1971 | Philip Embleton | 45 26.2 |
| 1972 | Philip Embleton | 44 26.8 |
| 1973 | Roger Mills | 44 38.6 |
| 1974 | Peter Marlow | 44 58.4 |
| 1975 | Brian Adams | 42 40.0 |
| 1976 | Brian Adams | 42 58.0 |
| 1977 | Brian Adams | 44 10.0 |
| 1978 | Brian Adams | 43 44.0 |
| 1979 | Brian Adams | 43 48.2 |

## AAA Relay Championships

### 1 MILE MEDLEY RELAY
**(880 yd, 220 yd, 220 yd, 440 yd)**

| | Team | min sec |
|---|---|---|
| 1911 | Blackheath Harriers | 3 33.8 |
| 1912 | Polytechnic Harriers | 3 32.2 |
| 1913 | Polytechnic Harriers | 3 34.0 |
| 1914 | Polytechnic Harriers | 3 31.6 |
| 1919 | Polytechnic Harriers | 3 37.8 |
| 1920 | Achilles Club | 3 39.6 |
| 1921 | Polytechnic Harriers | 3 35.6 |
| 1922 | Surrey AC | 3 35.2 |
| 1923 | Surrey AC | 3 36.8 |
| 1924 | Surrey AC | 3 36.2 |
| 1925 | Achilles Club | 3 35.2 |
| 1926 | Achilles Club | 3 36.2 |

### 4 × 110 YARDS RELAY

| | Team | sec |
|---|---|---|
| 1927 | CFC Preussen Krefeld (Germany) | 42.2 |
| 1928 | Frankfurter Sportgemeinde Eintracht (Germany) | 43.2 |
| 1929 | Polytechnic Harriers | 42.2 |
| 1930 | Polytechnic Harriers | 43.6 |
| 1931 | Achilles Club | 43.6 |
| 1932 | Blackheath Harriers | 43.6 |
| 1933 | SC Preussen Kreteld (Germany) | 43.0 |

| | | |
|---|---|---|
| 1934 | Budapesti Budai Torna Egylet (Hungary) | 43.0 |
| 1935 | Budapest Budai Torna Egylet (Hungary) | 42.6 |
| 1936 | ATC 'De Snelvoeters' (Netherlands) | 43.0 |
| 1937 | Blackheath Harriers | 42.9 |
| 1938 | Beracca (Italy) | 43.6 |
| 1939 | Blackheath Harriers | 43.0 |
| 1946 | South London Harriers | 44.2 |
| 1947 | South London Harriers | 43.4 |
| 1948 | Achilles Club | 43.6 |
| 1949 | Herne Hill Harriers | 42.9 |
| 1950 | Herne Hill Harriers | 42.6 |
| 1951 | KTSV Preussen 1855 (Germany) | 42.2 |
| 1952 | Polytechnic Harriers | 43.3 |
| 1953 | Polytechnic Harriers | 43.6 |
| 1954 | Belgrave Harriers | 42.6 |
| 1955 | Thames Valley Harriers | 43.5 |
| 1956 | Thames Valley Harriers | 43.0 |
| 1957 | Thames Valley Harriers | 42.9 |
| 1958 | Birchfield Harriers | 42.3 |
| 1959 | Thames Valley Harriers | 42.1 |
| 1960 | Birchfield Harriers | 42.4 |
| 1961 | Woodford Green AC | 41.5 |
| 1962 | Woodford Green AC | 41.7 |
| 1963 | Polytechnic Harriers | 41.4 |
| 1964 | Woodford Green AC | 41.7 |
| 1965 | Polytechnic Harriers | 42.4 |
| 1966 | Polytechnic Harriers | 41.4 |
| 1967 | Thames Valley Harriers | 41.7 |
| 1968 | Wolverhampton & Bilston AC | 41.9 |

### 4 × 100 METRES RELAY

| | Team | sec |
|---|---|---|
| 1969 | Warrington AC | 41.9 |
| 1970 | Warrington AC | 41.5 |
| 1971 | Wolverhampton & Bilston AC | 42.2 |
| 1972 | Wolverhampton & Bilston AC | 41.8 |
| 1973 | Warrington AC | 42.9 |
| 1974 | Thames Valley Harriers | 42.0 |
| 1977 | Wolverhampton & Bilston AC | 41.3 |

### 4 × 440 YARDS RELAY

| | Team | min | sec |
|---|---|---|---|
| 1927 | Achilles Club | 3 | 19.4 |
| 1928 | Achilles Club | 3 | 24.6 |
| 1929 | Achilles Club | 3 | 24.2 |
| 1930 | Achilles Club | 3 | 22.8 |
| 1931 | Polytechnic Harriers | 3 | 24.4 |
| 1932 | Milocarian AC | 3 | 20.8 |
| 1933 | London AC | 3 | 21.4 |
| 1934 | Milocarian AC | 3 | 18.4 |
| 1935 | London AC | 3 | 20.1 |
| 1936 | Achilles Club | 3 | 19.8 |
| 1937 | London AC | 3 | 24.8 |
| 1938 | Achilles Club | 3 | 19.4 |
| 1939 | South London Harriers | 3 | 26.2 |
| 1946 | South London Harriers | 3 | 27.4 |
| 1947 | Polytechnic Harriers | 3 | 20.6 |
| 1948 | Polytechnic Harriers | 3 | 20.8 |
| 1949 | Polytechnic Harriers | 3 | 18.0 |
| 1950 | Polytechnic Harriers | 3 | 20.4 |
| 1951 | Crefelder Sportverein (W. Germany) | 3 | 17.4 |
| 1952 | Polytechnic Harriers | 3 | 25.4 |
| 1953 | Polytechnic Harriers | 3 | 23.7 |
| 1954 | Herne Hill Harriers | 3 | 18.6 |
| 1955 | Mitcham AC | 3 | 20.6 |
| 1956 | Birchfield Harriers | 3 | 17.8 |
| 1957 | Olympischer Sportverein Horde 1931 EV (W. Germany) | 3 | 13.7 |
| 1958 | Birchfield Harriers | 3 | 15.1 |
| 1959 | Birchfield Harriers | 3 | 16.0 |
| 1960 | Birchfield Harriers | 3 | 14.0 |
| 1961 | Birchfield Harriers | 3 | 13.2 |
| 1962 | Lozells Harriers | 3 | 15.2 |
| 1963 | Birchfield Harriers | 3 | 13.0 |
| 1964 | Birchfield Harriers | 3 | 17.3 |
| 1965 | Woodford Green AC | 3 | 20.8 |
| 1966 | Polytechnic Harriers | 3 | 12.9 |
| 1967 | Thames Valley Harriers | 3 | 13.6 |
| 1968 | Wolverhampton & Bilston AC | 3 | 13.5 |

### 4 × 400 METRES RELAY

| | Team | min | sec |
|---|---|---|---|
| 1969 | Thames Valley Harriers | 3 | 13.8 |
| 1970 | Wolverhampton & Bilston AC | 3 | 11.5 |
| 1971 | Wolverhampton & Bilston AC | 3 | 15.2 |
| 1972 | Wolverhampton & Bilston AC | 3 | 13.6 |
| 1973 | Wolverhampton & Bilston AC | 3 | 16.7 |
| 1974 | Bournemouth AC | 3 | 20.8 |
| 1977 | Wolverhampton & Bilston AC | 3 | 21.3 |

### 1600 METRES MEDLEY RELAY (200 m, 200 m, 400 m, 800 m)

| | Team | min | sec |
|---|---|---|---|
| 1969 | Wolverhampton & Bilston AC | 3 | 22.3 |

### 4 × 880 YARDS RELAY

| | Team | min | sec |
|---|---|---|---|
| 1965 | N. Staffs & Stone Harriers | 7 | 30.4 |
| 1966 | N. Staffs & Stone Harriers | 7 | 31.6 |
| 1967 | Mitcham AC | 7 | 29.6 |
| 1968 | Sale Harriers | 7 | 28.4 |

### 4 × 800 METRES RELAY

| | Team | min | sec |
|---|---|---|---|
| 1969 | Sale Harriers | 7 | 26.4 |
| 1970 | Liverpool Harriers | 7 | 44.2 |

### 4 × 1 MILE RELAY

| | Team | min | sec |
|---|---|---|---|
| 1965 | Birchgrove Harriers | 16 | 59.8 |
| 1966 | Longwood Harriers | 16 | 46.2 |
| 1967 | Longwood Harriers | 17 | 02.4 |
| 1968 | Birchfield Harriers | 16 | 43.0 |

### 4 × 1500 METRES RELAY

| | Team | min | sec |
|---|---|---|---|
| 1969 | Polytechnic Harriers | 15 | 55.6 |
| 1970 | Manchester & District AC | 15 | 40.6 |
| 1971 | Liverpool Harriers | 15 | 57.6 |

## Road Running

### AAA 12-STAGE RELAY

| | |
|---|---|
| 1967 | Coventry Godiva H. |
| 1968 | Coventry Godiva H. |
| 1969 | Coventry Godiva H. |
| 1970 | Coventry Godiva H. |
| 1971 | Birchfield Harriers |
| 1972 | Tipton Harriers |
| 1973 | Birchfield Harriers |
| 1974 | Tipton Harriers |
| 1975 | Gateshead H. & AC |
| 1976 | Gateshead H. & AC |
| 1977 | Gateshead H. & AC |
| 1978 | Tipton Harriers |
| 1979 | Gateshead H. & AC |

### AAA 6-STAGE RELAY

| | |
|---|---|
| 1969 | City of Stoke AC |
| 1970 | City of Stoke AC |
| 1971 | City of Stoke AC |
| 1972 | City of Stoke AC |
| 1973 | Bolton United H. & AC |
| 1974 | Liverpool H. & AC |
| 1975 | Liverpool H. & AC |
| 1976 | Liverpool H. & AC |
| 1977 | Tipton Harriers |
| 1978 | Cambridge & Coleridge AC |

## Walking

### RWA Titles
### 10 MILES

| | | min | sec |
|---|---|---|---|
| 1947 | Harry Churcher | 81 | 23.0 |
| 1948 | Harry Churcher | 75 | 10.4 |
| 1949 | Laurence Allen | 75 | 09.0 |
| 1950 | Laurence Allen | 74 | 38.0 |
| 1951 | Laurence Allen | 75 | 41.0 |
| 1952 | Roland Hardy | 73 | 16.0 |
| 1953 | Roland Hardy | 74 | 53.4 |
| 1954 | Roland Hardy | 74 | 16.0 |
| 1955 | Roland Hardy | 74 | 47.0 |
| 1956 | Roland Hardy | 74 | 31.0 |
| 1957 | Stanley Vickers | 76 | 51.0 |
| 1958 | Stanley Vjckers | 73 | 44.0 |
| 1959* | Kenneth Matthews | 71 | 00.4 |
| 1960 | Kenneth Matthews | 70 | 57.0 |
| 1961 | Kenneth Matthews | 74 | 21.0 |
| 1962 | Kenneth Matthews | 76 | 10.0 |
| 1963 | Kenneth Matthews | 73 | 00.0 |
| 1964 | Kenneth Matthews | 70 | 22.0 |
| 1965 | Paul Nihill | 74 | 55.0 |
| 1966 | Peter McCullagh (Australia) | 74 | 05.0 |
| 1967 | Ronald Wallwork | 75 | 06.0 |
| 1968 | Paul Nihill | 72 | 28.0 |
| 1969 | Paul Nihill | 71 | 14.0 |
| 1970 | Wilfried Wesch (W. Germany) | 72 | 07.0 |
| 1971 | Philip Embleton | 69 | 29.0 |
| 1972 | Paul Nihill | 73 | 33.0 |
| 1973 | John Webb | 72 | 43.0 |
| 1974 | Peter Marlow | 72 | 58.0 |
| 1975 | Oliver Flynn | 71 | 15.0 |
| 1976 | Oliver Flynn | 69 | 59.0 |
| 1977 | Roger Mills | 72 | 36.0 |
| 1978† | Oliver Flynn | 67 | 29.0 |
| 1979 | Chris Harvey | 71 | 25.0 |

*Course about 350 yd short.
†Course about ½ mile short.

### 20 MILES

| | | hr | min | sec |
|---|---|---|---|---|
| 1908 | Harold Ross | 2 | 56 | 32 |
| 1909 | SCA Schofield | 2 | 56 | 48 |
| 1910 | Harold Ross | 2 | 53 | 45 |
| 1911 | Thomas Payne | 2 | 50 | 30 |
| 1912 | Harold Ross | 2 | 51 | 21 |
| 1913 | Harold Ross | 2 | 49 | 53 |
| 1914 | Harold Ross | 2 | 50 | 37 |
| 1920 | Harold Ross | 2 | 57 | 59 |
| 1921 | William Hehir | 2 | 58 | 56 |
| 1922 | William Hehir | 2 | 50 | 12 |
| 1923 | Fred Poynton | 2 | 51 | 35 |
| 1924 | Fred Poynton | 2 | 57 | 17 |
| 1925 | Fred Poynton | 2 | 48 | 17 |
| 1926 | No race | | | |
| 1927 | Tebbs Lloyd Johnson | 2 | 55 | 53 |
| 1928 | L. Stewart | 2 | 50 | 20 |
| 1929 | Albert Plumb | 2 | 50 | 18 |
| 1930 | Albert Plumb | 2 | 46 | 30 |
| 1931 | Tebbs Lloyd Johnson | 2 | 52 | 41 |
| 1932 | Albert Plumb | 2 | 43 | 38 |
| 1933 | Alfred Pope | 2 | 48 | 38 |
| 1934 | Tebbs Lloyd Johnson | 2 | 49 | 58 |
| 1935 | J. Medlicott | 2 | 47 | 46 |
| 1936 | Henry Hake | 2 | 47 | 23 |
| 1937 | SA Fletcher | 2 | 47 | 54 |
| 1938 | Julian Hopkins | 2 | 49 | 10 |
| 1939 | Harold Whitlock | 2 | 51 | 03 |
| 1946 | Harry Forbes | 2 | 50 | 43 |
| 1947 | Harry Forbes | 2 | 47 | 40 |
| 1948 | Rex Whitlock | 2 | 52 | 07 |
| 1949 | Laurence Allen | 2 | 51 | 18 |
| 1950 | Laurence Allen | 2 | 52 | 16 |
| 1951 | Laurence Allen | 2 | 51 | 52 |
| 1952 | John Proctor | 2 | 52 | 07 |
| 1953 | Robert Goodall | 2 | 50 | 40 |
| 1954 | Laurence Allen | 2 | 47 | 48 |
| 1955 | George Coleman | 2 | 40 | 08 |
| 1956 | Roland Hardy | 2 | 38 | 27 |
| 1957 | Eric Hall | 2 | 45 | 12 |
| 1958 | Laurence Allen | 2 | 43 | 21 |
| 1959 | Thomas Misson | 2 | 45 | 19 |
| 1960 | Stanley Vickers | 2 | 41 | 41 |
| 1961 | Donald Thompson | 2 | 44 | 49 |
| 1962 | Kenneth Matthews | 2 | 38 | 39 |
| 1963 | Paul Nihill | 2 | 39 | 43 |
| 1964 | Paul Nihill | 2 | 40 | 13 |
| 1965 | Paul Nihill | 2 | 44 | 03 |
| 1966 | Norman Read (New Zealand) | 2 | 39 | 33 |
| 1967 | Roy Lodge | 2 | 42 | 43 |
| 1968 | Paul Nihill | 2 | 35 | 07 |
| 1969 | Paul Nihill | 2 | 44 | 51 |
| 1970 | Wilfried Wesch (W. Germany) | 2 | 38 | 15 |
| 1971 | Paul Nihill | 2 | 30 | 35 |
| 1972 | John Warhurst | 2 | 35 | 19 |
| 1973 | Robert Dobson | 2 | 40 | 07 |
| 1974 | Roy Thorpe | 2 | 39 | 47 |
| 1975 | Robert Dobson | 2 | 36 | 26 |
| 1976 | Roger Mills | 2 | 32 | 13 |
| 1977 | Amos Seddon | 2 | 25 | 15 |

### 30 KILOMETRES

| | | hr | min | sec |
|---|---|---|---|---|
| 1978 | Oliver Flynn | 2 | 21 | 54 |

### 35 KILOMETRES

| | | hr | min | sec |
|---|---|---|---|---|
| 1979 | Roger Mills | 2 | 52 | 06 |

### 20 KILOMETRES

| | | hr | min | sec |
|---|---|---|---|---|
| 1965 | Paul Nihill | 1 | 33 | 33 |
| 1966 | Paul Nihill | 1 | 33 | 45 |
| 1967 | Ronald Wallwork | 1 | 37 | 21 |
| 1968 | Paul Nihill | 1 | 31 | 19 |
| 1969 | Paul Nihill | 1 | 30 | 07 |
| 1970 | Wilfried Wesch (W. Germany) | 1 | 31 | 47 |
| 1971 | Paul Nihill | 1 | 32 | 06 |
| 1972 | Paul Nihill | 1 | 28 | 45 |
| 1973 | Roger Mills | 1 | 31 | 13 |
| 1974 | Oliver Flynn | 1 | 32 | 06 |
| 1975 | Oliver Flynn | 1 | 28 | 58 |
| 1976 | Oliver Flynn | 1 | 30 | 00 |
| 1977 | Oliver Flynn | 1 | 28 | 42 |
| 1978 | Oliver Flynn | 1 | 28 | 54 |
| 1979 | Carl Lawton | 1 | 32 | 25 |

### 50 KILOMETRES

| | | hr | min | sec |
|---|---|---|---|---|
| 1930 | Thomas Green | 4 | 35 | 36 |
| 1931 | Tebbs Lloyd Johnson | 4 | 55 | 48 |
| 1932 | Francesco Pretti (Italy) | 4 | 41 | 54 |
| 1933 | Harold Whitlock | 4 | 39 | 00 |
| 1934 | Tebbs Lloyd Johnson | 4 | 36 | 30 |
| 1935 | Harold Whitlock | 4 | 39 | 08 |
| 1936 | Harold Whitlock | 4 | 30 | 38 |
| 1937 | Harold Whitlock | 4 | 38 | 43 |
| 1938 | Harold Whitlock | 4 | 43 | 01 |
| 1939 | Harold Whitlock | 4 | 40 | 43 |
| 1946 | Charles Megnin | 4 | 53 | 25 |
| 1947 | Harry Forbes | 4 | 40 | 06 |
| 1948 | Rex Whitlock | 4 | 35 | 35 |
| 1949 | Tebbs Lloyd Johnson | 4 | 51 | 50 |
| 1950 | John Proctor | 4 | 43 | 04 |
| 1951 | Donald Tunbridge | 4 | 45 | 34 |
| 1952 | Donald Tunbridge | 4 | 38 | 02 |
| 1953 | Frank Bailey | 4 | 46 | 10 |
| 1954 | John Ljunggren (Sweden) | 4 | 32 | 47 |
| 1955 | Albert Johnson | 4 | 31 | 32 |
| 1956 | Donald Thompson | 4 | 24 | 39 |
| 1957 | Donald Thompson | 4 | 41 | 48 |
| 1958 | Donald Thompson | 4 | 21 | 50 |
| 1959 | Donald Thompson | 4 | 12 | 19 |
| 1960 | Donald Thompson | 4 | 32 | 55 |

| | | |
|---|---|---|
| 1961 | Donald Thompson | 4 22 51 |
| 1962 | Donald Thompson | 4 27 26 |
| 1963 | Raymond Middleton | 4 16 43 |
| 1964 | Paul Nihill | 4 17 10 |
| 1965 | Raymond Middleton | 4 17 23 |
| 1966 | Donald Thompson | 4 28 26 |
| 1967 | Shaun Lightman | 4 26 56 |
| 1968 | Paul Nihill | 4 18 59 |
| 1969 | Brian Eley | 4 19 13 |
| 1970 | Robert Dobson | 4 20 22 |
| 1971 | Paul Nihill | 4 15 05 |
| 1972 | John Warhurst | 4 18 31 |
| 1973 | Robert Dobson | 4 14 29 |
| 1974 | Robert Dobson | 4 16 58 |
| 1975 | John Warhurst | 4 20 32 |
| 1976 | Roy Thorpe | 4 23 43 |
| 1977 | Brian Adams | 4 25 48 |
| 1978 | David Cotton | 4 14 25 |
| 1979 | Michael Parker (NZ) | 4 14 16 |

## Tug-of-War

### 90 STONE

1910 Central London Railway
1911 St. Vincent's AC, St. Helens
1913 2nd Batt. Coldstream Guards
1914 116th Batt., RFA

### 100 STONE

1923 R Division Metropolitan Police
1924 Royal Engineers (Training Batt.)
1925 Royal Engineers (Training Batt.)
1926 Royal Naval Barracks, Chatham
1927 N Division Metropolitan Police
1928 London Fire Brigade
1929 London Fire Brigade
1930 Royal Marines, Portsmouth
1931 Royal Marines, Portsmouth
1932 Royal Marines, Portsmouth
1933 Royal Marines, Portsmouth
1934 RAOC Feltham
1935 RAOC Feltham
1936 RAOC Feltham
1937 RAOC Feltham
1938 RAOC Feltham
1939 Royal Ulster Constabulary
1940–45 Not held
1946 No. 1 Central WS RANE, Ashford
1947 Wimpey, London Airport SC
1948 Wimpey, London Airport SC
1949 Wimpey, London Airport SC
1950 RAOC Feltham
1951 Wimpey, London Airport SC
1952 RAOC Feltham
1953 RAOC Feltham
1954 RAOC Feltham
1955 New Haw and Woodham
1956 New Haw and Woodham
1957 New Haw and Woodham
1958 New Haw and Woodham
1959 Hawker Aircraft
1960 Hawker Aircraft
1961 New Haw and Woodham
1962 Wood Treatment (Bosley) Limited
1963 Wood Treatment (Bosley) Limited
1964 Russell Green
1965 Russell Green
1966 Worcester Park
1967 Wood Treatment (Bosley) Limited
1968 Camberley
1969 Wood Treatment (Bosley) Limited
1970 Camberley

### 640 KG

1971 Wood Treatment (Bosley) Limited
1972 Wood Treatment (Bosley) Limited
1973 West Pinchbeck
1974 Wood Treatment (Bosley) Limited
1975 Wood Treatment (Bosley) Limited
1976 Wood Treatment (Bosley) Limited
1977 Camberley
1978 Beech Hill Blues

### CATCHWEIGHT

1911 City of London Police
1920 City of London Police
1923 City of London Police
1924 B Division Metropolitan Police
1925 Royal Engineers (Training Batt.)
1926 B Division Metropolitan Police
1927 B Division Metropolitan Police AC
1928 London Fire Brigade AA
1929 London Fire Brigade AA
1930 Luton Borough Police
1931 Royal Marines, Portsmouth
1932 Royal Marines, Portsmouth
1933 Royal Marines, Portsmouth
1934 Monmouth Constabulary
1935 Royal Ulster Constabulary
1936 Royal Ulster Constabulary
1937 Not held
1938 Royal Ulster Constabulary
1939 Royal Ulster Constabulary
1940–45 Not held
1946 Wimpey, London Airport SC
1947 Wimpey, London Airport SC
1948 Wimpey, London Airport SC
1949 Wimpey, London Airport SC
1950 Wimpey, London Airport SC
1951 Wimpey, London Airport SC
1952 RAOC Feltham
1953 RAOC Feltham
1954 RAOC Feltham
1955 RAOC Feltham
1956 New Haw and Woodham
1957 New Haw and Woodham
1958 New Haw and Woodham
1959 Wood Treatment (Bosley) Limited
1960 Wood Treatment (Bosley) Limited
1961 Wood Treatment (Bosley) Limited
1962 Wood Treatment (Bosley) Limited
1963 Wood Treatment (Bosley) Limited
1964 Wood Treatment (Bosley) Limited
1965 Wood Treatment (Bosley) Limited
1966 Wood Treatment (Bosley) Limited
1967 Wood Treatment (Bosley) Limited
1968 Wood Treatment (Bosley) Limited
1969 Wood Treatment (Bosley) Limited
1970 Wood Treatment (Bosley) Limited
1971 Wood Treatment (Bosley) Limited
1972 Wood Treatment (Bosley) Limited
1973 Wood Treatment (Bosley) Limited
1974 Wood Treatment (Bosley) Limited
1975 Wood Treatment (Bosley) Limited
1976 Wood Treatment (Bosley) Limited
1977 Wood Treatment (Bosley) Limited
1978 Wood Treatment (Bosley) Limited

## English Cross Country Championship

### INDIVIDUAL AND TEAM CHAMPIONS

| | Individual | Team |
|---|---|---|
| 1877 | Percy Stenning | Thames Hare and Hounds |
| 1878 | Percy Stenning | Spartan Harriers |
| 1879 | Percy Stenning | Thames Hare and Hounds |
| 1880 | Percy Stenning | Birchfield Harriers |
| 1881 | George Dunning | Moseley Harriers |
| 1882 | Walter G. George | Moseley Harriers |
| 1883 | George Dunning | Moseley Harriers |
| 1884 | Walter G. George | Moseley Harriers |
| 1885 | William Snook | Liverpool Harriers |
| 1886 | JE Hickman | Birchfield Harriers |
| 1887 | JE Hickman | Birchfield Harriers |

1888 Edward Parry Birchfield Harriers
1889 Edward Parry Salford Harriers
1890 Edward Parry Salford Harriers
1891 James Kibblewhite Birchfield Harriers
1892 Herbert Heath Birchfield Harriers
1893 Herbert Heath Essex Beagles
1894 George Crossland Salford Harriers
1895 S. Cottrill Birchfield Harriers
1896 George Crossland Salford Harriers
1897 Sydney J. Robinson Salford Harriers, Manchester Harriers
1898 Sydney J. Robinson Salford Harriers
1899 Charles Bennett Highgate Harriers
1900 Charles Bennett Finchley Harriers
1901 Alfred Shrubb Essex Beagles
1902 Alfred Shrubb Highgate Harriers
1903 Alfred Shrubb Birchfield Harriers
1904 Alfred Shrubb Highgate Harriers
1905 Albert Aldridge Highgate Harriers
1906 Charles Straw Sutton Harriers
1907 George Pearce Birchfield Harriers
1908 Arthur J. Robertson Hallamshire Harriers
1909 J. Murphy Birchfield Harriers
1910 Fred C. Neaves Hallamshire Harriers
1911 Fred N. Hibbins Hallamshire Harriers
1912 Fred N. Hibbins Hallamshire Harriers
1913 Ernest Glover Birchfield Harriers
1914 Charles Ruffell Surrey Athletic Club
1920* Charles Clibbon Birchfield Harriers
1921 Walter Freeman Birchfield Harriers
1922* H. Eckersley Birchfield Harriers
1923 Charles E. Blewitt Birchfield Harriers
1924 'Joe' Cotterell Birchfield Harriers
1925 'Joe' Cotterell Birchfield Harriers
1926 Jack E. Webster Birchfield Harriers
1927 Ernest Harper Hallamshire Harriers
1928 Jack E. Webster Birchfield Harriers
1929 Ernest Harper Birchfield Harriers
1930 WB Howard Birchfield Harriers
1931 John H. Potts Birchfield Harriers
1932 J. Alec Burns Birchfield Harriers
1933 Thomas Evenson Birchfield Harriers
1934 Sam Dodds Birchfield Harriers
1935 Frank Close Belgrave Harriers
1936 John H. Potts Birchfield Harriers
1937 Herbert Clark Birchfield Harriers
1938 Jack T. Holden Mitcham Athletic Club
1939 Jack T. Holden Belgrave Harriers
1946 Jack T. Holden Belgrave Harriers
1947 Archie Robertson Sutton Harriers
1948 Sydney C. Wooderson Belgrave Harriers
1949 Frank E. Aaron Sutton Harriers
1950 Frank E. Aaron Sutton Harriers
1951 Frank E. Aaron Sutton Harriers
1952 Walter Hesketh Victoria Park AAC
1953 DA Gordon Pirie Birchfield Harriers
1954 DA Gordon Pirie Bolton United Harriers
1955 DA Gordon Pirie South London Harriers
1956 Kenneth L. Norris Sheffield United Harriers
1957 Frank D. Sando South London Harriers
1958 Alan P. Perkins South London Harriers
1959 Fred Norris Sheffield United Harriers
1960 Basil B. Heatley Derby and County AC
1961 Basil B. Heatley Derby and County AC
1962 Gerry A. North Derby and County AC
1963 Basil B. Heatley Coventry Godiva Harriers
1964 Melvyn R. Batty Portsmouth AC
1965 Melvyn R. Batty Portsmouth AC
1966 Ron Hill North Staffs & Stone H
1967 Dick G. Taylor Portsmouth AC
1968 Ronald Hill Coventry Godiva Harriers
1969 Michael J. Tagg Tipton Harriers
1970 Trevor Wright City of Stoke AC
1971 David C. Bedford Shettleston Harriers
1972 Malcolm Thomas Tipton Harriers
1973† David C. Bedford Gateshead Harriers
1974 David J. Black Derby and County AC
1975 Tony D. Simmons Gateshead Harriers
1976 Bernard W. Ford Gateshead Harriers
1977 Brendan Foster Gateshead Harriers
1978 Bernard Ford Tipton Harriers
1979 Michael McLeod Gateshead Harriers

*Actual winner was J. Guillemot (France).
†Actual winner was R. Dixon (N.Z.)

## The Harvey Memorial Cup

Awarded annually to the competitor in the AAA Championships who is adjudged by the Championships Committee to be the best Champion of the year.
(Presented by the family of the late CC Harvey in June 1907.)

1907 [Alex Duncan / Jack Morton]
1908 Robert Kerr (Canada)
1909 Ernest Webb
1910 Ernest Webb
1911 Robert Pasemann (Germany)
1912 George Patching (S. Africa)
1913 Willie Applegarth
1914 Willie Applegarth
1919 Albert Hill
1920 Bevil Rudd (S. Africa)
1921 Albert Hill
1922 Harry Edward
1923 Eric Liddell
1924 Harold Abrahams
1925 [Harold Osborn (USA) / Jack Webster]
1926 Otto Peltzer (Germany)
1927 Douglas Lowe
1928 Douglas Lowe
1929 Cyril Ellis
1930 Lord Burghley
1931 Jozsef Daranyi (Hungary)
1932 Frederick Reid
1933 Lauri Lehtinen (Finland)
1934 Janusz Kusocinski (Poland)
1935 Harald Andersson (Sweden)
1936 Godfrey Brown
1937 William Roberts
1938 Donald Finlay
1939 Jean Chapelle (Belgium)
1946 Sydney Wooderson
1947 Emmanuel McDonald Bailey
1948 [Maurice Curotta (Australia) / Harold Parlett]
1949 William Nankeville
1950 [Frank Aaron / Roland Hardy]
1951 Arthur Wint (Jamaica)
1952 Jim Peters
1953 Gordon Pirie
1954 Frederick Green
1955 John Disley
1956 Kenneth Norris
1957 Derek Ibbotson
1958 Stanley Eldon
1959 Kenneth Matthews
1960 Stanley Vickers
1961 Basil Heatley
1962 Robbie Brightwell
1963 John Pennel (USA)
1964 Michael Bullivant
1965 Ronald Clarke (Australia)
1966 [Ronald Clarke (Australia) / Wendell Mottley (Trinidad)]
1967 Ronald Clarke (Australia)
1968 Ronald Hill
1969 Richard Taylor
1970 Howard Payne
1971 David Bedford
1972 David Bedford
1973 Andrew Carter
1974 Al Feuerbach (USA)
1975 David Black
1976 Donald Quarrie (Jamaica)
1977 Brendan Foster
1978 Brendan Foster

## The CN Jackson Memorial Cup

Awarded annually to the athlete born in the UK who is adjudged by the AAA Championships Committee to be the outstanding athlete of the year.
(Presented by friends in memory of CN Jackson, May 1926.)

|  |  |
|---|---|
| 1926 | Douglas Lowe |
| 1927 | Douglas Lowe |
| 1928 | Lord Burghley |
| 1929 | John Hanlon<br>Harry Payne |
| 1930 | Lord Burghley |
| 1931 | Godfrey Rampling |
| 1932 | Albert Cooper |
| 1933 | Albert Cooper<br>Reginald Thomas |
| 1934 | Donald Finlay |
| 1935 | Stanley West |
| 1936 | William Eaton |
| 1937 | William Roberts |
| 1938 | Donald Finlay |
| 1939 | Jack Emery |
| 1946 | Sydney Wooderson |
| 1947 | Jack Holden |
| 1948 | Alistair McCorquodale |
| 1949 | Harold Whittle |
| 1950 | Jack Holden |
| 1951 | Jim Peters |
| 1952 | John Disley |
| 1953 | Gordon Pirie |
| 1954 | Roger Bannister |
| 1955 | Brian Hewson |
| 1956 | Gordon Pirie |
| 1957 | Derek Ibbotson |
| 1958 | Arthur Rowe |
| 1959 | Brian Hewson |
| 1960 | Donald Thompson<br>Peter Radford |
| 1961 | Adrian Metcalfe |
| 1962 | Brian Kilby |
| 1963 | Maurice Herriott<br>Kenneth Matthews |
| 1964 | Lynn Davies<br>Kenneth Matthews |
| 1965 | Maurice Herriott<br>Alan Simpson |
| 1966 | Lynn Davies |
| 1967 | John Sherwood |
| 1968 | David Hemery |
| 1969 | Ronald Hill<br>Paul Nihill |
| 1970 | Ronald Hill |
| 1971 | David Bedford |
| 1972 | David Jenkins |
| 1973 | Brendan Foster |
| 1974 | Ian Thompson |
| 1975 | Alan Pascoe |
| 1976 | Brendan Foster |
| 1977 | Steven Ovett |
| 1978 | Steven Ovett<br>Daley Thompson |

# AAA Indoor Champions

### 60 YARDS

| | | sec |
|---|---|---|
| 1962 | David Jones | 6.5 |
| 1963 | Jochen Bender (W. Germany) | 6.4 |
| 1964 | Alfred Meakin | 6.4 |
| 1965 | Robert Frith | 6.3 |
| 1966 | Barrie Kelly | 6.3 |
| 1967 | Robert Frith | 6.3 |

### 60 METRES

| | | sec |
|---|---|---|
| 1968 | Robert Frith | 6.8 |
| 1969 | Robert Frith | 6.9 |
| 1970 | Paul Pinnington | 6.8 |
| 1971 | Donald Halliday | 6.8 |
| 1972 | Barrie Kelly | 6.8 |
| 1973 | Brian Green | 6.8 |
| 1974 | Donald Halliday | 6.7 |
| 1975 | David Roberts | 6.8 |
| 1976 | Chris Monk | 6.9 |
| 1977 | Allan Wells | 6.7 |
| 1978 | Peter Little | 6.84 |
| 1979 | Steven Green | 6.85 |

### 70 YARDS

| | | sec |
|---|---|---|
| 1935 | 'Sandy' Duncan | 7.5 |
| 1936 | Cyril Holmes | 7.4 |
| 1937 | Cyril Holmes | 7.3 |
| 1938 | Ernest Page | 7.4 |
| 1939 | Bernard Giles | 7.5 |

### 220 YARDS

| | | sec |
|---|---|---|
| 1965 | David Dear | 22.8 |
| 1966 | David Dear | 23.1 |
| 1967 | Trevor Smith | 22.7 |

### 200 METRES

| | | sec |
|---|---|---|
| 1968 | Ralph Banthorpe | 22.8 |
| 1969 | Peter Wiltshire | 22.6 |
| 1970 | Keith Meredith | 23.0 |
| 1975 | Chris Monk | 22.5 |
| 1976 | Andrew McMaster | 22.0 |
| 1977 | Glen Cohen | 22.0 |
| 1978 | Michael McFarlane | 21.9 |
| 1979 | Philip Brown | 22.1 |

### 440 YARDS

| | | sec |
|---|---|---|
| 1965 | Michael Rawson | 49.6 |
| 1966 | Wendell Mottley (Trinidad) | 47.3 |
| 1967 | Colin Campbell | 49.8 |

### 400 METRES

| | | sec |
|---|---|---|
| 1968 | Colin Campbell | 47.9 |
| 1969 | Gwynne Griffiths | 48.9 |
| 1970 | Gwynne Griffiths | 49.0 |
| 1971 | James Aukett | 48.2 |
| 1972 | James Aukett | 48.9 |
| 1973 | James Aukett | 47.9 |
| 1974 | James Aukett | 47.9 |
| 1975 | Joseph Chivers | 48.4 |
| 1976 | Steve Scutt | 49.0 |
| 1977 | Carl Hamilton | 49.3 |
| 1978 | Carl Hamilton | 49.3 |
| 1979 | Ainsley Bennett | 48.3 |

### 600 YARDS

| | | min | sec |
|---|---|---|---|
| 1936 | John Powell | 1 | 19.5 |
| 1962 | Brian Morris | 1 | 16.3 |
| 1963 | William Crothers (Canada) | 1 | 12.1 |
| 1964 | William Crothers (Canada) | 1 | 10.0 |

### 880 YARDS

| | | min | sec |
|---|---|---|---|
| 1937 | John Powell | 2 | 03.3 |
| 1938 | AC Pettit | 2 | 04.4 |
| 1939 | George Morris | 2 | 00.4 |
| 1965 | Peter Beacham | 1 | 52.5 |
| 1966 | John Gingell | 1 | 52.3 |
| 1967 | Duncan Middleton | 1 | 51.5 |

### 800 METRES

| | | min | sec |
|---|---|---|---|
| 1968 | John Gingell | 1 | 52.0 |
| 1969 | Robert Adams | 1 | 51.1 |
| 1970 | Colin Campbell | 1 | 49.6 |
| 1971 | Philip Lewis | 1 | 50.2 |
| 1972 | Colin Cusick | 1 | 51.2 |
| 1973 | Alan Gibson | 1 | 52.0 |
| 1974 | Raymond Weatherburn | 1 | 52.8 |
| 1975 | Peter Browne | 1 | 52.4 |
| 1976 | Peter Lewis | 1 | 50.0 |
| 1977 | Sebastian Coe | 1 | 49.1 |
| 1978 | Peter Hoffman | 1 | 51.4 |
| 1979 | Malcolm Edwards | 1 | 51.9 |

### 1000 YARDS

| | | min | sec |
|---|---|---|---|
| 1962 | Thomas Bryan | 2 | 17.9 |
| 1963 | William Crothers (Canada) | 2 | 14.0 |
| 1964 | John Whetton | 2 | 12.2 |

### 1 MILE

| | | min | sec |
|---|---|---|---|
| 1962 | Willie Olivier (S. Africa) | 4 | 12.1 |
| 1963 | John Whetton | 4 | 13.3 |
| 1964 | John Whetton | 4 | 07.9 |
| 1965 | John Whetton | 4 | 06.3 |
| 1966 | John Whetton | 4 | 04.7 |
| 1967 | John Whetton | 4 | 09.9 |

### 1500 METRES

| | | min | sec |
|---|---|---|---|
| 1968 | John Whetton | 3 | 51.0 |
| 1969 | Walter Wilkinson | 3 | 49.3 |
| 1970 | Walter Wilkinson | 3 | 48.0 |
| 1971 | John Davies | 3 | 46.9 |
| 1972 | Frank Clement | 3 | 46.4 |
| 1973 | James McGuinness | 3 | 50.6 |
| 1974 | Clive Thomas | 3 | 53.4 |
| 1975 | Philip Banning | 3 | 42.2 |
| 1976 | David Moorcroft | 3 | 45.6 |
| 1977 | Alan Mottershead | 3 | 50.7 |
| 1978 | Tim Hutchings | 3 | 48.4 |
| 1979 | Paul Williams | 3 | 46.6 |

### 2 MILES

| | | min | sec |
|---|---|---|---|
| 1937 | Robert Thorogood | 9 | 38.0 |
| 1938 | Robert Thorogood | 9 | 33.6 |
| 1939 | Thomas Rowe | 9 | 27.2 |
| 1962 | Derek Ibbotson | 8 | 52.2 |
| 1963 | John Cooke | 8 | 57.4 |
| 1964 | Bruce Kidd (Canada) | 8 | 39.0 |
| 1965 | Derek Ibbotson | 8 | 42.6 |
| 1966 | Alan Simpson | 8 | 45.6 |
| 1967 | Ian McCafferty | 8 | 36.4 |

### 3000 METRES

| | | min | sec |
|---|---|---|---|
| 1968 | Ian McCafferty | 8 | 00.4 |
| 1969 | Ian McCafferty | 8 | 08.4 |
| 1970 | Ricky Wilde | 7 | 59.2 |

| | | min sec |
|---|---|---|
| 1971 | Peter Stewart | 8 00.4 |
| 1972 | Ian Stewart | 7 50.0 |
| 1973 | Ian Stewart | 7 58.0 |
| 1974 | Raymond Smedley | 8 00.0 |
| 1975 | Ian Stewart | 8 01.0 |
| 1976 | Raymond Smedley | 7 59.2 |
| 1977 | Raymond Smedley | 7 59.2 |
| 1978 | Stephen Emson | 8 05.4 |
| 1979 | Sebastian Coe | 7 59.8 |

## 2000 METRES STEEPLECHASE

| | | min sec |
|---|---|---|
| 1967 | Ronald McAndrew | 5 42.4 |
| 1968 | Peter Morris | 5 35.0 |
| 1969 | Derek Blakeley | 5 36.6 |
| 1970 | Ronald McAndrew | 5 36.8 |
| 1971 | Bernard Hayward | 5 34.8 |
| 1972 | Ronald McAndrew | 5 32.4 |
| 1973 | Ronald McAndrew | 5 36.8 |
| 1974 | Ian Gilmour | 5 34.6 |
| 1975 | Dennis Coates | 5 30.8 |
| 1976 | Agust Asgeirsson (Iceland) | 5 38.8 |
| 1977 | Peter Griffiths | 5 34.2 |
| 1978 | Dennis Coates | 5 24.6 |
| 1979 | Ian Gilmour | 5 40.2 |

## 60 YARDS HURDLES

| | | sec |
|---|---|---|
| 1962 | Michael Hogan | 7.7 |
| 1963 | Lawrence Taitt | 7.6 |
| 1964 | Michael Parker | 7.4 |
| 1965 | Michael Parker | 7.4 |
| 1966 | Michael Parker | 7.4 |
| 1967 | Alan Pascoe | 7.5 |

## 60 METRES HURDLES

| | | sec |
|---|---|---|
| 1968 | Alan Pascoe | 8.1 |
| 1969 | Alan Pascoe | 7.8 |
| 1970 | Alan Pascoe | 7.8 |
| 1971 | Berwyn Price | 7.9 |
| 1972 | Graham Gower | 7.9 |
| 1973 | Alan Pascoe | 8.0 |
| 1974 | CJ Kirkpatrick | 8.0 |
| 1975 | Berwyn Price | 8.0 |
| 1976 | Berwyn Price | 8.1 |
| 1977 | Peter Kelly | 8.2 |
| 1978 | Berwyn Price | 7.90 |
| 1979 | Mark Holtom | 8.1 |

## 70 YARDS HURDLES

| | | sec |
|---|---|---|
| 1935 | Ashleigh Pilbrow | 9.0 |
| 1936 | ED Mitchell | 9.3 |
| 1937 | Donald Finlay | 9.0 |
| 1938 | Donald Finlay | 8.9 |
| 1939 | Thomas Lockton | 8.9 |

## HIGH JUMP

| | | metres |
|---|---|---|
| 1935 | Stanley West | 1.83 |
| 1936 | John Newman | 1.78 |
| 1937 | John Newman | 1.88 |
| 1938 | Robert Kennedy | 1.85 |
| 1939 | John Newman | 1.78 |
| 1962 | Gordon Miller | 2.03 |
| 1963 | Crawford Fairbrother | 2.00 |
| 1964 | Henry Wadsworth (USA) | 2.00 |
| 1965 | Gordon Miller | 2.03 |
| 1966 | Crawford Fairbrother | 2.00 |
| 1967 | Michael Campbell | 1.95 |
| 1968 | Michael Campbell | 1.95 |
| 1969 | Michael Campbell | 1.93 |
| 1970 | David Wilson | 1.95 |
| 1971 | David Livesey | 2.09 |
| 1972 | Michael Campbell | 2.00 |
| 1973 | Anthony Sneazwell (Australia) | 2.10 |
| 1974 | James Fanning (Ireland) | 2.01 |
| 1975 | Colin Boreham | 2.00 |
| 1976 | Michael Butterfield | 2.16 |
| 1977 | Mark Naylor | 2.10 |
| 1978 | Mark Naylor | 2.11 |
| 1979 | Mark Naylor | 2.15 |

## POLE VAULT

| | | metres |
|---|---|---|
| 1935 | Richard Webster | 3.73 |
| 1936 | Richard Webster | 3.73 |
| 1937 | Richard Webster | 3.90 |
| 1938 | Richard Webster | 3.73 |
| 1939 | Harry Yielder | 3.66 |
| 1962 | Trevor Burton | 4.19 |
| 1963 | Martin Higdon | 3.96 |
| 1964 | Rainer Schmelz (W. Germany) | 4.70 |
| 1965 | David Stevenson | 4.49 |
| 1966 | Martin Higdon | 4.26 |
| 1967 | Michael Bull | 4.60 |
| 1968 | Michael Bull | 4.75 |
| 1969 | Michael Bull | 4.95 |
| 1970 | Michael Bull | 4.90 |
| 1971 | Michael Bull | 4.73 |
| 1972 | Michael Bull | 4.90 |
| 1973 | Brian Hooper | 4.80 |
| 1974 | Michael Bull | 5.00 |
| 1975 | Brian Hooper | 5.20 |
| 1976 | Brian Hooper | 5.05 |
| 1977 | Michael Bull | 4.90 |
| 1978 | Brian Hooper | 5.21 |
| 1979 | Brian Hooper | 5.35 |

## LONG JUMP

| | | metres |
|---|---|---|
| 1935 | 'Sandy' Duncan | 6.93 |
| 1936 | Robert Crombie | 6.48 |
| 1937 | JP Daniel | 6.82 |
| 1938 | Rupert Powell | 6.63 |
| 1939 | Rupert Powell | 6.60 |
| 1962 | Fred Alsop | 7.19 |
| 1963 | Lynn Davies | 7.48 |
| 1964 | John Oladitan (Nigeria) | 7.33 |
| 1965 | Fred Alsop | 7.22 |
| 1966 | Lynn Davies | 7.85 |
| 1967 | Peter Templeton | 7.25 |
| 1968 | David Walker | 7.37 |
| 1969 | Philip Scott | 7.26 |
| 1970 | Alan Lerwill | 7.55 |
| 1971 | Alan Lerwill | 7.63 |
| 1972 | Lynn Davies | 7.51 |
| 1973 | Alan Lerwill | 7.63 |
| 1974 | Philip Scott | 7.33 |
| 1975 | Philip Scott | 7.28 |
| 1976 | Roy Mitchell | 7.69 |
| 1977 | Billie Kirkpatrick | 7.23 |
| 1978 | Tony Henry | 7.47 |
| 1979 | Billie Kirkpatrick | 7.42 |

## TRIPLE JUMP

| | | metres |
|---|---|---|
| 1965 | Fred Alsop | 15.51 |
| 1966 | Michael Ralph | 14.72 |
| 1967 | Fred Alsop | 15.09 |
| 1968 | Fred Alsop | 15.49 |
| 1969 | Derek Boosey | 15.47 |
| 1970 | Derek Boosey | 15.68 |
| 1971 | Anthony Wadhams | 15.43 |
| 1972 | Derek Boosey | 15.17 |
| 1973 | Christopher Colman | 15.40 |
| 1974 | Peter Blackburn | 15.54 |
| 1975 | David Johnson | 15.54 |
| 1976 | Aston Moore | 15.80 |
| 1977 | Aston Moore | 15.76 |
| 1978 | Keith Connor | 16.54 |
| 1979 | Richard Philps | 15.37 |

## SHOT

| | | metres |
|---|---|---|
| 1935 | Robert Howland | 12.84 |
| 1936 | Lawrence Reavell Carter | 13.14 |
| 1937 | Peter Hincks | 13.76 |
| 1938 | Robert Howland | 13.45 |

| | | |
|---|---|---|
| 1939 | H. Merz (Germany) | 12.81 |
| 1962 | Martyn Lucking | 17.88 |
| 1963 | Alan Carter | 15.73 |
| 1964 | Michael Lindsay | 17.54 |
| 1965 | Alan Carter | 17.44 |
| 1966 | Michael Lindsay | 16.83 |
| 1967 | Anthony Elvin | 16.57 |
| 1968 | Jeffrey Teale | 17.73 |
| 1969 | William Tancred | 17.31 |
| 1970 | Jeffrey Teale | 17.19 |
| 1971 | Geoffrey Capes | 18.07 |
| 1972 | Geoffrey Capes | 18.65 |
| 1973 | Michael Winch | 18.67 |
| 1974 | Geoffrey Capes | 20.28 |
| 1975 | Geoffrey Capes | 19.92 |
| 1976 | William Tancred | 18.01 |
| 1977 | Geoffrey Capes | 20.63 |
| 1978 | Geoffrey Capes | 20.32 |
| 1979 | Michael Winch | 18.60 |

### 1 MILE WALK

| | | min sec |
|---|---|---|
| 1936 | Albert Cooper | 6 59.4 |

## AAA Junior Champions (Under-20 from 1973)

### 100 YARDS

| | | sec |
|---|---|---|
| 1931 | William Heath | 10.3 |
| 1932 | John Glover | 10.4 |
| 1933 | Charles Chalk | 10.3 |
| 1934 | Alan Pennington | 10.3 |
| 1935 | William Loader | 10.1 |
| 1936 | Kenneth Richardson | 10.2 |
| 1937 | AW Elstrop | 10.2 |
| 1938 | Robert Roach | 10.1 |
| 1939 | Allan Watt | 10.0 |
| 1946 | William Ferguson | 10.6 |
| 1947 | William Jones | 10.2 |
| 1948 | Neil Scott | 10.2 |
| 1949 | Neil Scott | 10.0 |
| 1950 | Alan Lillington | 10.0 |
| 1951 | Keith Scott | 10.3 |
| 1952 | Alan Dunbar | 10.6 |
| 1953 | Hugh Morrison | 10.7 |
| 1954 | James Railton | 9.9 |
| 1955 | Edward McKeating | 10.0 |
| 1956 | John Young | 9.9 |
| 1957 | Alfred Meakin | 10.1 |
| 1958 | David Jones | 10.0 |
| 1959 | Ronald Nicholson | 9.9 |
| 1960 | Michael Hildrey | 10.0 |
| 1961 | Leonard Carter | 9.9 |
| 1962 | Gordon Shannon | 10.7 |
| 1963 | Robert Frith | 9.8 |
| 1964 | Patrick Morrison | 10.2 |
| 1965 | Paul Nash (S. Africa) | 9.9 |
| 1966 | Brian Simms | 10.1 |
| 1967 | David Thomas | 10.2 |
| 1968 | Peter Wiltshire | 9.7 |

### 100 METRES

| | | sec |
|---|---|---|
| 1969 | David Jenkins | 11.1 |
| 1970 | Christopher Monk | 11.1 |
| 1971 | Robert Munns | 10.8 |
| 1972 | Stephen Bailey | 11.2 |
| 1973 | Stephen Green | 10.8 |
| 1974 | Stephen Green | 10.6 |
| 1975 | Daley Thompson | 10.9 |
| 1976 | Robert Denham | 10.7 |
| 1977 | Peter Little | 10.5 |
| 1978 | Edwin Cutting | 10.92 |
| 1979 | Michael Powell | 10.4 |

### 220 YARDS

| | | sec |
|---|---|---|
| 1931 | William Heath | 23.7 |
| 1932 | Not held | |
| 1933 | Charles Chalk | 23.2 |
| 1934 | Alan Pennington | 22.9 |
| 1935 | David Higgins | 22.8 |
| 1936 | Edward Forsyth | 23.2 |
| 1937 | John Lockwood | 22.6 |
| 1938 | Cyril Holland | 23.6 |
| 1939 | Raymond Kirk | 23.1 |
| 1946 | William Ferguson | 23.4 |
| 1947 | AY Monahan | 23.0 |
| 1948 | Alan Sexton | 22.9 |
| 1949 | Alan Sexton | 22.1 |
| 1950 | George Ellis | 22.4 |
| 1951 | George Ellis | 21.9 |
| 1952 | John Booth | 23.1 |
| 1953 | D. Pulsford | 22.9 |
| 1954 | Michael Ruddy | 21.9 |
| 1955 | Ian Smith | 22.5 |
| 1956 | John Young | 22.6 |
| 1957 | Robbie Brightwell | 22.5 |
| 1958 | Melvyn Smith | 22.2 |
| 1959 | Michael Hildrey | 22.2 |
| 1960 | Michael Hildrey | 21.8 |
| 1961 | Leonard Carter | 21.8 |
| 1962 | David Edwards | 23.4 |
| 1963 | Andrew Ronay | 21.9 |
| 1964 | Patrick Morrison | 22.5 |
| 1965 | Paul Nash (S. Africa) | 21.7 |
| 1966 | Ralph Banthorpe | 22.3 |
| 1967 | Peter Wiltshire | 22.0 |
| 1968 | Trevor Rodwell | 21.8 |

### 200 METRES

| | | sec |
|---|---|---|
| 1969 | Ronald Griffiths | 21.7 |
| 1970 | Christopher Monk | 21.8 |
| 1971 | Robert Munns | 22.0 |
| 1972 | David Artley | 22.3 |
| 1973 | Stephen Green | 21.9 |
| 1974 | Andrew Harley | 21.5 |
| 1975 | Andrew Harley | 21.9 |
| 1976 | Andrew McMaster | 21.0 |
| 1977 | Peter Little | 21.0 |
| 1978 | Philip Cooke | 22.24 |
| 1979 | Philip Cooke | 21.5 |

### 440 YARDS

| | | sec |
|---|---|---|
| 1931 | John Anderson | 51.3 |
| 1932 | Geoffrey Blake | 52.4 |
| 1933 | Richard Wells | 52.8 |
| 1934 | George Nicholls | 52.6 |
| 1935 | Royston Chandler | 52.2 |
| 1936 | Royston Chandler | 51.0 |
| 1937 | Edward Forsyth | 52.5 |
| 1938 | Leslie Hatt | 52.2 |
| 1939 | Martin Pike | 50.8 |
| 1946 | Geoffrey Chester | 51.4 |
| 1947 | Allan Bannister | 51.7 |
| 1948 | Michael Paxton | 51.0 |
| 1949 | Maurice Wright | 51.1 |
| 1950 | Derek Johnson | 48.8 |
| 1951 | Derek Johnson | 49.1 |
| 1952 | Kenneth Chambers | 50.3 |
| 1953 | William Warmington | 51.0 |
| 1954 | Harold Smith | 50.1 |
| 1955 | Harold Smith | 50.8 |
| 1956 | David Jones | 51.2 |
| 1957 | John Holt | 49.5 |
| 1958 | Malcolm Yardley | 51.3 |
| 1959 | Brian Jackson | 48.7 |
| 1960 | Brian Jackson | 48.1 |
| 1961 | Nicholas Overhead | 49.3 |
| 1962 | Michael Hauck | 49.6 |
| 1963 | Edmund Jenkins | 48.7 |
| 1964 | John Sherwood | 47.7 |
| 1965 | Martin Winbolt-Lewis | 48.5 |
| 1966 | John Wilson | 49.1 |
| 1967 | Richard Green | 48.4 |
| 1968 | Jonathan English | 48.5 |

## 400 METRES

| | | sec |
|---|---|---|
| 1969 | David Jenkins | 47.3 |
| 1970 | Peter Beaven | 48.5 |
| 1971 | Desmond Coneys | 49.1 |
| 1972 | David Price | 49.0 |
| 1973 | Glendon Cohen | 47.5 |
| 1974 | Roger Jenkins | 47.3 |
| 1975 | Brian Jones | 47.3 |
| 1976 | Jeffrey Griffiths | 47.2 |
| 1977 | Andrew Kerr | 48.1 |
| 1978 | Steven Wymark | 48.19 |
| 1979 | Melvin Fowell | 48.6 |

## 880 YARDS

| | | min | sec |
|---|---|---|---|
| 1931 | Alfred Poole | 2 | 07.0 |
| 1932 | B. Jenkins | 2 | 02.4 |
| 1933 | Charles Oades | 2 | 04.2 |
| 1934 | Charles Oades | 2 | 01.4 |
| 1935 | Charles Oades | 2 | 02.6 |
| 1936 | Meredith Eliot | 1 | 58.8 |
| 1937 | Ronald Brown | 2 | 04.7 |
| 1938 | Arthur Smith | 2 | 00.1 |
| 1939 | Leslie Sarbutt | 2 | 00.1 |
| 1946 | D. Pickles | 2 | 02.0 |
| 1947 | Bob Goldie | 2 | 00.8 |
| 1948 | Peter Richards | 2 | 02.4 |
| 1949 | AJ Perry | 1 | 57.2 |
| 1950 | George Bunner | 2 | 04.2 |
| 1951 | Brian Hewson | 1 | 55.3 |
| 1952 | Brian Hewson | 1 | 55.5 |
| 1953 | Ronald Henderson | 1 | 57.7 |
| 1954 | Roy Beaumont | 1 | 59.0 |
| 1955 | Roy Beaumont | 1 | 56.7 |
| 1956 | Derek Haith | 1 | 57.6 |
| 1957 | Brian Linke | 1 | 57.1 |
| 1958 | Barrie Savory | 1 | 55.2 |
| 1959 | Anthony Harris | 1 | 54.3 |
| 1960 | Anthony Harris | 1 | 55.4 |
| 1961 | Terrance Naish | 1 | 55.0 |
| 1962 | Roger Dollimore | 1 | 56.0 |
| 1963 | David Hogg | 1 | 54.3 |
| 1964 | David Cropper | 1 | 55.4 |
| 1965 | Frank Murphy (Ireland) | 1 | 53.0 |
| 1966 | John Davies | 1 | 52.0 |
| 1967 | David Burden | 1 | 53.4 |
| 1968 | Peter Lewis | 1 | 54.4 |

## 800 METRES

| | | min | sec |
|---|---|---|---|
| 1969 | John Cherry | 1 | 51.0 |
| 1970 | Michael Fromant | 1 | 54.3 |
| 1971 | James Carroll | 1 | 53.5 |
| 1972 | Alan Mottershead | 1 | 55.6 |
| 1973 | Anthony Dyke | 1 | 52.0 |
| 1974 | Anthony Dyke | 1 | 51.1 |
| 1975 | Paul Forbes | 1 | 50.7 |
| 1976 | Stephen Caldwell | 1 | 50.4 |
| 1977 | Colin Szwed | 1 | 48.7 |
| 1978 | Julian Spooner | 1 | 51.0 |
| 1979 | Christopher McGeorge | 1 | 54.8 |

## 1 MILE

| | | min | sec |
|---|---|---|---|
| 1931 | AE Woodley | 4 | 36.6 |
| 1932 | Dennis Samuel | 4 | 32.6 |
| 1933 | Charles Jackson | 4 | 39.6 |
| 1934 | Austin Littler | 4 | 39.0 |
| 1935 | W. Moorcroft | 4 | 31.4 |
| 1936 | Anthony Noble | 4 | 29.6 |
| 1937 | Victor Foster | 4 | 30.6 |
| 1938 | Jack Timmins | 4 | 33.8 |
| 1939 | Raymond Goodbody | 4 | 25.0 |
| 1946 | Derek Burfitt | 4 | 23.2 |
| 1947 | Eddie Ellis | 4 | 32.6 |
| 1948 | Eddie Ellis | 4 | 29.6 |
| 1949 | Eddie Ellis | 4 | 28.8 |
| 1950 | Donald Seaman | 4 | 29.0 |
| 1951 | David Humphrey | 4 | 19.2 |
| 1952 | John Hendry | 4 | 21.2 |
| 1953 | Roger Dunkley | 4 | 25.8 |
| 1954 | Roger Dunkley | 4 | 15.6 |
| 1955 | Alan Cocking | 4 | 23.2 |
| 1956 | Roland Langridge | 4 | 18.4 |
| 1957 | William Cornell | 4 | 15.5 |
| 1958 | Patrick Montague | 4 | 25.0 |
| 1959 | Dick Jones | 4 | 10.0 |
| 1960 | Malcolm Browne | 4 | 17.3 |
| 1961 | Frank Martin | 4 | 14.0 |
| 1962 | Morris Jefferson | 4 | 14.4 |
| 1963 | Hugh Barrow | 4 | 08.9 |
| 1964 | Peter Abell | 4 | 11.7 |
| 1965 | Michael Tagg | 4 | 12.0 |
| 1966 | Andrew Herrity | 4 | 13.4 |
| 1967 | David Williams | 4 | 08.4 |
| 1968 | David Wright | 4 | 09.1 |

## 1500 METRES

| | | min | sec |
|---|---|---|---|
| 1969 | Phil Banning | 3 | 45.2 |
| 1970 | Ronald Macdonald | 3 | 50.5 |
| 1971 | David Moorcroft | 3 | 51.9 |
| 1972 | Stephen Lawrence | 3 | 55.0 |
| 1973 | Paul Lawther | 3 | 47.2 |
| 1974 | Paul Williams | 3 | 53.7 |
| 1975 | Sebastian Coe | 3 | 47.1 |
| 1976 | Ray Flynn (Ireland) | 3 | 44.1 |
| 1977 | Sean Cahill | 3 | 48.0 |
| 1978 | Graham Williamson | 3 | 39.7 |
| 1979 | Graham Williamson | 3 | 41.6 |

## 2 MILES

| | | min | sec |
|---|---|---|---|
| 1964 | Michael Tagg | 9 | 01.6 |
| 1965 | Colin Church | 9 | 01.8 |
| 1966 | Fanie Van Zyl (S. Africa) | 8 | 50.2 |
| 1967 | Tony Simmons | 8 | 50.4 |
| 1968 | David Bedford | 8 | 59.4 |

## 3000 METRES

| | | min | sec |
|---|---|---|---|
| 1969 | John Boggis | 8 | 17.4 |
| 1970 | David Black | 8 | 17.0 |
| 1971 | David Black | 8 | 00.7 |
| 1972 | Paul Bannon | 8 | 09.4 |
| 1973 | Mike Kearns | 8 | 06.8 |
| 1974 | John Treacy (Ireland) | 8 | 15.6 |
| 1975 | John Treacy (Ireland) | 8 | 15.0 |
| 1976 | Guy McCallum | 8 | 08.0 |
| 1977 | James Espir | 8 | 09.2 |
| 1978 | Michael Morton | 8 | 10.2 |
| 1979 | Stephen Cram | 8 | 03.2 |

## 5000 METRES

| | | min | sec |
|---|---|---|---|
| 1973 | Stephen Lawrence | 14 | 18.0 |
| 1974 | William Sheridan | 14 | 29.0 |
| 1975 | John Treacy (Ireland) | 14 | 04.6 |
| 1976 | Nicholas Lees | 14 | 13.2 |
| 1977 | Nicholas Lees | 14 | 01.0 |
| 1978 | Michael Morton | 14 | 03.9 |
| 1979 | Mark Scrutton | 14 | 08.6 |

## 120 YARDS HURDLES

| | | sec |
|---|---|---|
| 1931 | Francis Kingdon | 16.0 |
| 1932 | John Owen | 15.9 |
| 1933 | BC Ledeboer | 15.8 |
| 1934 | Maurice Carter | 15.9 |
| 1935 | Douglas Lock | 15.9 |
| 1936 | Thomas Lockton | 15.9 |
| 1937 | Denis Wilkinson | 15.5 |
| 1938 | Harry Hearn | 15.4 |
| 1939 | Tony Chadburn | 15.6 |
| 1946 | Harry Hodgkinson | 16.2 |
| 1947 | Joseph Birrell | 15.9 |
| 1948 | Joseph Birrell | 15.1 |
| 1949 | David Kay | 15.4 |
| 1950 | Geoffrey Parr | 15.7 |
| 1951 | Robert Shaw | 14.7 |

| | | |
|---|---|---|
| 1952 | Harry Kane | 15.4 |
| 1953 | Vic Matthews | 14.9 |
| 1954 | Roy Sutton | 15.2 |
| 1955 | Robin Woodland | 15.5 |
| 1956 | Robin Woodland | 14.8 |
| 1957 | Michael Stokely | 14.6 |
| 1958 | Stuart Tarrant | 14.9 |
| 1959 | Peter Sunderland | 14.9 |
| 1960 | George Tymms | 15.6 |
| 1961 | Michael Hogan | 14.6 |
| 1962 | Anthony Hogarth | 15.4 |
| 1963 | David Hemery | 14.6 |
| 1964 | John Lewis | 15.4 |
| 1965 | Chris de Nysschen (S. Africa) | 14.2 |
| 1966 | Andrew Todd | 14.3 |
| 1967 | Steve Black | 14.7 |
| 1968 | Philip Aylward | 14.8 |

## 110 METRES HURDLES (3 ft 3 in)

| | | sec |
|---|---|---|
| 1969 | Berwyn Price | 14.7 |
| 1970 | Peter Kelly | 14.5 |
| 1971 | Peter Kelly | 14.5 |
| 1972 | Angus McKenzie | 15.0 |

## 110 METRES HURDLES (3 ft 6 in)

| | | sec |
|---|---|---|
| 1973 | Angus McKenzie | 15.0 |
| 1974 | Anthony James | 15.0 |
| 1975 | Mark Hatton | 14.9 |
| 1976 | Mark Holtom | 14.5 |
| 1977 | Mark Holtom | 14.1 |
| 1978 | Philip Barthropp | 15.32 |
| 1979 | Trevor Carrington | 14.9 |

*400 METRES HURDLES — see p. 205

## 220 YARDS HURDLES

| | | sec |
|---|---|---|
| 1951 | Joseph Duffy | 23.3 |
| 1952 | Harry Kane | 23.3 |
| 1953 | H. Edwards | 24.0 |
| 1954 | William Thompson | 23.5 |
| 1955 | Alexander Hannah | 23.4 |
| 1956 | Michael Stokely | 24.0 |
| 1957 | Michael Stokely | 23.4 |
| 1958 | John Sams | 23.1 |
| 1959 | Orlando Baggott | 22.7 |
| 1960 | Francis Dick | 22.8 |
| 1961 | Clive Webb | 22.7 |
| 1962 | Clive Webb | 23.6 |
| 1963 | Michael Bell | 22.5 |
| 1964 | John Day | 23.2 |
| 1965 | Chris de Nysschen (S. Africa) | 22.9 |
| 1966 | Douglas Bruce | 23.0 |

## 1 MILE WALK

| | | min | sec |
|---|---|---|---|
| 1947 | Kenneth Harding | 7 | 30.2 |
| 1948 | E. Sharp | 7 | 22.6 |
| 1949 | Daniel Bolt | 7 | 06.0 |
| 1950 | Norman Read | 7 | 04.8 |
| 1951 | John Lowther | 6 | 59.2 |
| 1952 | Gareth Lewis | 6 | 53.6 |
| 1953 | Gareth Howell | 6 | 49.9 |
| 1954 | Gareth Howell | 6 | 54.0 |
| 1955 | John Edginton | 7 | 13.4 |
| 1956 | Michael Shannon | 7 | 07.4 |
| 1957 | Michael Shannon | 6 | 55.3 |
| 1958 | Dennis Read | 6 | 51.8 |
| 1959 | Peter Marlow | 7 | 05.4 |
| 1960 | Ron Wallwork | 6 | 59.1 |
| 1961 | Shaun Lightman | 6 | 54.5 |
| 1962 | Shaun Lightman | 6 | 46.2 |
| 1963 | Malcolm Tolley | 6 | 57.9 |
| 1964 | Christopher Trimming | 7 | 12.4 |
| 1965 | Robert Care | 6 | 58.2 |
| 1966 | Kevin Smith | 7 | 33.0 |
| 1967 | Phil Embleton | 7 | 04.9 |
| 1968 | Oliver Flynn | 6 | 58.4 |

## 3000 METRES WALK

| | | min | sec |
|---|---|---|---|
| 1969 | Richard Evans | 14 | 04.0 |
| 1970 | David Ward | 13 | 22.4 |
| 1971 | Brian Laver | 13 | 39.0 |
| 1972 | John Lord | 13 | 27.8 |

## 10 000 METRES WALK

| | | min | sec |
|---|---|---|---|
| 1973 | John Lord | 45 | 39.6 |
| 1974 | John Lord | 45 | 20.0 |
| 1975 | David Cotton | 46 | 29.6 |
| 1976 | Michael Dunion | 47 | 24.4 |
| 1977 | Graham Morris | 46 | 51.0 |
| 1978 | Michael Miley | 47 | 44.8 |
| 1979 | Gordon Vale | 45 | 55.2 |

## 4×110 YARDS RELAY

| | | sec |
|---|---|---|
| 1931 | Polytechnic H. | 46.4 |
| 1932 | Polytechnic H. | 45.6 |
| 1933 | South London H. | 46.0 |
| 1934 | Cambridge H. | 45.6 |
| 1935 | Polytechnic H. | 45.7 |
| 1936 | RAF, Halton | 46.4 |
| 1937 | Southgate H. | 46.0 |
| 1938 | Portsmouth AC | 45.9 |
| 1939 | RAF, Halton | 44.8 |
| 1946 | Merchant Taylors | 45.5 |
| 1947 | Polytechnic H. | 45.2 |
| 1948 | Cambridge H. | 44.9 |
| 1949 | Cambridge H. | 44.6 |
| 1950 | Portsmouth AC | 44.1 |
| 1951 | Mitcham AC | 44.6 |
| 1952 | Mitcham AC | 44.8 |
| 1953 | Polytechnic H. | 43.9 |
| 1954 | Liverpool Pembroke AC | 44.0 |
| 1955 | Victoria Park H. | 43.8 |
| 1956 | Blackheath H. | 43.8 |
| 1957 | Blackheath H. | 43.5 |
| 1958 | Coventry Godiva H. | 43.7 |
| 1959 | Shettleston H. | 43.7 |
| 1960 | London AC | 43.9 |
| 1961 | Watford H. | 43.4 |
| 1962 | Pilkington Rec. H. | 42.9 |
| 1963 | Woodford Green AC | 44.0 |
| 1964 | Thames Valley H. | 43.2 |
| 1965 | Belgrave H. | 42.8 |
| 1966 | Essex Beagles | 43.1 |
| 1967 | Birchfield H. | 44.0 |
| 1968 | Wolverhampton & Bilston AC | 42.5 |

## 4×100 METRES RELAY

| | | sec |
|---|---|---|
| 1969 | Wolverhampton & Bilston AC | 42.3 |
| 1970 | Thames Valley H. | 42.5 |
| 1971 | Wolverhampton & Bilston AC | 42.9 |
| 1972 | Thames Valley H. | 42.3 |
| 1973 | Epsom & Ewell H. | 44.6 |
| 1974 | Borough of Enfield H. | 43.4 |
| 1975 | Thames Valley H. | 42.6 |
| 1976 | Victoria Park H. | 41.30 |
| 1977 | Victoria Park H. | 42.75 |
| 1978 | Coventry Godiva H. | 42.40 |
| 1979 | Haringey AC | 41.80 |

## ¾ MILE STEEPLECHASE

| | | min | sec |
|---|---|---|---|
| 1931 | Richard Hainsworth | 3 | 55.4 |
| 1932 | Richard Hainsworth | 3 | 44.6 |
| 1933 | Jeffrey Preston Jones | 3 | 51.0 |
| 1934 | Edward Nankivell | 3 | 59.0 |
| 1935 | Hy. Dyall | 3 | 48.4 |
| 1936 | Hy. Dyall | 3 | 42.0 |

| | | |
|---|---|---|
| 1937 | Arthur Smith | 4 01.6 |
| 1938 | Arthur Smith | 4 46.6 |
| 1939 | Peter Burley | 3 33.6 |

### 1 MILE STEEPLECHASE

| | | min sec |
|---|---|---|
| 1956 | Brian Hall | 4 50.4 |
| 1957 | Maurice Herriott | 4 50.5 |

### 1500 METRES STEEPLECHASE

| | | min sec |
|---|---|---|
| 1958 | Maurice Herriott | 4 20.7 |
| 1959 | Anthony Yates | 4 23.0 |
| 1960 | James Catto | 4 19.3 |
| 1961 | Guy King | 4 17.6 |
| 1962 | Fred Stebbings | 4 15.2 |
| 1963 | Michael Williams | 4 20.0 |
| 1964 | Anthony Ashton | 4 19.7 |

### 2000 METRES STEEPLECHASE

| | | min sec |
|---|---|---|
| 1965 | Barry Davies | 5 51.8 |
| 1966 | Brendan Bryne | 6 00.4 |
| 1967 | Ian Foster | 5 55.6 |
| 1968 | Colin Taylor | 5 43.2 |
| 1969 | John Wheway | 5 40.2 |
| 1970 | Martin Jones | 5 43.8 |
| 1971 | Dennis Coates | 5 38.4 |
| 1972 | Neil Saunders | 5 59.0 |
| 1973 | John Tierney | 5 38.2 |
| 1974 | John Tierney | 5 49.6 |
| 1975 | Micky Morris | 5 37.8 |
| 1976 | John Wilson | 5 47.4 |
| 1977 | Paul Campbell | 5 40.2 |
| 1978 | Colin Reitz | 5 35.6 |
| 1979 | Colin Reitz | 5 31.6 |

### DECATHLON

| | | pts |
|---|---|---|
| 1971 | Patrick Bredin (junior implements) | 5072 |
| 1974 | John Howell | 6073 |
| 1975 | Daley Thompson | 7008 |
| 1976 | Graeme Watson | 6395 |
| 1977 | Peter Brugnani | 6204 |
| 1978 | Fidelis Obikwu | 6471 |
| 1979 | Eugene Gilkes | 6409 |

### HIGH JUMP

| | | metres |
|---|---|---|
| 1931 | Leslie Tovell | 1.70 |
| 1932 | Frederick Ford | 1.70 |
| | Harry Tate | 1.70 |
| 1933 | B. Ledeboer | 1.78 |
| 1934 | Edward Brewster | 1.75 |
| 1935 | John Newman | 1.80 |
| 1936 | JVH Gecks | 1.72 |
| 1937 | PL Tancred (Australia) | 1.78 |
| 1938 | Marcus Dowling | 1.72 |
| 1939 | Thomas J. Rumble | 1.78 |
| 1946 | Alan Paterson | 1.89 |
| 1947 | Peter Wells | 1.83 |
| 1948 | Geoffrey Elliott | 1.72 |
| 1949 | NP Kane | 1.78 |
| 1950 | Norman Finch | 1.78 |
| 1951 | Thomas Reynolds | 1.83 |
| 1952 | Thomas Reynolds | 1.83 |
| 1953 | Anthony Orton | 1.78 |
| 1954 | John Billington | 1.83 |
| 1955 | Michael Thatcher | 1.80 |
| 1956 | David Wilson | 1.78 |
| 1957 | Alan Houston | 1.85 |
| 1958 | Gordon Miller | 1.83 |
| 1959 | Alexander Davies | 1.93 |
| 1960 | James Russell | 1.88 |
| 1961 | Lloyd Foster | 1.78 |
| 1962 | Lloyd Foster | 1.88 |
| 1963 | Mike Selby | 1.88 |
| 1964 | Alan Murrell | 1.83 |
| 1965 | Robin Souter | 1.83 |
| 1966 | Robert Scott | 1.80 |
| 1967 | Robert Taylor | 1.85 |
| 1968 | Robert Bruynoogı | 1.83 |
| 1969 | David Wilson | 1.93 |
| 1970 | Chris Youngs | 1.83 |
| 1971 | Colin Boreham | 1.95 |
| 1972 | Angus McKenzie | 1.90 |
| 1973 | Martyn Shorten | 1.83 |
| 1974 | Milton Palmer | 2.01 |
| 1975 | Milton Palmer | 2.00 |
| 1976 | Milton Palmer | 2.11 |
| 1977 | Milton Palmer | 2.10 |
| 1978 | Tim Foulger | 2.05 |
| 1979 | Ousman Cham | 2.05 |

### POLE VAULT

| | | metres |
|---|---|---|
| 1931 | Leslie Tovell | 3.05 |
| | Leslie Edwards | 3.05 |
| 1932 | Richard Webster | 3.35 |
| 1933 | Richard Webster | 3.35 |
| 1934 | Henry Chalk | 2.82 |
| 1935 | F. Buck | 2.97 |
| | Cyril Aspinall | 2.97 |
| 1936 | Cyril Aspinall | 3.12 |
| 1937 | Lawrence Hamilton | 2.74 |
| 1938 | Aubrey Robinson | 3.05 |
| 1939 | Aubrey Robinson | 3.41 |
| 1946 | Ronald Ferris | 3.05 |
| 1947 | Raymond Petitjean | 3.25 |
| 1948 | Geoffrey Elliott | 3.05 |
| 1949 | William Piper | 3.35 |
| 1950 | Alan Hanlon | 3.35 |
| 1951 | George Broad | 3.66 |
| 1952 | George Broad | 3.50 |
| 1953 | Gerald Schmidt | 3.50 |
| 1954 | Michael Nugent | 3.58 |
| 1955 | Michael Nugent | 3.50 |
| 1956 | Anthony Pitt | 3.58 |
| 1957 | David Barnard | 3.58 |
| 1958 | David Barnard | 3.68 |
| 1959 | Robert Addis | 3.66 |
| 1960 | David Stevenson | 3.71 |
| 1961 | Brian Dixon | 3.50 |
| 1962 | Malcolm Higdon | 3.92 |
| 1963 | Norman Foster | 3.96 |
| 1964 | Jeffrey Fenge | 3.96 |
| 1965 | Neal Willson | 4.19 |
| 1966 | Mike Bryant | 4.06 |
| 1967 | Gordon Rule | 4.35 |
| 1968 | Gordon Rule | 3.96 |
| 1969 | Stuart Tufton | 4.27 |
| 1970 | Stephen Chappell | 4.09 |
| 1971 | Brian Hooper | 3.80 |
| 1972 | Girish Patel | 4.12 |
| 1973 | Girish Patel | 4.40 |
| 1974 | Keith Stock | 4.60 |
| 1975 | Keith Stock | 4.75 |
| 1976 | Rupert Goodall | 4.40 |
| 1977 | Andrew Jackson | 4.40 |
| 1978 | Tim Anstiss | 4.40 |
| 1979 | Allan Leiper | 4.50 |

### LONG JUMP

| | | metres |
|---|---|---|
| 1931 | Leslie Butler | 6.46 |
| 1932 | Cyril Shurmer | 6.32 |
| 1933 | Denis Higham | 6.30 |
| 1934 | William Breach | 6.88 |
| 1935 | Joseph Tate | 6.42 |
| 1936 | G. Pickthall | 6.33 |
| 1937 | Leslie Wise | 6.62 |
| 1938 | JE Wright | 6.45 |
| 1939 | Allan Watt | 6.78 |
| 1946 | Victor Tindall | 6.30 |
| 1947 | William Jones | 6.00 |
| 1948 | Derek Hulyer | 6.46 |
| 1949 | Ronald Sleigh | 6.72 |
| 1950 | Les Barton | 6.68 |
| 1951 | George Broad | 7.02 |
| 1952 | George Broad | 6.80 |
| 1953 | John Brown | 6.44 |
| 1954 | Derek Hadler | 6.81 |

| | | |
|---|---|---|
| 1955 | Bryan Woolley | 6.81 |
| 1956 | James Melville | 6.78 |
| 1957 | David Churchill | 6.55 |
| 1958 | David Whyte | 7.11 |
| 1959 | Lewis Birchall | 6.81 |
| 1960 | Alexander Davies | 6.79 |
| 1961 | Neil Humphries | 7.03 |
| 1962 | Geoffrey Beales | 6.68 |
| 1963 | Geoffrey Beales | 7.20 |
| 1964 | William Adams | 6.65 |
| 1965 | Hamish Robertson | 7.10 |
| 1966 | Colin O'Neill | 6.99 |
| 1967 | James Gray | 6.98 |
| 1968 | Geoff Hignett | 7.32 |
| 1969 | Geoff Hignett | 7.31 |
| 1970 | Stuart Atkins | 6.81 |
| 1971 | Jerry Gangadeen | 7.07 |
| 1972 | Steve Wright | 6.79 |
| 1973 | Trevor Paice | 7.16 |
| 1974 | Roy Mitchell | 7.30 |
| 1975 | Colm Cronin (Ireland) | 6.91 |
| 1976 | Leonard Tyson | 7.18 |
| 1977 | Colin Mitchell | 7.40 |
| 1978 | Colin Mitchell | 7.14 |
| 1979 | Edward Starrs | 7.56 |

### TRIPLE JUMP

| | | metres |
|---|---|---|
| 1950 | DJ Ashurst | 13.06 |
| 1951 | Kenneth Chambers | 13.50 |
| 1952 | Alan Reeve | 14.01 |
| 1953 | William Dawes | 13.65 |
| 1954 | John Darlington | 13.55 |
| 1955 | Ian Mitchell | 13.10 |
| 1956 | Aneurin Evans | 13.71 |
| 1957 | Fred Alsop | 14.15 |
| 1958 | John Welford | 13.18 |
| 1959 | David Stephens | 14.11 |
| 1960 | Roger Slaughter | 14.57 |
| 1961 | Lynn Davies | 13.76 |
| 1962 | Anthony Tymms | 13.68 |
| 1963 | John Vernon | 13.96 |
| 1964 | John Vernon | 14.24 |
| 1965 | Hamish Robertson | 14.63 |
| 1966 | Michael Gledhill | 13.89 |
| 1967 | John Thompson | 14.04 |
| 1968 | John Thompson | 14.53 |
| 1969 | Chris Colman | 14.17 |
| 1970 | John Short | 14.50 |
| 1971 | David Johnson | 14.34 |
| 1972 | Stefan Nowak | 13.77 |
| 1973 | Stefan Nowak | 14.96 |
| 1974 | Aston Moore | 15.56 |
| 1975 | Colm Cronin (Ireland) | 14.94 |
| 1976 | Keith Connor | 15.48 |
| 1977 | Megarry Effiong | 15.65 |
| 1978 | Megarry Effiong | 15.05 |
| 1979 | Conroy Brown | 15.24 |

### SHOT (12 lb)

| | | metres |
|---|---|---|
| 1931 | Charles Reidy | 11.75 |
| 1932 | Harry Tate | 11.83 |
| 1933 | Lawrence Reavell Carter | 13.92 |
| 1934 | Dudley Neilson | 12.70 |
| 1935 | H. Pietaru (France) | 15.39 |
| 1936 | L. Haas-Goerz (Germany) | 12.84 |
| 1937 | Michael Heath | 13.12 |
| 1938 | Albert Rosenberg | 12.98 |
| 1939 | Alexander Johnston | 14.76 |
| 1946 | Alan Topham-Steel | 12.58 |
| 1947 | John Banes | 13.90 |
| 1948 | Barry Dodd | 13.02 |
| 1949 | Alfred Wood | 15.64 |
| 1950 | David Chapple | 13.96 |
| 1951 | John Hutchinson | 14.04 |
| 1952 | Kenneth Jones | 14.75 |
| 1953 | Gerald Carr | 15.19 |
| 1954 | John Jones | 16.18 |
| 1955 | David Harrison | 15.54 |
| 1956 | Mike Lindsay | 16.86 |
| 1957 | Mike Lindsay | 18.26 |
| 1958 | John Davies | 16.41 |
| 1959 | John Davies | 16.20 |
| 1960 | James Todd | 16.94 |
| 1961 | Michael Bellingham | 17.35 |
| 1962 | Alan Carter | 17.47 |
| 1963 | Alan Carter | 18.69 |
| 1964 | John Holmes | 17.64 |
| 1965 | John van Reenen (S. Africa) | 19.55 |
| 1966 | Geoff Capes | 17.14 |
| 1967 | Geoff Capes | 18.15 |
| 1968 | Peter Tancred | 16.57 |
| 1969 | John Alderson | 17.08 |
| 1970 | John Alderson | 17.89 |

### SHOT ($6\frac{1}{4}$ kg)

| | | metres |
|---|---|---|
| 1971 | Tony Satchwell | 15.94 |
| 1972 | Stephen Archer | 14.88 |

### SHOT (16 lb)

| | | metres |
|---|---|---|
| 1973 | Ian Lindley | 14.52 |
| 1974 | Simon Rodhouse | 14.72 |
| 1975 | Paul Buxton | 16.11 |
| 1976 | Gerald McEvoy (Ireland) | 15.08 |
| 1977 | Andrew Vince | 15.26 |
| 1978 | Andrew Vince | 15.42 |
| 1979 | Graham Savory | 14.91 |

### DISCUS (3 lb 5 oz)

| | | metres |
|---|---|---|
| 1931 | Harold Eastwood | 35.14 |
| 1932 | Richard Webster | 33.02 |
| 1933 | Richard Webster | 35.16 |
| 1934 | Norman Downie | 40.22 |
| 1935 | JF Klein (France) | 44.38 |
| 1936 | Philip Dawson | 37.68 |
| 1937 | Jack Linaker | 40.44 |
| 1938 | Dudley Burges | 40.42 |
| 1939 | Marcus Dowling | 41.40 |
| 1946 | Alan Sadler | 40.36 |
| 1947 | Barry Dodd | 36.22 |
| 1948 | Barry Dodd | 44.34 |
| 1949 | Mark Pharoah | 46.22 |
| 1950 | Peter Atkinson | 40.74 |
| 1951 | Robert Shaw | 41.88 |
| 1952 | James Sampson | 43.58 |
| 1953 | Gerald Carr | 47.42 |
| 1954 | Gerald Carr | 47.66 |
| 1955 | John Pullinger | 45.70 |
| 1956 | Mike Lindsay | 55.48 |
| 1957 | Mike Lindsay | 53.90 |
| 1958 | John Sheldrick | 51.82 |
| 1959 | John Weightman | 46.92 |
| 1960 | Mike Bellingham | 50.30 |
| 1961 | Peter Nimmo | 51.60 |
| 1962 | Peter Nimmo | 53.44 |
| 1963 | John Hillier | 50.94 |
| 1964 | Brian Gillo | 53.10 |
| 1965 | John van Reenen (S. Africa) | 56.72 |
| 1966 | Michael Conway (Ireland) | 53.98 |
| 1967 | Peter Tancred | 49.00 |
| 1968 | Peter Tancred | 53.52 |
| 1969 | Guy Dirkin | 49.54 |
| 1970 | Guy Dirkin | 54.16 |

### DISCUS ($1\frac{3}{4}$ kg)

| | | metres |
|---|---|---|
| 1971 | Guy Dirkin | 50.38 |
| 1972 | Peter Sharman | 45.76 |

### DISCUS (2 kg)

| | | metres |
|---|---|---|
| 1973 | Peter Sharman | 43.24 |
| 1974 | Richard Slaney | 48.46 |
| 1975 | Paul Buxton | 52.68 |
| 1976 | Ian Strutt | 43.72 |
| 1977 | Craig Considine (Australia) | 46.74 |
| 1978 | Chris Dinsdale | 43.90 |
| 1979 | Chris Dinsdale | 48.68 |

### HAMMER (12 lb)

| | | metres |
|---|---|---|
| 1951 | Iain Bain | 43.86 |
| 1952 | Iain Bain | 47.66 |
| 1953 | Michael Martin | 51.40 |
| 1954 | Michael Ellis | 55.38 |
| 1955 | Michael Ellis | 58.16 |
| 1956 | Patrick Ritchie | 52.66 |
| 1957 | Peter Newton | 52.84 |
| 1958 | Peter Newton | 53.82 |
| 1959 | David Mitchell | 54.24 |
| 1960 | Leonard Martin | 47.04 |
| 1961 | Peter Gibbs | 58.02 |
| 1962 | Peter Aston | 53.66 |
| 1963 | Peter Aston | 60.96 |
| 1964 | Hugh Cameron | 55.94 |
| 1965 | Barry Williams | 56.28 |
| 1966 | Donald Harrigan (Ireland) | 54.26 |
| 1967 | Paul Dickenson | 60.30 |
| 1968 | Paul Dickenson | 61.36 |
| 1969 | Ian Chipchase | 63.46 |
| 1970 | Ian Chipchase | 59.28 |

### HAMMER ($6\frac{1}{4}$ lb)

| | | metres |
|---|---|---|
| 1971 | Karl Lasis | 53.74 |
| 1972 | Eric Berry | 63.28 |

### HAMMER ($7\frac{1}{4}$ kg)

| | | metres |
|---|---|---|
| 1973 | Eric Berry | 59.00 |
| 1974 | Philip Scott | 55.78 |
| 1975 | Paul Buxton | 60.00 |
| 1976 | Richard Gibson (Ireland) | 51.00 |
| 1977 | Declan Hegarty (Ireland) | 54.88 |
| 1978 | Ron James | 54.34 |
| 1979 | Martin Girvan | 66.14 |

### JAVELIN (700 gr)

| | | metres |
|---|---|---|
| 1931 | Leslie Edwards | 45.64 |
| 1932 | Joseph Heath | 54.16 |
| 1933 | Edward Finneron | 53.64 |
| 1934 | James MacKillop | 52.96 |
| 1935 | JF Klein (France) | 58.22 |
| 1936 | Frank Adams | 56.28 |
| 1937 | Robert Evans | 47.30 |
| 1938 | Robert Evans | 48.82 |
| 1939 | Malcolm Dalrymple | 49.00 |
| 1946 | Richard Williams | 56.64 |
| 1947 | John Swaisland | 55.32 |
| 1948 | G. Bell | 51.36 |
| 1949 | Michael Denley | 60.98 |
| 1950 | Maurice Morrell | 53.66 |
| 1951 | Malcolm Harradine | 61.30 |
| 1952 | John McDonald | 56.74 |
| 1953 | Colin Smith | 61.34 |
| 1954 | Michael Lanning | 55.74 |
| 1955 | Brian Whitaker | 60.78 |
| 1956 | Anthony Farmer | 64.32 |
| 1957 | Gary Bucknell | 61.26 |
| 1958 | John Andrews | 64.40 |
| 1959 | John McSorley | 62.72 |
| 1960 | James Todd | 63.60 |

### JAVELIN (800 gr)

| | | metres |
|---|---|---|
| 1961 | John Greasley | 71.58 |
| 1962 | William Peet | 58.40 |
| 1963 | William Peet | 61.50 |
| 1964 | Michael Nobbs | 60.52 |
| 1965 | Kenneth Holmes | 63.10 |
| 1966 | Richard Perkins | 68.92 |
| 1967 | Adrian Diffey | 56.44 |
| 1968 | Adrian Diffey | 65.20 |
| 1969 | Mladen Gavrilovic | 63.64 |
| 1970 | Nicholas Schofield | 61.34 |
| 1971 | Bogus Kawalko | 62.10 |
| 1972 | Derek Lee | 57.34 |
| 1973 | David Ottley | 66.44 |
| 1974 | Charles Clover | 75.50 |
| 1975 | Leonard Evans | 56.26 |
| 1976 | Jeff Brooks | 64.82 |
| 1977 | Chris Hodder (Rhodesia) | 67.38 |
| 1978 | Ian Marsh | 70.14 |
| 1979 | Ian Marsh | 68.32 |

## AAA Youth Championships

### 100 YARDS

| | | sec |
|---|---|---|
| 1968 | Adrian Thomas | 10.0 |

### 100 METRES

| | | sec |
|---|---|---|
| 1969 | Anthony Hadley | 11.1 |
| 1970 | Robert Munns | 11.2 |
| 1971 | Garry Peters | 11.2 |
| 1972 | Dennis Thompson | 11.4 |
| 1973 | Roy Sanderson | 11.2 |
| 1974 | David Hill | 10.9 |
| 1975 | David Baptiste | 11.0 |
| 1976 | Michael McFarlane | 10.8 |
| 1977 | Ezra Dennis | 11.0 |
| 1978 | Michael Powell | 10.94 |
| 1979 | Donovan Reid | 10.9 |

### 220 YARDS

| | | sec |
|---|---|---|
| 1967 | Richard Taylor | 22.8 |
| 1968 | David Jenkins | 22.5 |

### 200 METRES

| | | sec |
|---|---|---|
| 1969 | Anthony Hadley | 22.2 |
| 1970 | Robert Munns | 22.3 |
| 1971 | David Pink | 22.7 |
| 1972 | Garry Doerr | 23.2 |
| 1973 | Roy Sanderson | 22.5 |
| 1974 | Earl Tulloch | 22.1 |
| 1975 | David Baptiste | 22.4 |
| 1976 | Michael McFarlane | 21.4 |
| 1977 | Derek Butler | 22.1 |
| 1978 | Philip Brown | 22.61 |
| 1979 | Malcolm James | 22.0 |

### 440 YARDS

| | | sec |
|---|---|---|
| 1968 | David Jenkins | 49.0 |

### 400 METRES

| | | sec |
|---|---|---|
| 1969 | Peter Beaven | 48.5 |
| 1970 | Steve Marlow | 50.6 |
| 1971 | Steve Ovett | 49.8 |
| 1972 | Steve Ovett | 49.1 |
| 1973 | Cecil Moven | 49.6 |
| 1974 | Martin Francis | 49.5 |
| 1975 | Gregory Stewart | 49.7 |
| 1976 | Stephen Houlton | 49.9 |
| 1977 | Augustine Mbanu | 50.0 |
| 1978 | Anthony Morgan | 49.91 |
| 1979 | Malcolm James | 50.2 |

### 880 YARDS

| | | min | sec |
|---|---|---|---|
| 1967 | Michael Gordon | 1 | 54.1 |
| 1968 | Stephen Dodwell | 1 | 56.9 |

### 800 METRES

| | | min | sec |
|---|---|---|---|
| 1969 | Ian Whittle | 1 | 54.4 |
| 1970 | Anthony Settle | 1 | 54.6 |

| | | min | sec |
|---|---|---|---|
| 1971 | Anthony Dyke | 1 | 58.0 |
| 1972 | Anthony Dyke | 1 | 55.0 |
| 1973 | Wayne Tarquini | 1 | 53.8 |
| 1974 | Stephen Caldwell | 1 | 54.2 |
| 1975 | Dane Joseph | 1 | 55.4 |
| 1976 | Julian Spooner | 1 | 53.2 |
| 1977 | Julian Spooner | 1 | 53.6 |
| 1978 | Christopher McGeorge | 1 | 51.7 |
| 1979 | Peter Elliott | 1 | 55.6 |

### 1 MILE

| | | min | sec |
|---|---|---|---|
| 1968 | John Lees | 4 | 18.2 |

### 1500 METRES

| | | min | sec |
|---|---|---|---|
| 1969 | David Gibbon | 3 | 56.8 |
| 1970 | David Glassborrow | 3 | 55.9 |
| 1971 | Kevin Steere | 3 | 55.5 |
| 1972 | Paul Williams | 4 | 00.1 |
| 1973 | Sebastian Coe | 3 | 55.0 |
| 1974 | Mark Bateman | 3 | 53.2 |
| 1975 | Gary Nurse | 3 | 55.4 |
| 1976 | Roy Wood | 3 | 55.7 |
| 1977 | Steve Cram | 3 | 54.6 |
| 1978 | Nigel Harper | 3 | 56.2 |
| 1979 | Kelvin Newton | 3 | 57.0 |

### 1000 METRES STEEPLECHASE

| | | min | sec |
|---|---|---|---|
| 1967 | Christopher Barber | 2 | 46.1 |
| 1968 | Thomas Litherland | 2 | 39.9 |
| 1969 | David Jameson | 2 | 42.6 |
| 1970 | John O'Kane | 2 | 46.6 |
| 1971 | David Brewster | 2 | 43.1 |
| 1972 | Stephen Durnall | 2 | 48.0 |

### 1500 METRES STEEPLECHASE

| | | min | sec |
|---|---|---|---|
| 1973 | Stephen Edmonds | 4 | 21.6 |
| 1974 | Stephen Evans | 4 | 18.1 |
| 1978 | John Wilson | 4 | 15.3 |
| 1976 | Kevin Capper | 4 | 17.7 |
| 1977 | David Lewis | 4 | 13.6 |
| 1978 | David Lewis | 4 | 15.0 |
| 1979 | Michael Newby | 4 | 22.3 |

### 110 YARDS HURDLES

| | | sec |
|---|---|---|
| 1968 | Raymond Young | 13.5 |

### 100 METRES HURDLES

| | | sec |
|---|---|---|
| 1969 | Lindsay Smith | 13.2 |
| 1970 | Everette Thomas | 13.9 |
| 1971 | Angus McKenzie | 13.7 |
| 1972 | Anthony James | 13.9 |
| 1973 | Kenrick Cheong | 14.1 |
| 1974 | John Longman | 13.4 |
| 1975 | Geoffrey Thorp | 13.5 |
| 1976 | Nathaniel Augustin | 13.2 |
| 1977 | Peter Adams | 13.1 |
| 1978 | Denis Finnerty (Ireland) | 14.12 |
| 1979 | Desmond Wilkinson | 13.3 |

### 400 METRES HURDLES

| | | sec |
|---|---|---|
| 1978 | David Jones | 56.01 |
| 1979 | Philip Beattie | 56.0 |

### 1 MILE WALK

| | | min | sec |
|---|---|---|---|
| 1968 | Oliver Caviglioli | 7 | 04.0 |

### 2000 METRES WALK

| | | min | sec |
|---|---|---|---|
| 1969 | Peter Dallow | 9 | 00.8 |
| 1970 | Paul Sturdy | 8 | 41.8 |
| 1971 | Vincent Hands | 8 | 54.6 |
| 1972 | Kevin Sturdy | 8 | 36.6 |
| 1973 | Michael Dunion | 8 | 52.4 |
| 1974 | Michael Dunion | 8 | 33.4 |
| 1975 | Shaun Maxwell | 9 | 06.8 |

### 3000 METRES WALK

| | | min | sec |
|---|---|---|---|
| 1976 | Shaun Maxwell | 13 | 05.8 |
| 1977 | Ian McCombie | 13 | 28.8 |
| 1978 | Niall Troy | 13 | 10.6 |
| 1979 | Graham Maynard | 13 | 39.6 |

### HIGH JUMP

| | | metres |
|---|---|---|
| 1968 | David Wilson | 1.90 |
| 1969 | Paul Hambley | 1.75 |
| 1970 | Graham Barclay | 1.75 |
| 1971 | Eric Shirley | 1.85 |
| 1972 | Alan Dainton | 1.85 |
| 1973 | Brian Burgess | 1.95 |
| 1974 | Anthony Brewster | 1.90 |
| 1975 | Anthony Brewster | 2.03 |
| 1976 | Augustine Udo | 1.94 |
| 1977 | Ross Hepburn | 2.00 |
| 1978 | Edward Moore | 1.85 |
| 1979 | Ousman Cham | 2.05 |

### POLE VAULT

| | | metres |
|---|---|---|
| 1968 | Philip Goulding | 3.43 |
| 1969 | Brian Hooper | 3.50 |
| 1970 | Christopher Hyde | 3.55 |
| 1971 | Ray Kelly | 3.50 |
| 1972 | Keith Stock | 3.50 |
| 1973 | Keith Stock | 4.20 |
| 1974 | Liam Hennessy (Ireland) | 3.90 |
| 1975 | Neil Mcphee | 4.10 |
| 1976 | Mark Shippen | 3.90 |
| 1977 | John Ball | 4.10 |
| 1978 | Timothy Anstiss | 4.21 |
| 1979 | John Andrews | 4.22 |

### LONG JUMP

| | | metres |
|---|---|---|
| 1968 | Robert Nicholls | 6.49 |
| 1969 | Michael Ademola | 6.65 |
| 1970 | Paul McEwan | 6.47 |
| 1971 | Angus McKenzie | 6.76 |
| 1972 | Leslie Hoyte | 6.83 |
| 1973 | Michael Nangreave | 6.83 |
| 1974 | Albert Earle | 6.74 |
| 1975 | Cleve West | 6.43 |
| 1976 | Augustine Udo | 7.08 |
| 1977 | Trevor Sinclair | 6.89 |
| 1978 | Leroy White | 6.81 |
| 1979 | David Burgess | 6.97 |

### TRIPLE JUMP

| | | metres |
|---|---|---|
| 1968 | Peter Dale | 13.35 |
| 1969 | Barrie Hartshorn | 13.80 |
| 1970 | Richard Philps | 13.79 |
| 1971 | John Howell | 13.33 |
| 1972 | Frank Attoh | 13.93 |
| 1973 | Garry Ball | 13.94 |
| 1974 | Leigh McGinley | 13.85 |
| 1975 | Paul Rose | 14.30 |
| 1976 | Stephen Metcalfe | 14.20 |
| 1977 | Niall McCarthy (Ireland) | 14.22 |
| 1978 | Nicholas Leech | 13.85 |
| 1979 | Jeffrey Browne | 14.55 |

### SHOT (10 lb)

| | | metres |
|---|---|---|
| 1968 | John Corbett | 16.84 |
| 1969 | Stefan Purdy | 15.16 |
| 1970 | Geoffrey Hunt | 14.29 |

### SHOT (5 kg)

| | | metres |
|---|---|---|
| 1971 | Stephen Archer | 15.44 |
| 1972 | Ian Lindley | 16.48 |
| 1973 | Michael Eyres | 15.74 |
| 1974 | George Patience | 15.94 |
| 1975 | Kevan Sanderson | 16.18 |
| 1976 | Alan Husk | 15.85 |
| 1977 | Anthony Zaidman | 16.66 |
| 1978 | Anthony Zaidman | 17.61 |
| 1979 | George Brocklebank | 17.76 |

### DISCUS (1 kg)

| | | metres |
|---|---|---|
| 1968 | John Follett | 52.74 |
| 1969 | John Turton | 57.38 |
| 1970 | John Hartley | 54.90 |

### DISCUS (1½ kg)

| | | metres |
|---|---|---|
| 1971 | John Howell | 43.94 |
| 1972 | Stephen Berry | 46.02 |
| 1973 | Stephen Berry | 49.80 |
| 1974 | Joseph Brice | 44.62 |
| 1975 | David Allan | 45.94 |
| 1976 | Thomas Crotty (Ireland) | 46.12 |
| 1977 | Graham Savory | 46.28 |
| 1978 | Paul Mardle | 46.00 |
| 1979 | Paul Mardle | 47.90 |

### 3000 METRES

| | | min sec |
|---|---|---|
| 1978 | Gary Taylor | 8 34.2 |
| 1979 | Kelvin Newton | 8 38.3 |

### HAMMER (10 lb)

| | | metres |
|---|---|---|
| 1968 | David Rogers | 56.06 |
| 1969 | Philip Robinson | 55.74 |
| 1970 | Eric Berry | 60.70 |

### HAMMER (5 kg)

| | | metres |
|---|---|---|
| 1971 | Stephen Pinsent | 51.20 |
| 1972 | Trevor Minns | 50.44 |
| 1973 | Matthew Mileham | 52.46 |
| 1974 | Brian Riddles | 56.00 |
| 1975 | Stephen Watson | 59.84 |
| 1976 | Declan Hegarty (Ireland) | 61.90 |
| 1977 | Declan Hegarty (Ireland) | 66.16 |
| 1978 | Liam Hickey (Ireland) | 59.70 |
| 1979 | Anthony Kenneally | 66.72 |

### JAVELIN (700 gr)

| | | metres |
|---|---|---|
| 1968 | Adrian Tew | 58.30 |
| 1969 | Bogus Kawalko | 60.36 |
| 1970 | Stefan Jalowiecki | 54.46 |
| 1971 | Stefan Jalowiecki | 60.28 |
| 1972 | Gareth Brooks | 54.42 |
| 1973 | Jeffrey Brooks | 59.50 |
| 1974 | Leonard Evans | 60.12 |
| 1975 | Michael Pilling | 56.66 |
| 1976 | Craig Johnson | 61.54 |
| 1977 | Ian Marsh | 68.26 |
| 1978 | Marcus Humphries | 62.54 |
| 1979 | Mark O'Connor (Ireland) | 53.36 |

### 440 YARDS HURDLES — JUNIORS

| | | sec |
|---|---|---|
| 1967 | George Hilsdon | 55.6 |
| 1968 | Anthony Collins | 54.5 |

### 400 METRES HURDLES — JUNIORS

| | | sec |
|---|---|---|
| 1969 | Ricky Taylor | 53.2 |
| 1970 | Paul Young | 54.1 |
| 1971 | Peter Kelly | 53.4 |
| 1972 | Martin Ollier | 55.2 |
| 1973 | Stephen James | 54.1 |
| 1974 | Philip Mills (New Zealand) | 54.4 |
| 1975 | Wilbert Greaves | 54.3 |
| 1976 | Gary Oakes | 53.1 |
| 1977 | Gary Oakes | 51.7 |
| 1978 | Chris Preston | 53.68 |
| 1979 | Paul Goacher | 54.8 |

(See p. 200)

## AAA Championships, Venues and Dates, 1880–1979

| Year | Date | Venue |
|---|---|---|
| 1880 | 3 July | Lillie Bridge |
| 1881 | 16 July | Birmingham |
| 1882 | 1 July | Stoke on Trent |
| 1883 | 30 June | Lillie Bridge |
| 1884 | 21 June | Birmingham |
| 1885 | 27 June | Southport |
| 1886 | 3 July | Stamford Bridge |
| 1887 | 2 July | Stourbridge |
| 1888 | 30 June | Crewe |
| 1889 | 29 June | Stamford Bridge |
| 1890 | 12 July | Birmingham |
| 1891 | 27 June | Manchester |
| 1892 | 2 July | Stamford Bridge |
| 1893 | 1 July | Northampton |
| 1894 | 7 July | Huddersfield |
| 1895 | 6 July | Stamford Bridge |
| 1896 | 4 July | Northampton |
| 1897 | 3 July | Manchester |
| 1898 | 2 July | Stamford Bridge |
| 1899 | 1 July | Wolverhampton |
| 1900 | 7 July | Stamford Bridge |
| 1901 | 6 July | Huddersfield |
| 1902 | 5 July | Stamford Bridge |
| 1903 | 4 July | Northampton |
| 1904 | 2 July | Rochdale |
| 1905 | 1 July | Stamford Bridge |
| 1906 | 7 July | Stamford Bridge |
| 1907 | 6 July | Manchester |
| 1908 | 4 July | White City |
| 1909 | 3 July | Stamford Bridge |
| 1910 | 2 July | Stamford Bridge |
| 1911 | 1 July | Stamford Bridge |
| 1912 | 22 June | Stamford Bridge |
| 1913 | 5 July | Stamford Bridge |
| 1914 | 3/4 July | Stamford Bridge |
| 1915–1918 | | WORLD WAR I |
| 1919 | 5 July | Stamford Bridge |
| 1920 | 2/3 July | Stamford Bridge |
| 1921 | 1/2 July | Stamford Bridge |
| 1922 | 30 June/1 July | Stamford Bridge |
| 1923 | 6/7 July | Stamford Bridge |
| 1924 | 20/21 June | Stamford Bridge |
| 1925 | 17/18 July | Stamford Bridge |
| 1926 | 2/3 July | Stamford Bridge |
| 1927 | 1/2/4 July | Stamford Bridge |
| 1928 | 6/7 July | Stamford Bridge |
| 1929 | 5/6 July | Stamford Bridge |
| 1930 | 4/5 July | Stamford Bridge |
| 1931 | 3/4 July | Stamford Bridge |
| 1932 | 1/2 July | White City |
| 1933 | 7/8 July | White City |
| 1934 | 13/14 July | White City |
| 1935 | 12/13 July | White City |
| 1936 | 10/11 July | White City |
| 1937 | 16/17 July | White City |
| 1938 | 15/16 July | White City |
| 1939 | 7/8 July | White City |
| 1940–1945 | | WORLD WAR II |
| 1946 | 19/20 July | White City |
| 1947 | 18/19 July | White City |
| 1948 | 2/3 July | White City |
| 1949 | 15/16 July | White City |
| 1950 | 14/15 July | White City |
| 1951 | 13/14 July | White City |
| 1952 | 20/21 June | White City |
| 1953 | 10/11 July | White City |
| 1954 | 9/10 July | White City |
| 1955 | 15/16 July | White City |
| 1956 | 13/14 July | White City |
| 1957 | 12/13 July | White City |
| 1958 | 11/12 July | White City |
| 1959 | 10/11 July | White City |
| 1960 | 15/16 July | White City |
| 1961 | 14/15 July | White City |
| 1962 | 13/14 July | White City |
| 1963 | 12/13 July | White City |
| 1964 | 10/11 July | White City |
| 1965 | 9/10 July | White City |
| 1966 | 8/9 July | White City |
| 1967 | 14/15 July | White City |
| 1968 | 12/13 July | White City |
| 1969 | 1/2 August | White City |
| 1970 | 8/9 August | White City |
| 1971 | 23/24 July | Crystal Palace |
| 1972 | 14/15 July | Crystal Palace |
| 1973 | 13/14 July | Crystal Palace |
| 1974 | 12/13 July | Crystal Palace |
| 1975 | 1/2 August | Crystal Palace |
| 1976 | 13/14 August | Crystal Palace |
| 1977 | 22/23 July | Crystal Palace |
| 1978 | 23/24 June | Crystal Palace |
| 1979 | 13/14 July | Crystal Palace |

**Summary**
Including 1979, there have been 90 Meetings — 35 from 1880 to 1914; 21 from 1919 to 1939 and 34 from 1946 to 1979.
Total meetings held at the White City number 34, at Stamford Bridge 28, at Crystal Palace 9, and at Lillie Bridge 2. The remaining 17 meetings were held in the Provinces from 1881 to 1907.

| | 1880–1914 | 1919–1939 | 1946–1979 | Total |
|---|---|---|---|---|
| Lillie Bridge | 2 | nil | nil | 2 |
| Stamford Bridge | 15 | 13 | nil | 28 |
| Provincial | 17 | nil | nil | 17 |
| White City | 1 | 8 | 25 | 34 |
| Crystal Palace | nil | nil | 9 | 9 |
| TOTAL | 35 | 21 | 34 | 90 |

As Prince of Wales, the future King Edward VIII attended the 1908 Championships; King George V attended in 1922. Queen Elizabeth II has attended three Championship meetings: in 1952, accompanied by Princess Margaret, in 1956, the Duke of Edinburgh, and in 1968.

# Bibliography


## PERIODICALS

*Amateur Sport and Athletics, The Athlete, Athletic News, Athletics Arena, Athletics Weekly, Athletics World, Bell's Life in London, British Olympic Journal, The Field, CB Fry's Magazine, The Game, Illustrated Sporting and Dramatic News, Land and Water, The Modern Athlete, Modern Athletics, Olympic Review, The Sporting Gazette, Sports Quarterly Magazine, Sportsworld, World Sports.*

## BOOKS

ABRAHAMS, HM *Fifty Years of AAA Championships* (Carborundum Co, 1961)

ABRAHAMS, HM AND BRUCE KERR, J. *AAA Championships, 1880–1931* (AAA, 1932)

AMATEUR ATHLETIC ASSOCIATION *AAA Coming of Age Dinner* (AAA, 1902)

*Championship Programmes, Handbooks, Annual Reports and Miscellaneous Publications, 1880 onwards*

*Fifty Years of Progress, 1880–1930*, Edited by HF Pash (AAA, 1930)

BRASHER, CW (ED) *The Road to Rome* (Kimber, 1960)

BRITISH OLYMPIC ASSOCIATION *Olympic Reports, 1908 onwards*

BUCHANAN, I. *An Encyclopaedia of British Athletics Records* (Stanley Paul, 1961)

CROOME, ACM *Fifty Years of Sport at Oxford, Cambridge and the Great Public Schools* (Walter Southwood, 1913)

CRUMP, JCG *Running Round the World* (Hale, 1966)

GRIFFIN HH *Athletics* (Bell, 1889)

INTERNATIONAL AMATEUR ATHLETIC FEDERATION *Progressive World Record Lists 1913–1970 and supplements*

KILLANIN, LORD AND RODDA, J. *The Olympic Games* (Barrie and Jenkins, 1976)

MCWHIRTER, AR AND ND *Get To Your Marks!* (Nicholas Kaye, 1951)

*The Guinness Book of Olympic Records* (various edns 1964 onwards)

MEYER, HA (Ed) *Athletics by The Achilles Club* (Dent, 1938, 1951, 1955)

*Modern Athletics by The Achilles Club* (OUP, 1958)

NATIONAL UNION OF TRACK STATISTICIANS *British Athletics Annual* (1958 onwards)

PICKERING, R. *Athletics 1974* (Macdonald and Jane's, 1974 onwards)

QUERCETANI, RL *A World History of Track and Field Athletics* (OUP, 1964)

RACE WALKING ASSOCIATION *The Sport of Race Walking*, Edited by AA Harley (RWA, 1962)

RICHARDSON, LN *Jubilee History of the International Cross-Country Union, 1903–1953* (ICCU, 1953)

RYAN, J. AND FRASER, I. *The Annals of Thames Hare and Hounds* (TH&H, 1968)

SHEARMAN, M. *Athletics and Football* (Longman's, Green, 1889)

THOM, W. *Pedestrianism* (Brown and Frost, 1813)

TISDALL, RMN AND SHERIE, F. *The Young Athlete* (Blackie, 1934)

TOMLIN, S. (Ed) *Olympic Odyssey* (Modern Athletic Publications, 1956)

WALLIS, AJ *Olympics Cavalcade and Who's Who, 1948* (Background Books, 1948)

WATMAN, MF *The Encyclopaedia of Athletics* (Hale, 1964, 1967, 1973, 1977)

*History of British Athletics* (Hale, 1968)

WEBSTER, FAM *Athletics of Today* (Warne, 1929)

*Athletics Teaching and Training* (Pitman, 1948)

*The Evolution of the Olympic Games* (Heath, Cranton and Ouseley, 1914)

*Great Moments in Athletics* (Country Life, 1947)

WILKINSON, HF *Modern Athletics* (Warne, 1868, *The Field*, 1877)

# Index OF NAMES

*Birth and death dates shown where known* *Italicized numbers refer to illustrations*


A

Aaron, Dr Frank E. (b 30.3.20) 99
Abrahams, Harold M. (1899–1977) 67, 75, 76, 77, *77*, 79, 92, 95, 103, 125, 126, 129, 132, 155, 161, 162, 168, *175*, 175–7
Adams, Brian (b 13.3.49) 142, 143
Adedoyin, Prince Adegboyega F. (b 11.9.22) 95
Ahearne, Timothy J. (1885–1968) 55
Akii-bua, John (b 3.12.48) *147*, 148, 149
Alder, James NC (b 10.6.40) 131
Alexander, Sheila W. (see Lerwill)
Alford, James WLl (b 15.10.13) 88, *119*, 122
Allardice, RB Barclay (1779–1854) *15*, 15, 22
Allday, Suzanne (*née* Farmer) (b 26.11.34) 116
Allen, Laurence (Lol) (b 25.4.21) 140
Alsop, Frederick J. (b 20.10.38) 127, *128*
Alverstone, Lord (see Webster, Richard)
Anderson, Arthur ED (1886–1967) 75
Anderson, Gerard RL (1889–1914) 65
Anderson, Timothy D. (b 16.10.25) 99
Andersson, Arne (b 27.10.17) 92, 93
Andersson, Harald (b 2.4.07) *87*
Andrews, Thomas (b 15.6.54) 162
Ankio, Risto (b 15.4.37) 126
Anthony, Donald WJ (b 6.11.28) 105
Applegarth, William R. (1890–1958) *57*, 58, 105
Archer, John (Jack) (b 10.8.21) 89, 94, 97, 102
Armitage, Heather J. (b 17.3.33) (see Young)
Ashworth, Sir Herbert (b 30.1.10) 147
Astley, Arthur 60
Astley, Sir John D. (1828–94) 16
Atkinson, Sydney JM (b 14.3.01) 77, 78
Aukett, James W. (b 15.4.49) 158

B

Bacon, Frederick E. (b 1870) 44, 45
Bailey, Emmanuel McDonald (b 8.12.20) 89, 93–9, *102*, 102–5
Bailey, George W. 82, 83
Baker, Homer (b 1892) 70, 73
Baker, B. Howard (b 15.2.92) 68, *120*, 120
Baker, Philip J. (b 1.11.89) (now Lord Noel-Baker) 58, 69, 75
Bannister, Sir Roger G. (b 23.3.29) 58, 92, 96, 99, 101, 103–7, *107*, 108, *110*, 111, 114, 125, 126
Barclay, Captain (see Allardice RB)
Barclay, Sir Harry J. (1861–1933) 65, 67, 69, 82
Barnard, Adam P. (b 4.3.43) 155, 158
Barnard, William M. (1863–1932) 65
Barrett, John *60*
Barry, Dr William JM (b 23.9.1863) 47, 48
Barthel, Joseph (b 24.2.27) 96
Batty, Melvyn R. (b 9.4.40) 114
Bautista, Daniel (b 4.8.52) 142
Baxter, Irving K. (1876–1957) *52*, 52, *62*, 62
Baxter, Michael I. (b 28.5.45) 147
Bayi, Filbert (b 23.6.53) 163
Beavers, Walter J. (b 1903) 82, 84
Beccali, Luigi (b 19.11.07) 81, 83, 89
Bedford, David (b 30.12.49) *146*, 146–51, 155, 158, 163, 169, 171, *172*, 174
Bennett, Charles (1871–1949) *50*, 54, 170
Bennett, Louis (see 'Deerfoot')
Besson, Colette (b 7.4.46) 134
Binks, Joseph BW (1874–1966) *53*, 69, *170*
Birrell, Joseph R. (b 11.3.30) 96
Black, David J. (b 2.10.52) 158
Blair, Alexander (b 1877) 44, 45
Blankers, Jan (b 1904) 82
Blankers-Koen, Francina E. (Fanny) (b 26.4.18) 82
Blask, Erwin (b 20.3.10) 84
Blathwayt, Gerard W. (b 1855) *25*
Board, Lillian B. (1948–70) 134, 135
Bolding, James (b 3.11.49) 155
Bolotnikov, Pyotr (b 8.3.30) 127
Boothe, Lorna M. (b 5.12.54) 163
Borzov, Valeriy (b 20.10.49) 147
Boulter, John P. (b 18.11.40) 132
Bradley, Charles A. (1870–1940) 44
Brangwin, Kenneth C. 82
Brasher, Christopher W. (b 21.8.28) 106, 111, *113*, 113, 114, 116, 177
Brasser, R. Jan (b 20.11.12) *87*
Braun, Hans (1886–1918) *52*, 52, 65
Bredin, Edgar C. (1866–1939) 45, *49*, 68
Bridge, Robert (1883–1953) 68, 138, *139*, 140
Brightwell, Robbie I. (b 27.10.39) 125–9
Brookes, William Penny (1809–1895) 18
Brooks, Marshall J. (1855–1944) 32, 162
Brown, Audrey (b 1915) 87
Brown, A. Godfrey K. (b 21.2.15) 86, *88*, 88, 103
Brown, Keith S. (b 1915) 85, *86*
Brown, Ralph K. (b 28.8.09) 85
Browne, Peter M. (b 3.2.49) *155*
Brundage, Avery (1887–1975) 168
Buchner, Joachim (b 8.4.05) 77
Bulger, Daniel D. (b 1866) 48
Bull, Michael A. (b 11.9.46) 146, 148, *149*, *150*, 154
Bullivant, Michael J. (b 1.3.34) 126, 127
Burgess, Brian (b 30.9.57) 163
Burghley, Lord, 6th Marquess of Exeter (David GB Cecil) (b 9.2.05) 77, 78, *81*, 81, *82*, 82, 83, 91, 95, 103, 129, 161, *167*, 167, 168

Burke, Barbara HA (b 13.5.17) 87
Butler, Guy M. (b 25.8.99) 68, 69, 77
Byers, Lord (Charles) Frank (b 24.7.15) 131, 132
Bylehn, Erik 73

C

Campbell, Colin WA (b 20.6.46) *155*
Campbell, W. Menzies (Ming) (b 22.5.41) 127
Capes, Geoffrey L. (b 23.8.49) 149, *151*, 151, 154, *156*, 158, 163
Carpenter, John C. (b 1886) 54
Carr, Henry (b 27.11.42) 127
Carter, Andrew W. (b 29.1.49) *150*, 151, 154, *155*
Carter, Leonard W. (b 21.11.42) 127
Cawley, Shirley (b 26.4.32) 103, 122
Chambers, John G. (1843–83) *19–21*, 19–28, 29, 30, 31, 32, 36, 41, 59, 61, 63, 134, 136
Chapelle, Jean 89
Chapman, H. Anthony L. 122
Chataway, Christopher J. (b 31.1.31) 99, 103, 106, *108*, 108, *111*, *113*, 113, 114, 126, 170
Chinnery, Walter M. (1843–1905) 16, *25*
Chipchase, Ian A. (b 26.2.52) 154
Churcher, Harry G. (1910–72) 89, 96, 98
Clark, Duncan McDM (b 22.6.15) 99
Clarke, Ronald W. (b 21.2.37) *129*, 131, *132*, 132, 147, 148, 171
Clement, Frank J. (b 26.4.52) *153*, 154
Clifford, Col. the Hon. Henry H. (1826–83) 19
Clover, Charles P. (b 13.5.55) 154
Clynes, Ernest HL (1899–1973) 95, 131
Coe, Sebastian W. (b 29.9.56) 161, 165–6, *166*
Coghlan, Eamonn (b 21.11.52) 166
Cohen, Glendon H. (b 22.4.54) 158
Colbeck, Edward J. (1848–80) 23
Comstock, Boyd 120
Conneff, Thomas P. (1866–1912) 50
Connor, Keith L. (b 16.9.57) 161, 163
Consolini, Adolfo (1917–69) 88
Cooper, Albert A. (Bert) (1910–74) 82, 88, 89, 132, 139, *140*
Cooper, John H. (1940–74) 127, 129
Cornes, John F. (Jerry) (b 23.3.10) 81, 83, 84, *85*
Corts, Richard (1905–74) 77
Cotton, Alfred H. (b 21.8.14) *121*
Courtney, Thomas W. (b 17.8.33) 113
Cox, Stanley EW (b 15.7.18) 103
Cross, Francis JK (1865–1950) 68
Crossland, George 44, 45
Crump, Jack CG (1905–66) 123, 128–9, 140, 175
Csermak, Jozsef (b 14.2.32) 106
Cullen, Peter S. (b 24.8.32) 114
Cummings, William J. (1858–1919) 41, 43
Curtis, Harry 136, *137*, 137

D

Daft, Charles F. (1864–1918) 40
Dainton, Alan R. (b 6.1.56) 162
Daranyi, Jozsef (b 28.9.05) 82
Davies, John (b 20.11.52) 155
Davies, Lynn (b 20.5.42) 48, 117, *117*, 123, 127, 129, 131, 146, 149
Davin, Maurice (1842–1927) 36
Davin, Patrick (1857–1949) 36, 40, 48, 59
de Coubertin, Baron Pierre (1863–1937) 47, 54, 163
de Crespigny, Sir Claude Champion (1818–68) 28
Deerfoot, (Louis Bennett) (1828–97) 16, *17*, 22, 117
Delany, Ronald M. (b 6.3.35) 114
Denley, Michael J. (b 21.11.31) 103
Desborough, Lord (William H. Grenfell) (1855–1945) *55*, *90*, 90, 91
Desforges (now Pickering), Jean C. (b 4.7.29) 102, 108
Dick, Alan (b 15.4.30) 107
Dickinson, Richard D. (b 1867) 39, 62
Digby, Kenelm T. (1843–93) 28
Disley, John I. (b 20.11.28) 99, 103, 111, *113*, 114, *115*, 115, 122
Dixon, Rodney (b 13.7.50) *153*, 154, 161, 166
Dorando, (see Pietri)
Douda, Frantisek (b 25.10.08) 82
Downer, Alfred R. (1874–1912) 44, 45
Doyle, Sir Arthur Conan (1859–1930) 56
Driver, Peter B. (1932–71) 107
Duffey, Arthur F. (1878–1954) *51*, 51
Duncan, Kenneth S ('Sandy') (b 26.4.12) 122
Dunning, George A. (b 1855) 36
Dyce, Byron (b 27.3.48) *155*
Dyson, Geoffrey HG (b 22.6.14) 103, 106, *119*, 120, *121*, 122–4
Dyson, Maureen AJ (*née* Gardner) (1928–74) 98, 122

E

Eaton, William E. (b 20.4.09) 86, 114
Eby, Earl (1894–1971) 69
Edward, Harold FV (1902–45) *75*, 75
Edwards, Clancy (b 9.8.55) 166
Edwards, Philip (1907–71) 74
Elborough, Frederick T. (b 31.7.1852) 25
Eldon, Stanley E. (b 1.5.36) *105*, 115, 171
Elliott, Geoffrey M. (b 7.4.31) *101*, 106, 116, 122
Elliott, Herbert J. (b 25.2.38) *104*, 114–15
Ellis, Cyril (1904–73) 73, 78
Ellis, Michael J. (b 3.9.36) 114–16, 125
Emery, Carl AJ (Jack) (b 27.12.13) *88*, 89
Englehard, Hermann (b 21.6.03) 71, 73
Engelhart, Stanley E. 82
Etolu, Patrick 115
Evenson, Thomas (b 9.1.10) 83

Everett, Graham E. (b 20.1.34) 115
Exeter, Marquess of (see Burghley, Lord)
Eyre, Leonard (b 27.11.25) 99, *103*

F

Facelli, Luigi (b 10.5.1898) 78, *81*, 81
Fairbrother, Crawford W. (b 1.12.36) *109*, 126
Farnworth, JH 22
Farrell, Thomas S. (b 23.9.32) 114
Fattorini, Anthony (1862–1931) 178
Ferris, Samuel (b 29.8.1900) 77, 78, 83
Feuerbach, Al (b 14.1.48), 155
Figuerola, Enrique (b 15.7.39) 127
Finlay, Donald O. (1909–60) *82*, 82–6, *87*, 87–9, 96, *97*, 98, 103, 122, 132, 166
Fisher, Percy L. (1872–1930) 46, 55, *55*, 56, 65
FitzSimons, John HP (b 12.2.43) 131
Flanagan, John J. (1873–1938) *51*, 52
Flaxman, Alfred E. (1879–1916) *56*, 65
Flynn, Oliver T. (b 30.6.50) 143, 163
Foreman, Paul (b 25.1.39) 115
Foster, Brendan (b 12.1.48) 147, 151, 154, 155, 158, 162, 163, 166, 169, 170, *173*, 174
Foulds, June F. (see Paul)
Fowler, H. Roy (b 26.3.36) 126, 127
Fowler-Dixon, John E. (1850–1943) 62, 81, 145
Fraser, John 35
Freary, Michael (b 25.7.38) 171
Frigerio, Ugo (1901–68) 76, 138
Frost, Sydney *56*
Fryer, Peter G. (b 2.7.28) 107, 111
Fudge, Paula (*née* Yeoman) (b 30.3.52) 163
Fuller, William E. (1853–95) *25*

G

Gaby, Frederick R. (b 1895) 76–8, 81
Gale, Philip S. (1905–66) 125
Gammoudi, Mohamed (b 11.2.38) 131
Garay, Sandor (b 4.2.20) 95
Gardner, Keith A. St. H. (b 6.9.29) 115
Gardner, Maureen AJ (see Dyson)
Gay-Roberts, Edmund L. (b 1882) *170*
Gent, Harold (b 19.11.1861) 41
George, Alfred B. (1868–1934) 120
George, Walter G. (1858–1943) *13*, 13, 35, 36, 38, 40–4, 66, 68, 81, *169*, 169, 170
Gibson, John A. (b 1904) 78
Gold, Arthur A. (b 10.1.17) 123, 134, 149, 150, 163
Golding, Leslie H. (b 28.6.10) 123
Goodwin, G. Reginald (b 17.12.95) 139
Grace, Dr William G. (1848–1915) 22, 29, 43
Graham, Harold E. 52
Graham, Timothy JM (b 31.5.39) 129
Gray, George R. (b 1866) 50
Graybehl, Richard (b 19.7.56) *162*
Green, Andrew R. (b 26.11.42) 132
Green, Frederick (b 25.7.26) *103*, 106, 108, 170
Green, Thomas W. (1893–1975) 82, 103, 139
Greene, RA 47
Gregory, John A. (Jack) (b 22.6.23) 97
Grenfell, William H. (see Desborough, Lord)
Griffith, Thomas (1839–96) 36
Gruer, John 48
Gude, Helmut (b 23.11.25) 103
Gunn, Charles EJ (b 1885) 139

H

Hägg, Gunder (b 31.12.18) 92, 93, 174
Hahn, Lloyd (b 1898) 73
Halberg, Murray G. (b 7.7.35) 115
Hall, Dorothy G. (*née* Manley) (b 29.4.27) 98, 102
Halswelle, Wyndham (1882–1915) 55, 65
Hampson, Thomas (1907–65) 68 *72*, 73, 74, 81–3, 103
Hanlon, John AT 78
Hardy, Roland (b 3.12.27) 99, 103, 140
Harper, Ernest (b 2.8.02) 87
Harper, Peter (b 3.7.36) *121*
Harper, Lt Col Roland St.GT (b 23.4.07) 120, 122
Harris, Douglas (b 15.6.19) 96, *97*
Hart, Hendrik B. (Harry) (b 2.9.05) 82
Hartley, Donna M (*née* Murray) (b 1.5.55) 163
Hartley, William J, (b 27.6.50) *153*, 158
Harvey, Charles C. (1860–1906) 77
Harvey, Gordon C. (1858–1922) 77
Hassan, El Kasheef (b 1955) 166
Hassan, His Highness Prince (1855–84) 28, 155
Hawtrey, Henry C. (1882–1961) *53*, 54
Hay, Elspeth (b 24.4.30) 102
Healion, Bert (b 17.5.16) *89*
Heatley, Basil B. (b 25.12.33) *104*, 114, 129
Hein, Karl (b 11.6.08) 84, 87
Heino, Viljo J. (b 1.3.14) 94, 95, 105
Heljasz, Zygmunt (b 21.9.08) 83
Hemery, David P. (b 18.7.44) 131, 134, 146, *147*, 147–9
Hepburn, Ross (b 14.10.61) 161
Herbert, Charles (1846–1924) *47*, 47, 54, 60, 64, 91, 163
Herriott, Maurice (b 8.10.39) *112*, 116, 126–9, 132
Hewson, Brian S. (b 4.4.33) *104*, 111, 114, 116, 125
Hickman, JE 44
Hicks, Thomas J. (b 1876) 163
Higgins, F. Peter (b 16.11.28) 107, 113, 114
Hildreth, Peter B. (b 8.7.28) 103
Hill, Albert G. (1889–1969) *68*, 68, 69, *70*, 73, 74, 78, 87, 131
Hill, Henry W. (1852–1904) *25*
Hill, Dr Ron (b 21.9.38) 114, 127, 128, 135, *135*, 146

Hilton, CFR 120
Hiscock, Eileen M. (b 25.8.09) 87
Hodge, Percy (1890–1967) 75
Hodgson, WH *62*
Hoff, Charles (b 1902) 76, 120
Hogan, James J. (b 28.5.33) 131, 171
Höhne, Christoph (b 12.2.41) 142
Holden, John T. (Jack) (b 13.3.07) *83*, 84, 96, 98, *99*, 99, 102
Hollings, Stephen C. (b 23.11.46) 148
Holmes, Cyril B. (b 11.1.15) 88, *89*, 89, 92, 93
Holt, Ernest JH (Billy) (1883–1972) 95, 96
Homonnay, Dr Tamas (b 2.1.26) 106
Hopkins, Thelma E. (b 16.3.36) 108, 113
Horan, Frederick S. (1870–1956) 117
Horgan, Denis (1871–1922) *48*, 48, 52, 88, 105, 132, 140
Hoskin, Sheila H. (b 14.10.36) 116
Houghton, Harry (b 1901) 70
Howard, John (1824–75) 16
Howitt, William see (Jackson, William)
Howland, Robert L. (Bonzo) (b 25.3.05) 82
Hulley, John 16, 18
Hunter, F. Alan R. (b 1914) 85
Hunter, Charles Val (1843–1914) 55
Hunter, Evan A. (1887–1954) 85
Huseby, Gunnar (b 4.11.23) 103
Hutchens, Henry (Harry) (1858–1939) 41
Hutson, George W. (1889–1914) *57*, 65
Hyman, Dorothy (b 9.5.41) 127

I

Ibbotson, G. Derek (b 17.6.32) *105*, *111*, 113–15, 125, 126, 129
Inoue, Toshiaki (b 3.1.51) 155
Iqbal, Mohamed (b 12.7.27) 115
Iso-Hollo, Volmari (1907–69) 83, *84*

J

Jackson, Arnold NS (see Strode-Jackson)
Jackson, Clement N. (1846–1924) *29*, 29, 30, 31, 32, 35, 39–41, 56, 64, 65, 117
Jackson, William (b 15.2.1821) 16, *17*
Jacobs, Franklin (b 31.12.57) 163
Jarvis, Frank W. (b 1878) *51*, 51
Jazy, Michel (b 13.6.36) 125
Jenkins, David A. (b 25.5.52) 147–9, *158*, 158, 162
Jersey, 7th Earl of (Victor AGC Villiers) (1845–1915) 19, 22, 28, *34*, *63*, 63, *64*
Jeszensky, Laszlo (b 14.7.27) 106
Johnson, Bascom (1878–1954) 52
Johnson, Derek JN (b 5.1.33) 74, *101*, 106, 113
Johnson, Kenneth E. (b 14.10.28) 106, 107
Johnson, Tebbs Lloyd (b 7.4.1900) 97, 140
Johnston, Timothy FK (b 11.3.41) 134
Jones, David H. (b 11.3.40) 125, 127
Jones, Kenneth J. (b 30.12.21) 97
Juantorena, Alberto (b 3.12.51) 74, 161, 166
Junk, Bruno (b 27.9.29) 140
Junker, Louis (1854–90) 32
Just, Theodore H. (b 1886) 163

K

Kauser, F. Jakab *52*, 52
Kay, David R. (b 8.6.31) *121*
Keino, Kipchoge (b 17.1.40) 146
Kidd, Bruce (b 26.7.43) 126
Kiely, Thomas F. (b 25.8.1869) 48
Kilby, Brian L. (b 26.2.38) 127
Kimobwa, Samson (b 15.9.55) 163
Knight, George (b 12.3.33) *101*, *105*
Knox, Walter R. (1878–1951) 58, *119*, 119, 120, 122, 123
Kolehmainen, Johannes P. (Hannes) (1889–1966) 52, *53*, 76
Kraenzlein, Alvin C. (1876–1928) *50*, *51*, 51
Kuschmann, Manfred (b 27.7.50) 155
Kusocinski, Janusz (1907–40) 81, 84
Kuts, Vladimir P. (1927–75) 99, 108, 113, 171, 174

L

Land, William A. (b 24.11.14) 82
Landy, John M. (b 4.4.30) 103, 106, 107
Lane, John EJ (Jack) (b 14.12.50) 148
Lannaman, Sonia M. (b 24.3.56) 163
Larner, George E. (1875–1949) 55, *138*, 138, 141
Lawes, Charles B. (1843–1911) 19, 22, 28
Lawrence, George PC (b 1860) 38
Lawton, Barbara J. (*née* Inkpen) (b 28.10.49) 154
Lay, Peter (b 12.4.39) *121*
Lay, Stanley A. (b 1906) 78, 111
Leahy, Cornelius (Con) (b 1876) 48, 54, 55
Leahy, Patrick J. (1877–1926) 48, *49*
Lean, David F. (b 22.8.35) 115
Lee, Ambrose 18
Leeke, Henry A. (1879–1915) 65
Lehtinen, Lauri A. (1908–73) 83, *84*
Leigh-Wood, Roger 82
Le Masurier, John (b 24.7.17) 117, *119*, 120, *121*, 122, 123
Lerwill, Alan L. (b 15.11.46) 148, *154*, 154
Lerwill, Sheila W. (*née* Alexander) (b 16.8.28) 102, 103
Lewden, Pierre (b 21.2.01) 76, 120
Lewis, Leslie C. (b 26.12.24) 99, 102
Liddell, Eric H. (1902–45) *76*, 76, 77, 95
Lind, Carl-Johan (1883–1965) 76
Lindgren, Gerald P. (b 9.3.46) 131

Lindsay, Michael R. (b 2.11.38) *104*
Lines, Mary (b 3.12.1893) 66
Liquori, Martin (b 11.9.49) *152*
Livingstone-Learmonth, Thomas C. (1906–31) 78
Ljunggren, John A. (b 9.9.19) 140
Loader, William R. (b 1916) 78
Lockton, Charles L. (1856–1932) *25*, 32, 81
Lockton, Tom Langton (b 23.3.18) *88*
London, John E. (Jack) (1905–66) 77, *78*, 78
Long, Luz (1913–43) *87*, 87
Longden, Bruce (b 6.8.39) 124
Lovelock, John E. (Jack) (1910–49) 84, *85*, *86*, 86
Lowe, Douglas GA (b 17.8.02) 67–70, *71*, 71, 73, 74, 77, 78, 82, 103, 131, 161, *167*, 168, 176
Lowe, Patricia B. (now Cropper) (b 15.9.43) 135
Lucas, Charles JP 163
Lucking, Martyn T. (b 24.3.38) 127
Lutz, Mark (b 23.12.51) 155

Mc

McCorquodale, Alistair (b 5.12.25) 96, 97
McDonald Bailey, Emmanuel (see Bailey, Emmanuel McDonald)
McFarlane, Michael (b 2.5.60) 161
McGhee, Joseph (b 9.7.29) 108
McKenley, Herbert H. (b 10.7.22) 103
McLeod, Michael J. (b 25.1.52) 166
McMeekin, David (b 10.2.53) *155*
McNab, Thomas McI. (b 16.12.33) *121*, 123, 147
McNicol, Douglas E. (d 1915) 65
McPhee, Duncan (d 1950) 70
McSorley, John V. (b 18.9.41) 126

M

Macaulay Reginald H. (b 1858) 81
Macdonald, Robert (Bobby) 59
Macdonald, John E. (Jack) 16
MacIsaac, John (b 6.6.37) 116
Macquet, Michel PR (b 3.4.32) 126
Maiyoro, Nyandika (b 1930) 106
Malan, Daniël (b 26.6.50) 151, 158
Malcolm, Allan R. (b 21.10.19) 122
Manley, Dorothy G. (see Hall)
Mann, Ralph (b 16.6.49) 149
Marlow, William E. (b 4.2.19) *121*
Martell, F. John (b 18.8.17) 146, 147, 150, *178*
Martin, Paul (b 11.8.01) 70
Martin, Séraphin (b 2.7.06) 73
Marvalits, Kalman (b 1901) 78
Mason, Charles H. (1851–1902) *25*
Matthewman, Thomas (Tom) (b 1903) *76*
Matthews, Kenneth J. (b 21.6.34) 116, 125, 127, 129, 140, 141, 142, *145*
May, Rev. Ernest EB (b 14.9.1878) 60
Mays, Albert WJ (Mick) (1895–1956) 108
Meakin, Alfred F. (b 30.8.38) 127
Mecser, Lajos (b 23.9.42) 131
Meek, W. Henry 40
Melly, Charles P. (1829–88) 16, 18
Meredith, J. Edward, (Ted) (1892–1947) 71
Merrill, EE 35, 36, *38*, 50
Merriman, John L. (b 27.6.36) 116, 171
Metcalfe, Jack P. (b 3.2.12) 115
Metcalfe, Adrian P. (b 2.3.42) 114, 129
Michell, Edward B. (1843–1916) 19
Mikaelsson, John F. (b 6.12.13) 87, 140
Mikkola, Jaako (1886–1956) 120
Mills, Edward (1841–94) 16
Mills, Leslie R. (b 1.11.34) 147
Mills, Roger G. (b 11.2.48) 143, *144*, 162
Mitchell, James S. (1865–1921) 40, 48
Mitchell, Robert JC (b 1847) 32
Mitchell, Roy R. (b 1.1.55) 163
Monk, Christopher L. (b 29.9.51) 154
Montague, Evelyn A. (1900–48) 67
Moorcroft, David R. (b 10.4.53) *153*, 163
Moore, Aston L. (b 8.2.56) 163
Morgan, Norman D. (1866–1908) *50*
Morgan, William J. 25
Mountain, Edgar D. (b 2.4.01) *68*, 70
Moses, Edwin (b 31.7.55) 161, 166
Moss, Sidney G. (1882–1972) 56
Murphy, Frank (b 21.5.47) 134
Murphy, Michael C. (1861–1913) 117
Mussabini, Scipio A. (Sam) (1862–1927) 69, 75, 76, 78, 120
Myers, Lawrence E. (Lon) (1858–99) 35–40, *37*, 44, 50, 68, 131

N

Nankeville, G. William (b 24.3.25) 96, 98, *99*, 103
Nehan, George M. (b 1862) 36, 38, 39
Nelson, Alec (1872–1944) 119, 120
Neville, Ernest H. (1883–1972) 142
Newburn, Walter JM (1874–1919) 48
Nicolson, Thomas R. (1879–1951) *60*
Nichol, William P. (b 1901) *76*
Nicholas, Thomas L. (d 1924) 59
Nihill, V. Paul (b 5.9.39) 129, 134, 135, 142, *143*, 158
Nikiciuk, Wladyslaw (b 9.3.40) 134
Nikula, Pentii K. (b 3.2.29) 126
Noel-Baker, Lord (see Baker, P.)
Noji, Jozef (b 8.9.09) 86
Nokes, Malcolm C. (1897–1972) 67, 76, 82, 116, 120, 122
Norris, David S. (b 14.12.39) 115
Norris, Frederick. (b 4.9.21) *101*, 114
Norris, Kenneth L. (b 11.7.31) 111, *111*, 171
Nurmi, Paavo J. (1897–1973) 71, 75–6 *76*, 174, 177

## O


O'Brien, James 40
O'Callaghan, Dr Patrick (b 15.9.05) 84, *85*
O'Connor, Peter J. (1874–1957) 48, 51, *53*, 54, 76
Odam, Dorothy JB (see Tyler)
Oerter, Alfred (Al) (b 19.9.36) 166
Ogilvie, Patrick BB 82
Okuwobi, Oladipo (b 13.6.33) 114
Olney, Violet (b 22.5.11) 87
Olowu, Karim AB (b 7.6.24) 115
Olson, Gail (b 2.5.60) 163
O'Reilly, Brendan MP 106
Osborn, Harold M. (1899–1975) 77
Osendarp, Martinus B. (b 21.5.16) *85*, *89*
Ota, Tomio (b 21.10.36) 126
Ovett, Steven MJ (b 9.10.55) 151, *155*, 155, 158, 161, 163, *164*, *165*, 165, 166
Owens, JC (Jesse) (b 12.9.13) 87


## P


Packer, Ann E. (now Brightwell) (b 8.3.42) 129
Page, William Byrd (1866–1940) 50
Pain, Donald TP (b 14.9.04) 96
Paish, Wilfred HC (b 29.7.32) *121*
Palmer, W. Barclay L. (b 2.3.32) 111
Palmer, Milton G. (b 9.9.58) 161
Palmer, Samuel (b 15.12.1854) 38, 40
Parker, Frederick W. 56, 117, 119
Parker, F. John (Jack) (b 6.9.27) 122
Parlett, H. John (b 19.4.25) 74, 96, *97*, 98, 99, 102, 103
Pascoe, Alan P. (b 11.10.47) 148, 149, 154, 155, 158, *162*
Pashley, Anne (b 5.6.35) 113
Paterson, Alan S. (b 11.6.28) 98, 99, 102
Paul, June F. (*née* Foulds) (b 13.6.34) 102, 113
Paulus, Ernst (b 3.1.1897) 78
Pavitt, Ronald C. (b 15.9.26) 98, *102*, 103
Payne, Harry W. (1892–1969) 78
Payne, A. Howard (b 17.4.31) 127, *130*, 131, 146, 151, 154
Payne, C. Rosemary (*née* Charters) (b 19.5.33) 146
Pearce, Charles (b 3.10.1861) *61*, 62
Pell, Dennis B. (b 1916) *89*, 89
Pelling, Ernest H. (1866–1950) *59*, 59
Peltzer, Dr Otto (1900–70) *71*, 71, 73, 77, 131
Pennel, John T. (b 25.7.44) 127, 149
Pennington, Alan (b 4.4.16) *88*
Penny, Arthur W. (b 13.12.07) 84
Perry, Nathaniel (d 1899) *25*
Peters, James H. (b 24.10.18) 78, 103, 106, 107, *108*, 108, 127
Peters, Mary E. (b 6.7.39) 146, 149, 154
Peters, Willem (b 5.7.03) 78, 82
Pharaoh, Mark (b 18.7.31) 122
Phillips, William Page (1858–83) 35, 36, 39, 40
Pickering, Ronald J. (b 4.5.30) 117, 123
Pietri, Dorando (1885–1942) 54, 55, 107
Piggott, Leslie M (b 11.5.42) 149
Pike, Martin W. (b 12.7.20) 102
Pirie, DA Gordon (b 10.2.31) 99, *100*, *103*, 103, 105, 111, 113, 114, 115, 125, 126, 169, 170, *171*, 171
Platt, Susan M. (b 4.10.40) 127
Polhill, Anthony (b 15.12.47) 147
Poole, James 62
Pope, Alfred HG (b 24.3.04) 82, 139
Porhola, Ville (1897–1964) 76, 82
Porritt, Arthur E. (now Lord Porritt) (b 10.8.1900) 77
Porter, Alan C. (b 1933) *115*
Potts, John H. (b 17.9.06) 82
Powell, John (b 25.6.47) 155, 166
Power, W. David (b 14.7.28) 116, 126
Powles, Alfred (b 1853) *25*
Price, Berwyn (b 15.8.51) *148*, 163, 166
Price, William (1827–72) 16
Pritchard, Norman G. *51*, 51
Pugh, Derek C. (b 8.2.26) 102, 103, 111
Pullard, Robert (b 21.3.51) 163
Purcell, John (1862–1912) 48
Pym, C. Guy (1841–1918) 19


## Q


Quarrie, Donald (b 25.2.51) *160*, *161*, 161
Quax, Richard (b 1.1.48) *153*
Queensberry, Sir John Douglas, 8th Marquess of (1844–1900) 22


## R


Raby, James W. 36, 38, 39
Radford, Peter F. (b 20.9.39) *112*, 116, 125, 127
Rampling, Godfrey L. (b 14.5.09) 82–4, 87, 103
Rand, Mary D. (*née* Bignal, now Toomey) (b 10.2.40) 117, *118*, 123, 129, 131
Ravenstein, EG 18, 24
Rawson, Michael A. (b 26.5.34) 74, *104*, 114, 116
Ray, Joie (b 1894) 69
Ray, Thomas (1862–1904) 36, 38, *39*, 39, 40, 62
Read, Norman R. (b 13.8.31) 140
Reed, Henry A. (1825–74) 16
Reeve, Susan D. (b 17.9.51) 163
Reiff, Gaston EG (b 24.2.21) 94
Remigino, Lindy J. (b 3.6.31) 103
Remington, Mortimer (b 1868) *49*, 50
Reynolds, Martin E. (b 22.2.49) 146, 147, 149
Richards, Thomas (b 15.3.10) 97
Riddick, Steven (b 18.9.51) *159*

Ridley, John H. (1848–1904) 22, 111
Ridley, Rita (b 4.11.46) 146
Rimmer, John T. (1878–1962) *53*, 54, 170
Roberts, William (b 5.4.12) 87, *88*, 88, 95, 103
Robertson, Donald McNab (1905–49) *83*, 94
Rogers, GP 24
Rogers, Robert *25*
Romeo, Mario (b 7.4.15) 88
Rono, Henry (b 12.2.52) *157*, 163, 166
Rose, Nicholas H. (b 13.12.51) *152*, 163, *173*
Rowdon, George W. (b 1864) 50
Rowe, Arthur (b 17.8.36) *110*, 115, 116, 125, 126
Rudd, Bevil GD'U (1894–1948) *68*, 69, 70, 75
Russell, Arthur (b 1886) 55
Ryan, James M. (1871–1900) 48, 59
Rye, Walter (1843–1929) 24, 25, 30, 31, 32, 36, 79, 136, 169

S

Salisbury, John E. (b 26.1.34) 113, 115, 116
Salvat, Frank GJ (b 30.10.34) *105*, 125
Sampson, Edward J. (b 2.12.35) 116
Sanderson, Theresa I. (Tessa) (b 14.3.56) 163
Sando, Frank D. (b 14.3.31) *101*, 111
Santee, Wesley D. (b 25.3.32) 106
Savel, Ilie (b 25.8.27) 111
Savidge, John A. (b 18.12.34) 103, 106, *121*, 122
Saward, A. 24
Scarsbrook, Stanley C. 84
Schofield, George VA (1856–1933) 55
Schwab, Fritz (b 31.12.19) 140
Scott, Angus W. (b 16.8.27) 102
Scott, Walter (b 1886) *53*
Scrivens, Jean E. (b 15.10.35) 113
Segal, David H. (b 20.3.37) 125
Segedin, Petar (b 14.9.26) 99, 103
Seward, George (1817–83) 16
Shaw, David (b 19.10.36) 115, 163, 165
Shaw, Robert D. (b 27.12.32) 111
Shearman, Sir Montague (1857–1930) *25*, *29*, 29–31, *34*, 35, 38, 39, 41, 46, 62, 65, 66, 79, *80*, 80, 90, 91, 126, 136
Sheldon, Richard (b 9.7.1880) 48, 52
Shelley, Donald G. (b 3.12.36) *178*
Shenton, Brian (b 15.3.27) 102
Sherrill, Charles H. (1867–1936) 59
Sherwood, John (b 4.6.45) 134, 146, *147*
Sherwood, Sheila H. (*née* Parkin) (b 22.10.45) 134, 146
Shirley, Eric (b 3.4.29) 111, *115*, 115, 125
Shrubb, Alfred (1878–1964) *45*, 45, 46, 83, 86, 120, 169, *170*, 170, 171
Silvester, L. Jay (b 27.8.37) 126
Simmons, Anthony D. (b 6.10.48) 148, 150, 155
Simmons, WJ *78*
Simpson, Janet M. (b 2.9.44) 135
Singh, Milkha (b 17.10.35) 125
Slade, Walter (1854–1919) *25*
Sloane, William M. (1850–1928) 47
Slykhuis, Willem F. (b 13.1.23) *94*, 94
Smith, Colin G. (b 2.8.35) 114, 116
Smith, Frank 28
Snell, Peter G. (b 17.12.38) 74
Snook, William (1861–1916) 35, 36, 38, 41, *43*, 43, 44, 170
Southwell, Viscount Thomas A. (1836–78) 28
Spence, Malcolm C. (Mal) (b 4.9.37) 115
Stacey, Rev Nicolas D. (b 27.11.27) 102
Stallard Hyla B. (Henry) (1901–73) 69, *70*, 70, 71, 75
Stecher, Renate (b 12.5.50) 147
Stenning, Percy H. (Peter) (1854–92) 169
Stewart, Ian (b 15.1.49) 135, 146, 147, 149, *152*, 158, 171
Stewart, Mary (b 25.2.56) 163
Stewart, Peter J. (b 8.8.47) 147, 148
Stirling, Rosemary O. (now Wright) (b 11.12.47) 135, 146
Stoker, Abraham (Bram) (1847–1912) 136
Stone, Thomas (b 24.1.1852) *25*
Stoneley, Crew H. (b 1911) 83
Stones, Dwight (b 6.12.53) 155, *156*, 162
Storey, Edgar (1859–1909) 30
Strachan, Edward A. (1858–1953) 36
Strode-Jackson, Arnold N. (1891–1972) 56, 75
Stroud, Raymond L. (b 23.6.24) 131
Sturgess, William J. (1871–1945) *137*, 137, *138*
Sugawara, Takeo (b 23.5.38) 127
Sugioka, Kuniyoshi (b 10.2.42) 126
Sullivan, James E. (1860–1914) 54
Sutherland, Colin (b 16.11.55) 163
Sweeney, Arthur W. (1909–41) 84, *85*, *89*, 89
Szepes, Bela (b 5.9.03) 78

T

Taber, Norman S. (1891–1952) 69
Tabori, László (b 6.7.31) 125
Tagg, Michael J. (b 13.11.46) 148
Tancred, William R. (b 6.8.42) 149, 151, 158
Taylor, Richard G. (b 3.1.45) 171
Taylor, F. Morgan (1903–75) 78
Tewkesbury, John WB (1876–1968) *51*, 51
Thomas, HD 35
Thomas JW 24
Thomas, Reginald H. (d 1946) 81, 82
Thomas, Sidney (1868–1942) 45, 83
Thompson, Donald J. (b 20.1.33) 125, 136, 140, 141, *142*, 142
Thompson, Francis M. (Daley)(b 30.7.58) *124*, 124, 161, 163, 165
Thompson, Ian R. (b 6.10.49) *151*, 154, 155, 162

Thornton, John St. L. (1911–44) *87*
Thornton, Percy M. (1841–1918) 28
Tindall, Rev HC Lenox (1863–1940) 68, 87
Tisdall, Robert MN (b 16.5.07) 167
Toetti, Edgardo (b 10.7.10) *78*
Tomlin, Stanley A. (1905–69) 82
Tosi, Giuseppe, (b 25.5.16) 103
Tosswill, Alick C. (b 1844) 32
Townend, H. Stuart 82
Trafford, Alfred (1870–1951) *51*
Travis, David H. (b 9.9.45) *133*, 146
Treacy, John (b 5.6.57) 166
Treloar, John F. (b 19.1.28) 96
Truelove, Leslie R. (b 24.3.08) 116
Tsuburaya, Kokichi (1940–68) 129
Tulloh, M. Bruce S. (b 29.9.35) *105*, 116, 126, *127*, 127, 131, 135, 171
Tully, Michael (b 21.10.56) 166
Tuulos, Vilho (1895–1967) 76
Tuwei, Hilary 166
Tyler, Dorothy JB (*née* Odam) (b 14.3.20) 87, 88, 98, 99, 102
Tysoe, Alfred E. (1874–1901) 54, 70

V

Valkama, Jorma (1928–62) 126
Valste, Armas (b 7.8.05) 120
Vanin, Feodosi K. (b 25.2.14) 101
Van Reenen, Jan NR (John) (b 26.3.47) 158
Venn, Harry (1856–1913) *25*, 46, 55, 136, 137, 138
Venon, Judy (b 25.9.45) 154
Vickers, Stanley F. (b 18.6.32) 116, 125, 140, *141*, 141, *145*
Villiers, Victor AGC see Jersey, 7th Earl of
Vine, Paul AL (b 13.12.27) 111
Viren, Lasse (b 22.7.49) 150, 161, 174
Virtanen, Lauri (b 3.8.04) 81
Voigt, Emil R. (1882–1973) *55*, 55

W

Waddell, James *24*, 24, *25*, 25, 26–8, 30–2
Waddell, William *24*, 24, *25*, 25, 26–8, 30–2, 47, 59, 63
Walker, John (b 12.1.52) 161, 166
Wallwork, Ronald E. (b 26.5.41) 131
Ward, Peter D. (b 7.2.13) *88*
Warhurst, John (b 1.10.44) 154
Watkins, Harry (1872–1922) 44, 45
Watman, Melvyn F. (b 26.5.38) 158
Watts, Denis CV (b 31.7.20) 120, *121*, 122, 123
Webb, Ernest J. (1872–1937) *138*, 138
Webster, FA Michael (1887–1949) 56, 67, 86, 120
Webster, F. Richard (b 31.12.14) 86
Webster, Henry (Harry) (b 14.5.1854) 36, 40, 136
Webster, John E. (Jack) (1900–45) 77, *78*, 78
Webster, Richard E. (Lord Alverstone) (1842–1915) 19, 22, 23, 31, *34*, 47, *63*, 63, *64*, 79, 80
Weightman-Smith, George C. (b 1906) 77, 78
Weinberg, Raymond H. (b 5.10.26) 103
Wells, Allan W. (b 3.5.52) *161*, 161, 163
Wells, Peter (b 23.5.29) 98
Wharton, Arthur 40, 43
Wheeler, Alfred 22
Wheeler, Michael KV (b 14.2.35) 111, 113
Whetton, John H. (b 6.9.41) 135
White, John (Jack) (1838–1910) 117
Whitehead, J. Nicholas (b 29.5.33) 125
Whitfield, Malvin G. (b 11.10.24) 74, 98
Whitlock, H. Harold (b 16.12.03) 87, 89, 103, 139, *142*
Whittle, Harry (b 2.5.22) 95, 103, 105, *106*, 132
Whyatt, Henry 36
Wiggs, Michael E. (b 25.4.38) 125
Wilkinson, John CM (b 17.1.29) 102
Willers, Charles E. *61*
Williams, Archibald F. (Archie) (b 1.5.15) 86
Williams, Barry (b 5.3.47) 149
Williams, Steven (b 13.11.53) 155, 175
Williamson, Audrey D. (b 28.9.26) 98
Willis, Barry E. (b 7.8.24) 131
Wilmshurst, Kenneth SD (b 9.4.31) 106
Wilson, Alexander (b 1.12.07) 74
Wilson, Douglas G. (b 28.1.20) 92
Wint, Arthur S. (b 25.5.20) 93, 94, *95*, 96, 98, 99, 103, 105, 114
Winthrop, William Y. (1852–1912) *25*, 116
Winzenreid, Mark (b 13.10.49) *155*
Wise, Bernhard R. (1858–1916) *29*, 29–31, 35, 36, 38, 39
Wolff, Frederick F. (b 13.10.10) 87
Wöllke, Hans (1911–43) 87
Wooderson, Sydney C. (b 30.8.14) 74, 84, *85*, *86*, 86–9, *89*, 92, *93*, 93, *94*, 94, 95, 103, 105, 135, 166
Wright, Duncan McLeod (1896–1976) 82, *83*
Wrighton, John D. (b 10.3.33) 116

Y/Z

Yarrow, Squire S. (b 28.7.05) 94, *178*
Young, Heather J. (*née* Armitage) (b 17.3.33) 113, 116
Young, John RC (b 6.9.37) 111
Zabala, Juan C. (b 11.10.11) 83
Zamfir, Dumitru 111
Zander, John (1890–1967) *52*, 56
Zatopek, Emil (b 19.9.22) 94, 108, 111, 174

# Index OF SUBJECTS

This index includes general subjects and organizations mentioned in the text. Names are listed in the separate Name Index (p. 209). Where known, the date of origin or formation of each organization appears in brackets with the entry.


A

Achilles Club (1920) 66, 70, 75–8, 80–2, 91, 111, 113, 132
Agricultural Hall, Islington (1862) 86
Airedale Harriers 45
Alverstone Club (1920) 64
Amateur Athletic Association, formation (1880) 29–32; first rules (1880) 33; first Championships (1880) 13; first records (1887) 40; rules made compulsory (1889) 44; suspensions of 1896 44–5; and Olympic movement, (1894) 47; Olympic Games, (1908) 54; and IAAF (1912/13) 56; first professional coach (1914) 58; first home international (1914) 58; Reconstruction Committee (1919) 65; and County Associations (1919) 65; first international against France (1921) 66; formation of BAAB (1932) 66–7; Jubilee (1930) 81; and Commonwealth Games (1930) 81–2; move to White City (1932) 82; summer schools (1934) 120; Indoor Championships (1935), 86; and European Championships (1938) 88: and World War II (1939–45) 92: post-war planning scheme (1944) 94–5; coaching scheme (1946) 120–4; and Olympic Games (1948) 95–8; incorporation (1948) 96; first sponsorship (1961) 125; Byers report (1968) 132–4; financial crisis (1970) 146; move to Crystal Palace (1971) 147; Nationwide sponsorship (1972) 147
  Annual General Meeting 44, 60, 65, 67, 79, 91, 95, 114, 125, 134, 146, 161
  Athletes Consultative Committee (1956) 114
  Championship Results 179–206
  Championships (1880) 13, 28, 31, 32, 35–9, 47–58, 66, 68–73, 75–8, 81–9, 92–8, 99–116, 125–34, 136–42, 146–66, 169–74
  Coaching Scheme (1946) 116, 120–4, 132, 134
  Coming of Age Dinner (1901) 23, 30, 39
  Cycling Championships (1910–11) 62
  Finances 35, 39, 66, 94, 122, 125–6, 131, 132, 134–5, 146–7, 150
  General Committee 31, 39, 41, 43–6, 56, 59, 62–3, 65–9, 79, 91, 94, 120, 123–4, 176
  Indoor Championships (1935) 86, 126, 129, 196–8
  Jubilee (1930) 80–1
  Laws 41, 43–4, 54, 59–62, 65, 79
  Motto 68
  National Road Relay Championship (1967) 171
  Patrons 7, *7*, 66, 103, 134, 161–2
  Presidents *34*, *55*, 63–4, *63–4*, 65, 78–80, *80*, *90*, 90–1, 94–5, 161–2, *167*, 167–8, *175*, 175–7
  Principal Officers (1880–1979) 178
  Reconstruction Committee (1919) 65, 66
  Representative Matches (1911) 58, 92, 106
  Rules 33, 39, 43–4, 54, 59–62, 63, 65–6, 79, 116, 163
  Summer Schools (1934) 67, 120, 122–3
Amateur Athletic Club (1865) 19–32, 41, 61, 63, 75, 136
  Championship Meeting (1866) 19, 21–30, 32, 35, 59, 63, 79, 113, 136
Amateur Athletic Union (USA) (See United States)
Amateur Fencing Association (1902) 91
Amateur Field Events Association (1910) 55, 119–20
Amateur Swimming Association (1886) 44
Amateurism 18, 22, 24, 26, 28, 30–2, 43–5, 61–2, 93, 176
Announcing 92, 94–5
Area Associations 28, 30–1, 35, 39, 41, 43, 58, 65, 95, 123, 125, 132, 146
Area Boards of Control (1901) 61
Army Athletics 58, 92, 96, 122
Ashburnham Hall (1863) 86
Aston Lower Grounds, Birmingham, 35, 40
Athletic Association (1871) 24, 27, 31
*Athletic Journal* (Manchester) 59
*Athletic News* (Manchester) 138, 176
Athletic Society of Great Britain (1863) 18
*Athletics, 1978* 134
*Athletics Weekly* 122, 158
*Athletic World* 32
*Athletics and Football* 79
Attendance 99, 125, 127, 131
  Largest 92, 103, 125, 147
  Smallest 116, 126, 134, 146

B

*Ballet Exercises for Athletes* 123
Barrow Grammar School 96
Beaufort House ground (1864) 18, 22
*Bell's Life in London* 22, 36, 62
Betting 14–15, 24, 35–6, 41, 44, 46, 117
Bicycle Union (1878) 61
Birchfield Harriers (1876) 62, 77–8
Birmingham AC (1867) 28
Blackheath Harriers (1869) 95
Borough Road College 58
Bow ground (1863) 18
*Brendan Foster* 158
British Amateur Athletic Board (1932) 66–7, 114–16, 120, 123, 128, 132, 134, 149–50, 155, 163, 165, 176
British Athletic Federation, Proposed (1968) 132, 134
British Athletics Cup (see GRE Gold Cup)
British Athletics League (1969) 133–5

British Commonwealth Games (see Commonwealth Games)
British Empire Games (see Commonwealth Games)
British Empire v USA (1920) 75
British Olympic Association (1905) 54, 91, 95, 120, 122, 168, 176
British Women's Amateur Athletic Council (1959) 125
Broken Time 176
Brompton Road, Move to (1973) 150
Burnley Cricket Club (1833) 45
Byers Report (1968) 131–2, 134–5, 149–50

C

Cambridge University AC (1863) 16, 18–20, 22–4, 27–31, 41, 58, 63–4, 66, 70–1, 75, 92, 113–14, 117, 120, 168, 176
Carborundum Company, The (1911) 126
Central London Railway 116
Championship Wins in One Event, Most 48
Championship Wins, Most 105
Championship Wins, Most consecutive 88, 95, 105, 116, 132
Charterhouse School (1611) 63
Chief Athletic Adviser (1912) 55, 117, 119
Chief Coach (1914) 58, 119–20, 122–4, 132
Civil Service AC (1864) 18, 31, 136
Clubs 16, 41, 45–6, 60, 65–6, 79, 82, 92, 122–3, 125, 161
Coaches 29, 35, 55–6, 58, 69, 75–6, 78, 82, 92, 103, 106, 114, 117–24, *119, 121, 122*, 170
Coaching 55–6, 106, 116, 117–24, 132, 134, 150, 170
Commonwealth Games 47, 122
1930, Hamilton 73, 81–2, 168
1934, London 84–5
1938, Sydney 88, 99, 122
1950, Auckland 74, 99, 102
1954, Vancouver 74, 106–8
1958, Cardiff 114–16
1962, Perth 127
1966, Kingston 131
1970, Edinburgh 146, 174
1974, Christchurch 154
1978, Edmonton 124, 163, 165, 174
Counties Athletic Union (1926) 66
County Athletic Associations (1883) 43, 65–6
*County Gentleman, The* (see *Sporting Gazette*)
Coventry Godiva Harriers (1879) 44
Crick Run (1837) 14
Criticism of Administration 94, 114, 116, 123, 128, 132, 149, 175
Cross-Country 14, 31, 56, 95, 142, 169–71
Crouch Start 59, *59*
Crystal Palace ground, former 22, 66
Crystal Palace, National Sports Centre (1964) 23, 81, 146–7, 151, 162, 169, 174
Cups, Championship 28, 31–2, 155, *175*, 193, 194, *194*

D

*Daily Herald* 126
*Daily Sketch* 176
*Daily Telegraph* 91
Decathlon 105, 122, 124, 154, 163
Department of Education and Science 122, 129
*Dictionary of National Biography* 63
Director of British Athletics, Proposed (1968) 132, 149
Discus, history 55, 58, 68, 85, 122, 149, 155, 158
Distance Running, history 36, 41, 44–6, 64, 82–3, 95, 99, 106, 108, 111, 113–15, 126–7, 131, 134, 146–51, 155, 163–74
*Dracula* 136
Dress 15, 16, 35, 51, 65, 92
Drug Tests 163

E

Empire Pool, Wembley, (1934) 86, 126
England v France (1921) 66
England v Germany (1929) 73
England v Ireland (1877) 47
England v Ireland v Scotland (1914) 58, 66–7
English Championships (1923) 66
English Cross-Country Championships (see National CCCh)
English Cross-Country Union (1883) 132, 169
Entertainment Tax (1916) 96
Eton College (1440) 14, 19, 22, 35, 63, 91, 111
European Athletic Association (1932) 163
European Championships 99, 122
1938, Paris 88–9
1946, Oslo 94–5, 168
1950, Brussels 74, 102, 140
1954, Berne 108
1958, Stockholm 74, 116, 141
1962, Belgrade 126–7, 141
1966, Budapest 131, 142
1969, Athens 134–5
1971, Helsinki 147, 174
1974, Rome 155, 158, 174
1978, Prague 165
European Cup (1965) 154, 158, 163, 166, 174
European Indoor Championships (1966) 135
Exeter College, Oxford (1314) 14, 16
Expenses 45

F

Festival of Empire (1911) 58
Films, Coaching 120
First Claim Rule (1897) 45
*First Four Minutes* 92, 106
Five Star Award Scheme (1968) 123, 133, 135

*Flying Feet* 114
Football Association (1863) 23, 27, 43
Ford Sports Club 116
Foreign Competitors 32, 35–6, 38–9, 47–52 (then see AAA Championships)

G

Gateshead Harriers & AC 174
Gateshead Track 174
Gentlemen-Amateurs 16, 19, 22, 24–5, 28, 30–2, 36, 117
German Gymnastic Society (1861) 18, 24, 25, 31
Glasgow Rangers FC (1873) 92
Government Aid 122, 131, 146–7
GRE Gold Cup (1973) 154
Great Britain v France (1933) 98, 103
Great Britain v West Germany (indoors, 1962) 126
Greyhound Racing Association (1926) 81

H

Hackney Wick ground (1858) 16, 18
Hammer Circle (1952) 106, 122
Hammer Throw, history 18–19, 20, 59–60, 63–4, 84–5, 105–6, 114, 122, 131, 146, 149, 151, 154–5
Hampden Park, Glasgow (1903) 58
Handicappers, Licensed (1890) 61
Handicapping 16, 18, 41, 60–1
Harrow School (1571) 91
Harvey Cup (1906) 77, 82, 86, 89, 105, 126, 158, 161
High Jump, history 39, 48, 50, 59, 65, 77, 98, 120, 126, 155, 162–3
High Pavement School, Nottingham 89
Highgate Harriers (1879) 136
Highland Games 60, 119
Honorary Coaches 120–4
Hurdles, history 15, 20, 29, 38, 51, 55, 58, 65, 77–8, 82, 122, 127, 129, 131, 134, 146, 148–9, 154, 167–8

I

Iffley Road ground, Oxford (1876) 29, 106
Indoor Athletics 86, 126, 129, 131, 135
Instructional Booklets 123
Inter-County Championships (1925) 66
Inter University Athletic Board (1919) 66
International Amateur Athletic Federation (1913) 56, 66–7, 77, 84, 95, 114, 127, 163, 168, 170, 176
International Amateur Athletic Federation Congresses 56, 176
International Athletes' Club (1958) 114, 128
International Board (1932) 67, 176
International Cross-Country Championships (1903) 147, 166, 170–1
International Olympic Committee (1894) 54, 56, 91, 168
Ireland v England (1876) *25*, 26, 47, 79, 116
Irish Athletics 26, 47–8, 54, 59, 66–7, 84

J

Jackson Cup (1926) 82, 89, 105, 163, 194, *194*
Javelin, history 55, 58, 68, 78, 111, 114, 126, 131, 134, 154
Jogging 174
Junior Athletics 94, 123, 140, 151, 154–5, 161, 166

K

Kinnaird Trophy and Marathon (1909) 75
Knighthoods 67, 79, 91

L

Lambeth Baths 86
*Land and Water* 20, 23, 28, 30–2, 36, 41
Lanes 82
Law, The, and Athletics 29, 30, 41, 46, 63, 66, 68, 79, 85, 176
Lawn Tennis Association (1888) 91
League Competitions 132
Lillie Bridge ground (1869) 13, 22, 24–5, 27–8, 31–2, 40–1, *42*
Liverpool AC (1862) 16, 18
Liverpool Police 116
Local Officers (1884) 43, 45
London AC (1863) (see also Mincing Lane AC) 22, 24–8, 30–2, 35, 60, 80, 117, 136
London AC Amateur Championship Meeting (1879) 27–8, 30–1
London AC Schools Challenge Cups Meeting (1890) 70, 73
London to Brighton Walk (1886) 139
London Victoria band 81
London v Moscow (1954) 108
Long Jump, history 16, 32, 48, 59, 65, 115, 116, 123, 127, 131, 149, 154, 176
Lord's ground (1814) 14–15, 22
Loughborough College School of Athletics (1936) 120, 122
Loughborough Colleges (1930) 58, 67, 120
Lurgan AC (1871) 26

M

Malpractices 15, 30, 35, 41, 43–6, 60, 93, 116, 163
Manchester AC 47, 92

Manchester Harriers 45
Manhattan AC (USA) (1877) 35
Manly Exercises 14
Marathon 54–5, 78, 82–3, 94, 97–9, 102–3, 106–8, 127, 129, 131, 134–5, 151, 154–5, 163
Marston ground, Oxford (1867) 29
Marylebone Cricket Club (1787) 21, 91
Massage 117, 120
Megaphones 92
*Mémoires Olympiques* (1932) 54
Metric/Imperial Equivalents 11
Metric Measurements, Introduction of (1969) 134
Middle Distance 68–74, 77, 85–6, 106–7, 113, 116, 125, 132, 134, 147–8, 165–6
Middlesex County AAA 176
Midland Counties Amateur Athletic Association (1880) 28, 30–1, 35, 39, 41, 43–4, 56, 61, 95, 119, 122, 126
Midland Counties Cross-Country Championship (1879) 169
Mile, Four Minute (1954) 58, 99, 106, 114, 171
Milocarian AC (1930) 81
Mincing Lane AC (1863) (see also London AC) 16, 22
Ministry of Education see Dept of Education and Science
Monmouth AC 59
Monte Carlo Women's International (1921) 66
Moseley Harriers (1874) 35, 38, 170
Motspur Park track 74
Much Wenlock Olympian Society (1850) 18

N

National Administrator, AAA (1973) 150
National Amateur Wrestling Association (1904) 91
National Athletic and Cycling Association of Ireland 67, 84
National Coaches 103, 106, 114, 117–24
National Cross-Country Championships (1877) 44–6, 95, 147, 169–71, 174
National Cross-Country Union (1883) 66, 169
National Cyclists' Union (1878) 44, 46, 61–2, 79
National Fitness Council (1937) 120, 168
National Olympian Association (1865) 18, 20, 22
National Sports Centre (see Crystal Palace)
Nationwide Building Society (1884) 147, 162
New Haw & Woodham Tug-of-War Club 116
New York AC (1866) 116–17
New Zealand AAA (1887) 46
Newmarket 15, 20
*News Chronicle* 116
*News of the World* 122
Niagara Falls 90
Northampton ground 62
Northern Counties Athletic Association (1879) 28, 30–1, 41, 43, 56, 61, 77, 95, 119, 122, 126, 162
Northern Ireland AAA (1932) 67, 123, 125, 132, 134
Northern Ireland Amateur Athletic, Cycling and Cross-Country Association 67
Northern Ireland Women's AAA (1948) 134

O

*Observer* 177
Olympic Festival (1862) 16–18
Olympic Games 20, 47–8, 50–2, 54–6, 58–60, 62, 68–71, 73–5, 82, 90, 92, 99, 102, 122, 135, 142, 147 (see also below)
Olympic Games
1896, Athens 54
1900, Paris 50–1, 54, 116–17, 170
1904, St Louis 54, 163
1906, Athens 54, 91
1908, London 54–6, 59–60, 81, 91–2, 96, 107, 116–17, 136, 138
1912, Stockholm 56, 68, 69, 119, 138
1920, Antwerp 68–70, 75, 138–9
1924, Paris 70–1, 75–7, 120, 139, 175, 177
1928, Amsterdam 73, 78, 167, 176
1932, Los Angeles 73–4, 81–3, 120, 139, 142, 168
1936, Berlin 58, 86–7, 89, 91, 139, 168
1948, London 87–8, 95–8, 102, 122, 140, 142, 168
1952, Helsinki 87, 102–3, 105, 139–40
1956, Melbourne 113–16, 122, 125, 129, 142–3, 170–1
1960, Rome 123, 125–6, 136, 141
1964, Tokyo 117, 123, 127–9, 141–2
1968, Mexico City 134, 142
1972, Munich 142, 147–9, 174
1976, Montreal 143, 158, 161, 174
1980, Moscow 143, 165
*Olympic Review* 54
Oxford University AC (1866) 16, 18–19, 22, 24, 27–32, 35–6, 41, 58, 63–4, 66, 68–9, 71, 73, 75, 79, 84, 90–2, 106, 113–14, 117, 120, 170
Oxford v Cambridge Athletic Sports (1864) 18–19, 27–9, 41, 59–60, 63–4, 69–70, 73, 79, 91, 176
Oxford v Cambridge Boat Race (1829) 19, 23, 27–8, 30, 90–1

P

Pan-Britannic Contest 47
Paris Exposition Games (1900) (see Olympic Games, 1900)
Parliament 46, 56, 91, 122, 125
Pedestrianism (see Professional Athletics)
Pepsi-Cola Ltd. 127
Physical Education 65
Pole Vault, history 36, 39, 52, 59, 62, 65, 82, 85–6, 122, 127, 148–9, 163

Polytechnic Harriers (1883) 68, 75, 77–8, 83, 120, 131, 137
Principal National Coaches 114, 122
Professional Administrators 95, 146, 149–50
Professional Athletics 14–16, 22–3, 38–9, 41, 43–5, 59–62, 82, 117, 119, 169–70
Public Address Systems 92
Public Attitudes Survey Ltd (1957) 126
Public Schools Challenge Cups Meeting (see London AC Schools Challenge Cups Meeting)
Public Schools Relays (1923) 75
Pye Gold Cup (see GRE Gold Cup)

Q

Queensberry Rules (1867) 19, 22

R

Race Walking Association (1907) 65–6, 132, 138, 140, 142–3
Radio 95, 97, 162, 175–6
Randolph Hotel, Oxford, 31, 162
Reading AC (1881) 45
*Recollections of Bar and Bench* (1914) 63
Records, AAA National (1960) 11, 127, 162
Records, British (1887) 11, 40, 44, 69, 73, 76–9, 85–7, 89, 94, 136
Records, British All-Comers' (1948) 11, 99, 103, 111, 114–15
Records, British (National) (1948) 11, 98–9, 114–15
Records, English Native (1928) 11, 73, 81–2, 86, 98, 103, 105, 114, 176
Records, United Kingdom (All-Comers') (1960) 11, 125–7, 140–1, 151, 155, 163, 171
Records, United Kingdom (National) (1960) 11, 126–7, 134, 163, 171
Records, World, IAAF (1921) 11, 48, 56, 58, 70–1, 73–4, 77–8, 83, 86–7, 89, 103, 105–6, 108, 114, 131, 134, 147–8, 150, 163, 165–167, 170–1
Records, World Unofficial (Pre IAAF) 13, 16, 23, 29, 32, 35–6, 38–40, 44–5, 48, 50–1, 58, 64, 68, 99, 137, 169–70
Regent Street Polytechnic (1883) 86
Registration 132, 134
Relay Races 56, 58, 65, 75, 83, 87, 102, 115, 125, 129, 149, 158
*Reply to Certain Criticisms, A* (1908) 54
Road Runners Club (1952) 122–3, 171
Road Walking Association (1907) (see Race Walking Association)
*Rowing Almanack* 22
Royal Air Force Athletics 58, 77, 81, 92–3, 163
Royal Air Force, Cosford (1955) 129
Royal Air Force, Stanmore (1960) 126
Royal Family and Athletics 7, *7*, 14, 16, 32, *55*, 66, 102–3, 111, 134, 161–2
Rugby School (1567) 14
*Running Round the World* 128
Rural Sports 14

S

Salford Harriers 60, 83
Schools Athletic Association (1925) 66
Schools Athletics 14, 45, 56, 65–6, 75, 120, 122–3, 132, 150, 169
Scottish AAA (1883) 66–7, 123, 125, 132, 134
Scottish Women's AAA (1931) 134
Services Athletics 58, 65, 92
Shot Put, history 20, 48, 50, 55, 59, 63, 82, 115–16, 122, 126, 149, 154–5
Silver Jubilee Championships (1977) 161–3
South London Harriers (1871) 170–1
South Norwood AC 24
Southern Amateur Athletics League (1928) 131, 133
Southern Committee (1883) 43–6, 56, 61–2, 119, 136, 176
Southern Counties AAA (1961) 126, 150
Southern Counties Cross-Country Championship (1884) 45, 170
Southern Counties Road Walking Association (1907) 138
Special Coaching Scheme (1948) 122–3
Specialist Clubs 106, 122–3
Sponsorship 114, 122, 125–6, 131, 147, 165, 175
*Sport* (Dublin) 52
*Sporting Gazette, The* 19, 25, 30–2, 36, 169
*Sporting Life* 41, 46, 68
Sports Council (1965) 125, 131, 150
*Sportsview, BBC* 128
Sprinting, history 16, 35, 44, 51, 59, 75–8, 94, 102–3, 105, 125, 127, 147, 155
Stade Colombes, Paris 66
Stamford Bridge ground (1877) *26*, *27*, 27–8, 32, 40, 47, 50, 52, 58, 65–6, 71, 81, *81*, 176
Standards Scheme (1959) 123
Steeplechase, history 31, 56, 63, 75, 83, 99, 103, 106, 111, 113, 115, 122, 126–7, 129, 132, 148, 155, 171
Stoke-on-Trent AC 24
Stop-board 59–60
Street Betting Act (1907) 46
Style, running 36, 50, 59, 74–5, 103
Style, walking 36, 136–44
*Sunday Graphic* 176
*Sunday Times* 176
Suspensions, 41, 43–6, 67, 79, 93
*Svenska Idrottsförbund* (1895) 92–3
*Syllabus of Physical Training* (1909) 65

T

Tailteann Games (1829 BC) 47
Technical Developments 15, 19–20, 48, 50–1, 59–60, 63, 71, 82, 96, 105–6, 117–24, 147, 170
Television 97–8, 126, 128, 135, 146, 174
*Testament of a Runner* 78
Thames Hare & Hounds (1868) 24, 30–1, 169
Thames Rowing Club (1860) 169
Thames Valley Harriers (1887) 126
Timsbury Manor 128
Tracks, first 15
Trainers (see Coaches)
Training 50, 56, 73, 99, 114, 117–24, 136, 138, 141, 143, 158, 169–70
Triangular International (1914) 58, 66–7
Triple Jump 58, 68, 115, 155, 163
Tug-of-War 55, 116, 132
Tug-of-War Association (1958) 116, 132

U

*Union des Societés Françaises des Sports Athlétiques* (1887) 66
United Kingdom AAA, Proposed (1960) 125
United Kingdom National Championships (1977) 66, 163
United Kingdom Coaching Scheme (1972) 123, 134, 150
United States Amateur Athletic Union (1888) 35, 39, 48, 54, 59, 69
Universities Athletic Union (1919) 66
University of London AC 92

V

Volunteer Movement 16, 65

W

Walking, history 15, 19, 36, 56, 65–6, 82, 87, 97–9, 125, 127, 129, 131, 135, 136–44, 154, 162
Wall & Son (Ice Cream) Ltd, T. 123, 126
Walthamstow Harriers 45
*Weight Training for Athletes* 123
Welsh AAA (1948) 95, 116, 122–3, 126, 134
Welsh Women's AAA (1953) 134
Wembley Stadium (1923) 96
West London Cricket Ground, Brompton (1860) 16, 18
West London Rowing Club 16, 86
White City Stadium (1908) 54, 58, 81–2, 84, 92–3, 98–9, 103, 105–6, 125–6, 131, 134–5, 147
Wolfenden Committee on Sport and the Community (1960) 125
Wolverhampton and Bilston AC (1967) 154
Wolverhampton ground 62
Women's Amateur Athletic Association (1922) 66–7, 86, 114, 123, 125–6, 132, 134, 150
Women's Athletics 66–7, 126–7, 129, 131–2, 134–5, 146, 149
Wood Treatment, Bosley 116
Woodford Green AC (1908) 78, 139
Woolwich Garrison Sports 116
Working Agreements (AAU, 1925) 54 (WAAA, 1937) 67
World Cup Competition, IAAF (1977) 163
*World Sports* 123, 141
World War I (1914–18) 58, 65, 68–9, 120, 134, 138
World War II (1939–45) 58, 89, 92, 98, 120, 168

X

*XVII Olympiad, 1960* 176

Y

Yale University Athletic Association (1872) 117
Youngest Champion 32
Youth Athletics 123, 161, 166

## Facts and Feats Series:

**Air Facts and Feats,** *3rd ed.*
John WR Taylor, Michael JH Taylor and David Mondey

**Rail Facts and Feats,** *3rd ed.*
John Marshall

**Tank Facts and Feats,** *2nd ed.*
Kenneth Macksey

**Car Facts and Feats,** *3rd ed.*
edited by Anthony Harding

**Motorcycling Facts and Feats**
LJK Setright

**Motorboating Facts and Feats**
Kevin Desmond

**Yachting Facts and Feats**
Peter Johnson

**Business World**
Henry Button and Andrew Lampert

**Music Facts and Feats**
Robert and Celia Dearling with Brian Rust

**Art Facts and Feats**
John FitzMaurice Mills

**Antiques**
John FitzMaurice Mills

**Soccer Facts and Feats,** *2nd ed.*
Jack Rollin

**Animal Facts and Feats**
Gerald L. Wood FZS

**Plant Facts and Feats**
William G. Duncalf

**Structures — Bridges, Towers, Tunnels, Dams . . .**
John H. Stephens

**Weather Facts and Feats**
Ingrid Holford

**Astronomy Facts and Feats**
Patrick Moore

## Guide Series:

**Guide to French Country Cooking**
Christian Roland Délu

**Guide to Freshwater Angling**
Brian Harris and Paul Boyer

**Guide to Saltwater Angling**
Brian Harris

**Guide to Field Sports**
Wilson Stephens

**Guide to Motorcycling,** *2nd ed.*
Christian Lacombe

**Guide to Bicycling**
J. Durry and JB Wadley

**Guide to Equestrianism**
Dorian Williams

**Guide to Water Skiing**
David Nations OBE and Kevin Desmond

**Guide to Steeplechasing**
Gerry Cranham, Richard Pitman and John Oaksey

**Guide to Waterways of Western Europe**
Hugh McKnight

## Other Titles:

**History of Air Warfare**
David Brown, Christopher Shores and Kenneth Macksey

**History of Land Warfare**
Kenneth Macksey

**History of Sea Warfare**
Lt-Cmdr Gervis Frere-Cook and Kenneth Macksey

**The Guinness Book of 1952**
Kenneth Macksey

**The Guinness Book of 1953**
Kenneth Macksey

**The Guinness Book of 1954**
Kenneth Macksey

**The Guinness Book of Answers**
edited by Norris D. McWhirter

**The Guinness Book of Records**
edited by Norris D. McWhirter

**English Pottery and Porcelain**
Geoffrey Wills

**Antique Firearms**
Frederick Wilkinson

**The Guinness Book of Winners and Champions**
Chris Cook

**The Guinness Guide to Feminine Achievements**
Joan and Kenneth Macksey

**The Guinness Book of Names**
Leslie Dunkling

**Kings, Rulers and Statesmen**
Clive Carpenter

**The Guinness Book of British Hit Singles** *2nd ed.*
edited by Tim and Jo Rice, Paul Gambaccini and Mike Read

**The Guinness Book of World Autographs**
Ray Rawlins

**The Official Story of the Blue Riband of the Turf — Derby 200**
Michael Seth-Smith and Roger Mortimer

**100 Years of Wimbledon**
Lance Tingay